Microsoft

Microsoft Office
Step by Step
(Office 2021 and Microsoft 365)

Joan Lambert
Curtis Frye

Microsoft Office Step by Step (Office 2021 and Microsoft 365)
Published with the authorization of Microsoft Corporation by:
Pearson Education, Inc.

ISBN-13: 978-0-13-754476-9
ISBN-10: 0-13-754476-6

Library of Congress Control Number: 2022935442

4 2023

Trademarks
Microsoft and the trademarks listed at http://www.microsoft.com on the "Trademarks" webpage are trademarks of the Microsoft group of companies. All other marks are property of their respective owners.

Warning and Disclaimer
Every effort has been made to make this book as complete and as accurate as possible, but no warranty or fitness is implied. The information provided is on an "as is" basis. The author, the publisher, and Microsoft Corporation shall have neither liability nor responsibility to any person or entity with respect to any loss or damages arising from the information contained in this book or from the use of the programs accompanying it.

Special Sales
For information about buying this title in bulk quantities, or for special sales opportunities (which may include electronic versions; custom cover designs; and content particular to your business, training goals, marketing focus, or branding interests), please contact our corporate sales department at corpsales@pearsoned.com or (800) 382-3419.

For government sales inquiries, please contact governmentsales@pearsoned.com.

For questions about sales outside the U.S., please contact intlcs@pearson.com.

Editor-in-Chief
Brett Bartow

Executive Editor
Loretta Yates

Sponsoring Editor
Charvi Arora

Development Editor
Songlin Qiu

Managing Editor
Sandra Schroeder

Senior Project Editor
Tracey Croom

Project Editor/Proofreader
Dan Foster

Copy Editor
Susan Festa

Indexer
Valerie Haynes Perry

Technical Editor
Boyd Nolan

Editorial Assistant
Cindy Teeters

Cover Designer
Twist Creative, Seattle

Compositor
Danielle Foster

Pearson's Commitment to Diversity, Equity, and Inclusion

Pearson is dedicated to creating bias-free content that reflects the diversity of all learners. We embrace the many dimensions of diversity, including but not limited to race, ethnicity, gender, socioeconomic status, ability, age, sexual orientation, and religious or political beliefs.

Education is a powerful force for equity and change in our world. It has the potential to deliver opportunities that improve lives and enable economic mobility. As we work with authors to create content for every product and service, we acknowledge our responsibility to demonstrate inclusivity and incorporate diverse scholarship so that everyone can achieve their potential through learning. As the world's leading learning company, we have a duty to help drive change and live up to our purpose to help more people create a better life for themselves and to create a better world.

Our ambition is to purposefully contribute to a world where:

- Everyone has an equitable and lifelong opportunity to succeed through learning.

- Our educational products and services are inclusive and represent the rich diversity of learners.

- Our educational content accurately reflects the histories and experiences of the learners we serve.

- Our educational content prompts deeper discussions with learners and motivates them to expand their own learning (and worldview).

While we work hard to present unbiased content, we want to hear from you about any concerns or needs with this Pearson product so that we can investigate and address them.

Please contact us with concerns about any potential bias at https://www.pearson.com/report-bias.html.

Contents at a glance

Part 1: Microsoft Office (Microsoft 365 Apps)

    1: Explore Office. 3

    2: Create and manage files. 49

Part 2: Microsoft Word

    3: Modify the structure and appearance of text 79

    4: Collaborate on documents 125

    5: Merge data with documents and labels. 167

Part 3: Excel

    6: Perform calculations on data 205

    7: Manage worksheet data. 237

    8: Reorder and summarize data 259

    9: Analyze alternative data sets 275

Part 4: PowerPoint

    10: Create and manage slides 291

    11: Insert and manage simple graphics 323

    12: Add sound and movement to slides 361

Part 5: Microsoft Outlook

    13: Send and receive email messages 401

    14: Organize your Inbox 447

    15: Manage scheduling 477

    Appendix: Keyboard shortcuts 513

    Index. 521

Contents

Acknowledgments xv

About the authors: xvii

Introduction . . . . **xix**

Who this book is for xix

The Step by Step approach. xix

Features and conventions. xx

Download the practice files xxi

E-book edition xxv

Get support and give feedback. xxv

    Errata and support xxv

    Stay in touch xxv

    Adapt exercise steps. xxvi

Part 1: Microsoft Office (Microsoft 365 Apps)

1   **Explore Office**. **3**

Work in the Office user interface 4

    Identify app window elements 6

    Work with the ribbon and status bar. 12

    Adapt procedures for your environment 14

Discover new features 19

Change Office and app options 21

    Manage account information 21

    Microsoft account options 22

    Manage app options 25

Display and customize the Quick Access Toolbar 29

Customize the ribbon. 34

Get help and provide feedback. 38

Key points 43

Practice tasks 44

Create and manage files **49**

Create files. 50

Open and move around in files. 54

Display different views of files. 59

Display and edit file properties 63

File types and compatibility with earlier versions of Office apps 64

Save and close files 67

Save files to OneDrive 70

Key points 72

Practice tasks 73

Part 2: Microsoft Word

Modify the structure and appearance of text. **79**

Apply paragraph formatting 80

Configure alignment 81

Configure vertical spacing 82

Configure indents 85

Configure paragraph borders and shading. 88

Apply character formatting 89

Character formatting and case considerations. 94

Format the first letter of a paragraph as a drop cap. 96

Structure content manually 97

Create and modify lists 101

      Format text as you type 106

Apply built-in styles to text 107

      Apply styles 107

      Manage outline levels 112

Change the document theme 114

Key points 118

Practice tasks 119

Collaborate on documents 125

Mark up documents 126

      Insert comments 126

      Track changes 128

Display and review document markup 132

      Display markup 132

      Review and respond to comments 138

      Review and process tracked changes 140

      Remember to check for errors 142

Compare and combine documents 143

      Compare and combine separate copies of a document 143

      Compare separate versions of a document 146

Control content changes 147

      Restrict actions 148

      Restrict access by using a password 153

Coauthor documents 158

Key points 162

Practice tasks 163

5

Merge data with documents and labels **167**

Understand the mail merge process 168

Start the mail merge process... 169

    Get started with letters 170

    Get started with labels... 171

    Get started with email messages 174

    Attaching files to email merge messages............................ 175

Choose and refine the data source 176

    Select an existing data source 177

    Create a new data source 180

    Refine the data source records 181

    Refresh data 186

Insert merge fields 186

Preview and complete the merge 189

Create individual envelopes and labels................................ 191

    Generate individual envelopes 192

    Generate individual mailing labels.................................. 195

Key points 198

Practice tasks 199

Part 3: Excel

6

Perform calculations on data **205**

Name data ranges.. 206

    Operators and precedence.. 210

Create formulas to calculate values 210

Summarize data that meets specific conditions......................... 217

Copy and move formulas 221

Create array formulas. 224
Find and correct errors in calculations 226
Configure automatic and iterative calculation options 230
Key points 233
Practice tasks 234

Manage worksheet data **237**
Filter data ranges and tables 238
Summarize filtered data 243
    Randomly select list rows 249
Enforce data entry criteria 250
Key points 256
Practice tasks 257

Reorder and summarize data **259**
Sort worksheet data 260
Sort data by using custom lists 266
Outline and subtotal data 268
Key points 272
Practice tasks 273

Analyze alternative data sets **275**
Define and display alternative data sets. 276
Forecast data by using data tables. 281
Identify the input necessary to achieve a specific result 284
Key points 286
Practice tasks 287

Part 4: PowerPoint

10   **Create and manage slides** **291**

Add and remove slides 292

     Insert new slides.. 293

     Copy and import slides and content 294

     Hide and delete slides 300

Apply themes 301

Change slide backgrounds 305

     Non-theme colors... 313

Divide presentations into sections 314

Rearrange slides and sections 316

Key points 319

Practice tasks 320

11   **Insert and manage simple graphics** **323**

Insert, move, and resize pictures 324

     Graphic formats... 326

Edit and format pictures 329

Provide additional information about pictures 334

Create a photo album 337

Insert and format icons 342

     Work with scalable vector graphics 344

Draw and modify shapes.. 345

     Draw and add text to shapes 345

     Locate additional formatting commands.......................... 347

     Move and modify shapes 348

     Format shapes 350

     Connect shapes 354

Key points 355

Practice tasks 356

12

Add sound and movement to slides. 361

Animate text and pictures on slides. 362
  Animate this 368
  Morphing slide content into new forms 372
Customize animation effects 372
  Bookmark points of interest in media clips 378
Add audio content to slides 380
Add video content to slides 386
Compress media to decrease file size 390
  Hyperlink to additional resources. 393
Key points 394
Practice tasks 395

Part 5: Microsoft Outlook

13

Send and receive email messages. 401

Create and send messages 402
  Create messages 404
  Troubleshoot message addressing. 409
  Save and send messages. 414
  Send from a specific account. 415
Attach files and Outlook items to messages 418
  New mail notifications. 426
Display messages and message attachments. 427
  Display message content 427
  Display attachment content. 429
Display message participant information 433
Respond to messages 436
  Resending and recalling messages 440
Key points 442
Practice tasks 443

14 Organize your Inbox **447**

Display and manage messages 448

    Select the primary Inbox content 448

    Display and manage conversations 449

Arrange messages by specific attributes 455

Categorize items 459

    Store information in Outlook notes 464

Organize messages in folders 467

Print messages 471

Key points 473

Practice tasks 474

15 Manage scheduling **477**

Display different views of a calendar 478

    Use the Date Navigator 482

Schedule appointments and events 484

Convert calendar items 489

    Add holidays to your calendar 490

Configure calendar item options 493

Schedule and change meetings 498

Respond to meeting requests 506

Key points 508

Practice tasks 509

Appendix: Keyboard shortcuts 513

Index 521

Acknowledgments

Every book represents the combined efforts of many individuals. I'm thankful to Loretta Yates for the continuing opportunity to be part of this series, and to Charvi Arora for keeping things on track. Curt Frye wrote the original versions of this book and provided a solid starting point for this edition. It was a pleasure to work once again with the Scribe Tribe team, including Danielle Foster (compositor) and Dan Foster (project editor/proofreader). They are consummate professionals, and I learn something new each time I work with them. Scout Festa (copy editor) did a great job making sure no spelling errors got through to you, dear readers, and Valerie Haynes Perry (indexer) made it easy for you to find the information you're looking for. I've worked with this team, virtually, many times and am very grateful for their skills.

As always, many thanks and all my love to my divine daughter, Trinity Preppernau.

About the authors

Joan Lambert has worked closely with Microsoft technologies since 1986, and in the training and certification industry since 1997, guiding the translation of technical information and requirements into useful, relevant, and measurable resources for people seeking certification of their computer skills or who simply want to get things done efficiently. She has written more than 50 books about Windows, Office, and SharePoint technologies, including dozens of Step by Step books and several generations of Microsoft Office Specialist certification study guides. Students who use the GO! with Microsoft Office textbook products from Pearson may overhear her cheerfully demonstrating Office features in the videos that accompany the series.

A native of the Pacific Northwest, Joan has had the good fortune to live in many parts of the world—including Germany, New Zealand, Sweden, and Denmark—and many of our United States. She currently resides with her family—one daughter, two dogs, two cats, and seven chickens—in the Beehive State, where she enjoys the majestic mountain views, mostly blue skies, and occasional snowstorm.

Curtis Frye is the author of more than 30 books, including *Microsoft Excel 2019 Step by Step* and *Microsoft OneNote Step by Step* for Microsoft Press. He has also created and recorded more than 90 online training courses for lynda.com and LinkedIn Learning on topics such as Excel data analysis; supply chain, transportation, and inventory problems; and data visualization using Tableau. He lives in Portland, Oregon, with his wife, Virginia.

Introduction

Welcome to the wonderful world of Microsoft 365 apps, formerly known as Microsoft Office! This Step by Step book has been designed to make it easy for you to learn about key aspects of four of the Microsoft 365 apps: Word, Excel, PowerPoint, and Outlook. In each part of this book, you can start from the beginning and then build your skills as you learn to perform increasingly specialized procedures. Or, if you prefer, you can jump in wherever you need guidance for performing tasks. The how-to steps are delivered crisply and concisely—just the facts. You'll also find informative graphics that support the instructional content.

Who this book is for

Microsoft Office Step by Step is designed for use as a learning and reference resource by home and business users of Microsoft Office 365 or the individual Office apps who want to use Word, Excel, and PowerPoint to create and edit files, and Outlook to organize email, contact information, and calendar items. The content of the book is designed to be useful for people who have previously used earlier versions of the apps and for people who are discovering the apps for the first time.

The Step by Step approach

This book's coverage is divided into parts. Part 1 introduces the Microsoft 365 apps and the skills that are common to all of them. Parts 2–5 each provide a thorough introduction to one of the four apps covered in this book. Each part is divided into chapters representing skill set areas, and each chapter is divided into topics that group related skills. Each topic includes expository information followed by generic procedures. At the end of the chapter, you'll find a series of practice tasks you can complete on your own by using the skills taught in the chapter. You can use the practice files available from this book's website to work through the practice tasks, or you can use your own files.

Features and conventions

This book has been designed to lead you step by step through tasks you're likely to want to perform in Word, Excel, PowerPoint, and Outlook. The topics are all self-contained, so you can start at the beginning and work your way through all the procedures or reference them independently. If you have worked with previous versions of the apps, or if you complete all the exercises and later need help remembering how to perform a procedure, the following features of this book will help you locate specific information:

- **Detailed table of contents** Browse the listing of the topics, sections, and sidebars within each chapter.

- **Chapter thumb tabs and running heads** Identify the pages of each chapter by the thumb tabs on the book's open fore edge. Find a specific chapter by number or title by looking at the running heads at the top of even-numbered (verso) pages.

- **Topic-specific running heads** Within a chapter, quickly locate the topic you want by looking at the running heads at the top of odd-numbered (recto) pages.

- **Practice tasks page tabs** Easily locate the practice tasks at the end of each chapter by looking for the full-page stripe on the book's fore edge.

- **Detailed index** Look up coverage of specific tasks and features in the index at the back of the book.

You can save time when reading this book by understanding how the Step by Step series provides procedural instructions and auxiliary information and identifies on-screen and physical elements that you interact with. The following table lists content formatting conventions used in this book.

Convention	Meaning
TIP	This reader aid provides a helpful hint or shortcut to simplify a task.
IMPORTANT	This reader aid alerts you to a common problem or provides information necessary to successfully complete a procedure.
SEE ALSO	This reader aid directs you to more information about a topic in this book or elsewhere.

Convention	Meaning
1. Numbered steps 2. 3.	Numbered steps guide you through generic procedures in each topic and through hands-on practice tasks at the end of each chapter.
■ Bulleted lists	Bulleted lists indicate single-step procedures and sets of multiple alternative procedures.
Interface objects	In procedures and practice tasks, semibold black text indicates on-screen elements that you should select (click or tap).
User input	Light semibold formatting identifies specific information that you should enter when completing procedures or practice tasks.
Keyboard shortcuts	A plus sign between two keys indicates that you must select those keys at the same time. For example, "press Ctrl+P" directs you to hold down the Ctrl key while you press the P key.
Emphasis and *URLs*	In expository text, italic formatting identifies web addresses and words or phrases we want to emphasize.

Download the practice files

Before you can complete the practice tasks in this book, you must download the book's practice files to your computer from *MicrosoftPressStore.com/MSOfficeSBS365/downloads*. Follow the instructions on the webpage.

> ⚠ **IMPORTANT** Word, Excel, PowerPoint, Outlook, and other Microsoft 365 apps are not available from the book's website. You should install the apps before working through the procedures and practice tasks in this book.

You can open the files that are supplied for the practice tasks and save the finished versions of each file. If you want to repeat practice tasks later, you can download the original practice files again.

> 🔍 **SEE ALSO** For information about opening and saving files, see "Open and move around in files" and "Save and close files" in Chapter 2, "Create and manage files."

The following table lists the files available for use while working through the practice tasks in this book.

Chapter	Folder	File
Part 1: Microsoft Office (Microsoft 365 Apps)		
1: Explore Office	Office365SBS\Ch01	None
2: Create and manage files	Office365SBS\Ch02	DisplayProperties.xlsx
		DisplayViews.pptx
		NavigateFiles.docx
Part 2: Microsoft Word		
3: Modify the structure and appearance of text	Office365SBS\Ch03	ApplyStyles.docx
		ChangeTheme.docx
		CreateLists.docx
		FormatCharacters.docx
		FormatParagraphs.docx
		StructureContent.docx
4: Collaborate on documents	Office365SBS\Ch04	ControlChanges.docx
		MergeDocs1.docx
		MergeDocs2.docx
		ReviewComments.docx
		TrackChanges.docx
5: Merge data with documents and labels	Office365SBS\Ch05	CreateEnvelopes.docx
		CustomerList.csv
		CustomerList.xlsx
		InsertFields.docx
		PolicyholdersList.xlsx
		RefineData.docx
		StartMerge.docx

Chapter	Folder	File
Part 3: Microsoft Excel		
6: Perform calculations on data	Office365SBS\Ch06	AuditFormulas.xlsx
		BuildFormulas.xlsx
		CreateArrayFormulas.xlsx
		CreateConditonalFormulas.xlsx
		NameRanges.xlsx
		SetIterativeOptions.xlsx
7: Manage worksheet data	Office365SBS\Ch07	FilterData.xlsx
		SummarizeValues.xlsx
		ValidateData.xlsx
8: Reorder and summarize data	Office365SBS\Ch08	CustomSortData.xlsx
		OutlineData.xlsx
		SortData.xlsx
9: Analyze alternative data sets	Office365SBS\Ch09	CreateScenarios.xlsx
		DefineDataTables.xlsx
		PerformGoalSeekAnalysis.xlsx
Part 4: Microsoft PowerPoint		
10: Create and manage slides	Office365SBS\Ch10	AddRemoveSlides.pptx
		ApplyThemes.pptx
		ChangeBackgrounds.pptx
		CreateSections.pptx
		ImportOutline.docx
		RearrangeSlides.pptx
		ReuseSlides.pptx

Chapter	Folder	File
11: Insert and manage simple graphics	Office365SBS\Ch11	AccreditPictures.pptx
		Bouquets.jpg
		DrawShapes.pptx
		EditPictures.pptx
		InsertIcons.pptx
		InsertPictures.pptx
		InsertScreens.pptx
		Penguins01.jpg
		Penguins02.jpg
		PinkFlowers.jpg
		PurpleFlowers.jpg
		RedTree.jpg
		Tiger01.jpg
		Tiger02.jpg
		WhiteFlower.jpg
12: Add sound and movement to slides	Office365SBS\Ch12	AddAudio.pptx
		AddVideo.pptx
		AnimateSlides.pptx
		Butterfly.wmv
		CustomizeAnimation.pptx
		SoundTrack.wma
		Wildlife.wmv
Part 5: Microsoft Outlook		
13: Send and receive email messages	Office365SBS\Ch13	AttachFiles.docx
14: Organize your Inbox	Office365SBS\Ch14	None
15: Manage scheduling	Office365SBS\Ch15	None

E-book edition

If you're reading the e-book edition of this book, you can do the following:

- Search the full text
- Print
- Copy and paste

You can purchase and download the e-book edition from the Microsoft Press Store at *MicrosoftPressStore.com/MSOfficeSBS365/detail*.

Get support and give feedback

We've made every effort to ensure the accuracy of this book and its companion content. We welcome your feedback.

Errata and support

If you discover an error, please submit it to us at *MicrosoftPressStore.com/MSOfficeSBS365/errata*. We'll investigate all reported issues, update downloadable content if appropriate, and incorporate necessary changes into future editions of this book.

For additional book support and information, please visit *MicrosoftPressStore.com/Support*.

For assistance with Microsoft software and hardware, visit the Microsoft Support site at *support.microsoft.com*.

Stay in touch

Let's keep the conversation going! We're on Twitter at *twitter.com/MicrosoftPress*.

Part 1

Microsoft Office (Microsoft 365 Apps)

CHAPTER 1

Explore Office 3

CHAPTER 2

Create and manage files 49

Explore
Office

The Microsoft Office suite of apps (also called Microsoft 365 apps) includes many apps that serve different purposes but are designed to work together to maximize efficiency.

The elements that control the appearance of an app and the way you interact with it are collectively referred to as the *user interface*. Some user interface elements, such as the color scheme, are cosmetic. Others, such as toolbars, menus, and buttons, are functional. Each app has standard settings based on the way that most people work with the app. You can modify cosmetic and functional user interface elements in each app to suit your preferences and working style.

The Office apps share many common user-interface elements and functions. The ways in which you perform tasks such as opening, saving, searching, printing, and sharing files are standardized across the apps so that you can concentrate your learning efforts on the skills and features specific to the app or to the document, workbook, or presentation you're creating.

This chapter guides you through procedures common to Word, Excel, PowerPoint, and some aspects of Outlook. It includes procedures related to working in the Office user interface, changing options for Office and for specific apps, customizing the Quick Access Toolbar and ribbon, getting help, and sending feedback to the Microsoft Office team.

In this chapter

- Work in the Office user interface
- Discover new features
- Change Office and app options
- Display and customize the Quick Access Toolbar
- Customize the ribbon
- Get help and provide feedback

Work in the Office user interface

The goal of the Office working environment is to make working with Office files, including Word documents, Excel workbooks, PowerPoint presentations, and Outlook email messages, as intuitive as possible.

On a Windows computer, you can start an app from the Start menu app list or tile area, the Start screen, or the taskbar search box. You might also have shortcuts to apps on your desktop or on the Windows taskbar.

When you start Word, Excel, or PowerPoint without opening a specific file, the app Home page appears. The Home page is a hybrid of the Open and New pages of the Backstage view. It displays links to pinned and recent files in the left pane, and new file templates in the right pane.

The Home page presents a simple view of the options available when there is no open presentation

TIP The size of the Home, New, and Open page tabs in the left pane of the Backstage view changes based on the available space. At some screen resolutions and window sizes, these page tabs are short and labeled only with their names.

TIP You can suppress the Home page (also called the Start screen) if you want to go directly to a new, blank file when you start an app. For more information, see "Change Office and app options" later in this chapter.

When you're working with a file, the app window contains all the tools you need to add and format content.

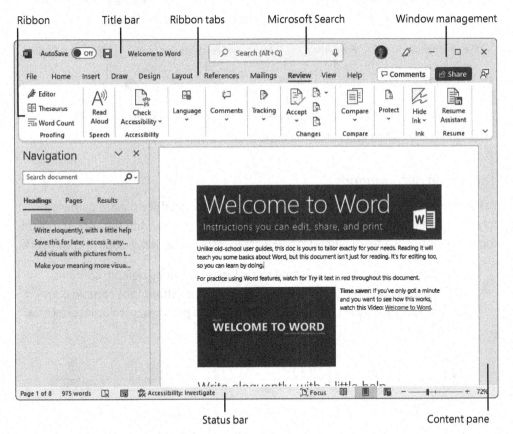

Elements specific to all Office app windows

Identify app window elements

A typical Office app window contains the elements described in this section. It might also display optional elements such as rulers, gridlines, navigation panes, and tool panes. Commands for tasks you perform often are readily available, and even those you might use infrequently are easy to find.

Title bar

At the top of the app window, this bar displays the name of the active file and provides tools for managing the app window and content. If the file is stored online in OneDrive or SharePoint, a dropdown menu adjacent to the file name provides a simple way to change the file name and access the storage location and version history.

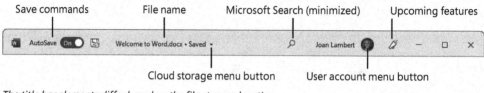

The title bar elements differ based on the file storage location

The ribbon of commands

Below the title bar, all the commands for working with an Office file are gathered together in this central location so that you can work efficiently with the app. Across the top of the ribbon is a set of named tabs. Each tab displays named groups of commands.

- **Standard ribbon tabs** The Home tab, which is active by default, contains the most frequently used commands for each app. Other tabs contain commands specific to the type of action you want to perform, such as Insert, Draw, and Design.

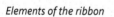

Elements of the ribbon

> **TIP** Your ribbon might look different from those shown in this book. You might have installed programs that add their own tabs to the ribbon, or your screen settings might be different. For more information, see "Customize the ribbon" later in this chapter.

- **Object-specific tool tabs** When a graphic element such as a picture, table, or chart is selected in a document, one or more *tool tabs* appear on which commands related to that specific object are located. Tool tabs are available only when the relevant object is selected. They are differentiated from the standard tabs by name and color, and are always located to the right of the standard tabs.

A typical tool tab

> **TIP** Some older commands no longer appear as buttons on the ribbon but are still available in the app. You can make these commands available by adding them to the Quick Access Toolbar or the ribbon. For more information, see "Display and Customize the Quick Access Toolbar" and "Customize the ribbon" later in this chapter.

On each tab, buttons representing commands are organized into named groups. You can point to any button to display a ScreenTip with the command name, its keyboard shortcut (if it has one), and a description of its function.

ScreenTips provide helpful information about commands

> **TIP** You can control the display of ScreenTips and of feature descriptions in ScreenTips. For more information, see "Change Office and app options" later in this chapter.

Some buttons include an arrow, which might be integrated with or separate from the button. To determine whether a button and its arrow are integrated, point to the button to activate it. If both the button and its arrow are shaded, selecting the button displays options for refining the action of the button. If only the button or arrow is shaded when you point to it, selecting the button carries out its default action or applies the current default formatting. Selecting the arrow and then an action carries out the action. Selecting the arrow and then a formatting option applies the formatting and sets it as the default for the button.

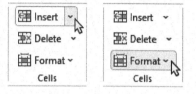

Buttons with separate and integrated arrows

When a formatting option includes several choices, they are often displayed in a gallery of images, called *thumbnails*, that provide a visual representation of each choice. When you point to a thumbnail in a gallery, the Live Preview feature shows you what the active content will look like if you select the thumbnail to apply the associated formatting. When a gallery contains more thumbnails than can be shown in the available ribbon space, you can display more content by selecting one of the scroll arrows or the More button located on the right edge of the gallery.

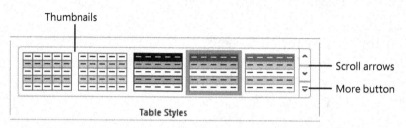

You can scroll gallery content or expand it as a pane

Related but less common commands are not represented as buttons in a group. Instead, they're available in a dialog or pane, which you display by selecting the dialog launcher located in the lower-right corner of the group.

> **TIP** To the right of the groups on the ribbon is the Ribbon Display Options button, which is shaped like a chevron. For more information, see "Work with the ribbon and status bar," later in this topic.

The Backstage view of an app

Commands related to managing the app and files (rather than file content) are gathered together in the Backstage view, which you display by selecting the File tab located at the left end of the ribbon. Commands available in the Backstage view are organized on named pages, which you display by selecting the page tabs in the left pane. You redisplay the document and the ribbon by selecting the Back arrow located above the page tabs.

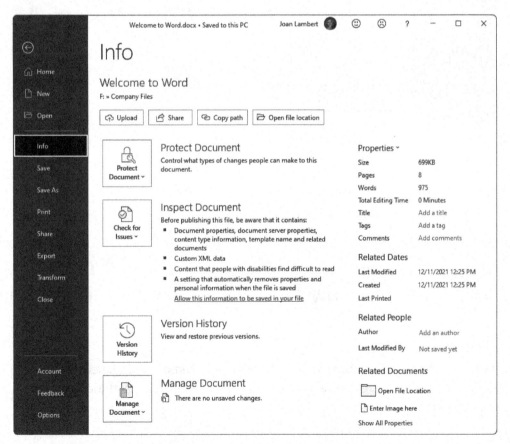

You manage files and app settings on various pages of the Backstage view

If all the page tabs don't fit vertically in the left pane because of the window size or screen resolution, "More" appears at the bottom of the left pane. Selecting the More button displays a menu of the hidden page tabs.

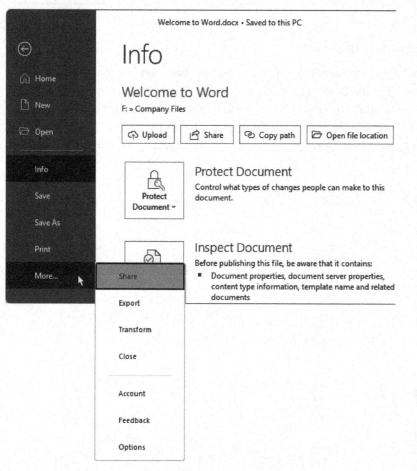

Accessing hidden pages in Backstage view

Collaboration tools

If you're using the Office apps through an Office 365 license, the Comments and Share buttons appear below the window-management commands, at the right end of the ribbon.

Comments   Share

*The available collaboration tools vary by file
storage location*

The Comments button opens the Comments pane, in which you can easily create,
review, respond to, and manage comments. The Share button makes it easy to quickly
share a link to, or a copy of, the file.

Status bar

Across the bottom of the app window, the status bar displays information about the
current file and provides access to certain app functions. You can choose the statistics and tools that appear on the status bar. Some items, such as Document Updates
Available, appear on the status bar only when that condition is true.

Page 20 of 54   10546 words   📖   🔊   ♿ Accessibility: Investigate

The left end of the Word status bar displays document information and tools

At the right end of the status bar are the View Shortcuts toolbar, the Zoom slider, and
the Zoom Level button. These tools provide you with convenient methods for adjusting the display of file content.

⬚ Focus   📖   📄   📃   –————▮————+   100%

Change the on-screen display of file content from the right end of the status bar

> 🔍 **SEE ALSO** On a touchscreen device, the appearance of the buttons on the View
> Shortcuts toolbar changes depending on whether you're in Mouse mode or Touch
> mode. For more information, see the next section, "Work with the ribbon and status bar."
> For information about changing the file content view, see "Display different views of files" in
> Chapter 2, "Create and manage files."

Work with the ribbon and status bar

The goal of the ribbon is to make working with file content as intuitive as possible. The ribbon is dynamic, meaning that as its width changes, its buttons adapt to the available space. As a result, a button might be large or small, it might or might not have a label, or it might even change to an entry in a list.

For example, when sufficient horizontal space is available, the buttons on the References tab of the Word app window are spread out, and you can review the commands available in each group.

At 1600 pixels wide, all button labels are visible

If you make the app window narrower (and decrease the horizontal space available to the ribbon), small button labels disappear, and entire groups of buttons might hide under one button that represents the entire group. Selecting the group button displays a list of the commands available in that group.

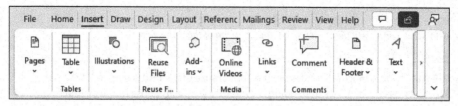

At 1200 pixels wide, command labels disappear, and groups collapse under buttons

When the ribbon becomes too narrow to display all the groups, a scroll arrow appears at its right end. Selecting the scroll arrow displays the hidden groups.

In narrow windows, scroll to display additional group buttons

The width of the ribbon depends on these three factors:

- **App window width** Maximizing the app window provides the most space for the ribbon.

- **Screen resolution** Screen resolution is the size of your screen display expressed as pixels wide × pixels high. The greater the screen resolution, the greater the amount of information that will fit on one screen. Your screen resolution options are dependent on the display adapter installed in your computer, and on your monitor. Common screen resolutions range from 800 × 600 to 2560 × 1440 (and some are larger). The greater the number of pixels wide (the first number), the greater the number of buttons that can be shown on the ribbon.

- **The magnification of your screen display** If you change the screen magnification setting in Windows, text and user interface elements are larger and therefore more legible, but fewer elements fit on the screen.

You can hide the ribbon completely if you don't need access to any of its buttons, or you can hide it so that only its tabs are visible. (This is a good way to gain vertical space when working on a smaller screen.) Then you can temporarily redisplay the ribbon to select a button, or permanently redisplay it if you need to select several buttons.

If you're working on a touchscreen device, you can turn on Touch mode, which provides more space between buttons on the ribbon and status bar. (It doesn't affect the layout of dialogs or panes.) The extra space is intended to lessen the possibility of accidentally tapping the wrong button with your finger. The same commands are available in Touch mode, but they're sometimes hidden under group buttons.

Touch spacing provides more room between ribbon, Navigation pane, and status bar elements

Adapt procedures for your environment

This book contains many images of user interface (UI) elements (such as the ribbons and the app windows) that you'll work with while performing tasks in Word, Excel, PowerPoint, or Outlook on a Windows computer. Depending on your operating system, screen resolution, or app window width, the app window ribbons on your screen might look different from those shown in this book. As a result, exercise instructions that involve the ribbon might require a little adaptation.

Simple procedural instructions use this format:

- On the **Insert** tab, in the **Illustrations** group, select the **Chart** button.

If the command is in a list, instructions use this format:

- On the **Home** tab, in the **Editing** group, select the **Find** arrow and then, in the **Find** list, select **Go To**.

A procedure that has multiple simple methods of completion uses this format:

- On the Quick Access Toolbar, select **Save**.
- In the left pane of the Backstage view, select **Save**.
- Press **Ctrl+S**.

If differences between your display settings and ours cause a button to appear differently on your screen than it does in this book, you can easily adapt the steps to locate the command. First select the specified tab, and then locate the specified group. If a group has been collapsed into a group list or under a group button, select the list or button to display the group's commands. If you can't immediately identify the button you want, point to likely candidates to display their names in ScreenTips.

Multistep procedural instructions use this format:

1. To select the paragraph that you want to format in columns, triple-click the paragraph.

2. On the **Layout** tab, in the **Page Setup** group, select the **Columns** button to display a menu of column layout options.

3. On the **Columns** menu, select **Three**.

On subsequent instances of instructions that require you to follow the same process, the instructions might be simplified in this format because the working location has already been established:

1. Select the paragraph that you want to format in columns.

2. On the **Columns** menu, select **Three**.

The instructions in this book assume that you're interacting with on-screen elements on your computer by selecting or clicking them with a mouse, or on a touchpad or other hardware device. If you're using a different method—for example, if your computer has a touchscreen interface and you're tapping the screen (with your finger or a stylus)—substitute the applicable tapping action when the book directs you to select a user interface element.

Instructions in this book refer to user interface elements that you select or tap on the screen as *buttons*, and to physical buttons that you press on a keyboard as *keys*, to conform to the standard terminology used in documentation for these products.

When the instructions tell you to enter information, you can do so by typing on a connected external keyboard, tapping an on-screen keyboard, or even speaking aloud, depending on your computer setup and your personal preferences.

You can switch between Touch mode and Mouse mode (the standard desktop app user interface) from the Quick Access Toolbar. Switching any one of the primary Office apps (Access, Excel, Outlook, PowerPoint, or Word) to Touch mode or Mouse mode effects the change in all of them.

To maximize the app window

- Select the **Maximize** button.

- Double-click the title bar.

- Drag the borders of a non-maximized window.

- Drag the window to the top of the screen. (When the pointer touches the top of the screen, an outline indicates the size the window will be when the pointer is released.)

To change the screen resolution

1. Do either of the following to open the Display pane of the System settings page:

   - Right-click or long-press (tap and hold) the Windows desktop, and then select **Display settings**.

   - Enter screen resolution in Windows Search, and then in the search results, select **Change the resolution of the display**.

2. In the **Display** pane, in the **Resolution** list, select the screen resolution you want. Windows displays a preview of the selected screen resolution.

3. If you like the change, select **Keep changes** in the message box that appears. If you don't, select **Revert** or wait for the screen resolution to automatically revert to the previous setting.

To change the magnification

1. Do either of the following to open the Display pane of the System settings page:

   - Right-click the Windows desktop, and then select **Display settings**.

   - Enter screen resolution in Windows Search, and then in the search results, select **Change the resolution of the display**.

2. In the **Display** pane, scroll to the **Scale and layout** area.

1

3. In the **Change the size of text, apps, and other items** list, do either of the following:

   - Select the standard scaling option you want.

   - Select **Custom scaling** and enter a custom scaling size from 100 percent to 500 percent.

To completely hide the ribbon

1. In the lower-right corner of the ribbon, select the **Ribbon Display Options** button.

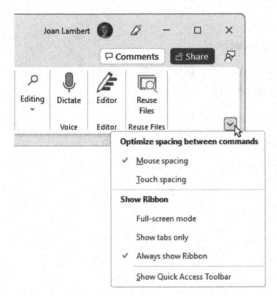

The new full-screen mode provides the largest work area

2. On the **Ribbon Display Options** menu, select **Full-screen mode.**

> ✓ **TIP** Select the ellipsis (...) near the upper-right corner of the full-screen app window to temporarily redisplay the ribbon, then select the Ribbon Display Options button and either Show Tabs Only or Always Show Ribbon to restore it.

To display only the ribbon tabs

- ■ Double-click any tab name.

- ■ In the lower-right corner of the ribbon, select the **Ribbon Display Options** button, and then select **Show tabs only.**

- ■ Press **Ctrl+F1.**

To temporarily redisplay the ribbon

- Select any tab to display the tab until you select a command or click away from the ribbon.

To permanently redisplay the ribbon

- Double-click any tab name.

- Select any tab name, then in the lower-right corner of the ribbon, select the **Ribbon Display Options** button, and then select **Always show Ribbon**.

- Press **Ctrl+F1**.

To optimize the ribbon for touch interaction

- In the lower-right corner of the ribbon, select the **Ribbon Display Options** button, and then select **Touch spacing**.

To specify the items that appear on the status bar

1. Right-click the status bar to display the Customize Status Bar menu.

Customize Status Bar				
	Formatted Page Number	13	Permissions	Off
	Section	1	Track Changes	Off
✓	Page Number	Page 13 of 53	Text Predictions	Text Predictions: Off
	Vertical Page Position		Caps Lock	Off
	Line Number		Overtype	Insert
	Column		Selection Mode	
✓	Word Count	10547 words	✓ Macro Recording	Not Recording
	Character Count (with spaces)	61172 characters	✓ Accessibility Checker	Accessibility: Investigate
✓	Spelling and Grammar Check	Errors	✓ Upload Status	
✓	Language		✓ Document Updates Available	
✓	Label		✓ Focus	
✓	Signatures	Off	✓ View Shortcuts	
	Information Management Policy	Off	✓ Zoom Slider	
			✓ Zoom	100%

A check mark indicates each active status bar tool

2. Click to activate or deactivate a status bar indicator or tool. The change is implemented immediately. The menu remains open to permit multiple selections.

3. When you finish, click away from the menu to close it.

Discover new features

1

To go along with the name change from Office 365, many new features have been incorporated into the Microsoft 365 apps since the previous edition of this book. These warrant special attention in this chapter because they might fall outside the range of the content that was selected from the individual Word, Excel, PowerPoint, and Outlook Step by Step books for this compilation.

- The user interface does not display the Quick Access Toolbar by default. You can display it above or below the ribbon and add controls to it from the Customize Quick Access Toolbar menu, the Options dialog, or the ribbon, just as before.

- The Save command that was previously on the Quick Access Toolbar is now located at the left end of the title bar, along with the new AutoSave toggle. AutoSave is available only for files that are stored in the Microsoft cloud (in OneDrive or SharePoint).

- Also for cloud-stored files, you can rename or move a file while editing it, display its version history, and display, compare, and restore previous file versions from the title bar.

- In the center of the title bar, the Microsoft Search feature provides quick access to file content, app features, Help articles, and previously edited files. You can type a search term into the search box or select the microphone and then speak the search term.

- If you prefer speaking to typing, you can enter content into files by using the Dictate feature that's available from the Home tab in Word documents, PowerPoint presentations, and Outlook message composition windows.

> ⚠️ **IMPORTANT** The audio search and dictation features require an audio card and an audio input device such as a built-in, headset, or USB-connected microphone.

- When you dock multiple panes on the right side of the app window—for example the Styles pane and the Alt Text pane, or even the Navigation pane— they arrange themselves on tabs, taking up only the space of one pane.

- You can increase the space between commands on the ribbon, menus, and the status bar to make it easier to access the right command when working on a touch-enabled device such as a tablet.

- Many accessibility features have been incorporated into the apps.

  - The Accessibility Checker runs by default in the background.

  - An Accessibility command on the status bar provides immediate feedback as to the accessibility of your document, presentation, or workbook and easy access to the Accessibility Pane, which displays the Accessibility Checker's findings and suggested solutions.

  - Alt text is automatically added to pictures that you insert into documents, presentations, and email messages. (You can, and should, review and refine the automatically generated alt text.)

  - Accessibility tools are available from a new Accessibility group on the Review tab of each app. From here you have quick access to app-specific accessibility-related options in the Options dialog.

> ⚠ **IMPORTANT** Accessibility is frequently associated with the availability of content to people with disabilities such as limited vision or hearing loss, or to people who use assistive technologies such as screen readers, screen magnifiers, or braille displays. In fact, a website or document that is designed for accessibility is easier for *all* people to navigate and comprehend, regardless of the method they use to access the content.

- The ribbon display options now support the display of the whole ribbon, only the tabs, or a full-screen display that entirely hides the ribbon.

- In Word, a new Focus mode displays document content against a black background with none of the app interface visible. You can turn on Focus mode from the status bar or View tab and turn it off by pressing the Esc key.

- An extensive library of professional-quality images, icons, and (in PowerPoint) videos is available from the Insert Pictures menu. The Online Pictures feature provides easy access to thousands of Creative Commons–licensed images that you can browse by category or locate by search term.

- The Help tab provides access to find information and training resources, contact Microsoft Support, provide feedback about features you like and don't like, and suggest features you'd like to see in future releases. You can also access the release notes for each recent release of the app.

- In Excel:

    - A new Navigation Pane provides easy access to tables, charts, and other elements. This is particularly helpful in workbooks that include a lot of worksheets.

    - The Analyze Data tool provides powerful analysis capabilities for the data you save in workbooks.

    - From the Help tab, you can drop in on or participate in Excel community groups and read blog posts from the product-development team.

Each new release of Office has new features, fixes, or just improvements. As with the certainty of death and taxes, the one thing we know is that we don't know what we don't know! Most people who use a new version of a product try to accomplish things the same way they did in the old version, but this might be more work than necessary. If you're a seasoned Office app user, review the ribbon tabs, Backstage view pages, and Options dialog for any new or modified features that will simplify the tasks you perform and support your productivity.

Change Office and app options

You access app settings from the Backstage view—specifically, from the Account page and the Options dialog.

Manage account information

The Account page of the Backstage view in each Office app (other than Outlook, in which it's called the Office Account page) displays information specific to your installation of the app. This information includes:

- Your Microsoft account and links to manage it.

- The current app window background and theme.

- Storage locations and services (such as OneDrive and SharePoint) that you've connected Office to.

- Your subscription information and links to manage the subscription, if you have Office through an Office 365 subscription.

- The installed app version and build number, update options, and links to information about the app and recent updates.

Account information in Word

Microsoft account options

If you use Microsoft 365, Office 365, Skype, OneDrive, or Xbox Live, or have an Outlook.com or Hotmail.com email address, you already have a Microsoft account. (Microsoft account credentials are also used by many non-Microsoft products and websites.) If you don't already have a Microsoft account, you can register any existing account as a Microsoft account, sign up for a free Outlook.com or Hotmail.com account and register that as a Microsoft account, or create an alias for an Outlook.com account and register the alias.

> **TIP** Many apps and websites authenticate transactions by using Microsoft account credentials. For that reason, it's a good idea to register a personal account that you control, rather than a business account that your employer controls, as your Microsoft account. That way, you won't risk losing access if you leave the company.

You can personalize the appearance of your Office app windows by choosing an Office theme. There are five Office theme options:

- **Dark Gray** Displays the title bar and ribbon tabs in dark gray, and the ribbon commands, status bar, and Backstage view in light gray.

- **Black** Displays the title bar, ribbon tabs, ribbon commands, and status bar in black and dark gray.

- **White** Displays the title bar, ribbon tabs, and ribbon commands in white, and the status bar in the app-specific color.

- **Use System Setting** Coordinates the Office app window settings with the Windows theme settings.

- **Colorful** Displays the title bar and ribbon tabs in a color specific to the app (such as blue for Word and green for Excel), and the ribbon commands, status bar, and Backstage view in light gray.

You can also choose an Office background, which is a subtle design that appears in the title bar area of the Backstage view. (In previous versions of the Office apps, it appeared in the title bar of the app window, regardless of the active tab.) There are 14 different backgrounds to choose from—Calligraphy, Circles and Stripes, Circuit, Clouds, Doodle Circles, Doodle Diamonds, Geometry, Lunchbox, School Supplies, Spring, Stars, Straws, Tree Rings, and Underwater. If you prefer to not clutter up the title bar, you can choose to not have a background.

From the Connected Services area of the page, you can connect Office to SharePoint sites and OneDrive storage locations to access the files you store there. You must already have an account with one of these services to connect Office to it.

Until you connect to storage locations, they aren't available to you from within Word. For example, when inserting a picture onto a page, you will have the option to insert a locally stored picture or to search online for a picture. After you connect to your SharePoint or OneDrive accounts, you can also insert pictures stored in those locations.

The changes you make on the Account page apply to all the Office apps installed on all the computers associated with your account. For example, changing the Office background in Word on one computer also changes it in Outlook on any other computer on which you've associated Office with the same account.

To display your Office account settings

1. Start Word, Excel, PowerPoint, or Outlook.

2. Select the **File** tab to display the Backstage view of the app, and then do either of the following:

   - In Word, Excel, or PowerPoint, select **Account**.

   - In Outlook, select **Office Account**.

To manage your Microsoft account connection

1. Display the **Account** or **Office Account** page of the Backstage view.

2. In the **User Information** area, select **Change photo**, **About me**, **Sign out**, or **Switch account** to begin the selected process.

To change the app window background for all Office apps

1. Display the **Account** or **Office Account** page of the Backstage view.

2. In the **Office Background** list, point to any background to display a live preview in the app window, and then select the background you want.

To change the app window color scheme for all Office apps

1. Display the **Account** or **Office Account** page of the Backstage view.

2. In the **Office Theme** list, select **Colorful**, **Dark Gray**, **Black**, or **White**.

To connect to a cloud storage location

1. Display the **Account** or **Office Account** page of the Backstage view.

2. At the bottom of the **Connected Services** area, select **Add a service**, **Storage**, and then the specific service you want to add.

Connect to personal and business cloud storage locations

To manage your Office 365 subscription

1. Display the **Account** or **Office Account** page of the Backstage view.

2. In the **Product Information** area, select **Manage Account** to display the sign-in page for your Office 365 management interface.

3. Provide your account credentials and sign in to access your options.

To manage Office updates

1. Display the **Account** or **Office Account** page of the Backstage view.

2. Select the **Update Options** button, and then select the action you want to take.

You can install available updates from the Backstage view before the automatic installation occurs

Manage app options

Selecting Options in the left pane of the Backstage view opens the app-specific Options dialog. Every Options dialog has a General tab where you can set user-specific information that is shared among the Office apps (some of this is the same information you can configure in the Backstage view) and configure high-level app-specific options.

Excel Options   ?   ✕

General		General options for working with Excel.
Formulas		
Data		
Proofing		
Save		
Language		
Accessibility		
Advanced		
Customize Ribbon		
Quick Access Toolbar		
Add-ins		
Trust Center		

User Interface options

When using multiple displays: ⓘ
- ◉ Optimize for best _appearance_
- ○ Optimize for _compatibility_ (application restart required)

☑ Show _M_ini Toolbar on selection ⓘ
☑ Show _Q_uick Analysis options on selection
☑ Show Convert to Da_t_a Types when typing ⓘ
☑ Enable _L_ive Preview ⓘ
☐ Collapse the ribbo_n_ automatically ⓘ
☐ Collapse the Microsoft Search box by default ⓘ

Scr_e_enTip style: [Show feature descriptions in ScreenTips   ▼]

When creating new workbooks

Use this as the default fo_n_t: [Body Font   ▼]
Font si_z_e: [11 ▼]
Default _v_iew for new sheets: [Normal View   ▼]
Include this many _s_heets: [1   ⌃⌄]

Personalize your copy of Microsoft Office

_U_ser name: [Joan Lambert]
☐ _A_lways use these values regardless of sign in to Office.
Office _B_ackground: [Doodle Circles   ▼]
Office _T_heme: [Use system setting ▼]

Privacy Settings

[Privacy Settings...]

LinkedIn Features

Use LinkedIn features in Office to stay connected with your professional network and keep up to date in your industry.
☑ Enable LinkedIn features in my Office applications ⓘ

About LinkedIn Features   Manage LinkedIn account associations

Start up options

Choose the extensions you want Excel to open by default: [_D_efault Programs...]
☑ _T_ell me if Microsoft Excel isn't the default program for viewing and editing spreadsheets.
☑ S_h_ow the Start screen when this application starts

[OK]   [Cancel]

You can customize the behavior of each app from its Options dialog

Each app's Options dialog contains hundreds of settings specific to that app. For example, you can make the following useful changes:

- **In Word** You can configure spelling and grammar-checking options including your writing style, change the default behavior when pasting content, and specify the view when opening an email attachment.

- **In Excel** You can change the default workbook font and number of worksheets, formula calculation and autocomplete options, error-checking rules, and the direction the cell selection moves when you press the Enter key.

- **In PowerPoint** You can turn on or off PowerPoint Designer suggestions and the automatic generation of alt text for pictures and configure the display of slideshow options such as the toolbar and blank ending slide.

- **In Outlook** You can configure the default appearance of outgoing messages, automatically create meetings as Teams meetings, customize your calendar so that the working days reflect your schedule, add the holidays of any country or region to your calendar, and store your Outlook settings in the cloud so they carry over to other computers on which you use Outlook.

There are also settings specific to the file you're working in. For example, you can hide spelling or grammar errors in a specific document or specify the image compression level for a document or presentation to increase image quality or decrease file size.

Some settings are available in all the app Options dialogs, including the following:

- Turn off the Mini Toolbar, which hosts common formatting commands and appears by default when you select content.

- Turn off the Live Preview feature if you find it distracting to have document formatting change when the pointer passes over a formatting command.

- Minimize or turn off the display of ScreenTips when you point to buttons.

- Specify the user name and initials you want to accompany your comments and tracked changes, and override the display of information from the account associated with your installation of Office.

- Turn off the Home pages for Word, Excel, and PowerPoint individually. When the Home page is turned off, starting the app without opening a specific file automatically creates a new, blank file.

After you work with an app for a while, you might want to refine more settings to tailor the app to the way you work. Knowing what options are available in the Options dialog is helpful in determining the changes that you can make to the app so that you can work most efficiently.

> ✅ **TIP** Although detailed coverage of each app's Options dialog is beyond the scope of this book, extensive information is available in the *Step by Step* book for each app, including *Microsoft Word Step by Step (Office 2021 and Microsoft 365)*, by Joan Lambert (Microsoft Press, 2022), and *Microsoft Excel Step by Step (Office 2021 and Microsoft 365)*, by Joan Lambert (Microsoft Press, 2021).

> ✅ **TIP** Two app elements you can customize from the Options dialog are the Quick Access Toolbar and the ribbon. For information, see "Display and Customize the Quick Access Toolbar" and "Customize the ribbon" later in this chapter.

To open an app-specific Options dialog

1. Select the **File** tab to display the Backstage view.

2. In the left pane, select **Options**.

To enable or disable the Mini Toolbar

1. Open the app-specific **Options** dialog.

2. On the **General** page, in the **User Interface options** area, select or clear the **Show Mini Toolbar on selection** checkbox. Then select **OK**.

To enable or disable the Live Preview feature

1. Open the app-specific **Options** dialog.

2. On the **General** page, in the **User Interface options** area, select or clear the **Enable Live Preview** checkbox. Then select **OK**.

To control the display of ScreenTips

1. Open the app-specific **Options** dialog.

2. On the **General** page, in the **User Interface options** area, display the **ScreenTip style** list, and then select any of the following:

   - **Show feature descriptions in ScreenTips**

   - **Don't show feature descriptions in ScreenTips**

   - **Don't show ScreenTips**

3. In the **Options** dialog, select **OK**.

To change the user identification that appears in comments and tracked changes

> ⚠️ **IMPORTANT** The User Name and Initials settings are shared by all the Office apps, so changing them in any one app changes them in all the apps.

1. Open the app-specific **Options** dialog.

2. On the **General** page, in the **Personalize your copy of Microsoft Office** area, do the following:

   - In the **User name** and **Initials** boxes, enter the information you want to use.

   - Select the **Always use these values regardless of sign in to Office** checkbox.

3. In the **Options** dialog, select **OK**.

To enable or disable the Home screen for the app

1. Open the app-specific **Options** dialog.

2. On the **General** page, in the **Start up options** area, select or clear the **Show the Start screen when this application starts** checkbox. Then select **OK**.

Display and customize the Quick Access Toolbar

The Quick Access Toolbar is a customizable toolbar that you can display above or below the ribbon. If you regularly use a few commands that are scattered on various tabs of the ribbon and you don't want to switch between tabs to access the commands, you might want to add them to the Quick Access Toolbar so that they're always available to you.

You can configure a separate Quick Access Toolbar for each Office app. By default, the Quick Access Toolbar is available in all files that you open in that app. You can also create a Quick Access Toolbar that is specific to a file and travels with it, so the commands are available to anyone who opens that file.

You can add commands to the Quick Access Toolbar from a menu on the toolbar, directly from the ribbon, or from the Quick Access Toolbar page of the app-specific Options dialog.

The Quick Access Toolbar is the most convenient command organization option

> **TIP** You can display a list of commands that do not appear on the ribbon by selecting Commands Not In The Ribbon in the Choose Commands From list on the Quick Access Toolbar or on the Customize Ribbon page of the app-specific Options dialog.

You can customize the Quick Access Toolbar in the following ways:

- Define a custom Quick Access Toolbar for all files opened in the app or for a specific file.

- Add any command from any group of any tab, including tool tabs, to the toolbar.

- Display a separator between different types of buttons.

- Move commands around on the toolbar until they are in the order you want.

- Reset everything back to the default Quick Access Toolbar configuration.

After you add commands to the Quick Access Toolbar, you can reorganize them and divide them into groups to simplify the process of locating the command you want.

As you add commands to the Quick Access Toolbar, it expands to accommodate them. If you add a lot of commands, it might become difficult to view the text in the title bar, or all the commands on the Quick Access Toolbar might not be visible, defeating the purpose of adding them. To resolve this problem and also position the Quick Access Toolbar closer to the file content, you can move the Quick Access Toolbar below the ribbon.

To display the Quick Access Toolbar

- Right-click any ribbon tab and then select **Show Quick Access Toolbar**.

- Right-click any command on the ribbon, and then select **Show Quick Access Toolbar**.

- In the left pane of the **Options** dialog, select **Quick Access Toolbar**. On the **Customize the Quick Access Toolbar** page, select the **Show Quick Access Toolbar** checkbox, and then select **OK**.

To add a popular command to the Quick Access Toolbar

- At the right end of the Quick Access Toolbar, select the **Customize Quick Access Toolbar** button. On the menu of commonly used commands, select a command you want to add.

Commonly used commands are available from the menu

To add a command to the Quick Access Toolbar from the ribbon

- Right-click a command on the ribbon, and then select **Add to Quick Access Toolbar**. You can add any type of command this way; you can even add a drop-down list of options or gallery of thumbnails.

To display the Quick Access Toolbar page of the Options dialog

- At the right end of the Quick Access Toolbar, select the **Customize Quick Access Toolbar** button, and then select **More Commands**.

- Select the **File** tab and then, in the left pane of the Backstage view, select **Options**. In the left pane of the **Options** dialog, select **Quick Access Toolbar**.

- Right-click any ribbon tab or empty area of the ribbon, and then select **Customize Quick Access Toolbar**.

To add a command to the Quick Access Toolbar from the Options dialog

1. Display the **Quick Access Toolbar** page of the **Options** dialog.

2. In the **Choose commands from** list, select the tab the command appears on, or select **Popular Commands**, **Commands Not in the Ribbon**, **All Commands**, or **Macros**.

3. In the left list, locate and select the command you want to add to the Quick Access Toolbar. Then select the **Add** button.

4. Make any other changes, and then select **OK** in the **Options** dialog.

To move the Quick Access Toolbar

- At the right end of the Quick Access Toolbar, select the **Customize Quick Access Toolbar** button, and then select **Show Below the Ribbon** or **Show Above the Ribbon**.

- Display the **Quick Access Toolbar** page of the **Options** dialog. Below the Choose Commands From pane, select or clear the **Show Quick Access Toolbar below the Ribbon** checkbox.

To define a custom Quick Access Toolbar for a specific file

1. Display the **Quick Access Toolbar** page of the **Options** dialog.

2. In the **Customize Quick Access Toolbar** list (above the right pane) select **For** *file name*.

3. Add the commands to the toolbar that you want to make available to anyone who edits the file, and then select **OK**. The app displays the file-specific Quick Access Toolbar to the right of the user's own Quick Access Toolbar.

> ✓ **TIP** If a command is on a user's Quick Access Toolbar and on a file-specific Quick Access Toolbar, it will be shown in both toolbars.

To display a separator on the Quick Access Toolbar

1. Display the **Quick Access Toolbar** page of the **Options** dialog.

2. In the right pane, select the command after which you want to insert the separator.

3. Do either of the following:

   - In the left pane, double-click **<Separator>**.

   - Select **<Separator>** in the left pane, and then select the **Add** button.

4. Make any other changes you want, and then select **OK**.

To move buttons on the Quick Access Toolbar

1. Display the **Quick Access Toolbar** page of the **Options** dialog.

2. In the right pane, select the button you want to move. Then select the **Move Up** or **Move Down** arrow until the button reaches the position you want.

To reset the Quick Access Toolbar to its default configuration

1. Display the **Quick Access Toolbar** page of the **Options** dialog.

2. In the lower-right corner of the page, select **Reset**, and then select either of the following:

   - **Reset only Quick Access Toolbar**

   - **Reset all customizations**

3. In the **Microsoft Office** message box verifying the change, select **Yes**.

> ⚠ **IMPORTANT** Resetting the Quick Access Toolbar does not change its location. You must manually move the Quick Access Toolbar by using either of the procedures described earlier.

Customize the ribbon

The ribbon was designed to make all the commonly used commands visible so that people can more easily discover the full potential of an Office app. But many people use the same app to perform the same set of tasks all the time, and for them, seeing buttons (or even entire groups of buttons) that they never use is just another form of clutter.

Would you prefer to display fewer commands, not more? Or would you prefer to display more specialized groups of commands? Well, you can. From the Customize Ribbon page of an app's Options dialog, you can control the tabs that appear on the ribbon, and the groups that appear on the tabs.

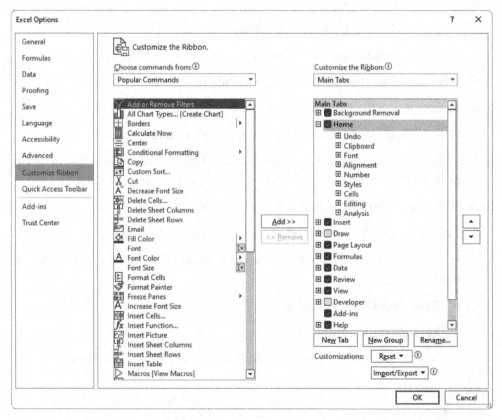

You can hide and display individual ribbon tabs

1

On this page, you can customize the ribbon in the following ways:

- Hide an entire tab.

- Remove a group of commands from a tab.'(The group is not removed from the app, only from the tab.)

- Move or copy a group of commands to another tab.

- Create a custom group on any tab and then add commands to it. (You cannot add commands to a predefined group.)

- Create a custom tab. For example, you might want to do this if you use only a few commands from each tab and you find it inefficient to flip between them.

Don't be afraid to experiment with the ribbon to come up with the configuration that best suits the way you work. If at any point you find that your new ribbon is harder to work with rather than easier, you can easily reset everything back to the default configuration.

> **IMPORTANT** Although customizing the default ribbon content might seem like a great way of making the app yours, it isn't recommended that you do so. A great deal of research has been done about the way that people use the commands in each app, and the ribbon has been organized to reflect the results of that research. If you modify the default ribbon settings, you might end up inadvertently hiding or moving commands that you need. Instead, consider the Quick Access Toolbar as the command area that you customize and make your own. If you add all the commands you use frequently to the Quick Access Toolbar, you can hide the ribbon and have extra vertical space for document display (this is very convenient when working on a smaller device). Or, if you really want to customize the ribbon, do so by gathering your most frequently used commands on a custom tab, and leave the others alone.

To display the Customize Ribbon page of the Options dialog

- Display the **Options** dialog, and in the left pane, select **Customize Ribbon**.

- Right-click any ribbon tab or empty area of the ribbon, and then select **Customize the Ribbon**.

To permit or prevent the display of a tab

1. Display the **Customize Ribbon** page of the **Options** dialog.

2. In the **Customize the Ribbon** list, select the tab set you want to manage:

   - All Tabs

   - Main Tabs

   - Tool Tabs

3. In the right pane, select or clear the checkbox of any tab other than the File tab. (You can't hide the File tab.)

To remove a group of commands from a tab

1. Display the **Customize Ribbon** page of the **Options** dialog.

2. In the **Customize the Ribbon** list, select the tab set you want to manage.

3. In the right pane, select the **Expand** button (+) to the left of the tab you want to modify.

4. Select the group you want to remove, and then in the center pane, select the **Remove** button.

To create a custom tab

1. Display the **Customize Ribbon** page of the **Options** dialog.

2. On the **Customize Ribbon** page, select the **New Tab** button to insert a new custom tab below the active tab in the right pane. The new tab includes an empty custom group.

Creating a new tab and group

To rename a custom tab

1. Select the custom tab, and then select the **Rename** button.

2. In the **Rename** dialog, replace the existing tab name with the tab name you want, and then select **OK**.

To rename a custom group

1. Select the custom group, and then select the **Rename** button to open a **Rename** dialog that includes hundreds of symbol options.

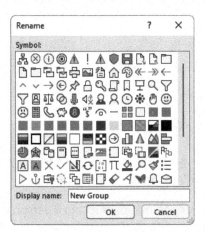

You can assign an icon to appear when the group is minimized

2. In the **Rename** dialog, change the display name, select the symbol you want to display when the ribbon is too narrow to display the group's commands, and then select **OK**.

To create a custom group

1. Display the **Customize Ribbon** page of the **Options** dialog.

2. On the **Customize Ribbon** page, in the right pane, select the tab you want to add the group to. Then select the **New Group** button to add an empty custom group.

To add commands to a custom group

1. Display the **Customize Ribbon** page of the **Options** dialog.

2. In the **Customize the Ribbon** list, expand the tab set you want to manage, and then select the group you want to add the commands to.

3. In the **Choose commands from** list, select the tab the command appears on, or select **Popular Commands**, **Commands Not in the Ribbon**, **All Commands**, or **Macros**.

4. In the left list, locate and select the command you want to add to the group. Then select the **Add** button.

5. Make any other changes, and then select **OK**.

To reset the ribbon to its default configuration

1. Display the **Customize Ribbon** page of the **Options** dialog.

2. In the lower-right corner of the page, select **Reset**, and then select either of the following:

   - **Reset only selected Ribbon tab**

   - **Reset all customizations**

Get help and provide feedback

The Office apps put help at your fingertips, quite literally, and make it easy for you to express your opinions and make requests about app features.

You can get information about a specific topic or command, or locate a person or file, by using the Microsoft Search feature that is conveniently located in the center of the title bar.

The easy path to help in any Office app

The Help tab provides access to app information and training resources, as well as a way to contact the Microsoft Support team or submit feedback about your Office experience. You can browse general information about the current app, and find links to additional training resources, in the Help pane.

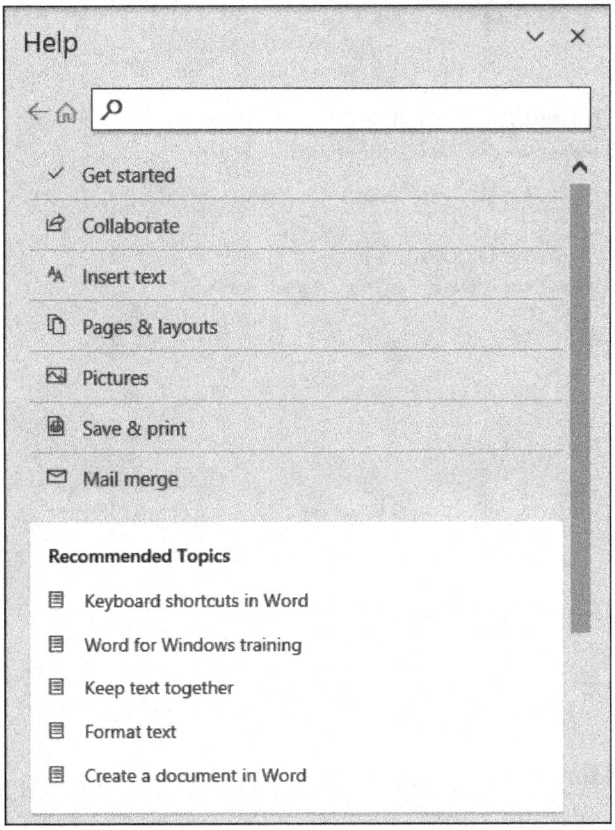

Help

Get started

Collaborate

Insert text

Pages & layouts

Pictures

Save & print

Mail merge

Recommended Topics

Keyboard shortcuts in Word

Word for Windows training

Keep text together

Format text

Create a document in Word

The Help pane displays online content from a variety of resources

As you use the apps and find things that work or don't work for you, you can provide feedback directly to Microsoft from within the program. You can review and vote for existing feature requests and add your own requests. This functionality has been available to early reviewers in the past but is now available to all Office users.

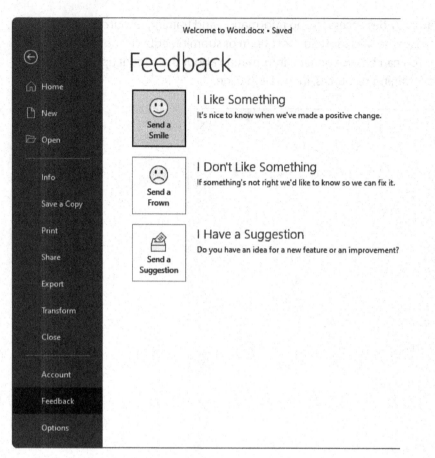

Send feedback and feature requests

To use the Microsoft Search feature

1. Do one of the following to activate the search box:

   - On the title bar, click in the **Search** box when it is maximized.

   - On the title bar, select the **Search** icon when the search box is minimized.

   - Press **Alt+Q**.

2. In the search box that appears, enter a search term to display a list of related commands and links to online resources, contacts, and files.

Or

1. On the title bar, in the maximized Search box, select the microphone icon.

2. When the search box displays "Listening..." speak your search term or question.

> ⚠️ **IMPORTANT** The audio search feature requires an audio card and an audio input device such as a built-in, headset, or USB-connected microphone.

To display the Help pane

- Press **F1**.
- On the **Help** tab, in the **Help** group, select **Help**.

To display the Feedback page of the Backstage view

- On the **Help** tab, in the **Help** group, select **Feedback**.
- Select the **File** tab to display the Backstage view, and then select the **Feedback** tab.

To send positive or negative feedback about an Office app feature

1. If you want to include a screenshot of something specific with your feedback, display it on the screen before proceeding.

2. Display the **Feedback** page of the Backstage view.

3. Select either **Send a Smile** or **Send a Frown** to open a feedback pane.

Send detailed feedback to the Office team

4. In the message box, enter your feedback. Be as specific as possible; if you're reporting a problem, detail the steps that led to the problem.

5. If you want to submit a screenshot of the current app window, select the **Include screenshot** checkbox.

6. If you want Microsoft to follow up with you on your query, select the **You can contact me about this feedback** checkbox and then enter your email address.

7. If you're submitting negative feedback, have not opted into optional diagnostics, and do not want Microsoft to receive system data that might help to diagnose a problem Office is having, clear the **Include diagnostic and usage data** checkbox.

8. Select **Submit** to send your feedback.

To suggest changes to an Office app

1. Display the **Feedback** page, and then select **Send a Suggestion** to go to the online feedback forum for the app you're working in.

2. In the **Enter your idea** box, enter basic terms related to your idea to filter the existing ideas.

3. If an existing idea is the suggestion you want to make, vote for it by selecting **Vote** to the left of the idea title.

4. If your idea hasn't already been suggested, select **Post a new idea**, enter a detailed yet succinct description of your idea, enter your email address (for Microsoft's use only), and then select **Post idea**.

 TIP Most Office Help content is stored online, so it isn't available to you when you don't have an internet connection.

Key points

- Word, Excel, PowerPoint, Outlook, and other Office apps share many common user interface elements.

- You can change the appearance and functionality of the Office apps. Changes to the color scheme or app header image affect all Office apps on all computers linked to your user account.

- You can specify the commands that you want to appear on the Quick Access Toolbar, put them in the order you want, and separate them into groups.

- You can create a file-specific Quick Access Toolbar that will be available to other people who open the file.

- You can move the Quick Access Toolbar below the ribbon and closer to the file content.

- You can specify the commands that you want to appear on the standard ribbon tabs, hide or display standard tabs other than the File tab, and create custom tabs and groups of commands.

- App information and training is now available from the Help tab within each app. Most help content is stored online, so it is not available to you when your computer or device is offline.

- You can send feedback and feature requests to the Office team, and review and vote for requests that other people have made.

Chapter 1

Practice tasks

No practice files are necessary to complete the practice tasks in this chapter.

Work in the Office user interface

Start Word, create a new blank document, maximize the app window, and then perform the following tasks:

1. On each tab of the ribbon, do the following:

   - Review the available groups and commands.

   - Display the ScreenTip of any command you're not familiar with. Notice the different levels of detail in the ScreenTips.

   - If a group has a dialog launcher in its lower-right corner, select the dialog launcher to display the associated dialog or pane.

2. Change the width of the app window and notice the effect it has on the ribbon. When the window is narrow, locate and select a group button to display the group of commands.

3. Maximize the app window. Hide the ribbon entirely and notice the change in the app window. Redisplay the ribbon tabs (but not the commands). Temporarily display the ribbon commands, and then click away from the ribbon to close it.

4. Use any of the procedures described in this chapter to permanently redisplay the ribbon tabs and commands.

5. Display the status bar shortcut menu, and identify the tools and statistics currently displayed on the status bar. Add any indicators to the status bar that will be useful to you.

6. Keep Word open for use in a later set of practice tasks.

Discover new features

Display the Word app window, and then perform the following tasks:

1. Display the **Account** page of the Backstage view and review the information available there.

2. Select the **Update Options** button and note whether updates are currently available to install.

> ✓ **TIP** The update process might require that you exit all the Office apps. If updates are available, apply them after you finish the practice tasks in this chapter.

3. On the **Update Options** menu, select **View Updates** to display the *What's New in Microsoft 365* webpage in your default browser. Review the information on this page to learn about the latest features of Word, Excel, PowerPoint, Outlook, and any other apps that interest you.

4. Keep Word open for use in a later set of practice tasks.

Change Office and app options

Start Excel, create a new blank workbook, and then perform the following tasks:

1. Display the **Account** page of the Backstage view and review the information available there.

2. Expand the **Office Background** list. Point to each theme to display a live preview of it. Then select the theme you want to apply.

3. Apply each of the Office themes and consider its merits. Then apply the theme you like best.

> ✓ **TIP** If you apply a theme other than Colorful, your interface colors will be different from the interface shown in the screenshots in this book, but the functionality will be the same.

4. Review the services that Office is currently connected to. Expand the **Add a service** menu and point to each of the menu items to display the available services. Connect to any of these that you want to use.

5. Return to Excel and open the **Excel Options** dialog.

6. Explore each page of the dialog. Notice the sections and the settings in each section. Note the settings that apply only to the current file.

7. Review the settings on the **General** page and modify them as necessary to fit the way you work. Then close the dialog.

8. Keep Excel open for use in the next set of practice tasks.

Display and customize the Quick Access Toolbar

Display the Excel app window, and then perform the following tasks:

1. Configure Excel to display the Quick Access Toolbar below the ribbon. Consider the merits of this location versus above the ribbon.

2. From the **Customize Quick Access Toolbar** menu, add the **Sort Ascending** command to the Quick Access Toolbar.

3. From the **Home** tab of the ribbon, add the following commands to the Quick Access Toolbar:

   - From the **Number** group, add the **Number Format** list.

   - From the **Styles** group, add the **Format as Table** command.

   Notice that each of the commands is represented on the Quick Access Toolbar exactly as it is on the ribbon. Selecting Number Format displays a list and selecting Format As Table displays a gallery.

4. From the **Sheet Options** group on the **Page Layout** tab, add the **View Gridlines** command and the **View Headings** command to the Quick Access Toolbar. Notice that the commands are represented on the Quick Access Toolbar as identically labeled checkboxes.

5. Point to each of the **View** commands on the Quick Access Toolbar and then on the ribbon to display its ScreenTip. Notice that ScreenTips for commands on the Quick Access Toolbar are identical to those for commands on the ribbon.

6. Display the **Quick Access Toolbar** page of the **Excel Options** dialog, and then do the following:

   - In the left pane, display the commands that appear on the **View** tab.

   - Add the **Page Break Preview** button from the **View** tab to the Quick Access Toolbar.

   - In the right pane, move the **Sort Ascending** button to the bottom of the list so that it will be the rightmost optional button on the Quick Access Toolbar (immediately to the left of the Customize Quick Access Toolbar button).

   - Insert a separator between the original commands and the commands you added in this task set.

   - Insert two separators between the **Number Format** and **Format As Table** commands.

7. Close the **Excel Options** dialog and observe your customized Quick Access Toolbar. Note the way that a single separator sets off commands, and the way that a double separator sets off commands.

8. Redisplay the **Quick Access Toolbar** page of the **Excel Options** dialog.

9. Reset the Quick Access Toolbar to its default configuration, and then close the dialog. Notice that resetting the Quick Access Toolbar does not change its location.

10. Close the workbook without saving it.

Customize the ribbon

Display the Word app window, and then perform the following tasks:

1. Display the **Customize Ribbon** page of the **Word Options** dialog.

2. Remove the **Mailings** tab from the ribbon and add the **Developer** tab (if it isn't already shown).

3. Create a custom tab and name it MyShapes.

4. Move the **MyShapes** tab to the top of the right pane so that it will be the leftmost optional ribbon tab (immediately to the right of the File tab).

5. Change the name of the custom group on the **MyShapes** tab to Curved Shapes and select a curved or circular icon to represent the group.

6. Create another custom group on the **MyShapes** tab. Name the group Angular Shapes and select a square or triangular icon to represent the group.

7. In the **Choose commands from** list, select **Commands Not in the Ribbon**. From the list, add the **Arc** and **Oval** commands to the **Curved Shapes** group. Then add the **Isosceles Triangle** and **Rectangle** commands to the **Angular Shapes** group.

8. Close the **Word Options** dialog and display your custom tab. Select the **Arc** command, and then drag on the page to draw an arc.

9. Change the width of the app window to collapse at least one custom group and verify that the group button displays the icon you selected.

10. Restore the app window to its original width and redisplay the **Customize Ribbon** page of the **Word Options** dialog.

11. Reset the ribbon to its default configuration, and then close the dialog.

12. Close the document without saving it.

Get help and provide feedback

Start PowerPoint, create a new blank presentation, and then perform the following tasks:

1. Using the Microsoft Search feature or Help pane, locate information about inserting 3D models onto PowerPoint slides. Then research any other topics that interest you.

2. From the ribbon, display the **Feedback** page of the Backstage view and review the options available there.

3. Select **Send a Suggestion** to go to the PowerPoint online Feedback forum. Review the feature requests that have already been made. If you find a feature request that would be particularly helpful to you, sign in and vote for it.

4. Close the webpage and return to the **Feedback** page.

5. If you've already found a feature that you like or dislike, display that feature or an example of it, and then send feedback that includes a screenshot.

Create and manage files

When working in Microsoft Word, Excel, or PowerPoint, you save content in individual files. In each app, you can save files as different types, depending on each file's purpose. The standard files are Word documents, Excel workbooks, and PowerPoint presentations. Regardless of the app or file type, you use similar techniques for creating and working in files, for changing the display of content, and for displaying and modifying the information stored with each file (its properties).

You don't often create freestanding files when working with Outlook items (although you can create template files and save messages and other Outlook items as files). The component of this chapter that relates to Outlook is the discussion of views. In Outlook, you choose views not of a file but of an entire module—such as the Calendar module. Displaying different views of modules can help you locate specific items or information more easily. Similarly, displaying different views of files or different file elements can make it easier to work in a document, on a worksheet, or on a slide. Each app offers a variety of content views.

This chapter guides you through procedures related to creating files, opening and moving around in files, displaying different views of files, displaying file properties, and saving and closing files, using techniques that are common to working in files created in Word, Excel, or PowerPoint.

In this chapter

- Create files
- Open and move around in files
- Display different views of files
- Display and edit file properties
- Save and close files

Create files

When creating a new document, workbook, or presentation, you can start with a blank file or a file based on a template. Word, Excel, and PowerPoint templates specify thematic elements (colors, fonts, and graphic effects) and often contain purpose-specific placeholder content to help you get started. PowerPoint templates also include customized slide layouts and images. You can customize the content and appearance of documents, workbooks, and presentations that you create from templates just as you can when you start from scratch. (The exception to this is when working with a protected file that limits the available styles or actions.)

- Word and Excel offer content templates that provide starting points for common types of documents (such as reports) or workbooks (such as budgets).

- PowerPoint offers some content templates, but most are design templates that control thematic elements and slide layouts.

Each template has an attached theme, so you can create a document, workbook, or presentation based on one template but then entirely change its appearance by applying a different theme, or by selecting a different set of theme fonts, theme colors, or theme effects.

As discussed in Chapter 1, "Explore Office," when you start Word, Excel, or PowerPoint without opening a file, the app displays a Home page that gives you options for opening and creating files. Additional options for creating new files are available from the New page of the Backstage view. The New page is available when you start the app without opening a file and when you're working in a file—the layout of the left pane of the Backstage view is different in these cases, but the content of the New page is the same.

> ✓ **TIP** The size of the Home, New, and Open page tabs in the left pane of the Backstage view changes based on the available space. At some screen resolutions and window sizes, the page tabs are as tall as they are wide.

> ⚠ **IMPORTANT** The templates that appear by default in your installation of Word, Excel, or PowerPoint might be different from those shown in images in this book. The templates change depending on your use of the app and the installation of app updates.

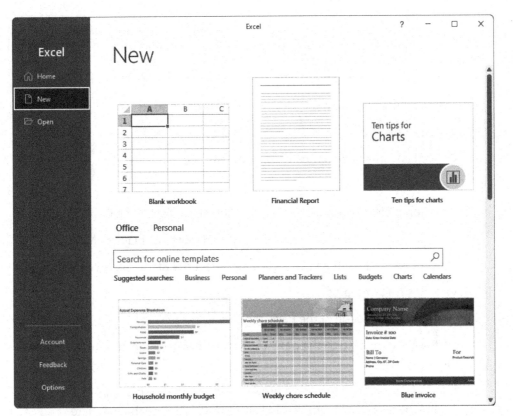

2

The New page of the Excel backstage view

You can start new files in different ways:

- You can start from a blank document, workbook, or presentation that contains one page, worksheet, or slide. You can then add content, apply structure and design elements, and make any necessary configuration changes.

- You can save time by basing your file on one of the many content and design templates that come with the Office apps. You can also preview and download many prepopulated templates from the Office website. These templates provide not only the design elements but also suggestions for content that is appropriate for different types of presentations, such as reports or product launches. After you download a template, you simply customize the content provided in the template to meet your needs.

> **TIP** You can suppress the Home page (also called the Start screen) if you want to go directly to a new, blank file when you start an app. For more information, see "Change Office and app options" in Chapter 1.

To create a new blank document, workbook, or presentation

1. Start the app.

2. When the Home page appears, press the **Esc** key.

Or

1. If the app is already running, select the **File** tab to display the Backstage view.

2. In the left pane of the Backstage view, select **New** to display the New page.

3. On the **New** page of the Backstage view, select the **Blank *file type*** thumbnail.

To preview design templates

1. Display the **New** page of the Backstage view.

2. On the **New** page, scroll the pane to view the design templates installed with the app.

3. Select any thumbnail to open a preview window that displays a sample document page, worksheet, or title slide and a description of the template.

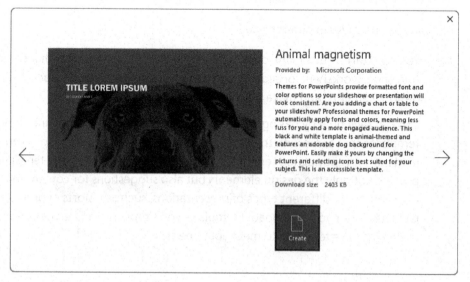

A template preview window for PowerPoint

> **TIP** Many templates display "lorem ipsum" text, which is placeholder text used to show the shape of text within a layout without distracting the reader with real content. Lorem ipsum text has been used for this purpose since the 1500s. The content is said to have been generated from a Latin work written by Cicero in 45 BC.

4. Do any of the following:

   - Select **Create** to create a document, workbook, or presentation based on the template in the preview window.

   - Select the arrow on the right side of the preview window to view the next template, or the arrow on the left side to view the previous template.

   - In the upper-right corner of the preview window, select the **Close** button (the **X**) to close the preview window without creating a document, workbook, or presentation.

To create a document, workbook, or presentation based on an installed template

1. Display the **New** page of the Backstage view.

2. Scroll the pane to locate the design template you want to use.

3. Double-click the thumbnail to create the file.

To create a document, workbook, or presentation based on an online template

1. Display the **New** page of the Backstage view.

2. To specify the initial search term, do either of the following:

   - In the Search box, enter one or more terms related to the template content or design you're looking for, and then select the **Search** button.

   - Below the search box, select one of the suggested searches.

3. Scroll the pane to locate a design that fits your needs.

4. Double-click any thumbnail to create a file based on the template.

> **TIP** If the app supports template preview, select any thumbnail to preview the design template, and then select Create in the preview window to create the file.

Open and move around in files

The Home page that appears by default when you start Word, Excel, or PowerPoint displays a list of files you worked on recently in that app, and a link to open other existing files. If the file you want to open appears on the Home page, you can open it directly from there. Otherwise, you open files from the Open page of the Backstage view.

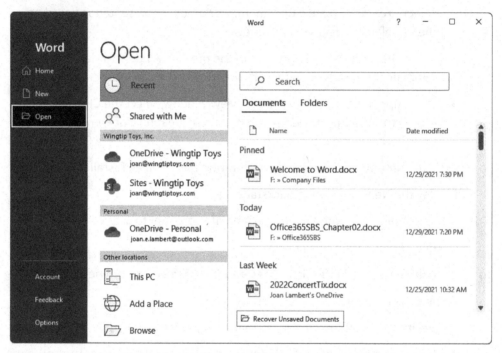

Open files from local, business, and personal storage locations

If you open a document that is too long to fit entirely on the screen, you can bring off-screen content into view without changing the location of the cursor by using the vertical scroll bar in the following ways:

- Select the scroll arrows to move up or down by one line.

- Select above or below the scroll box to move up or down by the height of one screen.

- Drag the scroll box on the scroll bar to display the part of the document corresponding to the location of the scroll box. For example, dragging the scroll box to the middle of the scroll bar displays the middle of the document.

If the document is too wide to fit on the screen, Word displays a horizontal scroll bar that you can use in similar ways to move from side to side.

You can also move around in a document by moving the cursor. To place the cursor in a specific location, you simply click there. You can also press a keyboard key to move the cursor. For example, pressing the Home key moves the cursor to the left end of a line.

The following table describes ways to move the cursor by using your keyboard.

Cursor movement	Key or keyboard shortcut
Left one character	Left Arrow
Right one character	Right Arrow
Up one line	Up Arrow
Down one line	Down Arrow
Left one word	Ctrl+Left Arrow
Right one word	Ctrl+Right Arrow
Up one paragraph	Ctrl+Up Arrow
Down one paragraph	Ctrl+Down Arrow
To the beginning of the current line	Home
To the end of the current line	End
To the beginning of the document	Ctrl+Home
To the end of the document	Ctrl+End
To the beginning of the previous page	Ctrl+Page Up
To the beginning of the next page	Ctrl+Page Down
Up one screen	Page Up
Down one screen	Page Down

In a long Word document, you might want to move quickly among elements of a certain type—for example, from heading to heading, from page to page, or from graphic to graphic. You can do this from the Navigation pane, which has three views—Headings, Pages, and Results—and a search box from which you can search for text, symbols, or objects.

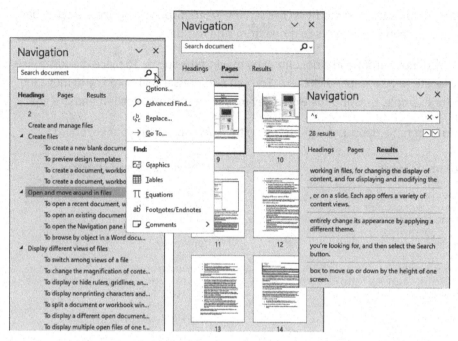

Move between objects of a specific type in Word

Similarly, in a presentation, you might want to move quickly to a specific slide or presentation section. You can do this from the Slide pane or from Slide Sorter view.

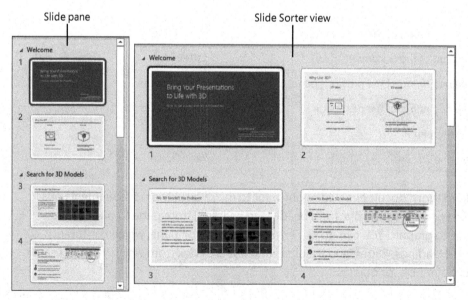

Move between slides and sections in PowerPoint

To open a recent document, workbook, or presentation

1. Start Word, Excel, or PowerPoint.

2. On the **Home** page, in the **Recent** list, select the file name of the file you want to open.

Or

1. With the app running, select the **File** tab to display the Backstage view.

2. In the left pane of the Backstage view, select **Open** to display the Open page.

3. In the right pane of the **Open** page, scroll the file list if necessary to locate the file you want to open, and then select the file name to open it.

To open an existing document, workbook, or presentation

1. Start Word, Excel, or PowerPoint.

2. Display the Open page of the Backstage view.

3. In the **Places** list, select the local or network storage location where the file is stored.

The Places list includes all the locations you've linked to from an Office app

4. Navigate to the file storage folder by using either of the following methods:

- In the right pane, select a recent folder. Then select any subfolders until you reach the folder you want.

- In the left pane, select **Browse** to open the Open dialog. Then select folders in the **Navigation** pane, double-click folders in the file pane, or enter the folder location in the **Address** bar.

5. Double-click the file you want to open.

> **TIP** In the Open dialog, selecting a file name and then selecting the Open arrow displays a list of alternative ways to open the selected file. To look through a file without making any inadvertent changes, you can open the file as read-only, open an independent copy of the file, or open it in Protected view. You can also open the file in a web browser. In the event of a computer crash or other similar incident, you can tell the app to open the file and try to repair any damage.

To open the Navigation pane in a Word document

- On the **View** tab, in the **Show** group, select the **Navigation Pane** checkbox.

To browse by object in a Word document

- Open the **Navigation** pane, and then do any of the following:

  - At the top of the **Navigation** pane, select **Headings**. Then select any heading to move directly to that location in the document.

  - At the top of the **Navigation** pane, select **Pages**. Then select any thumbnail to move directly to that page of the document.

  - At the right end of the search box, select the arrow. In the **Find** list, select the type of object you want to browse by. Then select the **Next** and **Previous** arrows to move among those objects.

Display different views of files

In each app, you can display the content of a file in a variety of views, each suited to a specific purpose. The views in each app are specific to that app's files.

Word includes the following views:

- **Print Layout view** This view displays a document on the screen the way it will look when printed. You can review elements such as margins, page breaks, headers and footers, and watermarks.

- **Read Mode view** This view displays as much document content as will fit on the screen at a comfortable size for reading. In this view, the ribbon is replaced by one toolbar at the top of the screen with buttons for searching and navigating in the document. You can view comments, but you can't edit the document in this view.

- **Web Layout view** This view displays the document the way it will look when viewed in a web browser. You can see backgrounds and other effects. You can also review how text wraps to fit the window and how graphics are positioned.

- **Outline view** This view displays the structure of a document as nested levels of headings and body text and provides tools for viewing and changing the hierarchy.

- **Draft view** This view displays the content of a document with a simplified layout so that you can quickly enter and edit text. You cannot view layout elements such as headers and footers.

Excel includes the following views:

- **Normal view** This view displays the worksheet with column and row headers.

- **Page Layout view** This view displays the worksheet on the screen the way it will look when printed, including page layout elements.

- **Page Break Preview view** This view displays only the portion of the worksheet that contains content, and any page breaks. You can drag page breaks in this view to move them.

You can also create custom views that apply a specific set of display and print settings to a worksheet.

PowerPoint includes the following views for use while developing a presentation:

- **Normal view** This view includes the Thumbnails pane on the left side of the app window, the Slide pane on the right side of the window, and an optional Notes pane at the bottom of the window. You insert, cut, copy, paste, duplicate, and delete slides in the Thumbnails pane, create slide content in the Slide pane, and record speaker notes in the Notes pane.

- **Notes Page view** This is the only view in which you can create speaker notes that contain elements other than text. Although you can add speaker notes in the Notes pane in Normal view, you must use Notes Page view to add graphics, tables, diagrams, or charts to your notes.

- **Outline view** This view displays a text outline of the presentation in the Outline pane and the active slide in the Slide pane. You can enter text either directly on the slide or in the outline.

- **Reading view** In this view, which is ideal for previewing the presentation, each slide fills the screen. You can select buttons on the navigation bar to move through or jump to specific slides.

- **Slide Sorter view** This view displays thumbnails of all the slides in the presentation. In this view, you manage the slides, rather than the slide content. You can easily reorganize the slides, group them into sections, and apply transitions to one or multiple slides. You can also apply transitions from one slide to another and specify how long each slide should remain on the screen.

While presenting a slide show, PowerPoint displays the slides in Slide Show view and presenter tools in Presenter view.

View options are available from the View Shortcuts toolbar near the right end of the status bar and from the View tab of the ribbon.

View Shortcuts

View options on the PowerPoint status bar; the active view is shaded

> **SEE ALSO** On a touchscreen device, the appearance of the buttons on the View Shortcuts toolbar changes depending on whether you're in Mouse mode or Touch mode. For more information, see "Work with the ribbon and status bar" in Chapter 1.

2

When you want to focus on the layout of a document, worksheet, or slide, you can display rulers and gridlines to help you position and align elements. You can also adjust the magnification of the content area by using the tools available in the Zoom group on the View tab, or the Zoom button or Zoom slider at the right end of the status bar.

If you want to work with different parts of a document or workbook, you can open the file in a second window and display both, or you can split a window into two panes and scroll through each pane independently. You're not limited to working with one file at a time. You can easily switch between open files, and you can display more than one app window simultaneously.

Not represented on the View tab is a feature that can be invaluable when you are fine-tuning the layout of a document in Word. Nonprinting characters, such as spaces, tabs, and paragraph marks, control the layout of your document, and hidden characters provide the structure for behind-the-scenes processes, such as indexing. You can control the display of these characters for each window.

To switch among views of a file

- On the **View Shortcuts** toolbar, select the view button you want.

- On the **View** tab, in the *File* Views group, select the view you want.

To change the magnification of content in the app window

1. On the **View** tab, in the **Zoom** group, select **Zoom** to open the Zoom dialog.

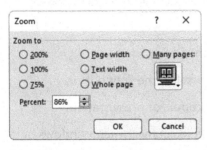

*Depending on the app, you can select
a magnification level, enter a specific
percentage, or select a page configuration*

2. In the **Zoom** dialog, select a **Zoom to** or **Magnification** option or enter a specific percentage in the **Percent** box, and then select **OK**.

Or

- Using the zoom controls at the right end of the status bar, do any of the following:

  - At the left end of the slider, select the **Zoom Out** button to decrease the zoom percentage.

  - At the right end of the slider, select the **Zoom In** button to increase the zoom percentage.

  - In PowerPoint, at the right end of the status bar, select the **Fit slide to current window** button.

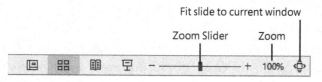

Fit Slide maximizes the slide on the canvas

To display or hide rulers, gridlines, and guides in a document or presentation

- On the **View** tab, in the **Show** group, do any of the following:

  - Select or clear the **Ruler** checkbox.

  - Select or clear the **Gridlines** checkbox.

  - In PowerPoint, select or clear the **Guides** checkbox.

To display nonprinting characters and formatting marks in a document

- On the **Home** tab, in the **Paragraph** group, select the **Show/Hide ¶** button.

To split a document or workbook window into two panes

- On the **View** tab, in the **Window** group, select the **Split** button.

To display a different open document, workbook, or presentation

- On the **View** tab, in the **Window** group, select the **Switch Windows** button, and then select the file you want to view.

- Point to the app button on the Windows taskbar, and then select the thumbnail of the presentation you want to display.

To display multiple open files of one type at the same time

- On the **View** tab, in the **Window** group, select the **Arrange All** button.

Display and edit file properties

Properties are file attributes or settings, such as the file name, size, created date, author, and read-only status. Some properties exist to provide information to computer operating systems and apps. You can display properties within a document, workbook, or presentation (for example, you can display the slide number on a slide). Word, Excel, and PowerPoint automatically track some of the properties for you, and you can set others.

You can examine the properties attached to a file from the Info page of the Backstage view.

Properties ˅	
Size	1.60MB
Slides	21
Hidden slides	1
Words	915
Notes	7
Title	Spring Catalog Kickoff
Tags	marketing
Comments	Add comments
Multimedia clips	0
Presentation format	Custom
Template	Office Theme
Status	Final
Categories	Add a category
Subject	Specify the subject
Hyperlink Base	wingtiptoys.com
Company	Wingtip Toys
Related Dates	
Last Modified	12/6/2021 6:03 PM
Created	12/22/2018 1:53 PM

Some of the properties stored with a typical PowerPoint presentation

File types and compatibility with earlier versions of Office apps

The Office 2021 apps use file formats based on a programming language called Extensible Markup Language, or more commonly, XML. These file formats, called the *Microsoft Office Open XML Formats*, were introduced with Microsoft Office 2007.

Each Office 2021 app offers a selection of file formats intended to provide specific benefits. The file formats and file name extensions for Word 2019 files include the following:

- Word Document (.docx)
- Word Macro-Enabled Document (.docm)
- Word Template (.dotx)
- Word Macro-Enabled Template (.dotm)
- Word XML Document (.xml)

The file formats and file name extensions for Excel 2021 files include the following:

- Excel Workbook (.xlsx)
- Excel Macro-Enabled Workbook (.xlsm)
- Excel Binary Workbook (.xlsb)
- Excel Template (.xltx)
- Excel Macro-Enabled Template (.xltm)
- Excel Add-In (.xlam)

2

The file formats and file name extensions for PowerPoint 2021 files include the following:

- PowerPoint Presentation (.pptx)

- PowerPoint Macro-Enabled Presentation (.pptm)

- PowerPoint Template (.potx)

- PowerPoint Macro-Enabled Template (.potm)

- PowerPoint Show (.ppsx)

- PowerPoint Macro-Enabled Show (.ppsm)

- PowerPoint Add-In (.ppam)

- PowerPoint XML Presentation (.xml)

- PowerPoint Picture Presentation (.pptx)

Other file types that are not specific to the Office apps, such as text files, webpages, PDF files, and XPS files, can be created from the Save As dialog of each app.

You can open a file created with Office 2010, Office 2003, Office XP, Office 2000, or Office 97 in an Office 2021 app, but new features will not be available. The file name appears in the title bar with [Compatibility Mode] to its right. You can work in Compatibility mode, or you can convert the document to the current file format by displaying the Info page of the Backstage view and selecting the Convert button in the Compatibility Mode section. You can also select Save As in the Backstage view to save a copy of the file in the current format.

If you work with people using a version of Office earlier than 2007, you can save your documents in a format that they will be able to use by choosing the corresponding 97–2003 file format in the Save As Type list, or they can download the Microsoft Office Compatibility Pack for Word, Excel, and PowerPoint File Formats from the Microsoft Download Center (located at *download.microsoft.com*) so that they can open current Office files in one of those versions of Office.

You can change or remove basic properties in the default Properties pane, expand the Properties pane to make more available, or display the Properties dialog to access even more properties.

To display file properties

1. Display the **Info** page of the Backstage view. The standard properties associated with the file are displayed in the Properties area of the right pane.

2. At the bottom of the **Properties** pane, select **Show All Properties** to expand the pane.

3. At the top of the **Properties** pane, select **Properties,** and then select **Advanced Properties** to display the Properties dialog.

To edit file properties

1. In the **Properties** pane, select the value for the property you want to edit to activate the content box.

2. Enter or replace the property value, and then press **Enter**.

Or

- In the **Properties** dialog, do either of the following:

  - On the **Summary** page, select the box to the right of the property you want to modify, and then enter or replace the property value.

  - On the **Custom** page, select the property you want to modify in the **Name** list, and then enter or replace the property value in the **Value** box.

Save and close files

You save a document, workbook, or presentation the first time by selecting the Save button on the Quick Access Toolbar or by displaying the Backstage view and then selecting Save As. Both actions open the Save As page, where you can select a storage location.

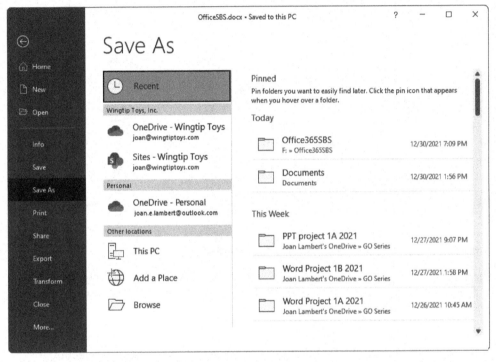

The Recent list shows places you've saved files from this app

You can save the file in a folder on your computer or, if you have an internet connection, in a folder on your Microsoft OneDrive. If your company is running Microsoft SharePoint, you can add a SharePoint site so that it's available from the Places pane of the Save As page, just like any other folder.

> 🔍 **SEE ALSO** For information about OneDrive, see the sidebar "Save files to OneDrive" later in this chapter.

Selecting Browse at the bottom of the left pane displays the Save As dialog, in which you assign a name to the file.

The Save As dialog displays only files of the same type as the one you're saving

> ✓ **TIP** If you want to create a new folder in which to store the file, select New Folder on the Save As dialog toolbar.

After you save a file for the first time, you can save changes simply by selecting the Save button on the Quick Access Toolbar. The new version of the file then overwrites the previous version.

> ✓ **TIP** By default, Word, Excel, and PowerPoint periodically save the file you are working on. To adjust the time interval between saves, display the Backstage view, and select Options. In the left pane of the Options dialog, select Save, and then specify the period of time in the Save AutoRecover Information Every box.

Every time you open a document, workbook, or presentation, a new instance of the app starts. You can close the file and exit that instance of the app. If you have only one document, workbook, or presentation open, you can close the file and exit the app, or you can close the file but leave the app running.

To save a document, workbook, or presentation for the first time

1. Select the **File** tab to display the Backstage view.

2. In the left pane of the Backstage view, select **Save As**.

3. On the **Save As** page of the Backstage view, select a storage location, and then select a recently accessed folder in the right pane, or select **Browse**.

4. In the **Save As** dialog, browse to the folder you want to save the file in.

5. In the **File name** box, enter a name for the file.

6. If you want to save a file in a format other than the one shown in the Save As Type box, select the **Save as type** arrow and then, in the **Save as type** list, select the file format you want.

7. In the **Save As** dialog, select **Save**.

To add a cloud storage location

1. On the **Save As** page of the Backstage view, select **Add a Place**.

2. In the **Add a Place** list, select **Office 365 SharePoint** or **OneDrive**.

3. In the **Add a service** window, enter the email address you use to sign in to the cloud storage service, and then select **Next**.

4. In the **Sign in** window, enter the password associated with the account, and then select **Sign In** to add the cloud storage location associated with that account to the Places list.

> ✓ **TIP** To save a copy of a file, display the **Save As** page of the Backstage view, and then save the file with a different name in the same location or with the same name in a different location. (You can't store two files of the same type with the same name in the same folder.)

Save files to OneDrive

When you save an Office file to OneDrive, you and other people with whom you share the file can work on it by using a local installation of the Office apps or by using the Office Online apps, which are available in the OneDrive environments.

If you're new to the world of OneDrive, here's a quick tutorial to help you get started.

OneDrive is a cloud-based storage solution. The purpose of OneDrive is to provide a single place for you to store and access all your files. Although this might seem like a simple concept, it provides major value for people who use Word or other Office products on multiple devices, including Windows computers, Mac computers, iPads and other tablets, and Windows, iPhone, and Android smartphones.

For example, you can create a file on your desktop computer at work, edit it on your laptop at home, and review it on your smartphone while you're waiting for your lunch to be served at a restaurant. If you use the full suite of Office products within your organization, you can even present the file in a Skype for Business meeting from your tablet PC, all while the file is stored in the same central location.

There are currently two types of OneDrive—one for personal use and one for business use:

- **OneDrive** A *personal* OneDrive storage site is provided free with every Microsoft account. Each OneDrive is linked to a specific account.

- **OneDrive for Business** An *organizational* OneDrive storage site, formerly part of SharePoint MySites, is provided with every business-level Office 365 subscription license. These storage locations are part of an organization's Office 365 online infrastructure.

2

You might have both types of OneDrive available to you; if you do, you can connect to both from the Office apps.

In this book, the personal and organizational versions are referred to generically as OneDrive sites.

At the time of this writing, Microsoft is providing 5 gigabytes (GB) of free OneDrive storage with your Microsoft account, or 1 terabyte (TB) for Office 365 subscribers. There are various ways to accumulate more storage. Go to *onedrive.live.com/about* and select See Plans to display the plans available for your location.

By default, files that you store on your OneDrive site are password-protected and available only to you. You can share specific files or folders with other people by sending a personalized invitation or a generic link that allows recipients to view or edit files. You can access files stored on your OneDrive in several ways:

- From within the Word, Excel, PowerPoint, or OneNote apps when opening or saving a file.

- Through File Explorer, when you synchronize your OneDrive site contents with the computer.

- Through a web browser. Personal OneDrive sites are available at *https:// onedrive.live.com*; organizational OneDrive sites have addresses linked to your Office 365 account, such as *https://contoso-my.sharepoint.com/ personal/joan_contoso_com*.

Because OneDrive and OneDrive for Business file storage locations are easily configurable in all versions of Word, Excel, PowerPoint, and OneNote, OneDrive is a simple and useful cloud storage option. And best of all, it's completely free!

To save a file without changing the name or location

- On the Quick Access Toolbar, select the **Save** button.

- In the left pane of the Backstage view, select **Save**.

- Press **Ctrl+S**.

To close a document, workbook, or presentation

- At the right end of the title bar, select the **Close** button to close the file and the app window.

- Display the Backstage view, and then select **Close** to close the file without exiting the app.

- On the Windows taskbar, point to the app button to display thumbnails of all open files of that type. Point to the thumbnail of the file you want to close, and then select the **Close** button that appears in its upper-right corner.

Key points

- You create new documents, workbooks, and presentations from the New page of the Backstage view. When creating Office files, you can choose a blank template, a template that includes preset formatting, or a template that includes starter content.

- You can open files from File Explorer or from the Open page of the Backstage view. The Recent list on the Open page displays files you've recently worked on or pinned for easy access.

- You can display different views of files, depending on your needs as you create the file and the purpose you're creating it for.

- Every file has properties; some are automatically tracked and updated, and others can be set by users.

- The first time you save a file, you specify its name, location, and file format. Each Office app offers several file formats; some are specific to the app, and others can be opened in third-party apps. You can save additional copies of a file by specifying a different name or location.

Practice tasks

Before you can complete these tasks, you must copy the book's practice files to your computer. The practice files for these tasks are in the **Office365SBS\Ch02** folder. You can save the results of the tasks in the same folder.

The introduction includes a complete list of practice files and download instructions.

Create files

Complete the following tasks:

1. Start PowerPoint and create a new, blank presentation.

2. Display the available presentation design templates.

3. Preview a template that you like.

4. Without closing the preview window, preview the next or previous template.

5. From the preview window, create a presentation based on the currently displayed template. Notice that the unsaved blank presentation closes.

6. Leave the presentation open for use in a later set of practice tasks.

Open and move around in files

Start Word, and then complete the following tasks:

1. From within Word, open the **NavigateFiles** document located in the practice file folder.

2. In the second line of the document title, click at the right end of the paragraph to position the cursor.

3. Use a keyboard method to move the cursor to the beginning of the line.

4. Use a keyboard method to move the cursor to the beginning of the word **Regulations**.

5. Use a keyboard method to move the cursor to the end of the document.

6. Use the scroll bar to move to the middle of the document.

> **TIP** If the vertical scroll bar is not visible, move the pointer to display the scroll bar.

7. Use the scroll bar to change the view of the document by one screen.

8. Open the **Navigation** pane and select **Headings** at the top if it isn't already selected.

9. In the **Navigation** pane, select **Landscaping** to move the cursor directly to the selected heading in the document.

10. At the top of the **Navigation** pane, select **Pages**. On the **Pages** page, scroll through the thumbnails to review the amount of visible detail, and then select the thumbnail for page **5** to move the cursor directly to the top of the selected page.

11. At the right end of the **Navigation** pane title bar, select the **Close** button to close the pane.

12. Close the document without saving it.

Display different views of files

Open the **DisplayViews** presentation, and complete the following tasks:

1. In Normal view, display slide **2** of the presentation. Then switch to Slide Show view.

2. Move forward through the presentation to its end. Then switch to Slide Sorter view and select slide **1**.

3. Display the presentation in Reading view. Use any method to navigate to slide **4**, and then use the most efficient method to return to slide **1**.

4. Display the presentation in Normal view.

5. Use commands on the **View** tab to arrange the **DisplayViews** presentation and the presentation you created in the first set of practice tasks side by side on the screen.

6. In the **DisplayViews** presentation, display the gridlines. Notice that they appear in both open presentations.

7. Switch to the presentation you created in the first set of practice tasks. Display the guides. Notice the effect of these actions in the other open presentation.

8. Set the magnification of the active presentation to **60%** and notice the effect of this action in the other open presentation.

9. Leave both presentations open for use in a later set of practice tasks.

Display and edit file properties

Start Excel, and then complete the following tasks:

1. Open the **DisplayProperties** workbook.

2. Display the workbook properties.

3. Expand the **Properties** list to display all properties. Then display the advanced properties.

4. In the **Properties** dialog, set the **Title** property to Shipping Costs. Then close the dialog.

5. Verify that the title appears in the **Properties** list on the **Info** page of the Backstage view.

6. Close the workbook and save your changes.

Save and close files

Complete the following tasks:

1. Save a copy of the **DisplayViews** presentation in the practice file folder as MyPresentation. Close the presentation and this instance of PowerPoint.

2. Close the presentation you created in the first task without exiting PowerPoint. Then exit the app.

Part 2

Microsoft Word

CHAPTER 3
Modify the structure and appearance of text 79

CHAPTER 4
Collaborate on documents 125

CHAPTER 5
Merge data with documents and labels 167

Modify the structure and appearance of text

Documents contain text that conveys information to readers, but the appearance of the document content also conveys a message. You can provide structure and meaning by formatting the text in various ways. Word 365 provides a variety of simple-to-use tools that you can use to apply sophisticated formatting and create a logical and meaningful navigational structure for your documents.

In a short document or one that doesn't require a complex navigational structure, you can easily format words and paragraphs so that key points stand out and the structure of your document is clear. You can achieve dramatic flair by applying predefined WordArt text effects. To keep the appearance of documents and other Microsoft 365 files consistent, you can format document elements by applying predefined sets of formatting called *styles*. In addition, you can change the fonts, colors, and effects throughout a document with one click or tap by applying a theme.

This chapter guides you through procedures related to applying paragraph and character formatting, structuring content manually, creating and modifying lists, applying styles to text, and changing a document's theme.

In this chapter

- Apply paragraph formatting
- Apply character formatting
- Structure content manually
- Create and modify lists
- Apply built-in styles to text
- Change the document theme

Apply paragraph formatting

You create a paragraph by entering text and then pressing the Enter key. A paragraph can contain one word, one sentence, or multiple sentences. Every paragraph ends with a paragraph mark, which looks like a backward P (¶). Paragraph marks and other structural characters (such as spaces, line breaks, and tabs) are usually hidden, but you can display them. Sometimes displaying these hidden characters makes it easier to accomplish a task or understand a structural problem.

> **SEE ALSO** For information about working with hidden structural characters, see "Structure content manually" later in this chapter.

You can change the look of a paragraph by changing its indentation, alignment, and line spacing, in addition to the space before and after it. You can also put borders around it and shade its background. Collectively, the settings you use to vary the look of a paragraph are called *paragraph formatting*.

You can modify a paragraph's left and right edge alignment and internal line spacing, and the spacing above and below the paragraph, by using tools on the Home tab of the ribbon or in the Paragraph dialog, and its left and right indents from the Home tab, the Layout tab, the Paragraph dialog, or the horizontal ruler. The ruler is often hidden to provide more space for the document content.

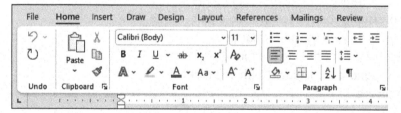

The left indent can be changed from the Home tab, the Layout tab, or the ruler

If you modify a paragraph and aren't happy with the changes, you can restore the original paragraph and character settings by clearing the formatting to reset the paragraph to its base style.

> **SEE ALSO** For information about styles, see "Apply built-in styles to text" later in this chapter.

When you want to make several adjustments to the alignment, indentation, and spacing of selected paragraphs, it's sometimes quicker to make changes in the Paragraph dialog than to select buttons and drag markers.

Indent and spacing settings in the Paragraph dialog

Configure alignment

The alignment settings control the horizontal position of the paragraph text between the page margins. There are four alignment options:

- **Align Left** This is the default paragraph alignment. It sets the left end of each line of the paragraph at the left page margin or left indent. It results in a straight left edge and a ragged right edge.

- **Align Right** This option sets the right end of each line of the paragraph at the right page margin or right indent. It results in a straight right edge and a ragged left edge.

- **Center** This option centers each line of the paragraph between the left and right page margins or indents. It results in ragged left and right edges.

- **Justify** This option adjusts the spacing between words so that the left end of each line of the paragraph is at the left page margin or indent, and the right end of each line of the paragraph (other than the last line) is at the right margin or indent. It results in straight left and right edges.

The icons on the alignment buttons on the ribbon depict the effect of each alignment option.

To open the Paragraph dialog

- On the **Home** tab or the **Layout** tab, in the **Paragraph** group, select the **Paragraph Settings** dialog launcher.

- On the **Home** tab, in the **Paragraph** group, select the **Line and Paragraph Spacing** button and then **Line Spacing Options**.

- Right-click anywhere in the paragraph and then select **Paragraph**.

To set paragraph alignment

- Position the cursor anywhere in the paragraph or select all the paragraphs you want to adjust. Then do either of the following:

  - On the **Home** tab, in the **Paragraph** group, select the **Align Left**, **Center**, **Align Right**, or **Justify** button.

  - Open the **Paragraph** dialog. On the **Indents and Spacing** tab, in the **General** area, select **Left**, **Centered**, **Right**, or **Justified** in the **Alignment** list.

Configure vertical spacing

Paragraphs have two types of vertical spacing:

- **Paragraph spacing** This is the space between paragraphs, defined by setting the space before and after each paragraph. This space is usually measured in points. (One point is 1/72 of an inch, or approximately 0.035 centimeters.)

- **Line spacing** This is the space between the lines within a paragraph, defined by setting the height of the lines either in relation to the height of the text (single, double, or a specific number of lines) or by specifying a minimum or exact point measurement.

The default line spacing for documents created in Word 365 is 1.08 lines. Changing the line spacing alters the appearance and readability of the text in the paragraph and the amount of space it occupies on the page.

> *The line spacing of this left-aligned paragraph is set to Single (1 line).* A paragraph can contain one word, one sentence, or multiple sentences. You can change the look of a paragraph by changing its indentation, alignment, and line spacing, as well as the space before and after it. You can also put borders around it and shade its background. Collectively, the settings you use to vary the look of a paragraph are called *paragraph formatting*.
>
> *The line spacing of this justified paragraph is set to Double (2 lines).* A paragraph can contain one word, one sentence, or multiple sentences. You can change the look of a paragraph by changing its indentation, alignment, and line spacing, as well as the space before and after it. You can also put borders around it and shade its background. Collectively, the settings you use to vary the look of a paragraph are called *paragraph formatting*.

3

The effect of changing line spacing

You can set the paragraph and line spacing for individual paragraphs and for paragraph styles. You can quickly adjust the spacing of most content in a document by selecting an option from the Paragraph Spacing menu on the Design tab. (Although the menu is named Paragraph Spacing, the menu options control both paragraph spacing and line spacing.) These options, which are named by effect rather than by specific measurements, work by modifying the spacing of the Normal paragraph style and any other styles that depend on the Normal style for their spacing. (In standard templates, most other styles are based on the Normal style.) The Paragraph Spacing options modify the Normal style in the current document only and do not affect other documents.

The following table describes the effect of each Paragraph Spacing option on the paragraph and line spacing settings.

Paragraph spacing option	Before paragraph	After paragraph	Line spacing
Default	Controlled by style set	Controlled by style set	Controlled by style set
No Paragraph Space	0 points	0 points	1 line
Compact	0 points	4 points	1 line
Tight	0 points	6 points	1.15 lines
Open	0 points	10 points	1.15 lines
Relaxed	0 points	6 points	1.5 lines
Double	0 points	8 points	2 lines

To quickly adjust the vertical spacing before, after, and within all paragraphs in a document

1. On the **Design** tab, in the **Document Formatting** group, select **Paragraph Spacing** to display the Paragraph Spacing menu.

Each paragraph spacing option controls space around and within the paragraph

2. Select the option you want to apply to all the paragraphs in the document.

To adjust the spacing between paragraphs

1. Select all the paragraphs you want to adjust.

2. On the **Layout** tab, in the **Paragraph** group, adjust the **Spacing Before** and **Spacing After** settings.

Spacing is measured in points

To adjust spacing between the lines of paragraphs

- Position the cursor anywhere in the paragraph or select all the paragraphs you want to adjust. Do either of the following:

  - To make a quick adjustment to the selected paragraphs, on the **Home** tab, in the **Paragraph** group, select the **Line and Paragraph Spacing** button, and then select any of the line-spacing commands on the menu.

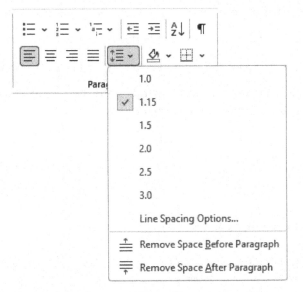

You can choose from preset internal line-spacing options or adjust paragraph spacing

> ✓ **TIP** You can also adjust the space before and after selected paragraphs from the Line And Paragraph Spacing menu. Selecting one of the last two options adds or removes a preset amount of space between the selected paragraphs.

  - To make a more-specific adjustment, open the **Paragraph** dialog. Then, on the **Indents and Spacing** tab, in the **Spacing** area, make the adjustments you want to the paragraph spacing, and then select **OK**.

Configure indents

In Word, you don't define the width of paragraphs and the length of pages by defining the area occupied by the text. Instead, you define the size of the white space—the left, right, top, and bottom margins—around the text.

Although the left and right margins are set for a whole document or for a section of a document, you can vary the position of a paragraph between the margins by indenting the left or right edge of the paragraph.

A paragraph indent is the space from the page margin to the text. You can change the left indent by selecting buttons on the Home tab, or you can set the indents directly on the ruler. Three indent markers are always present on the ruler:

- **Left Indent** This defines the outermost left edge of each line of the paragraph.

- **Right Indent** This defines the outermost right edge of each line of the paragraph.

- **First Line Indent** This defines the starting point of the first line of the paragraph.

The ruler indicates the space between the left and right page margins in a lighter color than is used in the space outside of the page margins.

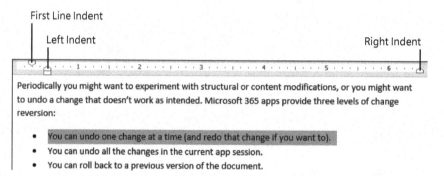

The indent markers on the ruler

The default setting for the Left Indent and First Line Indent markers is 0.0", which aligns with the left page margin. The default setting for the Right Indent marker is the distance from the left margin to the right margin. For example, if the page size is set to 8.5 inches wide and the left and right margins are set to 1.0 inch, the default Right Indent marker is at 6.5 inches.

You can arrange the Left Indent and First Line Indent markers to create a hanging indent or a first line indent. Hanging indents are most commonly used for bulleted and numbered lists, in which the bullet or number is indented less than the main text (essentially, it is *out*dented). First line indents are frequently used to distinguish the beginning of each subsequent paragraph in documents that consist of many consecutive paragraphs of text. Both types of indents are set by using the First Line Indent marker on the ruler.

> **TIP** The First Line Indent marker is linked to the Left Indent marker. Moving the Left Indent marker also moves the First Line Indent marker to maintain the first line indent distance. You can move the First Line Indent marker independently of the Left Indent marker to change the first line indent distance.

To display the ruler

- On the **View** tab, in the **Show** group, select the **Ruler** checkbox.

> **TIP** In this book, we show measurements in inches. If you want to change the measurement units Word uses, open the Word Options dialog. On the Advanced page, in the Display area, select the units you want in the Show Measurements In Units Of list. Then select OK.

To indent or outdent the left edge of a paragraph

- Position the cursor anywhere in the paragraph, or select all the paragraphs you want to adjust. Then do any of the following:

  - On the **Home** tab, in the **Paragraph** group, select the **Increase Indent** or **Decrease Indent** button to move the left edge of the paragraph in 0.25-inch increments.

  > **TIP** You cannot increase or decrease the indent beyond the margins by using the Increase Indent and Decrease Indent buttons. If you need to extend an indent beyond the margins, you can do so by setting negative indentation measurements in the Paragraph dialog.

  - Open the **Paragraph** dialog. Then, on the **Indents and Spacing** tab, in the **Indentation** area, set the indent in the **Left** box, and then select **OK**.

  - On the ruler, drag the **Left Indent** marker to the ruler measurement at which you want to position the left edge of the body of the paragraph.

To create a hanging indent or first line indent

1. Position the cursor anywhere in the paragraph, or select all the paragraphs you want to adjust.

2. Open the **Paragraph** dialog. Then, on the **Indents and Spacing** tab, in the **Indents** area, select **First line** or **Hanging** in the **Special** box.

3. In the **By** box, set the amount of the indent, and then select **OK**.

Or

1. Set the left indent of the paragraph body.

2. On the ruler, drag the **First Line Indent** marker to the ruler measurement at which you want to begin the first line of the paragraph.

Configure paragraph borders and shading

To make a paragraph really stand out, you might want to put a border around it or shade its background. (For real drama, you can do both.) You can select a predefined border from the Borders menu or design a custom border in the Borders And Shading dialog.

You can customize many aspects of the border

After you select the style, color, width, and location of the border, you can select Options to specify its distance from the text.

To indent or outdent the right edge of a paragraph

- Position the cursor anywhere in the paragraph or select all the paragraphs you want to adjust. Then do either of the following:

  - On the ruler, drag the **Right Indent** marker to the ruler measurement at which you want to set the maximum right edge of the paragraph.

  - Open the **Paragraph** dialog. Then, on the **Indents and Spacing** tab, in the **Indentation** area, set the right indent in the **Right** box, and then select **OK**.

> **TIP** Unless the paragraph alignment is justified, the right edge of the paragraph will be ragged, but no line will extend beyond the right indent or outdent.

Apply character formatting

The appearance of your document helps convey not only the document's message but also information about the document's creator: you. A neatly organized document that contains consistently formatted content and appropriate graphic elements, and that doesn't contain spelling or grammatical errors, invokes greater confidence in your ability to provide any product or service.

Earlier in this chapter, you learned about methods of applying formatting to paragraphs. This topic covers methods of formatting the text of a document. Formatting that you apply to text is referred to as *character formatting*.

In Word documents, you can apply three types of character formatting:

- Individual character formats, including font, font size, font color, bold, italic, underline, strikethrough, subscript, superscript, and highlight color

- Artistic text effects that incorporate character outline and fill colors

- Preformatted styles associated with the document template, many of which not only affect the appearance of the text but also convey structural information (such as titles and headings)

When you enter text in a document, it's displayed in a specific font. By default, the font used for text in a new blank document is 11-point Calibri, but you can change the font of any text element at any time. The available fonts vary from one computer to another, depending on the apps installed. Common fonts include Arial, Verdana, and Times New Roman.

You can vary the look of a font by changing the following attributes:

- **Size** Almost every font has a range of sizes you can select from. (Sometimes you can set additional sizes beyond those listed.) The font size is measured in points, from the top of the ascenders (the letter parts that go up, like the left line of the letter *h*) to the bottom of the descenders (the letter parts that drop down, like the left line of the letter *p*).

- **Style** Almost every font has a range of font styles. The most common are regular (or plain), italic, bold, and bold italic.

- **Effects** Fonts can be enhanced by applying effects, such as underlining, small capital letters (small caps), or shadows.

- **Character spacing** You can alter the spacing between characters by pushing them apart or squeezing them together.

Although some attributes might cancel each other out, they are usually cumulative. For example, you might use a bold font style in various sizes and colors to make words stand out in a newsletter.

You apply character formatting from three locations:

- **Mini Toolbar** Several common formatting buttons are available on the Mini Toolbar that appears temporarily when you select text.

The Mini Toolbar appears temporarily when you select text, becomes transparent when you move the pointer away from the selected text, and disappears if not used

- **Font group on the Home tab** This group includes buttons for changing the font and most of the font attributes you are likely to use.

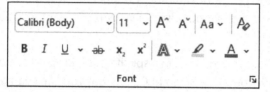

The most common font formatting commands are available on the Home tab

■ **Font dialog** Less commonly applied attributes such as small caps and special
underlining are available from the Font dialog.

Less-common font and character attributes can be set in the Font dialog

In addition to applying character formatting to change the look of characters, you can
apply predefined text effects (sometimes referred to as *WordArt*) to a selection to add
more zing. The available effects match the current theme colors.

*You can apply any predefined effect in
the gallery or define a custom effect*

These effects are somewhat dramatic, so you'll probably want to restrict their use to document titles and similar elements to which you want to draw particular attention.

To change the font of selected text

- On the **Mini Toolbar** or in the **Font** group on the **Home** tab, in the **Font** list, select the font you want to apply.

To change the font size of selected text

- Do any of the following on the **Mini Toolbar** or in the **Font** group on the **Home** tab:

  - In the **Font Size** list, select the font size you want to apply.

  - In the **Font Size** box, enter the font size you want to apply (even a size that doesn't appear in the list). Then press the **Enter** key.

  - To increase the font size in set increments, select the **Increase Font Size** button or press **Ctrl+>**.

  - To decrease the font size in set increments, select the **Decrease Font Size** button or press **Ctrl+<**.

To format selected text as bold, italic, or underlined

- On the **Mini Toolbar**, select the **Bold**, **Italic**, or **Underline** button.

- On the **Home** tab, in the **Font** group, select the **Bold**, **Italic**, or **Underline** button.

- Press **Ctrl+B** to format the text as bold.

- Press **Ctrl+I** to format the text as italic.

- Press **Ctrl+U** to underline the text.

> ✓ **TIP** To quickly apply a different underline style to selected text, select the arrow next to the Underline button on the Home tab, and then in the list, select the underline style you want to apply.

To cross out selected text by drawing a line through it

- On the **Home** tab, in the **Font** group, select the **Strikethrough** button.

To display superscript or subscript characters

1. Select the characters you want to display in superscript or subscript form.

2. On the **Home** tab, in the **Font** group, do either of the following:

- Select the **Subscript** button to decrease the size of the selected characters and shift them to the bottom of the line.

- Select the **Superscript** button to decrease the size of the selected characters and shift them to the top of the line.

3

To apply artistic effects to selected text

■ On the **Home** tab, in the **Font** group, select the **Text Effects and Typography** button, and then do either of the following:

- In the **Text Effects and Typography** gallery, select the preformatted effect combination that you want to apply.

- On the **Text Effects and Typography** menu, select **Outline**, **Shadow**, **Reflection**, **Glow**, **Number Styles**, **Ligatures**, or **Stylistic Sets**. Then make selections on the submenus to apply and modify those effects.

To change the font color of selected text

1. On the **Mini Toolbar**, or in the **Font** group on the **Home** tab, select the **Font Color** arrow to display the **Font Color** menu.

2. In the **Theme Colors** or **Standard Colors** palette, select a color swatch to apply that color to the selected text.

> **TIP** To apply the Font Color button's current color, you can simply select the button (not its arrow). If you want to apply a color that's not shown in the Theme Colors or Standard Colors palette, select More Colors. In the Colors dialog, select the color you want in the honeycomb on the Standard page, select the color gradient, or enter values for a color on the Custom page.

To change the case of selected text

■ On the **Home** tab, in the **Font** group, select the **Change Case** button and then select **Sentence case**, **lowercase**, **UPPERCASE**, **Capitalize Each Word**, or **tOGGLE cASE**.

■ Press **Shift+F3** repeatedly to cycle through the standard case options (Sentence case, UPPERCASE, lowercase, and Capitalize Each Word).

> **IMPORTANT** The case options vary based on the selected text. If the selection ends in a period, Word does not include the Capitalize Each Word option in the rotation. If the selection does not end in a period, Word does not include Sentence case in the rotation.

Character formatting and case considerations

The way you use character formatting in a document can influence the document's visual impact on your readers. Used judiciously, character formatting can make a plain document look attractive and professional, but excessive use can make it look amateurish and detract from the message. For example, using too many fonts in the same document is a mark of inexperience, so don't use more than two or three.

Bear in mind that lowercase letters tend to recede, so using all uppercase (capital) letters can be useful for titles and headings or for certain kinds of emphasis. However, large blocks of uppercase letters are tiring to the eye.

TIP Where do the terms *uppercase* and *lowercase* come from? Until the advent of computers, individual characters made of lead were assembled to form the words that would appear on a printed page. The characters were stored alphabetically in cases, with the capital letters in the upper case and the small letters in the lower case.

To highlight text

- Select the text you want to highlight, and then do either of the following:

    - On the **Mini Toolbar** or in the **Font** group on the **Home** tab, select the **Text Highlight Color** button to apply the default highlight color.

    - On the **Mini Toolbar** or in the **Font** group on the **Home** tab, select the **Text Highlight Color** arrow, and then select a color swatch to apply the selected highlight color and change the default highlight color.

Or

1. Without first selecting text, do either of the following:

    - Select the **Text Highlight Color** button to select the default highlight color.

    - Select the **Text Highlight Color** arrow and then select a color swatch to select that highlight color.

2. When the pointer changes to a highlighter, drag it across one or more sections of text to apply the highlight.

3. Select the **Text Highlight Color** button or press the **Esc** key to deactivate the highlighter.

3

To copy formatting to other text

1. Click or tap anywhere in the text that has the formatting you want to copy.

2. On the **Home** tab, in the **Clipboard** group, do either of the following:

   - If you want to apply the formatting to only one target, select **Format Painter** once.

   - If you want to apply the formatting to multiple targets, double-click **Format Painter**.

3. When the pointer changes to a paintbrush, select or drag across the text you want to apply the copied formatting to.

4. If you activated the Format Painter for multiple targets, repeat step 3 until you finish applying the formatting. Then select the **Format Painter** button once or press the **Esc** key to deactivate the tool.

To repeat the previous formatting command

- Select the text to which you want to apply the repeated formatting. Then do any of the following to repeat the previous formatting command:

  - On the **Quick Access Toolbar**, select the **Repeat** button.

  - Press **Ctrl+Y**.

  - Press **F4**.

To open the Font dialog

- On the **Home** tab, in the **Font** group, select the **Font** dialog launcher.

- Press **Ctrl+Shift+F**.

To remove character formatting

- Select the text you want to clear the formatting from. Then do any of the following:

  - Press **Ctrl+Spacebar** to remove manually applied formatting (but not styles).

  - On the **Home** tab, in the **Font** group, select the **Clear All Formatting** button to remove all styles and formatting other than highlighting from selected text.

  > ⚠ **IMPORTANT** If you select an entire paragraph, the Clear All Formatting command will clear character and paragraph formatting from the paragraph and reset it to the default paragraph style.

  - On the **Home** tab, in the **Font** group, select the **Text Highlight Color** arrow and then, on the menu, select **No Color** to remove highlighting.

Format the first letter of a paragraph as a drop cap

Many books, magazines, and reports begin the first paragraph of a section or chapter by using an enlarged, decorative capital letter. Called a dropped capital, or simply a *drop cap*, this effect can be an easy way to give a document a finished, professional look. When you format a paragraph to start with a drop cap, Word inserts the first letter of the paragraph in a text box and formats its height and font in accordance with the Drop Cap options.

> **W**ith the Room Planner, you'll never make a design mistake again. Created by acclaimed interior designers to simplify the redecorating process, this planning tool incorporates elements of color, dimension, and style to guide your project. It includes a furniture location guide; room grid; drawing tools; and miniature furniture, rugs, accessories, and color swatches that match our large in-store selection. Here's how to use the planner to create the room of your dreams!

By default, a drop-cap letter is the height of three lines of text

Word 365 has two basic drop-cap styles:

- **Dropped** The letter is embedded in the original paragraph.

- **In margin** The letter occupies its own column, and the remaining paragraph text is moved to the right.

To format the first letter of a paragraph as a drop cap:

1. Click anywhere in the paragraph.

2. On the **Insert** tab, in the **Text** group, select the **Drop Cap** button and then select the drop-cap style you want to apply.

To change the font, height, or distance between the drop cap and the paragraph text, select Drop Cap Options on the Drop Cap menu, and then select the options you want in the Drop Cap dialog.

If you want to apply the drop-cap format to more than the first letter of the paragraph, add the drop cap to the paragraph, click to the right of the letter in the text box, and enter the rest of the word or text that you want to make stand out. If you do this, don't forget to delete the word from the beginning of the paragraph!

To change the character spacing

1. Select the text you want to change.

2. Open the **Font** dialog, and then select the **Advanced** tab to display character spacing and typographic features.

3. In the **Spacing** list, select **Expanded** or **Condensed**.

4. In the adjacent **By** box, set the number of points you want to expand or condense the character spacing.

5. In the **Font** dialog, select **OK**.

Structure content manually

At times, it's necessary to manually position text within a paragraph. You can do this by using two different hidden characters: line breaks and tabs. These characters are visible only when the option to show paragraph marks and formatting symbols is turned on.

These hidden characters have distinctive appearances:

- A line break character looks like a bent left-pointing arrow (↵)

- A tab character looks like a right-pointing arrow (→)

You can use a soft line break, also known as a *soft return*, to wrap a line of a paragraph in a specific location without ending the paragraph. You might use this technique to display only specific text on a line, or to break a line before a word that would otherwise be hyphenated.

> **TIP** Inserting a line break does not start a new paragraph, so when you apply paragraph formatting to a line of text that ends with a line break, the formatting is applied to the entire paragraph, not only to that line.

A tab stop defines the space between two document elements. For example, you can separate numbers from list items, or columns of text, by using tabs. You can then set tab stops that define the location and alignment of the tabbed text.

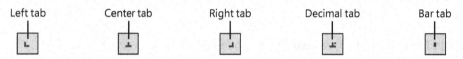

You can align text in different ways by using tabs

You can align lines of text in different locations across the page by using tab stops. The easiest way to set tab stops is directly on the horizontal ruler. By default, Word sets left-aligned tab stops every half inch (1.27 centimeters). These default tab stops aren't shown on the ruler. To set a custom tab stop, start by selecting the Tab button (located at the intersection of the vertical and horizontal rulers) until the type of tab stop you want appears.

Tab setting options

You have the following tab options:

- **Left tab** Aligns the left end of the text with the tab stop.

- **Center tab** Aligns the center of the text with the tab stop.

- **Right tab** Aligns the right end of the text with the tab stop.

- **Decimal tab** Aligns the decimal point in the text (usually a numeric value) with the tab stop.

- **Bar tab** Draws a vertical line at the position of the tab stop.

If you find it too difficult to position tab stops on the ruler, you can set, clear, align, and format tab stops from the Tabs dialog.

3

Tabs   ?   ✕

Tab stop position:

1.2"

| 1.2" |
| 3.5" |
| 4.6" |
| 6.25" |

Default tab stops:

0.5"

Tab stops to be cleared:

Alignment

◉ Left   ○ Center   ○ Right
○ Decimal   ○ Bar

Leader

◉ 1 None   ○ 2 ....   ○ 3 -------
○ 4 ___

Set   Clear   Clear All

OK   Cancel

You can specify the alignment and tab leader for each tab

You might also work from this dialog if you want to use tab leaders—visible marks such as dots or dashes connecting the text before the tab with the text after it. For example, tab leaders are useful in a table of contents to carry the eye from the text to the page number.

When you insert tab characters, the text to the right of the tab character aligns on the tab stop according to its type. For example, if you set a center tab stop, pressing the Tab key moves the text so that its center is aligned with the tab stop.

To display or hide paragraph marks and other structural characters

- On the **Home** tab, in the **Paragraph** group, select the **Show/Hide ¶** button.

- Press **Ctrl+Shift+8 (Ctrl+*)**.

To insert a line break

- Position the cursor where you want to break the line. Then do either of the following:

  - On the **Layout** tab, in the **Page Setup** group, select **Breaks** and then **Text Wrapping**.

  - Press **Shift+Enter**.

To insert a tab character

- Position the cursor where you want to add the tab character, and then press the **Tab** key.

To open the Tabs dialog

1. Select any portion of one or more paragraphs that you want to manage tab stops for.

2. Open the **Paragraph** dialog.

3. In the lower-left corner of the **Indents and Spacing** tab, select the **Tabs** button.

To align a tab and set a tab stop

1. Select any portion of one or more paragraphs that you want to set the tab stop for.

2. Display the ruler, if it isn't shown, by selecting the **Ruler** checkbox in the **Show** group on the **View** tab.

3. Select the **Tab** button at the left end of the ruler to cycle through the tab stop alignments, in this order:

   - Left

   - Center

   - Right

   - Decimal

   - Bar

4. When the **Tab** button shows the alignment you want, select the ruler at the point where you want to set the tab.

> **TIP** When you manually align a tab and set a tab stop, Word removes any default tab stops to the left of the one you set. (It doesn't remove any manually set tab stops.)

Or

1. Open the **Tabs** dialog.

2. In the **Tab stop position** box, enter the position for the new tab stop.

3. In the **Alignment** and **Leader** areas, set the options you want for this tab stop.

4. Select **Set** to set the tab, and then select **OK**.

To change the position of an existing custom tab stop

- Drag the tab marker on the ruler to the left or right.

- Open the **Tabs** dialog. In the **Tab stop position** list, select the tab stop you want to change. Select the **Clear** button to clear the existing tab stop. Enter the replacement tab stop position in the **Tab stop position** box, select **Set**, and then select **OK**.

To remove a custom tab stop

- Drag the tab marker off of the ruler.

- In the **Tabs** dialog, select the custom tab stop in the **Tab stop position** list, select **Clear**, and then select **OK**.

Create and modify lists

Lists are paragraphs that start with a character—usually a number or bullet—and are formatted with a hanging indent so that the character stands out on the left end of each list item. Fortunately, Word takes care of the formatting of lists for you. You simply indicate the type of list you want to create.

When the order of items is not important—for example, for a list of people or supplies—a bulleted list is the best choice. When the order is important—for example, for sequential steps in a procedure—you should create a numbered list.

You can format an existing set of paragraphs as a list or create the list as you enter text into the document. After you create a list, you can modify, format, and customize the list as follows:

- You can move items around in a list, insert new items, or delete unwanted items. If the list is numbered, Word automatically updates the numbers.

- You can modify the indentation of the list. You can change both the overall indentation of the list and the relationship of the first line to the other lines.

- For a bulleted list, you can sort list items alphabetically in ascending or descending order, change the bullet symbol, or define a custom bullet (even a picture bullet).

- For a numbered list, you can change the number style to use different punctuation, roman numerals, or letters, or define a custom style, and you can specify the starting number.

To format a new bulleted or numbered list as you enter content

- With the cursor at the position in the document where you want to start the list, do either of the following:

  - To start a new bulleted list, enter * (an asterisk) at the beginning of a paragraph, and then press the **Spacebar** or the **Tab** key before entering the list item text.

  - To start a new numbered list, enter 1. (the number 1 followed by a period) at the beginning of a paragraph, and then press the **Spacebar** or the **Tab** key before entering the list item text.

When you start a list in this fashion, Word automatically formats the text as a bulleted or numbered list.

When you press Enter to start a new item, Word continues the formatting to the new paragraph. Typing text and pressing Enter adds subsequent bulleted or numbered items. To end the list, press Enter twice, or select the Bullets arrow or Numbering arrow in the Paragraph group on the Home tab, and then in the gallery, select None.

> **TIP** If you want to start a paragraph with an asterisk or number but don't want to format the paragraph as a bulleted or numbered list, select the AutoCorrect Options button that appears after Word changes the formatting, and then in the list, select the appropriate Undo option. You can also select the Undo button on the Quick Access Toolbar or press Ctrl+Z.

To convert paragraphs to bulleted or numbered list items

1. Select the paragraphs that you want to convert to list items.

2. On the **Home** tab, in the **Paragraph** group, do either of the following:

   - Select the **Bullets** button to convert the selection to a bulleted list.

   - Select the **Numbering** button to convert the selection to a numbered list.

To create a list with multiple levels

1. Start creating a bulleted or numbered list.

2. When you want the next list item to be at a different level, do either of the following:

   - To create the next item one level lower (indented more), press the **Tab** key at the beginning of that paragraph before you enter the lower-level list item text.

   - To create the next item one level higher (indented less), press **Shift+Tab** at the beginning of the paragraph before you enter the higher-level list item text.

   In the case of a bulleted list, Word changes the bullet character for each item level. In the case of a numbered list, Word changes the type of numbering used, based on a predefined numbering scheme.

> **TIP** For a multilevel list, you can change the numbering pattern or bullets by selecting the Multilevel List button in the Paragraph group on the Home tab and then selecting the pattern you want, or you can define a custom pattern by selecting Define New Multilevel List.

To modify the indentation of a list

- Select the list items whose indentation you want to change, and do any of the following:

   - On the **Home** tab, in the **Paragraph** group, select the **Increase Indent** button to move the list items to the right.

   - In the **Paragraph** group, select the **Decrease Indent** button to move the list items to the left.

   - Display the ruler and drag the indent markers to the left or right.

> **TIP** You can adjust the space between the bullets and their text by dragging only the Hanging Indent marker.

> **SEE ALSO** For information about paragraph indentation, see "Apply paragraph formatting" earlier in this chapter.

To sort bulleted list items alphabetically

1. Select the bulleted list items whose sort order you want to change.

2. On the **Home** tab, in the **Paragraph** group, select the **Sort** button to open the Sort Text dialog.

3. In the **Sort by** area, select **Ascending** or **Descending**. Then select **OK**.

To change the bullet symbol

1. Select the bulleted list whose bullet symbol you want to change.

2. On the **Home** tab, in the **Paragraph** group, select the **Bullets** arrow.

3. In the **Bullets** gallery, select the new symbol you want to use to replace the bullet character that begins each item in the selected list.

To define a custom bullet

1. In the **Bullets** gallery, select **Define New Bullet**.

2. In the **Define New Bullet** dialog, select the **Symbol**, **Picture**, or **Font** button, and then select from the wide range of options.

3. Select **OK** to apply the new bullet style to the list.

To change the number style

1. Select the numbered list whose number style you want to change.

2. On the **Home** tab, in the **Paragraph** group, select the **Numbering** arrow to display the Numbering gallery.

3. Make a new selection to change the style of the number that begins each item in the selected list.

To define a custom number style

1. In the **Numbering** gallery, select **Define New Number Format**.

2. In the **Define New Number Format** dialog, do either of the following:

   - Change the selections in the **Number Style**, **Number Format**, or **Alignment** boxes.

   - Select the **Font** button and then select from the wide range of options.

3. Select **OK** to apply the new numbering style to the list.

To start a list or part of a list at a predefined number

1. Place the cursor within an existing list, in the list paragraph whose number you want to set.

2. Display the **Numbering** gallery, and then select **Set Numbering Value** to open the Set Numbering Value dialog.

3. Do either of the following to permit custom numbering:

   - Select **Start new list**.

   - Select **Continue from previous list**, and then select the **Advance value (skip numbers)** checkbox.

4. In the **Set value to** box, enter the number you want to assign to the list item. Then select **OK**.

3

Set Numbering Value   ?   ×

● Start new list
○ Continue from previous list
☐ Advance value (skip numbers)

Set value to:
3 ⬍

Preview: 3.

OK   Cancel

You can start or restart a numbered list at any number

Format text as you type

The Word list capabilities are only one example of the app's ability to intuit how you want to format an element based on what you type. You can learn more about these and other AutoFormatting options by exploring the AutoCorrect dialog, which you can open from the Proofing page of the Word Options dialog.

The AutoFormat As You Type page shows the options Word implements by default, including bulleted and numbered lists.

You can select and clear options to control automatic formatting behavior

One interesting option in this dialog is Border Lines. When this checkbox is selected, typing three consecutive hyphens (---) or three consecutive under-scores (___) and pressing Enter draws a single line across the page. Typing three consecutive equals signs (===) and pressing Enter draws a double line. Typing three consecutive tildes (~~~) and pressing Enter draws a zigzag line.

Apply built-in styles to text

You don't have to know much about character and paragraph formatting to format your documents in ways that will make them easier to read and more professional looking. With a couple of mouse clicks or screen taps, you can easily change the look of words, phrases, and paragraphs by using styles. More importantly, you can build a document outline that is reflected in the Navigation pane and use it to create a table of contents.

3

Apply styles

Styles can include character formatting (such as font, size, and color), paragraph formatting (such as line spacing and outline level), or a combination of both. Styles are stored in the template that is attached to a document.

By default, blank new documents are based on the Normal template. The Normal template includes a standard selection of styles that fit the basic needs of most documents. These styles include nine heading levels, various text styles including those for multiple levels of bulleted and numbered lists, index and table of contents entry styles, and many specialized styles such as those for hyperlinks, quotations, placeholders, captions, and other elements.

By default, the most common predefined styles are available in the Styles gallery on the Home tab. You can add styles to the gallery or remove those that you don't often use.

Normal	No Spacing	Heading 1	Heading 2
Title	Subtitle	*Subtle Emphasis*	*Emphasis*
Intense Emphasis	**Strong**	Quote	*Intense Quote*
SUBTLE REFERENCE	INTENSE REFERENCE	***Book Title***	List Paragraph

A₊ Create a Style
A∅ Clear Formatting
A→ Apply Styles...

The Styles gallery in a new, blank document based on the Normal template

Styles stored in a template are usually based on the Normal style and use only the default body and heading fonts associated with the document's theme, so they all go together well. For this reason, formatting document content by using styles produces a harmonious effect. After you apply named styles, you can easily change the look of an entire document by switching to a different style set that contains styles with the same names but different formatting.

> 🔍 **SEE ALSO** For information about document theme elements, see "Change the document theme" later in this chapter.

Style sets are available from the Document Formatting gallery on the Design tab.

Pointing to a style set in the gallery displays a live preview of the effects of applying that style set to the entire document

> ✓ **TIP** Style sets provide a quick and easy way to change the look of an existing document. You can also modify style definitions by changing the template on which the document is based.

To open the Styles pane

- On the **Home** tab, select the **Styles** dialog launcher.

Styles ▼ ✕	Styles ▼ ✕
Clear All	**Title** ¶a
Normal ¶	Subtitle ¶a
No Spacing ¶	*Subtle Emphasis* a
Heading 1 ¶a	*Emphasis* a
Heading 2 ¶a	*Intense Emphasis* a
Title ¶a	**Strong** a
Subtitle ¶a	*Quote* ¶a
Subtle Emphasis a	*Intense Quote* ¶a
Emphasis a	SUBTLE REFERENCE a
Intense Emphasis a	INTENSE REFERENCE a
Strong a	***Book Title*** a
Quote ¶a	List Paragraph ¶
Intense Quote ¶a	☑ Show Preview
Subtle Reference a	☐ Disable Linked Styles
Intense Reference a	A₊ A₍ₐ A✓ Options...
Book Title a	
List Paragraph ¶	
Footer ¶a	
Header ¶a	
☐ Show Preview	
☐ Disable Linked Styles	
A₊ A₍ₐ A✓ Options...	

The Styles pane can display style names or previews

> ✓ **TIP** If the Styles pane floats above the page, you can drag it by its title bar to the right or left edge of the app window to dock it.

To change which styles are displayed in the Styles pane

1. Open the Styles pane, and then select **Options**.

Style Pane Options	?	×

Se̲lect styles to show:

Recommended ⌄

S̲elect how list is sorted:

As Recommended ⌄

Select formatting to show as styles:
- ☐ P̲aragraph level formatting
- ☐ F̲ont formatting
- ☐ B̲ullet and numbering formatting

Select how built-in style names are shown
- ☑ Sho̲w next heading when previous level is used
- ☐ H̲ide built-in name when alternate name exists

◉ Only in this document   ○ New documents based on this template

OK	Cancel

To make it easier to find specific styles, sort the list alphabetically

2. In the **Style Pane Options** dialog, do any of the following, and then select **OK**:

   - In the **Select styles to show** list, select one of the following:

     - **Recommended** Displays styles that are tagged in the template as recommended for use

     - **In use** Displays styles that are applied to content in the current document

     - **In current document** Displays styles that are in the template that is attached to the current document

     - **All styles** Displays built-in styles, styles that are in the attached template, and styles that were brought into the document from other templates

   - In the **Select how list is sorted** list, select **Alphabetical**, **As Recommended**, **Font**, **Based on**, or **By type**.

   - In the **Select formatting to show as styles** area, select each checkbox for which you want to display variations from named styles.

   - In the **Select how built-in style names are shown** area, select the checkbox for each option you want to turn on.

3

Style Pane Options

Select styles to show:

In use

Select how list is sorted:

Alphabetical

Select formatting to show as styles:

☑ Paragraph level formatting

☑ Font formatting

☐ Bullet and numbering formatting

Select how built-in style names are shown

☐ Show next heading when previous level is used

☐ Hide built-in name when alternate name exists

🔘 Only in this document   ⚪ New documents based on this template

OK   Cancel

Displaying paragraph-level and font formatting exposes deviations from style definitions

To display or hide style previews in the Styles pane

- Open the Styles pane, and then select or clear the **Show Preview** checkbox.

To add a style to the Styles gallery

- In the Styles pane, point to the style, select the arrow that appears, and then select **Add to Style Gallery**.

To remove a style from the Styles gallery

- In the Styles pane, point to the style, select the arrow that appears, and then select **Remove from Style Gallery**.

- In the **Styles** gallery, right-click or long-press (tap and hold) the style, and then select **Remove from Style Gallery**.

To apply a built-in style

1. Select the text or paragraph to which you want to apply the style.

> ✔ **TIP** If the style you want to apply is a paragraph style, you can position the cursor anywhere in the paragraph. If the style you want to apply is a character style, you must select the text.

2. In the **Styles** gallery on the **Home** tab, or in the Styles pane, select the style you want to apply.

To change the style set

1. On the **Design** tab, in the **Document Formatting** group, select the **More** button to display all the style sets (if necessary).

2. Point to any style set to preview its effect on the document.

3. Select the style set you want to apply.

Manage outline levels

Styles can be used for multiple purposes: to affect the appearance of the content, to build a document outline, and to tag content as a certain type so that you can easily locate it.

Heading styles define a document's outline

Each paragraph style has an associated Outline Level setting. Outline levels include Body Text and Level 1 through Level 9. Most documents use only body text and the first two, three, or four outline levels.

3

Paragraph　　　　　　　　　　　？　✕

Indents and Spacing　　**Line and Page Breaks**

General

Alignment:　[Left　∨]

Outline level:　[Level 1　∨]　☐ Collapsed by default

| Body Text ▲ |
| Level 1 |
| Level 2 |
| Level 3 |

Indentation

Left:　| Level 4 |

Right:　| Level 5 |
| Level 6 |

☐ Mirror inde| Level 7 |
| Level 8 |
| Level 9 ▼ |

Special:　[Hanging　∨]　By:　[0.25" ⊞]

Most documents use only two to four of the outline levels

Paragraphs that have the Level 1 through Level 9 outline levels become part of the hierarchical structure of the document. They appear as headings in the Navigation pane and act as handles for the content that appears below them in the hierarchy. You can collapse and expand the content below each heading and move entire sections of content by dragging the headings in the Navigation pane.

To display the document outline in the Navigation pane

- In the Navigation pane, select **Headings** to display the document structure.

 TIP Only headings that are styled by using document heading styles, or other styles that have outline levels applied, appear in the Navigation pane.

To expand or collapse the outline in the Navigation pane

- In the Navigation pane, do either of the following:

  - If there is a white triangle to the left of a heading, select it to expand that heading to show its subheadings.

  - If there is a downward-angled black triangle to the left of a heading, select it to collapse the subheadings under that heading.

 TIP If there is no triangle next to a heading, that heading does not have subheadings.

To expand or collapse sections in the document

- In a document that contains styles, point to a heading to display a triangle to its left. Then do either of the following:

  - If the triangle is a downward-angled gray triangle, select the triangle to hide the content that is within the heading.

  - If the triangle is a white triangle, select the triangle to display the hidden document content.

Change the document theme

Every document you create is based on a template, and the look of the template is controlled by a theme. The theme is a combination of coordinated colors, fonts, and effects that visually convey a certain tone. To change the look of a document, you can apply a different theme from the Themes gallery.

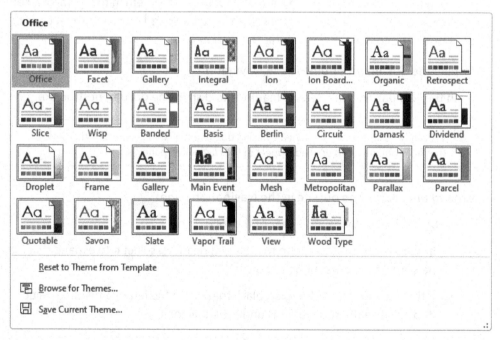

The default installation of Word 365 offers 30 themes to choose from

3

Each theme has a built-in font set and color set, and an associated effect style.

- Each font set includes two font definitions: one for headings and one for body text. In some font sets, the heading and body fonts are the same.

- Each color in a color set has a specific role in the formatting of styled elements. For example, the first color in each set is applied to the Title and Intense Reference styles, and different shades of the third color are applied to the Subtitle, Heading 1, and Heading 2 styles.

If you like the background elements of a theme but not the colors or fonts, you can mix and match theme elements.

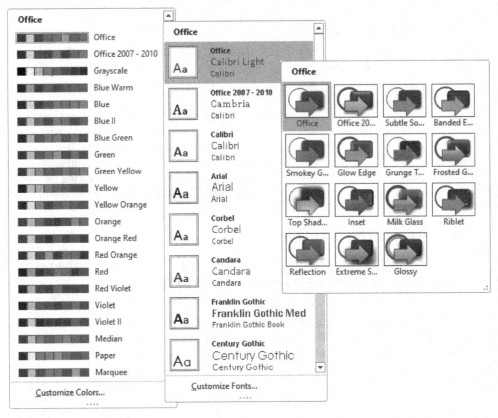

Word 365 offers thousands of different combinations for creating a custom theme that meets your exact needs

> **TIP** In addition to colors and fonts, you can control the subtler design elements associated with a theme, such as paragraph spacing and visual effects.

If you create a combination of theme elements that you would like to use with other documents, you can save the combination as a new theme. By saving the theme in the default Document Themes folder, you make the theme available in the Themes gallery. However, you don't have to store custom themes in the Document Themes folder; you can store them anywhere on your hard disk, on removable media, or in a network location.

> **TIP** The default Document Themes folder is stored within your user profile. On a default freestanding installation, the folder is located at C:\Users\<*user name*>\ AppData\Roaming\Microsoft\Templates\Document Themes. In a corporate environment with managed computer configurations, the user profile folder might be located elsewhere.

By default, Word applies the Office theme to all new, blank documents. In Word 365, the Office theme uses a primarily blue palette, the Calibri font for body text, and Calibri Light for headings. If you plan to frequently use a theme other than the Office theme, you can make that the default theme.

> **TIP** If multiple people create corporate documents for your company, you can ensure that everyone's documents have a common look and feel by assembling a custom theme and making it available to everyone. Use theme elements that reflect your corporate colors, fonts, and visual style, and then save the theme to a central location or send the theme file by email and instruct your colleagues to save it to the default Document Themes folder.

To apply a built-in theme to a document

- On the **Design** tab, in the **Document Formatting** group, select the **Themes** button, and then select the theme you want to apply.

> **TIP** If you have manually applied formatting to document content, the theme does not override the manual formatting. To ensure that all document elements are controlled by the theme, select Reset To The Default Style Set on the Document Formatting menu.

3

To change theme elements in a document

- On the **Design** tab, in the **Document Formatting** group, do any of the following:

  - Select **Colors** (the ScreenTip says *Theme Colors*), and then select the color set you want to apply.

  - Select **Fonts** (the ScreenTip says *Theme Fonts*), and then select the font set you want to apply.

  - Select **Effects** (the ScreenTip says *Theme Effects*), and then select the effect style you want to apply.

To save a custom theme

1. Apply a base theme, and then modify the theme colors, fonts, and effects as you want them.

2. On the **Design** tab, in the **Document Formatting** group, select **Themes**.

3. At the bottom of the **Themes** menu, select **Save Current Theme** to display the contents of the Document Themes folder in the **Save Current Theme** dialog.

4. Accept the theme name that's in the **File name** box or replace the suggested name with one that's more descriptive. Then select **Save**.

To apply a custom theme

1. Display the **Themes** menu. If you have created a custom theme, the Themes menu now includes a Custom area that contains your theme.

2. Select the theme to apply it to the document.

To change the default theme

1. In the document, apply the theme you want to use as the default theme.

2. On the **Design** tab, in the **Document Formatting** group, select **Set as Default**.

To apply a theme from a nonstandard location

1. On the **Design** tab, in the **Document Formatting** group, select **Themes**.

2. At the bottom of the **Themes** menu, select **Browse for Themes**.

3. In the **Choose Theme or Themed Document** dialog, browse to the theme you want to apply, and then select **Open**.

To find the location of your Document Themes folder

1. On the **Design** tab, in the **Document Formatting** group, select **Themes**.

2. At the bottom of the **Themes** menu, select **Save Current Theme**.

3. In the **Save Current Theme** dialog, select the icon at the left end of the address bar to display the full path to the Document Themes folder.

To delete a custom theme

- Open File Explorer, browse to the **Document Themes** folder, and delete the theme file.

- In Word, display the **Themes** menu, right-click the custom theme, and then select **Delete**.

Note that the second method removes the theme choice from the gallery but does not remove the theme file from the Document Themes folder.

Key points

- You can format many aspects of a paragraph, including its indentation, alignment, internal line spacing, preceding and following space, border, and background. Within a paragraph, you can control the content structure by using hidden line breaks and tabs, and the appearance of the content by changing the size, color, style, effects, and spacing of the text.

- You can apply paragraph and character formatting manually, or you can format multiple elements of a paragraph, and control the outline level of the content, by using styles.

- You can change the formatting applied by all the styles within a document by changing the document theme or any individual element of the theme, such as the theme colors, theme fonts, or theme effects.

- To make a set of items or instructions stand out from the surrounding text, you can format it as an ordered (numbered) or unordered (bulleted) list.

> **SEE ALSO** This chapter is from the full-length book *Microsoft Word Step by Step (Office 2021 and Microsoft 365)* (Microsoft Press, 2022). Please consult that book for information about features of Word that aren't discussed in this book.

Practice tasks

Before you can complete these tasks, you must copy the book's practice files to your computer. The practice files for these tasks are in the **Office365SBS\Ch03** folder. You can save the results of the tasks in the same folder.

The introduction includes a complete list of practice files and download instructions.

Apply paragraph formatting

Open the **FormatParagraphs** document, display formatting marks, and then perform the following tasks:

1. Display the rulers and adjust the zoom level to display most or all of the paragraphs in the document.

2. Select the first two paragraphs (*Welcome!* and the next paragraph) and center them between the margins.

3. Select the second paragraph (*We would like...*) and apply a first-line indent.

4. Select the third paragraph (*Please take a few...*). Format the paragraph so its edges are flush against the left and right margins. Then indent the paragraph by a half inch on the left and on the right.

5. Indent the *Be careful* paragraph by 0.25 inches.

6. Simultaneously select the *Pillows*, *Blankets*, *Towels*, *Limousine winery tour*, and *In-home massage* paragraphs. Change the paragraph spacing to remove the space after the paragraphs.

7. At the top of the document, apply an outside border to the *Please take a few minutes* paragraph.

8. Save and close the document.

Apply character formatting

Open the **FormatCharacters** document, and then perform the following tasks:

1. In the second bullet point, underline the word *natural*. Then repeat the formatting command to underline the word *all* in the fourth bullet point.

2. In the fourth bullet point, select anywhere in the word *across*. Apply a thick underline to the word in a way that also assigns the **Thick underline** format to the **Underline** button. Then apply the thick underline to the word *departments*.

3. Apply bold formatting to the *Employee Orientation* heading.

4. Copy the formatting, and then paint it onto the *Guidelines* subtitle, to make the subtitle a heading.

5. Select the *Guidelines* heading, and apply the following formatting:

   - Change the font to **Impact**.

   - Set the font size to **20** points.

   - Apply the **Small caps** font effect.

   - Expand the character spacing by **10** points.

6. Change the font color of the words *Employee Orientation* to **Green, Accent 6**.

7. Select the *Community Service Committee* heading, and apply the following formatting:

   - Outline the letters in the same color you applied to *Employee Orientation*.

   - Apply an **Offset Diagonal Bottom Left** outer shadow. Change the shadow color to **Green, Accent 6, Darker 50%**.

   - Fill the letters with the **Green, Accent 6** color, and then change the text outline to **Green, Accent 6, Darker 25%**.

   You have now applied three text effects to the selected text by using three shades of the same green.

8. In the first bullet point, select the phrase *the concept of service* and apply a **Bright Green** highlight.

9. In the fifth bullet point, simultaneously select the words *brainstorming*, *planning*, and *leadership*, and change the case of all the letters to uppercase.

10. Save and close the document.

Structure content manually

Open the **StructureContent** document, display formatting marks, and then perform the following tasks:

1. Display the rulers and adjust the zoom level to display most or all of the paragraphs in the document.

2. In the second paragraph (*We would like…*), insert a line break immediately after the comma and space that follow the word *cottage*.

3. Select the *Pillows*, *Blankets*, *Towels*, and *Dish towels* paragraphs. Insert a left tab stop at the **2**-inch mark and clear any tab stops to the left of that location.

4. In the *Pillows* paragraph, replace the space before the word *There* with a tab marker. Repeat the process to insert tabs in each of the next three paragraphs. The part of each paragraph that follows the colon is now aligned at the 2-inch mark, producing more space than you need.

5. Select the four paragraphs containing tabs. Change the left tab stop from the 2-inch mark to the **1.25**-inch mark. Then, on the ruler, drag the **Hanging Indent** marker to the tab stop at the **1.25-inch** mark (the Left Indent marker moves with it) to cause the second line of the paragraphs to start in the same location as the first line. Finally, press the **Home** key to release the selection so you can review the results.

6. At the bottom of the document, select the three paragraphs containing dollar amounts. Set a **Decimal Tab** stop at the **3**-inch mark. Then replace the space to the left of each dollar sign with a tab to align the prices on the decimal points.

7. Hide the formatting marks to better display the results of your work.

8. Save and close the document.

Create and modify lists

Open the **CreateLists** document, display formatting marks and rulers, and then perform the following tasks:

1. Select the first four paragraphs below *The rules fall into four categories*. Format the selected paragraphs as a bulleted list. Then change the bullet character for the four list items to the one composed of four diamonds.

2. Select the two paragraphs below the *Definitions* heading. Format the selected paragraphs as a numbered list.

3. Select the first four paragraphs below the *General Rules* heading. Format the paragraphs as a second numbered list. Ensure that the new list starts with the number 1.

4. Format the next three paragraphs as a bulleted list. (Notice that Word uses the bullet symbol you specified earlier.) Indent the bulleted list as a subset of the preceding numbered list item.

5. Format the remaining three paragraphs as a numbered list. Ensure that the list numbering continues from the previous numbered list.

6. Locate the *No large dogs* numbered list item. Create a new second-level numbered list item (**a**) from the text that begins with the word *Seeing*. Then create a second item (**b**) and enter **The Board reserves the right to make exceptions to this rule.**

7. Create a third list item (**c**). Promote the new list item to a first-level item, and enter **All pets must reside within their Owners' Apartments.** Notice that the *General Rules* list is now organized hierarchically.

8. Sort the three bulleted list items in ascending alphabetical order.

9. Save and close the document.

Apply built-in styles to text

Open the **ApplyStyles** document in Print Layout view, and then perform the following tasks:

1. Scroll through the document to review its content. Notice that the document begins with a centered title and subtitle, and there are several headings throughout.

2. Display the Navigation pane. Notice that the Headings page of the pane does not reflect the headings in the document because the headings are formatted with manually applied formatting instead of styles.

3. Open the Styles pane and dock it to the right edge of the app window.

4. Set the zoom level of the page to fit the page content between the Navigation pane and the Styles pane.

5. Apply the **Title** style to the document title, *All About Bamboo*.

6. Apply the **Subtitle** style to the *Information Sheet* paragraph.

7. Apply the **Heading 1** style to the first bold heading, *Moving to a New Home*. Notice that the heading appears in the Navigation pane.

8. Hide the content that follows the heading. Then redisplay it.

9. Apply the **Heading 1** style to *Staying Healthy*. Then repeat the formatting to apply the same style to *Keeping Bugs at Bay*.

10. Scroll the page so that both underlined headings are visible. Select the *Mites* and *Mealy Bugs* headings. Then simultaneously apply the **Heading 2** style to both selections.

11. Configure the Styles pane to display all styles, in alphabetical order.

12. Move to the beginning of the document.

13. In the first paragraph of the document, select the company name *Wide World Importers*, and apply the **Intense Reference** style.

14. In the second paragraph, near the end of the first sentence, select the word *clumping*, and apply the **Emphasis** style. Then, at the end of the sentence, apply the same style to the word *running*.

15. Close the Navigation pane and the Styles pane. Then configure the view setting to display both pages of the document in the window.

16. Apply the **Basic (Elegant)** style set to the document. Change the view to **Page Width** and notice the changes to the styled content.

17. Save and close the document.

Change the document theme

Open the **ChangeTheme** document, and then perform the following tasks:

1. Apply the **Facet** theme to the document.

2. Change the theme colors to the **Orange** color scheme.

3. Change the theme fonts to the **Georgia** theme set.

4. Save the modified theme in the default folder as a custom theme named My Theme. Verify that the custom theme is available on the **Themes** menu.

5. Save and close the document.

Collaborate on documents

It's not unusual for several people to collaborate on the development of a document. Collaboration is simplest when contributors review electronic documents in files on a computer screen rather than review paper printouts. On-screen review is very efficient; you can provide legible feedback, implement specific changes, and save trees at the same time.

If you save a file in a shared location, multiple people can review and edit the document at the same time. This highly efficient method of collaboration is called *coauthoring*. Another method of gathering feedback from multiple reviewers is to send a file to each reviewer and then merge the reviewed versions into one file that displays all the changes. This is less efficient but has its benefits.

Word has many tools that simplify the process of collaboratively creating documents. You can make changes without deleting the original content, provide feedback in comments, and respond to comments and queries from other reviewers. To protect a document from unwanted changes, you can restrict the editing options so that Word tracks all changes, allows only certain types of changes, or doesn't allow changes at all.

In this chapter

- Mark up documents
- Display and review document markup
- Compare and combine documents
- Control content changes
- Coauthor documents

This chapter guides you through procedures related to marking up and reviewing documents, comparing and merging document versions, restricting the changes that people can make to documents that you share with them, and coauthoring documents.

Mark up documents

Comments and tracked changes are collectively referred to as *markup*. Markup is used during the content-development and review processes and is particularly useful for bringing changes, suggestions, and comments to the attention of multiple members of a collaborative authoring group.

Insert comments

A comment is a note attached to an anchor within the text. The anchor can be text or any type of object, or simply a location; wherever it is, Word displays the comment in the right margin of the document.

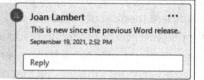

Word automatically adds your name and a time stamp to the comment

Each comment is inside a container that is fully visible when the comment is active (when you point to or select it). Comment containers are referred to as *balloons*. Balloons can be used for the display of various types of markup.

You can insert comments for many reasons, such as to ask questions, make suggestions, provide reference information, or explain edits. You insert and work with comments by using the commands in the Comments group on the Review tab and on the Comments menu at the right end of the ribbon.

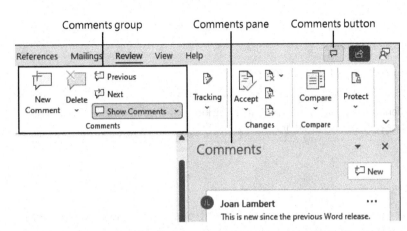

The commands in the Comments group make it easy to navigate and remove comments

---

⚠ **IMPORTANT** Word uses standard colors to mark content moves, edits, and structural changes in tables but doesn't track the editor, time, or date of the change. It is possible to customize these markup colors, but there really isn't any point to doing so because the custom colors don't travel with the document.

✓ **TIP** Display documents in Print Layout view so that all the collaboration commands are available.

To display the Comments pane

- To the right of the ribbon tabs, select the **Comments** button.

- On the **Review** tab, in the **Comments** group, select the **Show Comments** arrow (not the button), and then in the list, select **List**.

To insert a comment

1. Select the text or object you want to anchor the comment to.

2. Do one of the following:

   - On the **Review** tab, in the **Comments** group, select **New Comment**.

   - In the **Comments** pane, select **New**.

   - Press **Alt+I+M**.

3. In the comment balloon that appears in the right margin or in the **Comments** pane, enter the comment.

4. Press **Ctrl+Enter** to post the comment.

 TIP Comments are usually simple text but can include other elements and formatting, such as images and active hyperlinks.

Track changes

When two or more people collaborate on a document, one person usually creates and "owns" the document, and the others review it—adding or revising content to make it more accurate, logical, or readable. When reviewing a document in Word, you can track your changes so they are available for review and retain the original text for comparison or reversion. You manage change tracking from the Tracking group on the Review tab.

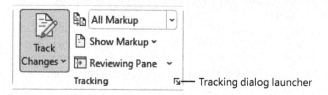

A shaded button indicates that change tracking is active

 TIP Turning on the change-tracking feature tracks changes only in the active document, not in any other open documents.

When change tracking is on, Word tracks insertions and deletions and the movement and formatting of content. When you display a document in All Markup view, tracked changes are indicated by different font colors and formatting. The default formatting is as follows:

- Insertions are in the reviewer-specific color and underlined.

- Deletions are in the reviewer-specific color and crossed out (struck through).

- Formatting changes are indicated in balloons in the markup area.

- Moves are green and double-underlined.

- In All Markup view or Simple Markup view, all changes are indicated in the left margin by a vertical line.

As with comments, m~~Multiple people can track changes in a document.~~ Word tracks insertions and deletions and the movement and formatting of content. When you display a document in All Markup view, tracked changes are indicated by different font colors and formatting. The default formatting is as follows:

- Insertions are in the reviewer-specific color and underlined.
- Deletions are in the reviewer-specific color and crossed out.
- Formatting changes are indicated in balloons in the markup area.
- Moves are green and double-underlined.
- All changes are indicated in the left margin by a vertical line.

~~Multiple people can track changes in a document.~~ Word assigns a color to each person's changes and uses that color to format inserted and deleted text. ~~If you prefer to select a color for your own changes, you can do so.~~ You can also modify the formatting that indicates each type of change. For example, you could have Word indicate inserted text by formatting it as bold, italic, or with a double underline. Note, however, that this change would be valid only for your profile on the computer you make the change on and would not affect change formatting on other computers.

Moved text is green, and a double underline indicates its new location

Multiple people can track changes in a document. Word assigns a color to each person's changes and uses that color to format inserted and deleted text. If you prefer to select a color for your own changes, you can do so. You can also modify the formatting that indicates each type of change. For example, you could have Word indicate inserted text by formatting it as bold, as italic, or with a double underline. Note, however, that this change would be valid only for your profile on the computer you make the change on and would not affect change formatting on other computers.

You can modify the types of changes that are tracked and the markup colors

If you want to ensure that other reviewers track their changes to a document, you can turn on and lock the change-tracking feature and (optionally) require that reviewers enter a password to turn it off.

A new feature in this version of Word allows you to turn on change tracking only for yourself or for everyone who edits the document.

> **SEE ALSO** For information about forcing change tracking by restricting editing, see "Control content changes" later in this chapter.

To turn on change tracking for everyone

- On the **Review** tab, in the **Tracking** group, select the **Track Changes** button (not its arrow).

- On the **Review** tab, in the **Tracking** group, select the **Track Changes** arrow, and then select **For Everyone**.

- Press **Ctrl+Shift+E**.

> **SEE ALSO** For information about keyboard shortcuts, see the appendix, "Keyboard shortcuts."

To turn on change tracking for only yourself

- On the **Review** tab, in the **Tracking** group, select the **Track Changes** arrow, and then select **Just Mine**.

To turn off change tracking

- On the **Review** tab, in the **Tracking** group, select the **Track Changes** button (not its arrow).

To track changes without displaying them on the screen

1. On the **Review** tab, in the **Tracking** group, select the **Display for Review** arrow.

2. In the **Display for Review** list, select **Simple Markup** or **No Markup**.

> **SEE ALSO** For more information about the markup views, see "Display and review document markup" later in this chapter.

To specify the color of the changes you track in any document

1. On the **Review** tab, select the **Tracking** dialog launcher to open the **Track Changes Options** dialog.

2. Select **Advanced Options** to open the **Advanced Track Changes Options** dialog.

3. In the **Color** lists adjacent to **Insertions**, **Deletions**, and **Formatting**, select the color you want to use for that type of change in Word documents on the current computer.

4. Select **OK** in each open dialog to close them and save your changes.

To prevent reviewers from turning off change tracking

1. On the **Review** tab, in the **Tracking** group, select the **Track Changes** arrow, and then select **Lock Tracking**.

2. In the **Lock Tracking** dialog, enter and reenter a password to prevent other people from turning off change tracking.

Lock Tracking	?	X

Prevent other authors from turning off Track Changes.

Enter password (optional): `****`

Reenter to confirm: `****`

(This is not a security feature.)

OK   Cancel

Use a password that you will remember, or make a note of it in a secure location so you can find it later

3. In the **Lock Tracking** dialog, select **OK**. The Track Changes button becomes unavailable.

To unlock change tracking

1. On the **Review** tab, in the **Tracking** group, select the **Track Changes** arrow, and then select **Lock Tracking**.

2. In the **Unlock Tracking** dialog, enter the password you assigned when you enabled this feature, and then select **OK**.

Unlocking tracking doesn't turn off change tracking; you must do that separately

Display and review document markup

After reviewers provide feedback by making changes and entering comments, you can review the tracked changes and comments and choose how you would like to process them.

Display markup

Usually you would display and review all types of markup at one time—insertions, deletions, moves, formatting changes, and comments. However, if you prefer, you can choose to display only certain types of markup, or only markup from specific reviewers.

Word has four basic Display For Review options that govern the display of tracked changes in a document. The settings are as follows:

- **Simple Markup** This default markup view displays a red vertical line in the left margin adjacent to each tracked change. Markup is hidden.

- **All Markup** This view displays a gray vertical line in the left margin adjacent to each tracked change, and formats inserted, deleted, and moved content to reflect the settings in the Advanced Track Changes Options dialog.

> **SEE ALSO** For information about controlling markup formatting, see "Mark up documents" earlier in this chapter.

- **No Markup** This view hides comments and displays the current document content as though all changes have been accepted. Changes that you make in this view are tracked (if change tracking is turned on) and visible when markup is shown.

- **Original** This view displays the original document content without any markup.

Depending on your view settings, comments are shown in the following ways:

- In balloons in the Comments pane

- In balloons in the right margin

- Hidden and indicated by highlighting in the text

You can select the comment icon or point to the highlight to display the comment text.

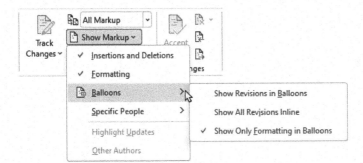

The individual markup display options

After you select a Display For Review option, you can additionally filter the display of markup in these ways:

- You can individually control the display of comments, insertions and deletions, and formatting.

- You can show all markup inline or in balloons, or keep comments in balloons and insertions, deletions, and moves inline.

- You can display or hide markup by reviewer.

You can display and manage all the comments in the document in the new Comments pane, which opens to the right of the document text. From within the Comments pane, you can create, edit, reply to, resolve, and delete comment threads.

Manage comment threads in the Comments pane

If you prefer to display all comments and tracked changes in a document at one time, you can do so in the Revisions pane. By default, this pane opens to the left of the document text (and to the right of the Navigation pane, if that is open) at the same height as the document content area. If you want to, you can dock it on the right side of the window instead.

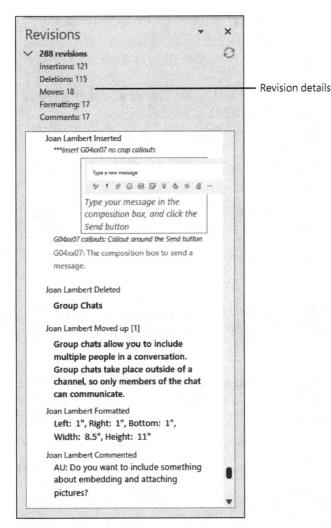

Revision details

Information about the number and type of revisions is available at the top of the Revisions pane

From the ribbon, you can also display the Revisions pane horizontally. By default, the horizontal pane stretches across the bottom of the Word app window. If you prefer, you can drag it to the top of the window.

When the Comments pane or Revisions pane is docked, the content pane becomes narrower (or shorter, if you display the horizontal Revisions pane) to make space for the pane. You can undock the pane so that it floats independently of the app window and doesn't take space away from the content pane. The floating pane has a vertical format, but you can change its height and width to fit wherever it's convenient. The best display location depends on the amount of space you have available on your device screen or screens.

To change the display of markup in a document

- To switch between Simple Markup view and All Markup view, select the red or gray vertical line in the margin to the left of any tracked change.

Or

1. On the **Review** tab, in the **Tracking** group, select the **Display for Review** arrow (to the right of the current markup view).

2. In the **Display for Review** list, select **Simple Markup**, **All Markup**, **No Markup**, or **Original**.

To display specific types of markup in balloons

1. In the **Display for Review** list, select **All Markup**.

2. In the **Show Markup** list, select **Balloons**, and then select **Show Revisions in Balloons**, **Show All Revisions Inline**, or **Show Only Formatting in Balloons**.

To hide or display all markup of a specific type

- On the **Review** tab, in the **Tracking** group, select **Show Markup**, and then select **Comments, Insertions and Deletions**, or **Formatting**.

> **TIP** A check mark to the left of a markup type indicates that elements of that type are visible in views of the document that display those elements.

To display only markup by a specific person

1. On the **Review** tab, in the **Tracking** group, select **Show Markup**.

2. In the **Show Markup** list, point to **Specific People**. If a check mark appears to the left of All Reviewers, select it to remove the check mark. Then select the name of the reviewer whose comments you want to display.

To display individual comments in Simple Markup view

- Select a comment icon to display the comments on that line in comment balloons.

- Point to a comment icon to highlight the comments on that line in the colors associated with the comments' authors.

> **TIP** The reviewer name is taken from the user information stored with the user account. If you're signed in to Word with a Microsoft account, Word tracks revisions by the name associated with your Microsoft account. If the instance of Word you're working in is not linked to a Microsoft account, you can change the stored user information on the General page of the Word Options dialog. Changing your user information affects revision tracking only when you aren't signed in with a Microsoft account.

4

To display comments in the margin

- On the **Review** tab, in the **Comments** group, select the **Show Comments** button.

- On the **Review** tab, in the **Comments** group, select the **Show Comments** arrow (not the button), and then select **Contextual**.

To display the Comments pane

- To the right of the ribbon tabs, select the **Comments** button.

- On the **Review** tab, in the **Comments** group, select the **Show Comments** arrow (not the button), and then in the list, select **List**.

To display the Revisions pane

- On the **Review** tab, in the **Tracking** group, select the **Reviewing Pane** button (not the arrow).

> **TIP** Selecting the button opens the Revisions pane in its most recent location. The default location in each new Word session is to the left of the page.

Or

1. In the **Tracking** group, select the **Reviewing Pane** arrow.

2. In the **Reviewing Pane** list, do either of the following:

   - Select **Reviewing Pane Vertical** to display the pane to the left or right of the document.

   - Select **Reviewing Pane Horizontal** to display the pane below the ribbon or above the status bar.

To display a breakdown of revision types

- In the **Revisions** pane, to the left of the revision summary, select the **Expand** button (the **v**).

To change the location of the Comments pane or Revisions pane

- Drag the pane by its header to any of the following locations:

  - Dock the pane vertically to the left or right side of the app window or against any other vertical pane.

  - Dock the pane horizontally below the ribbon or above the status bar.

  - Drag the pane inside or outside the app window to float it independently.

To change the width or height of the floating Comments pane or Revisions pane

1. Point to the right or top border of the pane.

2. When the pointer changes to a double-headed arrow, drag the border.

To close the Comments pane or Revisions pane

- In the upper-right corner of the pane, select the **Close** button.

- On the **Review** tab, in the **Tracking** group, select **Reviewing Pane**.

Review and respond to comments

All the comments in a document are available for review, regardless of who created them. You can scroll through a document and review the comments as you come to them, or you can jump from comment to comment by selecting comments in the Comments pane or buttons on the ribbon, or by using the commands on the Comments menu.

> **TIP** If a document contains both comments and tracked changes, selecting the Next or Previous button in the Changes group on the Review tab moves sequentially among these elements, whereas selecting the Next or Previous button in the Comments group or Comments menu moves only among comments.

When reviewing comments, you can take the following actions:

- Respond to individual comments to provide further information or request clarification.

- Mark individual comments or comment threads as Resolved to indicate that you've processed them and retain them for later reference.

- Delete individual comments that you no longer require.

- Filter the comments by author.

- Delete all visible comments at the same time.

- Delete all comments in the document at the same time.

The ability to mark comments as Resolved is a useful feature. Marking a comment as Resolved leaves the comment intact but minimizes and recolors the comment elements so that it doesn't distract from the document content in the way that an active comment does.

An example of a tracked comment before and after being marked as Resolved

To move only among comments

- In the **Comments** pane or **Revisions** pane, select any comment to move to that comment in the document.

- On the **Review** tab, in the **Comments** group, select the **Next** or **Previous** button to jump from balloon to balloon.

- Scroll through the document to visually locate comment balloons.

To activate a comment for editing

- In the comment balloon, select the **Edit comment** icon (the pencil).

To respond to a comment

- In the comment balloon, enter your comment in the **Reply** box and then select the **Post reply** button or press **Ctrl+Enter** to post your reply.

To mark a comment as Resolved or reactivate a Resolved comment

- Right-click or long-press (tap and hold) the comment highlight (in the text), and then select **Resolve Comment**.

- In the comment balloon, select the **More thread actions** button (…) and then select **Resolve thread**.

> **TIP** It isn't possible to resolve individual comments in a multi-comment thread. The first comment in a thread is treated as a thread.

To delete a comment

- In the comment balloon, select the **More thread actions** button (…) for a comment without replies, and then select **Delete thread**.

- In the comment balloon, select the **More comment actions** button (…) for any reply within a thread, and then select **Delete comment**.

- Right-click the comment highlight (in the text) or the comment balloon, and then select **Delete Comment**.

To delete a comment thread

- Activate the comment balloon, and then on the **Review** tab, in the **Comments** group, select the **Delete** button.

- In the comment balloon, select the **More thread actions** button (…) for the first comment in a thread, and then select **Delete thread**.

Review and process tracked changes

As with comments, you can scroll through a document and review insertions, deletions, content moves, and formatting changes as you come to them, or you can jump from change to change by selecting buttons on the ribbon or using the Revisions pane. You also have the option of accepting or rejecting multiple changes at the same time.

Here are some typical scenarios for reviewing and processing changes that you might consider:

- Display a document in Simple Markup view or No Markup view so you're viewing the final content. If you are happy with the document content in that view, accept all the changes at the same time.

- Display a document in All Markup view. Scan the individual changes visually. Individually reject any change that doesn't meet your requirements. As you complete the review of a section that meets your requirements, select the content of that section and approve all the changes within your selection.

- Display a document in All Markup view. Move to the first change. Accept or reject the change to move to the next. (You can perform both actions with one click.)

When reviewing tracked changes, you can take the following actions:

- Accept or reject individual changes.

- Select a section of content and accept or reject all changes therein at the same time.

- Filter the changes and then accept or reject all visible changes at the same time.

- Accept or reject all changes in the document at the same time.

To move among tracked changes and comments

- On the **Review** tab, in the **Changes** group, select the **Next** or **Previous** button.

- In the **Revisions** pane, select any change or comment to move to it in the document.

To display the time and author of a tracked change

- Point to any revision in the text to display a ScreenTip identifying the name of the reviewer who made the change, and when the change was made.

To incorporate a selected change into the document and move to the next change

- On the **Review** tab, in the **Changes** group, select the **Accept** button.

Or

1. On the **Review** tab, in the **Changes** group, select the **Accept** arrow.

2. In the **Accept** list, select **Accept and Move to Next**.

To incorporate a selected change into the document and remain in the same location

- Right-click the change, and then select **Accept Deletion** or **Accept Insertion**.

- On the **Review** tab, in the **Accept** list, select **Accept This Change**.

To remove the selected change, restore the original text, and move to the next change

- On the **Review** tab, in the **Changes** group, select the **Reject** button.

- On the **Review** tab, in the **Reject** list, select **Reject and Move to Next**.

4

To remove the selected change, restore the original text, and remain in the same location

- Right-click the change, and then select **Reject Deletion** or **Reject Insertion**.

- On the **Review** tab, in the **Reject** list, select **Reject This Change**.

To accept or reject all the changes in a section of text

- Select the text. Then do either of the following:

  - On the **Review** tab, in the **Changes** group, select the **Accept** button or the **Reject** button.

  - Right-click the selected text, and then select **Accept Change** or **Reject Change**.

To accept or reject all the changes in a document

- On the **Review** tab, in the **Accept** list, select **Accept All Changes**.

- On the **Review** tab, in the **Reject** list, select **Reject All Changes**.

To accept or reject all the changes of a certain type or from a certain reviewer

- Configure the review display settings to display only the changes you want to accept or reject. Then do either of the following:

  - On the **Review** tab, in the **Accept** list, select **Accept All Changes Shown**.

  - On the **Review** tab, in the **Reject** list, select **Reject All Changes Shown**.

Remember to check for errors

It's a good idea to check for spelling issues in a document after you finish processing changes because, for example, it's easy to accidentally end up with a missing or extra space in the document. If the Check Spelling As You Type option is on (as it is by default), you can scroll through the document and visually scan for wavy red underlines that indicate suspected spelling errors or double blue underlines that indicate suspected grammar errors. To be entirely thorough, you can run the Editor tool (from the Proofing group on the Review tab) and respond to each spelling or grammar issue or writing suggestion it identifies.

Compare and combine documents

Sometimes you might want to compare several versions of the same document. Word supports two types of document-version comparison:

- Comparing a document to a separate copy of the document.

- Comparing a document to a previous version of the same document.

Compare and combine separate copies of a document

If you have sent a document out for review by several colleagues, you might want to compare their edited versions with the original document. Or if you've made changes to a document and you want to compare it to a previous version of the document, you can do that, too.

Instead of comparing multiple open documents visually, you can tell Word to compare the documents and either move the changes from one document into the other or create a new document that contains the changes from both documents.

By default, when you compare documents, Word generates a composite document that shows all the differences between the two documents as tracked changes. If you want to review the specific changes and the before-and-after versions independently, you can display the source documents in the same window.

Scrolling any version of the documents you're comparing or combining scrolls all three

If you're working on a document that's stored in a SharePoint document library, the Compare menu also includes options for comparing the open document to other versions of itself.

> **TIP** Word can't compare or combine documents that have Protection turned on to restrict changes.

You can compare any two documents. To compare multiple edited documents to one original, combine all the edited documents into one and then compare them with the original.

To compare or combine two documents and annotate changes

1. Start from a blank document or any existing document.

2. On the **Review** tab, in the **Compare** group, select **Compare** to track changes from only one document or **Combine** to track changes from both documents.

3. In the **Compare Documents** or **Combine Documents** dialog, under **Original document**, select the arrow to expand the alphabetical list of documents you've recently worked with.

4. If the document you want to designate as the first document appears in the list, select it. If not, select **Browse** (the first item in the list) to display the **Open** dialog. In the dialog, navigate to the document you want, select it, and then select **Open**.

5. Use the same technique in the **Revised document** area to select the document you want to designate as the second document.

6. In the **Label changes with** box or boxes, enter the name or names you want Word to assign as the reviewer when marking differences between the documents.

> **TIP** When comparing documents, you specify the reviewer for only the revised document; when combining documents, you specify reviewers for both documents.

| Compare Documents | ? | × |

Original document
OldDocument.docx

Revised document
NewDocument.docx

Label changes with

Label changes with Updates

<< Less   OK   Cancel

Comparison settings

☑ Insertions and deletions   ☑ Tables
☑ Moves   ☑ Headers and footers
☑ Comments   ☑ Footnotes and endnotes
☑ Formatting   ☑ Textboxes
☑ Case changes   ☑ Fields
☑ White space

Show changes

Show changes at: Show changes in:
○ Character level   ○ Original document
● Word level   ○ Revised document
                                    ● New document

You can indicate the differences to identify and how to label them

7. If the dialog doesn't include the **Comparison settings** and **Show changes** areas, select the **More** button to display them.

8. In the **Comparison settings** area of the dialog, select the checkboxes of the content differences you want to annotate.

> **TIP** By default, Word marks changes at the word level in a new document. You have the option to show changes at the character level and to show them in one of the two documents rather than in a third document. Until you're comfortable with the compare and combine operations, it's safest to retain the default settings in the Show Changes area.

9. In the **Compare Documents** or **Combine Documents** dialog, select **OK** to create the combined document.

> **TIP** If you compare documents that contain conflicting formatting, a message box will ask you to confirm which document's formatting should be used.

To hide or display comparison source documents

- In the **Compare Result** document window, on the **Review** tab, in the **Compare** group, select **Show Source Documents**, and then select **Hide Source Documents** or the option to show one or both source documents.

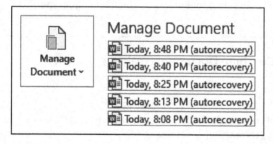

Word shows both source documents by default

Compare separate versions of a document

Word automatically saves a temporary copy of your open documents every 10 minutes. Automatically saved versions of the document are displayed in the Manage Document area of the Info page of the Backstage view.

Manage Document	
Manage Document ⌄	Today, 8:48 PM (autorecovery)
	Today, 8:40 PM (autorecovery)
	Today, 8:25 PM (autorecovery)
	Today, 8:13 PM (autorecovery)
	Today, 8:08 PM (autorecovery)

You can easily review or recover an earlier version of a document

To display a previous version of a document

- On the **Info** page of the Backstage view, in the **Manage Document** list, select the version you want to display.

To compare a document to a previous version

1. Display the previous version of the document.

2. On the information bar at the top of the previous version, select **Compare**.

To roll back to a previous version of a document

1. Display the previous version of the document.

2. On the information bar at the top of the previous version, select the **Restore** button.

To change how often Word automatically saves document recovery versions

1. Display the **Save** page of the **Word Options** dialog.

2. In the **Save AutoRecover information every** box, enter the number of minutes Word should allow to pass before saving a recovery version of the document.

3. Select **OK** to close the dialog.

Control content changes

Sometimes you'll want to allow people to display the contents of a document but not make changes to it. Other times you'll want to allow changes, but only of certain types, or only if they're tracked for your review. This section includes information about ways that you can protect the content of a document.

> **TIP** When considering content protection options, keep in mind that storing documents within a document-management system that has version control can save you a lot of trouble. Word includes a built-in version-tracking system that you can use to compare and restore previous versions of a document that are stored on your computer. Microsoft SharePoint document libraries provide access to previous versions of documents checked in by any team member.

Restrict actions

To prevent people from introducing inconsistent formatting or unwanted changes into a document, you can restrict the types of changes that an individual document permits, in the following ways:

- **Restrict formatting** You can limit formatting changes to a specific list of styles that you select or to the recommended minimum style set, which consists of all the styles needed by Word for features such as tables of contents. (The recommended minimum set doesn't necessarily include all the styles used in the document.) Restricting formatting prevents anyone from adding or applying styles that you don't want in your document.

> **SEE ALSO** For more information about styles, see "Apply character formatting" and "Apply built-in styles to text" in Chapter 3, "Modify the structure and appearance of text."

- **Restrict editing** You can limit changes to comments, tracked changes, or form field content, or you can permit no changes at all.

You can implement these types of restrictions from the Restrict Editing pane. When restrictions are turned on, the Restrict Editing pane provides information about the actions you can perform in the document. Ribbon buttons that apply restricted formats are unavailable (grayed out).

You can restrict formatting so that other people don't make unapproved content or formatting changes

> 🔍 **SEE ALSO** For information about locking the change-tracking feature without restricting editing, see "Track changes" earlier in this chapter.

To display the Restrict Editing pane

- On the **Info** page of the Backstage view, select **Protect Document**, and then select **Restrict Editing**.

- On the **Review** tab or **Developer** tab, in the **Protect** group, select the **Restrict Editing** button.

To restrict the styles permitted in a document

1. Display the **Restrict Editing** pane.

2. In the **Formatting restrictions** area of the **Restrict Editing** pane, select the **Limit formatting to a selection of styles** checkbox, and then select **Settings** to display the **Formatting Restrictions** dialog.

The Allow AutoFormat option permits Word to apply automatic formatting, such as list formatting

3. Select the permitted styles by doing one of the following:

   - To allow only the recommended minimum style set, select **Recommended Minimum**.

   - To allow only specific styles, select **None** and then, in the **Checked styles are currently allowed** list box, select the checkboxes of the styles you want to allow.

   - To allow all styles and restrict only formatting, select **All**.

4. Select the permitted formatting by doing any of the following:

   - To permit Word to automatically format elements such as hyperlinks, bulleted lists, and numbered lists that aren't specified by a style, select the **Allow AutoFormat to override formatting restrictions** checkbox.

   - To permit only the current document theme, theme colors, and theme fonts, select the **Block Theme or Scheme switching** checkbox.

   - To permit only the current style set, select the **Block Quick Style Set switching** checkbox.

5. Select **OK** to implement the restricted set of styles. Word displays a message warning you that restricted styles will be removed.

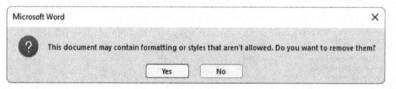

Word displays this warning regardless of whether the document contains restricted styles

6. In the message box, select **Yes** to remove any restricted formatting and revert restricted styles to Normal.

7. In the **Start enforcement** area of the **Restrict Editing** pane, select **Yes, Start Enforcing Protection** to open the **Start Enforcing Protection** dialog.

Start Enforcing Protection   ?   ✕

Protection method

● Password

(The document is not encrypted. Malicious users can edit the file and remove the password.)

Enter new password (optional): ••••

Reenter password to confirm: ••••

○ User authentication

(Authenticated owners can remove document protection. The document is encrypted and Restricted Access is enabled.)

OK   Cancel

People who don't know the password can't turn off the restrictions

8. If you want to require a password to turn off the restrictions, enter the password in the **Enter new password** and **Reenter password to confirm** boxes. Otherwise, leave the boxes blank.

9. In the **Start Enforcing Protection** dialog, select **OK** to turn on the restrictions.

To restrict the editing permitted in a document

1. Display the **Restrict Editing** pane.

2. In the **Editing restrictions** area of the pane, select the **Allow only this type of editing in the document** checkbox.

3. In the **Allow only this type of editing in the document** list, select one of the following:

    - **Tracked changes**

    - **Comments**

    - **Filling in forms**

    - **No changes (Read only)**

4. In the **Start enforcement** area of the **Restrict Editing** pane, select **Yes, Start Enforcing Protection** to open the Start Enforcing Protection dialog.

5. If you want to require a password to turn off the restrictions, enter the password in the **Enter new password** and **Reenter password to confirm** boxes. Otherwise, leave the boxes blank.

6. In the **Start Enforcing Protection** dialog, select **OK** to turn on the restrictions.

To remove restrictions for specific people

1. Display the **Restrict Editing** pane.

2. In the **Editing restrictions** area of the pane, select the **Allow only this type of editing in the document** checkbox and then select either **Comments** or **No changes (Read only)** as the type of editing you want to permit for all users. An Exceptions section appears in the pane.

3. In the document, select the content that you want to permit a specific person or specific people to freely edit.

4. In the **Exceptions** area, if the **Groups** or **Individuals** box does *not* list the people or person you want to permit to edit the selection, do the following:

   a. Select **More users** to open the **Add Users** dialog.

   b. Enter the user credentials of the person or people you want to allow to freely edit the selection.

   When granting restriction exceptions to multiple people, separate the entries by using semicolons

   c. In the **Add Users** dialog, select **OK**.

5. In the **Exceptions** area, select the checkbox that precedes each group or person you want to permit to edit the selection.

6. If you want to permit the editing of additional sections of content, repeat steps 3 through 5.

7. In the **Start enforcement** area of the **Restrict Editing** pane, select **Yes, Start Enforcing Protection** to open the **Start Enforcing Protection** dialog shown in the earlier procedure to restrict the styles permitted in a document.

8. In the **Start Enforcing Protection** dialog, select **User authentication**, and then select **OK** to turn on the restrictions.

To remove editing and formatting restrictions

1. Display the **Restrict Editing** pane.

2. At the bottom of the pane, select **Stop Protection**.

3. The **Unprotect Document** dialog opens regardless of whether a password is required.

When protecting a document, always use a password you can remember, because it can't be reset

4. In the **Unprotect Document** dialog, enter a password in the **Password** box if one is required. Otherwise, leave the **Password** box blank. Then select **OK** to remove the restrictions.

Restrict access by using a password

Sometimes, you might want to allow only certain people to open and change a document. The simplest way to do this for an individual document is to assign a password to protect the file. Then, anyone who wants to modify the document must enter a password when opening it.

You can assign a password to a document while working in the document or when saving the document. Word offers two levels of password protection:

- **Encrypted** The document is saved in such a way that people who do not know the password cannot open it at all.

- **Unencrypted** The document is saved in such a way that only people who know the password can open it, make changes, and save the file. People who don't know the password can open a read-only version. If they make changes and want to save them, they must save the document with a different name or in a different location, preserving the original.

General Options ? ✕

General Options

File encryption options for this document

Password to open: ••••••••

File sharing options for this document

Password to modify: ••••|

☑ Read-only recommended

Assigning a password to open a document encrypts the document; assigning a password to modify the document does not encrypt it

> ⚠ **IMPORTANT** Don't use common words or phrases as passwords, and don't use the same password for multiple documents. After assigning a password, make a note of it in a safe place. If you forget it, you won't be able to open the password-protected document.

To recommend against changes to a document

1. Display the **Save As** page of the Backstage view.

2. Using locations in the **Places** list, the current folder, or recent folders as a starting point, navigate to the folder you want to save the document in. If necessary, select **Browse** to display the Save As dialog.

3. If you want to protect a copy of the document instead of the original, enter a name for the copy in the **File name** box.

4. Near the lower-right corner of the **Save As** dialog, select **Tools**. Then in the **Tools** list, select **General Options**.

5. In the **General Options** dialog, select the **Read-only recommended** checkbox, and then select **OK**.

To prevent unauthorized changes by setting a password

1. On the **Save As** page of the Backstage view, navigate to the folder you want to save the password-protected document in. If necessary, select **Browse** to display the Save As dialog.

2. If you want to protect a copy of the document instead of the original, enter a name for the copy in the **File name** box.

3. Near the lower-right corner of the **Save As** dialog, select **Tools**. Then in the **Tools** list, select **General Options**.

4. In the **General Options** dialog, enter the password you want to assign to the document in the **Password to modify** box. Then select **OK** to display the Confirm Password dialog.

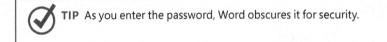 **TIP** As you enter the password, Word obscures it for security.

5. In the **Confirm Password** dialog, enter the same password in the **Reenter password to modify** box, and then select **OK** to set the password.

6. In the **Save As** dialog, select **Save**. If Word prompts you to overwrite the original document, select **Yes**.

To test the security of a password-protected document

1. Open the document and verify that Word displays the **Password** dialog.

2. Enter an incorrect password, select **OK**, and verify that Word denies you access to the document.

To open a password-protected document for reading

1. Open the document.

2. In the **Password** dialog, select the **Read Only** button to open a read-only version of the document.

 TIP When using the default settings, Word opens the document in Read Mode.

To open a password-protected document for editing

1. Open the document.

2. In the **Password** dialog, enter the password that you assigned to the document, and then select **OK** to open a read/write version of the document.

To remove password protection from an unencrypted document

1. On the **Save As** page of the Backstage view, in the **Current Folder** area, select the current folder.

2. At the bottom of the **Save As** dialog, in the **Tools** list, select **General Options**.

3. In the **General Options** dialog, select the contents of the **Password to modify** box, press **Delete**, and then select **OK**.

4. In the **Save As** dialog, select **Save**.

To prevent document access by setting a password

1. Display the **Info** page of the Backstage view.

2. Select **Protect Document**, and then select **Encrypt with Password**.

After you assign the password, you will no longer be able to open the document without it

3. In the **Encrypt Document** dialog, enter the password you want to assign in the **Password** box, and then select **OK**.

4. In the **Confirm Password** dialog, enter the same password in the **Password** box, and then select **OK**.

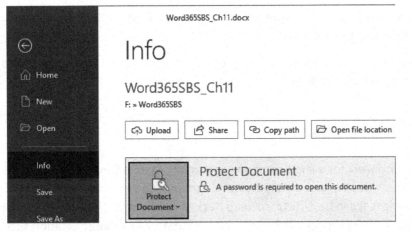

The Info page of the Backstage view displays the protected status of the document

5. Close the document and save your changes.

Or

1. On the **Save As** page of the Backstage view, navigate to the folder you want to save the password-protected document in. If necessary, select **Browse** to display the **Save As** dialog.

2. If you want to make a password-protected copy of the document, enter a name for the copy in the **File name** box.

3. Near the lower-right corner of the **Save As** dialog, select **Tools**. Then in the **Tools** list, select **General Options**.

4. In the **General Options** dialog, enter the password you want to assign to the document in the **Password to open** box. Then select **OK** to display the **Confirm Password** dialog.

5. Enter the same password in the **Reenter password to modify** box, and then select **OK** to set the password.

6. In the **Save As** dialog, select **Save**. If Word prompts you to overwrite the original document, select **Yes**.

To remove password encryption from a document

1. Open the document and enter the correct password.

2. On the **Info** page of the Backstage view, in the **Protect Document** list, select **Encrypt with Password**.

3. In the **Encrypt Document** dialog, delete the password from the **Password** box, and then select **OK**.

Coauthor documents

Whether you work for a large company or a small organization, you might need to collaborate with other people on the development of a document. Regardless of the circumstances, it can be difficult to keep track of different versions of a document produced by different people. If you store a document in a shared location such as a SharePoint document library or Microsoft OneDrive folder, multiple people can edit the document simultaneously.

After you save a document to a shared location, you can open and edit the document just as you would if it were stored on your computer. Other people can also open and edit the document either by browsing to it or from an invitation that you send. This facilitates efficient collaboration between people regardless of location, schedule, or time zone.

The process of inviting people to edit a shared file depends on the storage location. The file is automatically shared with other people who have access to the SharePoint document library or OneDrive folder. You can invite other people to edit or view the file from the Share pane.

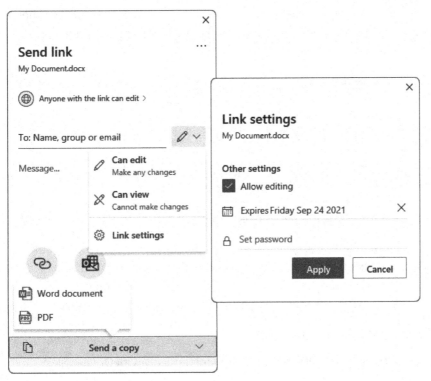

You can send a copy or provide read or write access to an online file

When other people open a shared file for editing, Word alerts you to their presence by displaying their user badge (a round badge displaying a photo or initials) on the ribbon.

Selecting an editor's user badge displays options for tracking the work that person is doing in the document and communicating with him or her. If the file is stored on SharePoint, you have the option of chatting with other editors directly in the document. Otherwise, you have an email option.

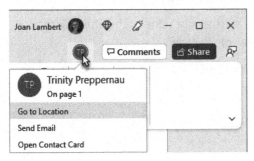

An alert appears as each editor opens the document

Word keeps track of the content that people are editing so you can see where other people are working in a document. If change tracking is turned on, you can see the changes they're making.

Active editing point

You can use Outlook 2019 to manage multiple email accounts, including multiple Microsoft Exchange accounts Server or Office 365 accounts, internet mail accounts (such as Gmail), and their associated contacts, calendars, and other elements. Even if you use Outlook only for sending and receiving email messages, it can be challenging to keep track of them and to locate specific information that you're looking for. Fortunately, Outlook provides many simple yet useful features that you can use to organize messages and other Outlook items and to quickly find information you need.

Word indicates the areas of the document that are being edited

When you turn on change tracking in a Word document, you can turn it on for all editors or only for yourself. If each person working in the document tracks his or her changes, the tracked changes remain available so that the document owner can accept or reject them when the team has finished working on the document.

To make a document available for coauthoring

- Save the document to a SharePoint document library or OneDrive folder.

To begin coauthoring a document

1. If the document is stored in a SharePoint document library, do *not* check it out.

2. Open the document directly from the document library or OneDrive folder.

3. Edit the document as you would normally. Other editors can join the document from the same location.

To display the Share pane

- To the right of the ribbon tabs, select the **Share** button.

- In the left pane of the Backstage view, in the right pane of the **Share with People** page, select the **Share with People** button.

To invite other people to edit a file stored in OneDrive

1. Display the **Share** pane.

2. In the **Invite people** box, enter the names or email addresses of the people you want to invite to edit the document.

3. In the permissions list, select **Can edit** to allow the recipients to make changes to the document.

4. In the message box, enter any message you want to include in the sharing invitation.

5. Select **Share** to send an email message that contains a link to the document on OneDrive.

Or

1. Display the **Share** pane.

2. At the bottom of the pane, select **Get a sharing link**, and then select **Create an edit link**.

3. To the right of the link that is created, select **Copy**.

4. Paste the copied link into an email message, instant message, or other communication form, and send it to the people you want to invite to edit the file.

To move to the location in a document where another editor is working

1. On the ribbon, select the user badge of the editor you want to locate.

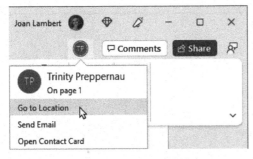

You can easily locate edits other people are making

2. On the menu, select **Go to Location**.

To begin a chat in a document stored on SharePoint

- On the ribbon, select the user badge of the editor you want to chat with, and then select **Chat**.

Key points

- You can insert comments in a document to ask questions or explain suggested edits.

- You can track the revisions you make to a document without losing the original text. Word assigns different revision-tracking colors to multiple reviewers, so you can easily identify change sources.

- You can merge multiple versions of a document so that the changes in all versions are tracked in one document.

- If only specific people should work on a document, you can protect it with a password. You can also restrict the types of changes people can make or force all changes to be tracked.

- Multiple people can simultaneously edit a document stored in a SharePoint document library or on OneDrive.

> **SEE ALSO** This chapter is from the full-length book *Microsoft Word Step by Step (Office 2021 and Microsoft 365)* (Microsoft Press, 2022). Please consult that book for information about features of Word that aren't discussed in this book.

Practice tasks

Before you can complete these tasks, you must copy the book's practice files to your computer. The practice files for these tasks are in the **Office365SBS\Ch04** folder. You can save the results of the tasks in the same folder.

The introduction includes a complete list of practice files and download instructions.

Mark up documents

Open the **TrackChanges** document in Word, display the document in Print Layout view, and then perform the following tasks:

1. Turn on change tracking.

2. Display the Comments pane.

3. In the last column of the table, select the words *some good*, and then attach the comment They carry the new Ultra line.

4. Configure the review settings to display the **All Markup** view of changes and to display only formatting in balloons.

5. If necessary, scroll through the document to display the table. Perform these tasks in the *Fabrikam* row of the table:

    *   In the *Prices* column, delete the word *much* from the phrase *Some much lower.*

    *   In the *Service* column, insert but slow after the word *Adequate*.

6. Perform these tasks in the *Northwind Traders* row of the table:

    *   In the *Quality* column, replace the word *Poor* with Substandard.

    *   Point to the deleted word and then to the inserted word to display information about the changes in ScreenTips.

7. Configure the review settings to display revisions in balloons instead of inline.

8. Restore the inline revision indicators and remove the balloons.

9. Move the last sentence of the paragraph (Traveling for business...) to the beginning of the paragraph. If necessary, insert a space after the sentence.

10. Turn off change tracking.

11. Configure the review settings to display the Simple Markup view.

12. Save and close the document.

Display and review document markup

Open the **ReviewComments** document in Word, display the document in Print Layout view, and then perform the following tasks:

1. Configure the review settings to display the **Simple Markup** view of changes.

2. Display only revisions made by Elizabeth Jones.

3. Move to the first comment shown in the document, which is attached to the word *competitors*. Delete the comment.

4. Move to the second comment, which is attached to the word *Adequate* in the *Service* column of the table. Point to the word in the table to display a ScreenTip that contains the name of the person who inserted the comment and the date and time the comment was inserted. Notice that the ScreenTip displays more information than the comment bubble.

5. Select the **Reply to Comment** button in the second comment bubble. In the reply box, enter If you had been a real customer, would you have left?

6. Display the **Revisions** pane on the left side of the app window. Then drag the pane away from the side of the window so that it floats independently.

7. In the **Revisions** pane, expand the detailed summary of revisions and note the types of revisions in the document.

8. Configure the review settings to display revisions made by all reviewers.

9. Scroll through the revisions in the pane, and then close it.

10. Configure the review settings to display the **All Markup** view of changes.

11. Hide all comments in the document.

12. Move between the tracked changes in the document.

    - Accept all the changes in the text paragraph.

    - Process the changes in the table as follows:

        - Reject the table formatting change.

        - Accept the deletion of the word *much*.

        - Reject the changes associated with the addition of the words *but slow*.

        - Accept both changes associated with the replacement of *Poor* with *Substandard*.

13. Configure the review settings to display the **No Markup** view of changes. Then change the balloon setting to the one you like best.

14. Save and close the document.

Compare and combine documents

Open a new, blank document in Word, and then perform the following tasks:

1. Compare the **MergeDocs1** and **MergeDocs2** documents by using the following settings:

    - Label unmarked changes from **MergeDocs2** with your name.

    - Select all available comparison settings.

    - Mark the differences in a separate document.

2. When Word completes the comparison, ensure that the **Revisions** pane is open on the left, the merged document in the center, and the two original documents on the right.

> **TIP** If the Revisions pane is not open, select Reviewing Pane in the Tracking group on the Review tab. If the source documents are not displayed, select the Compare button, select Show Source Documents, and then select Show Both.

3. In the center pane, scroll through the document to review all the revisions, and then in the **Revisions** pane, scroll through the individual revisions. Before changes can be accepted in the document, conflicting changes must be resolved.

4. In the **Revisions** pane, locate the deleted instance of *March* and then accept the deletion.

5. Select each change that remains in the **Revisions** pane to display that location in the three document panes.

6. Select the merged document in the center pane to activate it. Then accept all the changes in the document at the same time.

7. Close the **Revisions** pane, and then close the two windows on the right side of the screen.

8. Save the merged document as MyMergedDocument, and then close it.

Control content changes

Open the **ControlChanges** document, and then perform the following tasks:

1. Save a copy of the document, naming the copy MyControlChanges, and require the password P@ssw0rd1 to modify the document but no password to read the document.

2. Configure the document options to recommend that people open a read-only copy of the document.

3. Close the document, and then open a read-only version of it.

4. Attempt to make a change and verify that you can't save the changed document.

5. Close the document, and then use the password to open an editable version of it.

6. Remove the password protection from the document.

7. Encrypt the document and require the password P@ssw0rd2 to open it.

8. Restrict the formatting in the document to only the recommended minimum styles.

9. Block users from switching schemes or style sets.

10. Turn on the restrictions and remove any formatting and styles that don't meet the requirements you selected. Notice the changes to the document.

11. Configure the editing restrictions so that you can edit only the first paragraph of the document and other people aren't permitted to make any changes.

12. Save and close the document.

Coauthor documents

There is no practice task for this topic because it requires that documents be stored in a shared location.

Merge data with documents and labels

Many organizations communicate with customers or members by means of letters, newsletters, and promotional pieces that are sent to everyone on a mailing list. You can use a reasonably simple process called *mail merge* to easily insert specific information from a data source into a Word document to create personalized individual items such as form letters, labels, envelopes, or email messages. You can also use this process to create a directory, catalog, or other listing that incorporates information from the data source.

The primary requirement for a mail merge operation is a well-structured data source. You can pull information from a variety of data sources—even your Microsoft Outlook address book—and merge it with a starting document or a content template to create the output you want. Word provides a wizard that can guide you through the processes, but this chapter provides information about each of the individual processes so you can quickly get started with your merging projects.

This chapter guides you through procedures related to starting the mail merge process, choosing and refining data sources, choosing the output type and starting documents, previewing the results and completing the merge, and creating individual envelopes and labels.

In this chapter

- Understand the mail merge process
- Start the mail merge process
- Choose and refine the data source
- Insert merge fields
- Preview and complete the merge
- Create individual envelopes and labels

Understand the mail merge process

The process for creating a mail merge document is straightforward and logical. All the tools for performing mail merge operations are available from the Mailings tab. From this tab, you can run the wizard or perform individual steps of the mail merge process on your own.

Mail merge tools are located on the Mailings tab

Three important terms used when discussing mail merge processes include:

- **Data source** The file or storage entity that contains the variable information you want to pull into the merge output.

- **Field** A specific category of information, such as a first name, last name, birthdate, customer number, item number, or price.

- **Record** A set of the information that goes in the fields—for example, information about a specific person or transaction. A record doesn't have to contain information for every field, but it must have a placeholder for any missing information.

The mail merge process varies slightly depending on whether you're creating one document per record or one document containing all the records. However, the basic process is this:

1. Identify a data source that contains the records you want to use.

2. Create a document into which you want to merge the records.

3. In the document, identify the fields from the data source that you want to merge into the document.

4. Preview the results and make any necessary adjustments.

5. Merge the data into the document to either create one or more new documents or to print the merge results directly to the printer.

You can perform the mail merge process by using the commands on the Mailings tab of the ribbon, or you can get step-by-step guidance from the Mail Merge wizard. The wizard displays options in a series of panes, and you choose the options you want. If you're new to mail merge, the wizard can provide a helpful framework. If you're comfortable with the mail merge process and know what you want to create, it can be faster to perform the steps manually.

To use the Mail Merge wizard

1. Start Word and display the **Mailings** tab.

2. In the **Start Mail Merge** group, select **Start Mail Merge**, and then select **Step-by-Step Mail Merge Wizard**.

3. In each of the six panes of the wizard, select an option or provide the requested information.

4. In the last pane, specify whether to send the merge output directly to the printer or to create one or more documents that you can review and save.

5

Start the mail merge process

For most mail merge projects, you need a starting document that provides structure and common content, and that identifies the locations where you want to insert data. You specify the data to merge into each location by inserting *merge fields*. The merge fields pull data from the data source fields into the starting document. To identify the data fields available for the mail merge operation, you must select the data source and import its records into the Mail Merge Recipients list.

The best starting point varies based on the type of output that you want to create. The output categories include letters, email messages, envelopes, labels, and directories.

In this topic, we discuss ways of getting started with a mail merge process based on the output type.

> ⊘ **TIP** If you find that you need help, you can start the wizard from any point in the process and move back to make changes or forward to keep the work you've done.

Get started with letters

If you're creating a form letter or similar document, you can write the document, connect to the data source, and then insert the merge fields, or you can start with a blank document, connect to the data source, and then insert the merge fields as you write the document. Either way, you can't insert merge fields in a document until you connect to the data source.

If you're creating a document that needs to go through a review process, it's easier to do that before you connect to the data source; otherwise, the document tries to connect to the data source each time a reviewer opens it. When that's the case, you can insert placeholders in the document where you plan to insert merge fields later. You can set off the placeholders from the real text by using brackets or highlighting to indicate to reviewers that the placeholders aren't final content, and to make them easy to locate later.

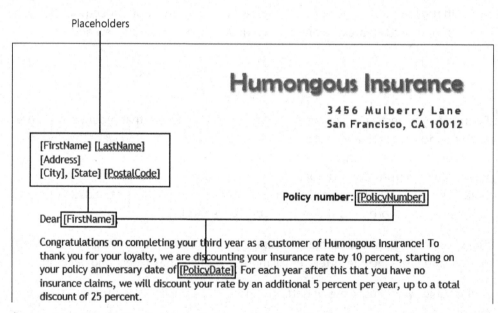

It's easiest to write and edit your document before starting the mail merge process

If you need help creating a document for your intended purpose, you can use any of the Word content templates. A wide variety of templates is available from the New page of the Backstage view.

To start a letter mail merge

1. Open a blank document or a document that contains the static content you want to pull data into.

2. On the **Mailings** tab, in the **Start Mail Merge** group, select **Start Mail Merge**.

3. On the **Start Mail Merge** menu, select **Letters**. There is no visible change to the document.

4. To continue and complete the process:

    a. Use the procedures described in "Choose and refine the data source" later in this chapter to identify the data source and available fields.

    b. Create or edit the document content, and use the procedures described in "Insert merge fields" later in this chapter to insert the merge fields.

    c. Use the procedures described in "Preview and complete the merge" later in this chapter to finish creating the letter.

Get started with labels

The mail merge processes for labels are designed not only for stickers but also for name tags, badge inserts, business cards, tab inserts for page dividers, CD labels, postcards, notecards, printable magnets, and anything else that you print onto paper or other sheet-fed media that is divided into fixed areas. Many of these products are available from office supply and craft supply retailers. Common manufacturers of label materials include Avery and 3M, but there are many others.

> **SEE ALSO** For more information about creating mailing labels, see "Create individual envelopes and labels" later in this chapter.

When generating labels from a data source, you're usually printing data from multiple records onto each sheet, but you can also print a full sheet of each record.

When creating labels, you select the manufacturer and product number of the specific printing media, and then Word creates a table that defines the printable area of the label sheet. You insert merge fields into the first cell as a template for all the other cells, format the content as you want it, and then copy the cell content to the other fields. If you're making sheets of labels that pull data from multiple records, each additional field starts with a «Next Record» tag that signals Word to move to the next record.

«AddressBlock»   «AddressBlock»   «AddressBlock»

«AddressBlock»   «AddressBlock»   «AddressBlock»

«AddressBlock»   «AddressBlock»   «AddressBlock»

The starting document for an address label mail merge

It's important that you select the correct manufacturer and product because the document page setup is very precisely controlled to match the media.

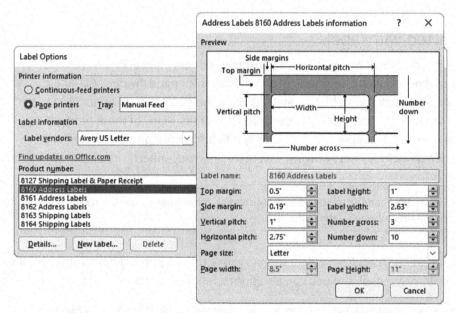

The definition for each label product includes the dimensions of the printable and nonprintable areas of the sheet

To start a label mail merge

1. Open a blank document and display paragraph marks and formatting symbols.

2. On the **Mailings** tab, in the **Start Mail Merge** group, select **Start Mail Merge**.

3. On the **Start Mail Merge** menu, select **Labels**. The Label Options dialog opens.

Thousands of label products are available from this dialog

4. In the **Printer information** area, choose the correct printer type for the label forms and, for standard printers, choose the input tray (or manual feed) for the label sheets.

5. On the label package, identify the manufacturer and product number of the labels you will use. In the **Label information** area, do the following:

   • In the **Label vendors** list, select the label manufacturer.

   • In the **Product number** list, select the product number.

> **TIP** To save time, select in the Product Number box and then press the keyboard key corresponding to the first character of the product number to jump to that section of the list. Then scroll to locate the specific product number. If the label product you're using doesn't already appear in the list, select the Find Updates On Office.com link to refresh the list.

6. In the **Label Options** dialog, select **OK** to return to the document. Word creates the label form in which you will enter the merge fields and any static content.

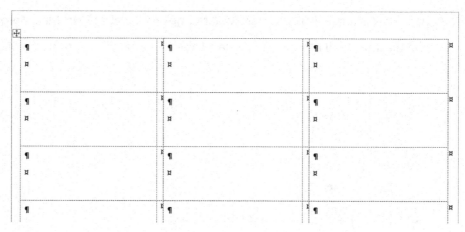

Ensure that paragraph symbols and formatting marks are shown before continuing

7. To continue and complete the process:

   a. Use the procedures described in "Choose and refine the data source" later in this chapter to identify the data source and available fields.

   b. Create or edit the static label content, and use the procedures described in "Insert merge fields" later in this chapter to insert the merge fields.

   c. Use the procedures described in "Preview and complete the merge" later in this chapter to finish creating the labels.

Get started with email messages

When you want to send the same information to all the people on a list—for example, all your customers, or all the members of a club or your family—you don't have to print letters and physically mail them. Instead, you can use mail merge to create a personalized email message for each person in a data source. As with a form letter that will be printed, you can either use the Mail Merge wizard or use the buttons on the Mailings tab to insert merge fields into a document. These merge fields will be replaced with information from the specified data source, and the starting document will be converted to individual email messages.

Many email messages need no merge fields other than a greeting line.

«GreetingLine»

Thank you for your recent visit to our store. It was a pleasure to discuss your decorating plans and offer suggestions.

As you requested, we have added your name to our online mailing list. You will receive our monthly newsletter, as well as advance notice of upcoming sales and special in-store events. You can also visit our website at www.wideworldimporters.com for a schedule of events, links to online decorating resources, articles on furniture care, and more.

Questions? Contact us by email at customerservice@wideworldimporters.com, or call (925) 555-0167 during business hours.

If you want to edit the custom greeting, right-click the merge field and then select Edit Greeting Line

5

Because email messages tend to be less formal than printed letters, you might want to start the messages with a custom greeting rather than one of the predefined greeting options (*Dear* and *To*).

Word connects to Outlook to send the email messages. You can find the sent messages in your Outlook Sent Mail folder.

Attaching files to email merge messages

The native mail merge features of Word don't provide a method for attaching a file or files to the email messages that you generate from Word. If this is something that you want to do, however, there is a workaround.

If you're looking for a simpler method of attaching files to outgoing email merge message, there are many third-party add-ins that enable you to do this, either for free or for a fee, depending on the number of messages you send. Search online for "mail merge with attachments" to return a current list of solution providers.

To start an email mail merge

1. Open a blank document or a document that contains the static content you want to pull data into.

2. On the **Mailings** tab, in the **Start Mail Merge** group, select **Start Mail Merge**.

3. On the **Start Mail Merge** menu, select **E-mail Messages**. Word displays the current content in Web view.

> **SEE ALSO** For information about the available views, see "Display different views of files" in Chapter 2, "Create and manage documents."

4. To continue and complete the process:

   a. Use the procedures described in the next section ("Choose and refine the data source") to identify the data source and available fields.

   b. Create or edit the document content, and use the procedures described in "Insert merge fields" later in this chapter to insert the merge fields.

   c. Use the procedures described in "Preview and complete the merge" later in this chapter to finish creating the messages.

Choose and refine the data source

The mail merge process combines variable information from a data source with static information in a starting document. The basic data source requirement is the same regardless of the output format: it must be a container that stores information in a consistent structure.

	A	B	C	D	E	F
1	FirstName	LastName	Address	City	State	PostalCode
2	Patrick	Wedge	151 Fir Drive	Bangor	AK	10136
3	Pia	Westermann	221 Mahogany Dr	San Antonio	ND	10218
4	Greg	Yvkoff	791 Beech			
5	Lee	Chia	79 Beech R			
6	Joseph	Matthews	895 Gum B			
7	James	Van Eaton	742 Madro			
8	Humberto	Acevedo	421 Hawth			
9	Anette	Grohsmüller	956 Cypres			
10	David	Hodgson	292 Maple			
11	Jim	Wickham	547 Gum A			
12	Paulo	Lisboa	855 Beech			
13	Ty	Carlson	760 Willow			
14	Amy	Recker	566 Yucca			

```
FirstName,LastName,Address,City,State,PostalCode
Patrick,Wedge,151 Fir Drive,Bangor,AK,10136
Pia,Westermann,221 Mahogany Dr,San Antonio,ND,10218
Greg,Yvkoff,791 Beech Terrace,Toledo,MT,10367
Lee,Chia,79 Beech Rd,Houston,ND,10537
Joseph,Matthews,895 Gum Bay,Evansville,OK,10826
James,Van Eaton,742 Madrone St,Rockford,IN,11374
Humberto,Acevedo,421 Hawthorn Ct,Tucson,MA,11491
Anette,Grohsmüller,956 Cypress Ln,Denver,AL,12097
David,Hodgson,292 Maple Terrace,Youngstown,WY,12642
Jim,Wickham,547 Gum Ave,St. Louis,VT,12864
Paulo,Lisboa,855 Beech Bay,Gainesville,NM,12999
Ty,Carlson,760 Willow Ave,Chattanooga,SC,13291
Amy,Recker,566 Yucca Ct,Montgomery,LA,13322
```

Data sources store information in a consistent structure

Most data source structures store data in a tabular format, with fields identified at the top and records following. The most straightforward example of this, and the one we work with throughout this chapter, is a Microsoft Excel worksheet.

Each field in a data source must be identified by a unique name so you can pull data from the field into the starting document. In Excel, the field names are the table headers or column headers.

The Mail Merge Recipients dialog displays all the records from the data source

Select an existing data source

The full list of acceptable data source file types is lengthy. Typical data sources include Excel worksheets and delimited text files (text files that contain data in which fields are separated by commas, tabs, or other delimiters), but you can also pull data from tables in Microsoft Word, Access, or SQL Server; from a Microsoft Outlook contact list; or from a variety of other, less common sources.

```
All Files (*.*)
All Data Sources (*.odc;*.mdb;*.mde;*.accdb;*.accde;*.ols;*.udl;*.dsn;*.xlsx;*.xlsm;...
Office Database Connections (*.odc)
Access Databases (*.mdb;*.mde)
Access 2007 Database (*.accdb;*.accde)
Microsoft Office Address Lists (*.mdb)
Microsoft Office List Shortcuts (*.ols)
Microsoft Data links (*.udl)
ODBC File DSNs (*.dsn)
Excel Files (*.xlsx;*.xlsm;*.xlsb;*.xls)
Web Pages (*.htm;*.html;*.asp;*.mht;*.mhtml)
Rich Text Format (*.rtf)
Word Documents (*.docx;*.doc;*.docm)
All Word Documents (*.docx;*.doc;*.docm;*.dotx;*.dot;*.dotm;*.rtf;*.htm;*.html)
Text Files (*.txt;*.prn;*.csv;*.tab;*.asc)
Database Queries (*.dqy;*.rqy)
OpenDocument Text Files (*.odt)
```

All the file types that are accepted as data sources

> **TIP** If your company or organization uses another contact-management system, you can probably export information to one of these formats. Delimited text files are the most basic format of structured information storage and should be an export option from any other information storage system.

The data source doesn't have to be stored on your computer; the wizard can link to remotely stored data. If the data source is stored on a server that requires you to log on, you can provide your credentials and, optionally, store your password.

> **TIP** It isn't necessary for the data source file to be closed during the import operation; you can import records from an open file, edit and save the file, and refresh the list with the changes.

If you use Outlook to manage your Microsoft Exchange or Exchange Online email, contacts, and calendar information, you can import data from an Exchange account contact folder to use as a mail merge data source. The Mail Merge wizard polls your Outlook data folders and provides a list of contact folders that you can use. When you choose a contact folder, the wizard imports the contact list.

It's likely that your contact list contains a variety of contacts—clients, employees, friends, relatives, and other people you have corresponded with. Many of these contacts might not be current, and many of them might not be people to whom you want to direct the specific form letter or email message that you're creating. But that's

OK; you can import the entire contact list and then use the filtering function in the Mail Merge Recipients dialog to identify only those people you want to include in your current mail merge project.

Data Source	☑	Last Name ▾	First Name ▾	Address ▾	City ▾	Sta
CustomerList.xlsx	☑	Wedge	Patrick	151 Fir Drive	Bangor	AK
CustomerList.xlsx	☑	Westermann	Pia	221 Mahogany Dr	San Antonio	ND
CustomerList.xlsx	☑	Yvkoff	Greg	791 Beech Terrace	Toledo	MT
CustomerList.xlsx	☑	Chia	Lee	79 Beech Rd	Houston	ND
CustomerList.xlsx	☑	Matthews	Joseph	895 Gum Bay	Evansville	OK
CustomerList.xlsx	☑	Van Eaton	James	742 Madrone St	Rockford	IN
CustomerList.xlsx	☑	Acevedo	Humberto	421 Hawthorn Ct	Tucson	MA
CustomerList.xlsx	☑	Grohsmüller	Anette	956 Cypress Ln	Denver	AL
CustomerList.xlsx	☑	Hodgson	David	292 Maple Terrace	Youngstown	WV

Mail Merge Recipients

This is the list of recipients that will be used in your merge. Use the options below to add to or change your list. Use the checkboxes to add or remove recipients from the merge. When your list is ready, click OK.

Data Source

CustomerList.xlsx

Edit...   Refresh

Refine recipient list

A↓ Sort...
Filter...
Find duplicates...
Find recipient...
Validate addresses...

OK

A selected checkbox indicates that a record will be included in the mail merge

> **SEE ALSO** For information about filtering records for a mail merge, see "Refine the data source records" later in this topic.

To select an existing data source

1. On the **Mailings** tab, in the **Start Mail Merge** group, select **Select Recipients** to display the data source options.

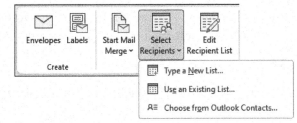

Envelopes Labels Start Mail Merge ▾ Select Recipients ▾ Edit Recipient List

Create

    Type a New List...
    Use an Existing List...
    Choose from Outlook Contacts...

You can either choose or create a data source file

2. On the **Select Recipients** menu, do either of the following:

- Select **Use an Existing List**. In the **Select Data Source** dialog, browse to and select the data source file, and then select **Open**.

- Select **Choose from Outlook Contacts**. In the **Select Contacts** dialog, select the contact folder that you want to import, and then select **OK**.

Create a new data source

If the information that you want to include in your data source isn't already stored in a file or address list, you can create a Microsoft Office Address List while working in the Mail Merge wizard. The wizard saves your list as a table in an Access database (.mdb) file in the My Data Sources subfolder of your Documents folder.

The process of entering information through the Address List interface is somewhat tedious, because you must manually populate each field—so if you have a lot of records, it's easier to enter your data into an Excel worksheet. However, it's fine for a small impromptu mail merge process, such as creating a set of nametags for a meeting.

Creating a simple list in the wizard

You're not limited to collecting contact information; you can add, remove, and reorder the fields to store the type of data that's pertinent to your mail merge process.

To create a data source from the Mailings tab

1. On the **Mailings** tab, in the **Start Mail Merge** group, select **Select Recipients**, and then select **Type a New List**.

2. In the **New Address List** dialog, do the following:

   a. Select **Customize Columns**. Add any fields to the column list that you plan to include in the mail merge operation. To keep things tidy, you can remove fields that you don't plan to use.

   b. Enter the information for each record, selecting **New Entry** to create another.

3. When you finish, select **OK**.

4. In the **Save Address List** dialog, provide a name for the database file, and then select **Save**.

Refine the data source records

The data source you choose doesn't have to be specific to the item you're creating. For example, you could create postcards announcing an in-store sale only for customers who live in that area or create gift certificates only for people who have birthdays in the next month.

If you don't want to include all the data source records in your mail merge operation, you can now whittle down the list to those you want. You can use the following processes to remove a record from the recipient list:

- **Filter the list on one or more fields** You can filter the list to display only the records that you want to include, or to locate (and then remove) the records that you want to exclude.

- **Remove duplicates** The wizard can help to identify entries that might be duplicates. You can either clear the checkboxes for the duplicate versions that you don't want to use, or you can remove the entries from the data source file, save the file, and refresh the recipients list.

- **Manually exclude records** Each record has a checkbox. Clearing the checkbox removes the record from the mail merge operation.

Excluding records from the mail merge operation does not remove them from the Mail Merge Recipients list or from the original data source file. They will still be available for you to use in this or another mail merge operation.

In addition to limiting the set of information used in a mail merge, you can also sort the records to specify the order in which they appear in the mail merge document— for example, in postal code order for a bulk mailing.

> ⚠️ **IMPORTANT** The Refine Recipient List area of the Mail Merge Recipients dialog includes a Validate Addresses link. A third-party address-validation tool is required to validate addresses. If you don't already have one of these tools, selecting the link displays a message that an address validation add-in is required and provides a link to a list of validation tools that work with Word. You can use these tools to validate mailing addresses against US postal regulation standards to filter out recipients whose mailing addresses don't appear to be valid.

To display the Mail Merge Recipients list

- On the **Mailings** tab, in the **Start Mail Merge** group, select **Edit Recipient List**.

To filter the recipients list to display only records you want to include

1. Display the **Mail Merge Recipients** list.

2. In the **Refine recipient list** area, select **Filter** to display the Filter Records tab of the Filter And Sort dialog.

3. In the **Field** list, select the field you want to filter by.

4. In the **Comparison** list, select one of the following:

   - Equal to

   - Not equal to

   - Less than

   - Greater than

   - Less than or equal

   - Greater than or equal

   - Is blank

   - Is not blank

   - Contains

   - Does not contain

5. In the **Compare to** list, enter the criterion for the field filter.

6. To apply multiple criteria, select **And** or **Or** in the leftmost list and then enter the additional criteria.

A multi-filter operation that returns only specific insurance policy subscribers

7. In the **Filter and Sort** dialog, select **OK**. Records not displayed in the filtered list are not included in the mail merge operation.

To filter records out of the recipients list

1. Following the instructions in the previous procedure, filter the **Mail Merge Recipients** list to display the records you want to exclude.

2. Select the checkbox in the column heading area (twice if necessary) to clear the checkboxes of all the records returned by the filter operation.

Clearing a checkbox removes a record from the recipient list but not from the data source

3. In the **Refine recipient list** area, select **Filter** to redisplay the Filter Records tab of the Filter And Sort dialog.

4. On the **Filter Records** tab, select the **Clear All** button, and then select **OK** to remove the filter. The records that you excluded while the filter was applied are still excluded.

To remove duplicate records from the recipients list

1. Display the **Mail Merge Recipients** list.

2. In the **Refine recipient list** area, select **Find duplicates** to display records that have similar field entries.

Find Duplicates					? ✕

The following entries appear to be duplicates. Use the checkboxes to select the entries you want to include in your merge.

Data Source		LastName	FirstName	Address	City	State
Policyholders.xl...	☑	Charles	Mathew	14 Lilac Court	Zanesville	LA
Policyholders.xl...	☑	Charles	Matthew	14 Lilac Court	Zanesville	LA
Policyholders.xl...	☑	Clayton	Jane	290 Willow Drive	Newark	TX
Policyholders.xl...	☑	Clayton	Jane			
Policyholders.xl...	☑	Untch	Hans-Walter	483 Conifer Drive	Las Vegas	LA
Policyholders.xl...	☑	Untch	Hans-Walter	483 Conifer Drive	Las Vegas	LA

	OK	Cancel

Review possible duplicates

3. In the **Find Duplicates** dialog, clear the checkboxes of any records that you want to exclude from the mail merge operation. Then select **OK**.

To sort records in a data source

1. Display the **Mail Merge Recipients** list.

2. To sort the records by one field, select the field name (the column header) of the field you want to sort by. (Select the field name again to sort in the opposite order.)

   Or

2. To sort the records by multiple fields, do the following:

    a. In the **Refine recipient list** area, select **Sort** to display the Sort Records tab of the Filter And Sort dialog.

You can sort by up to three fields

    b. In the **Sort by** list, select the first field you want to sort by. Then select the adjacent **Ascending** or **Descending** option to specify the sort order.

    c. In the first **Then by** list, select the second field you want to sort by, and then select the adjacent **Ascending** or **Descending** option.

    d. In the second **Then by** list, specify the third sort field and order, or select **(None)**.

    e. In the **Filter and Sort** dialog, select **OK**.

To manually exclude records from the recipients list

1. Display the **Mail Merge Recipients** list.

2. If necessary, sort or filter the list to locate records.

3. Clear the checkboxes of any records that you want to exclude from the mail merge operation.

Refresh data

You can save and close the document at any point in the mail merge process. When you reopen the document, if you've already connected to the data source and inserted merge fields, Word prompts you to refresh the data connection.

Microsoft Word ✕

⚠ Opening this document will run the following SQL command:

SELECT * FROM `PolicyholdersList$`

Data from your database will be placed in the document. Do you want to continue?

[Yes] [No]

The recipient list reflects changes to the source data when you reopen the document

You can also refresh the data manually at any time from within the document by selecting the Refresh button in the Data Source area of the Mail Merge Recipients dialog.

Insert merge fields

In the document, merge fields are enclosed in chevrons (« and »). However, you can't simply type the chevrons and the field name; you must insert the merge field by using the commands on the Mailings tab. This creates a link from the merge field to the data source field.

The commands that you use to insert merge fields in a starting document are in the Write & Insert Fields group on the Mailings tab.

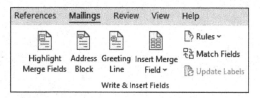

The tools for inserting fields in mail merge documents

Every field in the data source is available to insert as an individual merge field. Two additional merge fields that pull information from the data source are available to save you time:

- **Address Block** This merge field inserts elements of a standard address block (the recipient's name, company name, and postal address) that you select so you can insert all the information with one merge field.

You can customize the Address Block merge field

- **Greeting Line** This merge field inserts a personalized salutation or substitutes a generic salutation for records that are missing the necessary information.

You can select from multiple greetings and name forms

After you insert the first merge field in a document, the Highlight Merge Fields button in the Write & Insert Fields group on the Mailings tab becomes active. Select this button to highlight (in gray) all the merge fields in the document so they're easier to locate.

Humongous Insurance

3456 Mulberry Lane
San Francisco, CA 10012

«AddressBlock»

Policy number: «PolicyNumber»

Dear «FirstName»,

Congratulations on completing your third year as a customer of Humongous Insurance! To thank you for your loyalty, we are discounting your insurance rate by 10 percent, starting on your policy anniversary date of «PolicyDate». For each year after this that you have no insurance claims, we will discount your rate by an additional 5 percent per year, up to a total discount of 25 percent.

Thank you for your continued support of Humongous Insurance. Because of loyal customers like you, our business is growing steadily and the future looks brighter than ever.

If you have any questions, please contact your personal agent, «Agent», or visit our website at www.humongousinsurance.com. On the website, you can also find information about our referral program, through which you can earn additional discounts and other rewards.

Highlight the merge fields to more easily locate them and verify that they aren't placeholders

> ⚠ **IMPORTANT** Before you can perform the procedures in this topic, you must select a data source. For more information, see "Choose and refine the data source" earlier in this chapter.

To insert a single merge field

1. Position the cursor in the location where you want to insert the merge field.

2. On the **Mailings** tab, in the **Write & Insert Fields** group, select **Insert Merge Field**, and then select the field you want to insert.

To insert a customized address block

1. Position the cursor in the location where you want to insert the address block.

2. On the **Mailings** tab, in the **Write & Insert Fields** group, select **Address Block**.

3. In the **Insert Address Block** dialog, select the address block elements you want to include and select the format for the recipient's name.

4. In the **Preview** box displaying your first data record, check that the address block looks correct. You can move through additional records to check further.

5. When you finish, select **OK**.

To insert a customized greeting line

1. Position the cursor in the location where you want to insert the Greeting Line merge field.

2. On the **Mailings** tab, in the **Write & Insert Fields** group, select **Greeting Line**.

3. In the **Insert Greeting Line** dialog, select the greeting line elements you want to include and the generic format for records that don't have the elements you specify.

4. In the **Preview** box displaying your first data record, check that the greeting looks correct. You can move through additional records to check further.

5. When you finish, select **OK**.

To modify a customized merge field

- Right-click or long-press (tap and hold) the merge field and then select **Edit Address Block** or **Edit Greeting Line**.

Preview and complete the merge

After you specify the data source you want to use and enter merge fields in the main document, you can preview the effect of merging the records into the documents and then perform the actual merge. You can further filter the source data during the preview process. When you're ready, you can either send the merged documents directly to the printer or merge the records into a new document. If you merge to a new document, you have another chance to review and, if necessary, edit the merged documents before sending them to the printer.

> ⚠ **IMPORTANT** Before you can perform the procedures in this topic, you must select a data source and insert merge fields. For more information, see "Choose and refine the data source" and "Insert merge fields" earlier in this chapter.

To preview merged documents

1. Display the starting document with merge fields in place and the data source attached.

2. On the **Mailings** tab, in the **Preview Results** group, select **Preview Results** to display the data source information in place of the merge fields.

3. In the **Preview Results** group, do any of the following:

   - Select the **Next Record** or **Previous Record** button to move through the data source one record at a time.

   - Select the **First Record** or **Last Record** button to move to the first or last record in the data source.

   - Select **Preview Results** again to redisplay the merge fields.

To merge data to a new document

1. On the **Mailings** tab, in the **Finish** group, select **Finish & Merge**, and then **Edit Individual Documents**. The Merge To New Document dialog opens.

You can limit the merge to one record or a range of records

2. In the **Merge to New Document** dialog, indicate the record or records that you want to merge, and then select **OK**.

To merge data and print the resulting file

1. On the **Mailings** tab, in the **Finish** group, select **Finish & Merge**, and then **Print Documents**.

2. In the **Merge to Printer** dialog, indicate the record or records that you want to merge, and then select **OK**.

3. In the **Print** dialog, select your printer, configure any additional printer settings that are necessary, and then select **OK**.

To merge data and email the resulting messages

1. On the **Mailings** tab, in the **Finish** group, select **Finish & Merge**, and then **Send Email Messages**. The Merge To E-mail dialog opens.

Merge to E-mail	?	✕

Message options

To: EmailAddress ⌄

Subject line: Thank you for your business!

Mail format: HTML ⌄

Send records

● All
○ Current record
○ From: ☐ To: ☐

[OK] [Cancel]

You specify the address field and subject line before sending the messages

2. In the **Message options** area, do the following:

   a. In the **To** list, select the field that contains the recipients' email addresses.

   b. In the **Subject line** box, enter the message subject you want the email message to display.

   c. In the **Mail format** list, select **Attachment**, **Plain text**, or **HTML**.

3. In the **Send records** area, indicate the record or records that you want to merge. Then select **OK**.

Create individual envelopes and labels

If you want to print a lot of envelopes or mailing labels based on data source fields, you can use the mail merge function to create documents, and then print the documents onto envelopes or sheet-fed labels rather than regular paper.

However, you can also use the Envelopes and Labels commands to create one or more individually addressed envelopes or address labels. Because these functions are related to "mailing" envelopes or packages, they are located on the Mailing tab of the ribbon with the mail merge functionality.

Generate individual envelopes

The Envelope function prints a delivery address and can also print a return address and electronic postage, if you have the necessary software installed. You can manually enter the delivery address, or you can pick it up from a document (usually a letter) that contains an address.

Elizabeth Jones
123 Plumeria Court
Hibiscus Hill, UT 98765

October 31, 2021

Principal Max Amillion
Hibiscus Hill High School
321 Orchid Street
Hibiscus Hill, UT 98765

Dear Principal Amillion,

I am writing to inform you that my daughter
Although the educational value of this trip w
regular schoolwork during this time. I will ma
in a timely manner.

Envelopes and Labels   ?   ✕

Envelopes | Labels

Delivery address:

Principal Max Amillion
Hibiscus Hill High School
321 Orchid Street
Hibiscus Hill, UT 98765

☐ Add electronic postage

Return address: ☐ O_mit

Elizabeth Jones
123 Plumeria Court
Hibiscus Hill, UT 98765

Preview | Feed

When prompted by the printer, insert an envelope in your printer's manual feeder.

Print | Add to Document | Options... | E-postage Properties...

Cancel

You can edit the address information before creating or printing the envelope

> **⊘ TIP** You can save time by storing the return address with your user information. The address then appears by default as the return address in the Envelopes And Labels dialog.

When creating envelopes, you can specify the envelope size, the address locations, and the fonts for the addresses. You can also specify the paper source, the envelope feed method (horizontally or vertically and face up or face down), and the alignment of the envelope. Then Word configures the page layout options and print options as required for your selections.

You can position the addresses on the envelope exactly where you want them

When you create an envelope based on an address in a letter, you can print the envelope immediately, or add the envelope page to the document and then print the envelope and letter later.

Adding the envelope to the document inserts it as a separate document section with unique page layout settings

> ⚠️ **IMPORTANT** The electronic postage options on the Envelopes tab of the Envelopes And Labels dialog require the installation of an electronic postage add-in. Selecting an electronic postage option displays a message box that directs you to a list of electronic postage providers. However, at the time of this writing, the only available add-in works only with Word 2013. Additional add-ins might be available by the time you read this book; when they are, you can print electronic postage directly onto envelopes.

To save your mailing address for use in Word documents

1. Open the **Word Options** dialog, and then select the **Advanced** tab.

2. On the **Advanced** page, in the **General** section, enter your name and address in the **Mailing Address** box. Then select **OK**.

To set up an envelope with a manually entered address

1. Open any document.

2. On the **Mailings** tab, in the **Create** group, select **Envelopes** to open the Envelopes And Labels dialog.

   The Return Address box contains your user name and your mailing address, if you saved that in the Word Options dialog. (If you saved and then deleted your mailing address, the Return Address box might be blank.)

3. In the **Return address** area, do either of the following:

   - Review the return address information and modify it as necessary.

   - If you plan to print to envelopes that have a preprinted return address, select the **Omit** checkbox.

4. In the **Delivery address** box, enter the name and address that you want Word to print on the envelope.

To set up an envelope from an address in a document

1. Open the document and select the address.

2. On the **Mailings** tab, in the **Create** group, select **Envelopes** to open the Envelopes And Labels dialog with the selected address in the Delivery Address box. The Return Address box contains your user name, and your return address if you've saved that in Word.

Create individual envelopes and labels

3. Review the addresses and make any changes you want. If you plan to print on an envelope that has a preprinted return address, select the **Omit** checkbox in the **Return address** area.

To configure or confirm the envelope printing options

1. At the bottom of the **Envelopes** tab of the **Envelopes and Labels** dialog, select **Options** to open the Envelope Options dialog.

2. On the **Envelope Options** tab, set the envelope size, delivery address font and position, and return address font and position.

3. On the **Printing Options** tab, set the feed method, rotation, and paper source.

> ⚠️ **IMPORTANT** If the printer shown at the top of the Printing Options tab is not the correct printer, select OK in each of the open dialogs to save your settings and return to the source document. Then select the correct printer in the source document and return to the Envelopes And Labels dialog to finish creating the envelope.

4. Select **OK** to return to the Envelopes And Labels dialog.

To print or save an envelope

- After you set up the envelope and configure the envelope printing options, do either of the following:

  - Load an envelope into the printer in the orientation configured in the Envelope Options dialog. Then at the bottom of the **Envelopes and Labels** dialog, select **Print** to print the envelope.

  - At the bottom of the **Envelopes and Labels** dialog, select **Add to Document** to insert the envelope content as a separately formatted section at the beginning of the current document. Then save the document.

Generate individual mailing labels

The Labels function is designed to print one address (a delivery address or a return address) onto a sheet of labels, to create either a single label or a full sheet of the same label. Instead of selecting an envelope size, you select a label form by first selecting the label manufacturer and then selecting the specific product number. Word sets up a document to precisely match the content layout areas of the selected form.

Elizabeth Jones 123 Plumeria Court Hibiscus Hill, UT 98765	Elizabeth Jones 123 Plumeria Court Hibiscus Hill, UT 98765	Elizabeth Jones 123 Plumeria Court Hibiscus Hill, UT 98765
Elizabeth Jones 123 Plumeria Court Hibiscus Hill, UT 98765	Elizabeth Jones 123 Plumeria Court Hibiscus Hill, UT 98765	Elizabeth Jones 123 Plumeria Court Hibiscus Hill, UT 98765
Elizabeth Jones 123 Plumeria Court Hibiscus Hill, UT 98765	Elizabeth Jones 123 Plumeria Court Hibiscus Hill, UT 98765	Elizabeth Jones 123 Plumeria Court Hibiscus Hill, UT 98765
Elizabeth Jones 123 Plumeria Court	Elizabeth Jones 123 Plumeria Court	Elizabeth Jones 123 Plumeria Court

The content cells defined by the table match the printing areas of the label sheets

As discussed in "Get started with labels" earlier in this chapter, the term "labels" refers not only to rectangular stickers but also to many other things that you print onto sheet-fed media that is divided into fixed areas. You can use the Labels function to print on any of these. It's important that you select the correct form, because the print areas are very specifically defined.

To set up individual mailing labels

1. Open any document.

2. On the **Mailings** tab, in the **Create** group, select **Labels** to open the Envelopes And Labels dialog.

3. In the **Address** area, do either of the following:

   - If you've saved your return address information in Word and you want to create a return address label, select the **Use return address** checkbox to insert the saved address into the Address box. Then review the return address information and modify it as necessary.

   - Enter the name and address that you want Word to print on the label.

Envelopes and Labels ? ✕

Envelopes | **Labels**

Address: ▦ ▼ ☐ Use return address

Elizabeth Jones
123 Plumeria court
Hibiscus Hill, UT 98765|

Print
● Full page of the same label
○ Single label
Row: 1 ⬍ Column: 1 ⬍

Label
Avery US Letter, 8160 Address La...
Address Labels

Before printing, insert labels in your printer's manual feeder.

[Print]   [New Document]   [Options...]   [E-postage Properties...]

[Cancel]

5

Although the field specifies an address, you can print any text on the labels

4. In the **Print** area, do either of the following to correctly configure the label output:

    - If you want to print one full sheet of labels, select **Full page of the same label**.

    - If you want to print only one label, select **Single label** and then enter the row and column of the position on the sheet of the label you want to print on.

> ✅ **TIP** This feature permits you to easily reuse a partial sheet of blank labels.

5. In the **Label** area, confirm that the label type is the correct one for the printed label forms you're using. If it's not, configure the label settings in the **Label Options** dialog.

> **SEE ALSO** For information about configuring label settings, see "Get started with labels" earlier in this chapter.

To print or save a mailing label

- After you set up the label and configure the label printing options, do either of the following:

  - Load a label form into the printer in the manner configured in the Label Options dialog. Then at the bottom of the **Envelopes and Labels** dialog, select **Print** to print the label.

  - At the bottom of the **Envelopes and Labels** dialog, select **New Document** to generate a new document that contains the merged labels. Then save the document.

Key points

- The mail merge process is that of merging variable information from a data source into the static content of a main document such as a letter, envelope, sheet of labels, or email message.

- Mail merge data sources are organized into sets of information, called records, with each record containing the same items of information, called fields.

- You insert merge field placeholders into the main document to tell Word where to merge fields from the data source.

- You don't have to use all the records from a data source for a mail merge; you can filter the data and exclude specific records.

- The mail merge process can create a new document that you can edit or save, or you can send the results directly to your printer or to email recipients.

> **SEE ALSO** This chapter is from the full-length book *Microsoft Word Step by Step (Office 2021 and Microsoft 365)* (Microsoft Press, 2022). Please consult that book for information about features of Word that aren't discussed in this book.

Practice tasks

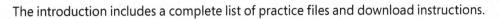

Before you can complete these tasks, you must copy the book's practice files to your computer. The practice files for these tasks are in the **Office365SBS\Ch05** folder. You can save the results of the tasks in the same folder.

The introduction includes a complete list of practice files and download instructions.

Understand the mail merge process

Start Word, open a new blank document, and then perform the following tasks:

1. Start the Mail Merge wizard and investigate the options provided therein.

2. Using the wizard, create any mail merge item you want to. Use the **CustomerList** workbook from the practice file folder as your data source.

3. If you create a mail merge document, save it as MyMerge, and then close it.

Start the mail merge process

Open the **StartMerge** document from the practice file folder, and then perform the following tasks:

1. Start a letter mail merge. Notice that the document does not change.

2. Start an email mail merge. Notice that the document view changes to Web Layout.

3. Start a label mail merge and investigate the options in the Label Options dialog. Choose a label vendor and product number, and display the label details.

4. Create the label sheet and allow Word to replace the contents of the **StartMerge** document when prompted to do so.

5. Close the document without saving it.

Choose and refine the data source

Open the **RefineData** document, and then perform the following tasks:

1. Start a letter mail merge. Select the **CustomerList** workbook from the practice file folder as the data source and select the **Customers$** table of the workbook when prompted to do so.

2. Sort the recipient list alphabetically, in ascending order, by the customers' last names.

3. Remove duplicate records from the recipient list.

4. Filter the list to display only those records for customers who live in either the state of Texas (TX) or the state of Louisiana (LA).

5. Manually exclude all the Louisiana (LA) records from the recipient list, and then return to the letter.

6. From the **Select Recipients** menu, create a new data source. Add your name and the names of two other people. Add any other information you want, and then save the new list as PracticeList.mdb.

7. Save and close the document.

Insert merge fields

Open the **InsertFields** document, and then perform the following tasks:

1. Start a letter mail merge. Select the **PolicyholdersList** workbook from the practice file folder as the data source, and select the **PolicyHolders$** table of the workbook when prompted to do so.

2. Replace each placeholder in the document with its corresponding merge field.

3. Save the **InsertFields** document, but don't close it.

4. Create a new blank document and start a new letter mail merge. Use the same data source as in step 1.

5. Open the **Insert Address Block** dialog. Review the settings and make any changes you want, and then insert the merge field.

6. In the document, two lines below the address block, insert a **Greeting Line** merge field.

7. Save the document as **MyFields**, and then close it. Leave the **InsertFields** document open for the next set of practice tasks.

Preview and complete the merge

Complete the previous set of practice tasks to modify the **InsertFields** document. Then perform the following tasks:

1. Use the tools in the **Preview Results** group on the **Mailings** tab to preview the results of completing the mail merge. Then redisplay the merge fields.

2. Merge the data source into the document to create a new document. Save the document as **MyLetter**, and then close it.

3. Redisplay the **InsertFields** document and follow the procedure to merge the output directly to the printer. (If you don't want to print the file, select **Cancel** in the final dialog.)

4. Follow the procedure to merge the output to email messages. Explore the settings, and then select **Cancel**.

5. Save and close the document.

Create individual envelopes and labels

Open the **CreateEnvelopes** document, and then perform the following tasks:

1. Open the **Word Options** dialog and display the **Advanced** page. In the **General** section, check whether you have saved your mailing address. If you have not, do so now.

2. In the document, select the letter recipient's name and address, and then open the **Envelopes and Labels** dialog. Verify that the **Return Address** box contains your mailing address and that the **Delivery Address** box contains the letter recipient's name and address.

3. In the **Envelope Options** dialog, configure the envelope printing options and then, if you want, load an envelope into your printer and print the addresses onto the envelope.

4. Save and close the **CreateEnvelopes** document.

5. Create a new blank document.

6. Display the **Labels** tab of the **Envelopes and Labels** dialog. If your saved mailing address is not already shown in the Address box, select the **Use return address** checkbox to add your saved information to the **Address** box.

7. Configure the merge output to print one full sheet of labels.

8. Do either of the following:

   - If you have a sheet of labels to print to, configure the label settings. Then load a sheet of labels into the printer and print the addresses onto the labels.

   - If you don't have a sheet of labels, generate a new document that contains the merged labels. Then save the document as MyLabels, and close it.

Part 3

Excel

CHAPTER 6
Perform calculations on data 205

CHAPTER 7
Manage worksheet data 237

CHAPTER 8
Reorder and summarize data 259

CHAPTER 9
Analyze alternative data sets 275

Perform calculations on data

Excel workbooks provide an easy interface for storing and organizing data, but Excel can do so much more than that. Using the built-in functions, you can easily perform a variety of calculations—from simple tasks such as calculating totals to complex financial calculations. Excel can report information such as the current date and time, the maximum value or number of blank cells in a data set, and the cells that meet specific conditions, and it can use this information when performing calculations. To simplify the process of referencing cells or data ranges in your calculations, you can name them. Excel provides guidance for creating formulas to perform calculations and for identifying and fixing any errors in the calculations.

This chapter guides you through procedures related to naming data ranges, creating formulas to calculate values, summarizing data in one or more cells, copying and moving formulas, creating array formulas, troubleshooting issues with formula calculations, and configuring automatic and iterative calculation options.

In this chapter

- Name data ranges
- Create formulas to calculate values
- Summarize data that meets specific conditions
- Copy and move formulas
- Create array formulas
- Find and correct errors in calculations
- Configure automatic and iterative calculation options

Name data ranges

When you work with large amounts of data, it's often useful to identify groups of cells that contain related data. For example, you might have a worksheet for a delivery service in which:

- Each column of data summarizes the number of packages handled during one hour of the day.

- Each row of data represents a region that handled packages.

	A	B	C	D	E	F	G	H	I
1									
2			5:00 PM	6:00 PM	7:00 PM	8:00 PM	9:00 PM	10:00 PM	11:00 PM
3		Northeast	53,587	41,438	36,599	43,023	37,664	44,030	36,930
4		Atlantic	8,896	14,467	9,209	10,767	11,277	10,786	14,838
5		Southeast	7,207	13,475	13,589	14,702	7,769	10,979	10,919
6		North Central	9,829	9,959	10,367	8,962	14,847	12,085	8,015
7		Midwest	7,397	7,811	10,292	7,776	14,805	8,777	14,480
8		Southwest	7,735	11,352	7,222	11,412	14,948	10,686	14,741
9		Mountain West	9,721	8,404	11,944	8,162	14,531	11,348	8,559
10		Northwest	9,240	10,995	7,836	9,702	9,265	14,240	9,798
11		Central	11,810	13,625	8,921	13,593	11,042	10,223	13,338

Worksheets often contain logical groups of data

Instead of specifying a cell or range of cells individually every time you want to reference the data they contain, you can name the cell or cells—in other words, create a *named range*. For example, you could group the packages handled in the Northeast region during all time periods into a range named *Northeast*. Whenever you want to use the contents of that range in a calculation, you can reference Northeast instead of $C$3:$I$3. That way, you don't need to remember the cell range or even the worksheet it's on.

	A	B	C	D	E	F	G	H	I
1									
2			5:00 PM	6:00 PM	7:00 PM	8:00 PM	9:00 PM	10:00 PM	11:00 PM
3		Northeast	53,587	41,438	36,599	43,023	37,664	44,030	36,930
4		Atlantic	8,896	14,467	9,209	10,767	11,277	10,786	14,838
5		Southeast	7,207	13,475	13,589	14,702	7,769	10,979	10,919

Select a group of cells to create a named range

> 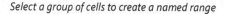 **TIP** Range names can be simple or complex. In a workbook that contains different kinds of data, a more descriptive name such as *NortheastVolume* can help you remember the data the range includes.

If you have a range of data with consistent row or column headings, you can create a series of ranges at one time instead of having to create each individually.

By default, when you create a named range, its scope is the entire workbook. This means that you can reference the name in a formula on any worksheet in the workbook. If a workbook contains a series of worksheets with the same content—for example, sales data worksheets for each month of a year—you might want to set the scope of ranges on those worksheets to the worksheet instead of to the workbook.

After you create a named range, you can edit the name, the cells the range includes, or the scope in which the range exists, or delete a range you no longer need, in the Name Manager.

Name	Value	Refers To	Scope	Comment
Atlantic	[" 8,896 "," 14,467 ",...	=Sheet1!$C$4:$I$4	Workbook	
Central	[" 11,810 "," 13,625 ...	=Sheet1!$C$11:$I$11	Workbook	
Midwest	[" 7,397 "," 7,811 "," ...	=Sheet1!$C$7:$I$7	Workbook	
Mountain_West	[" 9,721 "," 8,404 "," ...	=Sheet1!$C$9:$I$9	Workbook	
NorthCentral	[" 9,829 "," 9,959 "," ...	=Sheet1!$C$6:$I$6	Workbook	
Northeast	[" 53,587 "," 41,438 ...	=Sheet1!$C$3:$I$3	Workbook	
Northwest	[" 9,240 "," 10,995 ",...	=Sheet1!$C$10:$I$10	Workbook	
Southeast	[" 7,207 "," 13,475 ",...	=Sheet1!$C$5:$I$5	Workbook	
Southwest	[" 7,735 "," 11,352 ",...	=Sheet1!$C$8:$I$8	Workbook	

Refers to: =Sheet1!$C$4:$I$4

Manage named ranges in the Name Manager

> **TIP** If your workbook contains a lot of named ranges, tables, or other objects, you can filter the Name Manager list to locate objects more easily.

To create a named range

1. Select the cells you want to include in the named range.

2. In the **Name Box**, next to the formula bar, enter a name for your named range.

Or

1. Select the cells you want to include in the named range.

2. On the **Formulas** tab, in the **Defined Names** group, select **Define Name**.

3. In the **New Name** dialog, do the following:

    a. In the **Name** box, enter a name for the range. The name must begin with a letter or underscore and may not contain spaces.

    b. If you want to restrict the range to use on a specific worksheet, select that worksheet in the **Scope** list.

    c. If you want to provide additional information to help workbook users identify the range, enter a description of up to 255 characters in the **Comment** box.

    d. Verify that the **Refers to** box includes the cells you want to include in the range.

    e. Select **OK**.

To create a series of named ranges from data with headings

1. Select the cells that contain the headings and data you want to include in the named ranges.

2. On the **Formulas** tab, in the **Defined Names** group, select **Create from Selection**.

3. In the **Create Names from Selection** dialog, select the checkbox next to the location of the heading text from which you want to create the range names.

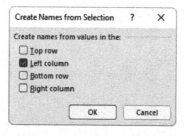

Name ranges by any outer row or column in the selection

4. Select **OK**.

To open the Name Manager

■ On the **Formulas** tab, in the **Defined Names** group, select **Name Manager**.

To change the name of a named range

1. Open the **Name Manager**.

2. Select the range you want to rename, and then select **Edit**.

3. In the **Edit Name** dialog, in the **Name** box, change the range name, and then select **OK**.

To change the cells in a named range

1. Open the **Name Manager**.

2. Select the range you want to edit, and then do either of the following:

   - In the **Refers to** box, change the cell range.

   - Select **Edit**. In the **Edit Name** dialog, in the **Refers to** box, change the cell range, and then select **OK**.

To change the scope of a named range

1. Select the range you want to change the scope of and note the range name shown in the **Name Box**.

2. On the **Formulas** tab, in the **Defined Names** group, select **Define Name**.

3. In the **New Name** dialog, do the following:

   a. In the **Name** box, enter the existing range name that you noted in step 1.

   b. In the **Scope** list, select the new scope.

   c. If you want to provide additional information to help workbook users identify the range, enter a description of up to 255 characters in the **Comment** box.

   d. Verify that the **Refers to** box includes the cells you want to include in the range.

   e. Select **OK**.

To delete a named range

1. Open the **Name Manager**.

2. Select the range you want to delete, and then select **Delete**.

3. In the Microsoft Excel dialog prompting you to confirm the deletion, select **OK**.

Create formulas to calculate values

After you enter data on a worksheet and, optionally, define ranges to simplify data references, you can create formulas to performs calculations on your data. For example, you can calculate the total cost of a customer's shipments, figure the average number of packages for all Wednesdays in the month of January, or find the highest and lowest daily package volumes for a week, month, or year.

You can enter a formula directly into a cell or into the formula bar located between the ribbon and the worksheet area.

Every formula begins with an equal sign (=), which tells Excel to interpret the expression after the equal sign as a calculation instead of as text. The formula that you enter after the equal sign can include simple references and mathematical operators, or it can begin with an Excel function. For example, you can find the sum of the numbers in cells C2 and C3 by using the formula =C2+C3. You can edit formulas by selecting the cell and then editing the formula in the cell or in the formula bar.

Operators and precedence

When you create an Excel formula, you use the built-in functions and arithmetic operators that define operations such as addition and multiplication. The following table displays the order in which Excel evaluates mathematical operations.

Precedence	Operator	Description
1	-	Negation
2	%	Percentage
3	^	Exponentiation
4	* and /	Multiplication and division
5	+ and –	Addition and subtraction
6	&	Concatenation

If two operators at the same level, such as + and −, occur in the same equation, Excel evaluates them from left to right.

For example, Excel evaluates the operations in the formula $= 4 + 8 * 3 - 6$ in this order:

1. $8 * 3 = 24$

2. $4 + 24$, with a result of 28

3. $28 - 6$, with a final result of 22

You can control the order in which Excel evaluates operations by using parentheses. Excel always evaluates operations in parentheses first.

For example, if the previous equation were rewritten as $= (4 + 8) * 3 - 6$, Excel would evaluate the operations in this order:

1. $(4 + 8)$, with a result of 12

2. $12 * 3$, with a result of 36

3. $36 - 6$, with a final result of 30

In a formula that has multiple levels of parentheses, Excel evaluates the expressions within the innermost set of parentheses first and works its way out. As with operations on the same level, expressions at the same parenthetical level are evaluated from left to right.

For example, Excel evaluates the formula $= 4 + (3 + 8 * (2 + 5)) - 7$ in this order:

1. $(2 + 5)$, with a result of 7

2. $7 * 8$, with a result of 56

3. $56 + 3$, with a result of 59

4. $4 + 59$, with a result of 63

5. $63 - 7$, with a final result of 56

6

You can perform mathematical operations on numbers by using the mathematical operators for addition (+), subtraction (–), multiplication (*), division (/), negation (-), and exponentiation (^). You can perform other operations on a range of numbers by using the following Excel functions:

- **SUM** Returns the sum of the numbers.

- **AVERAGE** Returns the average of the numbers.

- **COUNT** Returns the number of entries in the cell range.

- **MAX** Returns the largest number.

- **MIN** Returns the smallest number.

These functions are available from the AutoSum list, which is in the Editing group on the Home tab of the ribbon and in the Function Library group on the Formulas tab. The Function Library is also where you'll find the rest of the Excel functions, organized into categories.

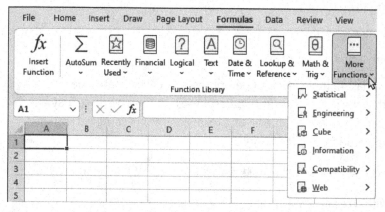

Excel includes a wide variety of functions

The Formula AutoComplete feature simplifies the process of referencing functions, named ranges, and tables in formulas. It provides a template for you to follow and suggests entries for each function argument. Here's how it works:

1. As you begin to enter a function name after the equal sign, Excel displays a list of functions matching the characters you've entered. You can select a function from the list and then press Tab to enter the function name and the opening parenthesis in the cell or formula bar.

	A	B	C	D	E	F	G	H	I	J
1	Delivery Exceptions									
2										
3	Route ▼	Count ▼		=SU						
4	101	4		*fx* SUBSTITUTE		Replaces existing text with new text in a text string				
5	102	9		*fx* SUBTOTAL						
6	103	12		*fx* SUM						
7	104	8		*fx* SUMIF						
8	105	5		*fx* SUMIFS						
9	106	6		*fx* SUMPRODUCT						
10	107	6		*fx* SUMSQ						
11	108	5		*fx* SUMX2MY2						
12	109	14		*fx* SUMX2PY2						
13	110	7		*fx* SUMXMY2						

Select a function from the list

2. After the opening parenthesis, Excel displays the arguments that the selected function accepts. Bold indicates required arguments and square brackets enclose optional arguments. You can simply follow the prompts to enter or select the necessary information, and then enter a closing parenthesis to finish the formula.

	A	B	C	D	E	F
1	Delivery Exceptions					
2						
3	Route ▼	Count ▼		=SUM(		
4	101	4		SUM(**number1**, [number2], ...)		
5	102	9				
6	103	12				

Excel prompts you for required and optional information

3. To reference a named range, table, or table element, start entering the name (or an opening square bracket to indicate a table element) and Excel displays a list of options to choose from.

> ✓ **TIP** You can reference a series of contiguous cells in a formula by entering the cell range or by dragging through the cells. If the cells aren't contiguous, hold down the Ctrl key and select each cell. For information about using keyboard shortcuts to select cell ranges, see the appendix, "Keyboard shortcuts."

▲	A	B	C	D	E	F	G	H	I	J	K
1	**Delivery Exceptions**										
2											
3	Route ▾	Count ▾		=SUM(Exceptions[							
4	101	4		SUM(number1, [number2], ...)							
5	102	9				@ - This Row	Choose only this row of the specified column				
6	103	12				(...) Route					
7	104	8				(...) Count					
8	105	5				#All					
9	106	6				#Data					
10	107	6				#Headers					
						#Totals					

Excel displays the available table elements

If you're creating a more complex formula and want extra guidance, you can assemble the formula in the Insert Function dialog. All the Excel functions are available from within the dialog.

Create formulas in the Insert Function dialog

If you're uncertain which function to use, you can search for one by entering a simple description of what you'd like to accomplish. Selecting any function displays the function's arguments and description.

Activate any field to display a description of the argument

After you select a function, Excel displays an interface in which you can enter all the function arguments. The complexity of the interface depends on the function.

Whether you enter a formula directly or assemble it in the Insert Function dialog, you can reference data in cells (A3) or cell ranges (A3:J12), in named ranges (Northeast), or in table columns (TableName[ColumnName]). For example, if the Northeast range refers to cells C3:I3, you can calculate the average of cells C3:I3 by using the formula =AVERAGE(Northeast).

To create a formula manually

1. Select the cell in which you want to create the formula.

2. In the cell or in the formula bar, enter an equal sign (=).

3. If the formula will call a function, enter the function name and an opening parenthesis to begin the formula and display the required and optional arguments.

4. Enter the remainder of the formula:

   - Reference cells by entering the cell reference or selecting the cell.

   - Reference cell ranges by entering the cell range or dragging across the range.

   - Reference named ranges and tables by entering the range or table name.

   - Reference table elements by entering [after the table name, selecting the element from the list, and then entering].

5. If the formula includes a function, enter the closing parenthesis to end it.

6. Press **Enter** to enter the formula in the cell and return the results.

To open the Insert Function dialog

- On the formula bar, to the left of the text entry box, select the **Insert Function** button (*fx*).

- On the **Formulas** tab, in the **Function Library** group, select **Insert Function**.

- Press **Shift+F3**.

To locate a function in the Insert Function dialog

- In the **Search for a function** box, enter a brief description of the operation you want to perform, and then select **Go**.

Or

1. In the **Or select a category** list, select the function category.

2. Scroll down the **Select a function** list to the function.

To create a formula in the Insert Function dialog

1. Open the **Insert Function** dialog.

2. Select the function you want to use in the formula, and then select **OK**.

3. In the **Function Arguments** dialog, enter the function's arguments, and then select **OK**.

To reference a named range in a formula

- Enter the range name in place of the cell range.

To reference an Excel table column in a formula

- Enter the table name followed by an opening bracket ([), the column name, and a closing bracket (]).

Summarize data that meets specific conditions

Another use for formulas is to display messages when certain conditions are met. This kind of formula is called a *conditional formula*. One way to create a conditional formula in Excel is to use the IF function. Selecting the Insert Function button next to the formula bar and then choosing the IF function displays the Function Arguments dialog with the fields required to create an IF formula.

The Function Arguments dialog for an IF formula

When you work with an IF function, the Function Arguments dialog displays three input boxes:

- **Logical_test** The condition you want to check.

- **Value_if_true** The value to display if the condition is met. This could be a cell reference, or a number or text enclosed in quotes.

- **Value_if_false** The value to display if the condition is not met.

The following table displays other conditional functions you can use to summarize data.

Function	Description
AVERAGEIF	Finds the average of values within a cell range that meet a specified criterion
AVERAGEIFS	Finds the average of values within a cell range that meet multiple criteria
COUNT	Counts the cells in a range that contain numerical values
COUNTA	Counts the cells in a range that are not empty
COUNTBLANK	Counts the cells in a range that are empty
COUNTIF	Counts the cells in a range that meet a specified criterion
COUNTIFS	Counts the cells in a range that meet multiple criteria
IFERROR	Displays one value if a formula results in an error and another if it doesn't
SUMIF	Adds the values in a range that meet a single criterion
SUMIFS	Adds the values in a range that meet multiple criteria

To create a formula that uses the AVERAGEIF function, you define the range to be examined for the criterion, the criterion, and, if required, the range from which to draw the values. As an example, consider a worksheet that lists each customer's ID number, name, state, and total monthly shipping bill. If you want to find the average order of customers from the state of Washington (abbreviated in the worksheet as WA), you can create the formula =AVERAGEIF(C3:C6, "WA", D3:D6).

	A	B	C	D
1	CustomerID	CustomerName	State	Total
2	CN100	Contoso	WA	$118,476.00
3	CN101	Fabrikam	WA	$125,511.00
4	CN102	Northwind Traders	OR	$103,228.00
5	CN103	Adventure Works	WA	$ 86,552.00

Sample data that illustrates the preceding example

The AVERAGEIFS, SUMIFS, and COUNTIFS functions extend the capabilities of the AVERAGEIF, SUMIF, and COUNTIF functions to allow for multiple criteria. For example, if you want to find the sum of all orders of at least $100,000 placed by companies in Washington, you can create the formula =SUMIFS(D2:D5, C2:C5, "=WA", D2:D5, ">=100000").

The AVERAGEIFS and SUMIFS functions start with a data range that contains values that the formula summarizes. You then list the data ranges and the criteria to apply to that range. In generic terms, the syntax is =AVERAGEIFS(data_range, criteria_range1, criteria1[,criteria_range2, criteria2...]). The part of the syntax in brackets (which aren't used when you create the formula) is optional, so an AVERAGEIFS or SUMIFS formula that contains a single criterion will work. The COUNTIFS function, which doesn't perform any calculations, doesn't need a data range; you just provide the criteria ranges and criteria. For example, you could find the number of customers from Washington who were billed at least $100,000 by using the formula =COUNTIFS(C2:C5, "=WA", D2:D5, ">=100000").

You can use the IFERROR function to display a custom error message instead of relying on the default Excel error messages to explain what happened. For example, you could create this type of formula to employ the VLOOKUP function to look up a customer's name in the second column of a table named Customers based on the customer identification number entered into cell G8. That formula might look like this: =IFERROR(VLOOKUP(G8,Customers,2,FALSE),"Customer not found"). If the function finds a match for the customer ID in cell G8, it displays the customer's name; if not, it displays the text "Customer not found."

6

> ✅ **TIP** The last two arguments in the VLOOKUP function tell the formula to look in the Customers table's second column and to require an exact match. For more information about the VLOOKUP function, see *the full-length book Microsoft Excel Step by Step (Office 2021 and Microsoft 365) (Microsoft Press, 2021).*

To summarize data by using the IF function

- Use the syntax =IF(*logical_test, value_if_true, value_if_false*) where:
  - *logical_test* is the logical test to be performed.
  - *value_if_true* is the value the formula returns if the test is true.
  - *value_if_false* is the value the formula returns if the test is false.

To count cells that contain numbers in a range

- Use the syntax =COUNT(*range*), where *range* is the cell range in which you want to count cells.

To count cells that are non-blank

- Use the syntax =COUNTA(*range*), where *range* is the cell range in which you want to count cells.

To count cells that contain a blank value

- Use the syntax =COUNTBLANK(*range*), where *range* is the cell range in which you want to count cells.

To count cells that meet one condition

- Use the syntax =COUNTIF(*range, criteria*) where:

  - *range* is the cell range that might contain the criteria value.

  - *criteria* is the logical test used to determine whether to count the cell.

To count cells that meet multiple conditions

- Use the syntax =COUNTIFS(*criteria_range1, criteria1, criteria_range2, criteria2,...*) where for each *criteria_range* and *criteria* pair:

  - *criteria_range* is the cell range that might contain the criteria value.

  - *criteria* is the logical test used to determine whether to count the cell.

To find the sum of data that meets one condition

- Use the syntax =SUMIF(*range, criteria, sum_range*) where:

  - *range* is the cell range that might contain the criteria value.

  - *criteria* is the logical test used to determine whether to include the cell.

  - *sum_range* is the range that contains the values to be included if the range cell in the same row meets the criterion.

To find the sum of data that meets multiple conditions

- Use the syntax =SUMIFS(*sum_range, criteria_range1, criteria1, criteria_range2, criteria2,...*) where:

  - *sum_range* is the range that contains the values to be included if all *criteria_range* cells in the same row meet all criteria.

  - *criteria_range* is the cell range that might contain the criteria value.

  - *criteria* is the logical test used to determine whether to include the cell.

To find the average of data that meets one condition

- Use the syntax =AVERAGEIF(*range, criteria, average_range*) where:

    - *range* is the cell range that might contain the *criteria* value.

    - *criteria* is the logical test used to determine whether to include the cell.

    - *average_range* is the range that contains the values to be included if the *range* cell in the same row meets the criterion.

To find the average of data that meets multiple conditions

- Use the syntax =AVERAGEIFS(*average_range, criteria_range1, criteria1, criteria_range2, criteria2,...*) where:

    - *average_range* is the range that contains the values to be included if all *criteria_range* cells in the same row meet all criteria.

    - *criteria_range* is the cell range that might contain the *criteria* value.

    - *criteria* is the logical test used to determine whether to include the cell.

To display a custom message if a cell contains an error

- Use the syntax =IFERROR(*value, value_if_error*) where:

    - *value* is a cell reference or formula.

    - *value_if_error* is the value to be displayed if the *value* argument returns an error.

Copy and move formulas

After you create a formula, you can copy it and paste it into another cell. When you do, Excel changes the formula to work in the new cells. For instance, suppose you have a worksheet in which cell C7 contains the formula =SUM(C2:C6). If you copy cell C7 and paste the copied formula into cell D7, Excel enters =SUM(D2:D6). Excel knows to change the cells used in the formula because the formula uses a *relative reference*—a reference that can change if the formula is copied to another cell. Relative references are written with just the cell row and column—for example, C14.

Relative references are useful when you summarize rows of data and want to use the same formula for each row. As an example, suppose you have a worksheet with two columns of data, labeled Sale Price and Rate, and you want to calculate a sales representative's commission by multiplying the two values in a row. To calculate the commission for the first sale, you would enter the formula =A2*B2 in cell C2.

	A	B	C	D
	Sale Price	Rate	Commission	
1	Sale Price	Rate	Commission	
2	$ 19,720	6%	$ 1,183.20	
3	$ 11,287	6%		
4	$ 18,926	6%		
5	$ 5,722	5.5%		
6	$ 15,785	6%		
7	$ 10,445	6%		
8				

C2 =A2*B2

Use formulas to calculate values such as commissions

Selecting cell C2 and dragging the fill handle down through cell C7 copies the formula from cell C2 into each of the other cells. Because you created the formula by using relative references, Excel updates each cell's formula to reflect its position relative to the starting cell (in this case, cell C2). The formula in cell C7, for example, is =A7*B7.

C7 =A7*B7

	A	B	C	D
1	Sale Price	Rate	Commission	
2	$ 19,720	6%	$ 1,183.20	
3	$ 11,287	6%	$ 677.22	
4	$ 18,926	6%	$ 1,135.56	
5	$ 5,722	5.5%	$ 314.71	
6	$ 15,785	6%	$ 947.10	
7	$ 10,445	6%	$ 626.70	
8				

Copying formulas to other cells to summarize additional data

When you enter a formula in a cell of an Excel table column, Excel automatically copies the formula to the rest of the column and updates any relative references in the formula.

If you want a cell reference to remain constant when you copy a formula to another cell, use an *absolute reference* by inserting a dollar sign ($) before the column letter and row number or a *mixed reference* by inserting a dollar sign before either the column letter or row number.

> ✓ **TIP** In addition to using an absolute reference, another way to ensure that your cell references don't change when you copy a formula to another cell is to select the cell that contains the formula, copy the formula's text in the formula bar, press the Esc key to exit cut-and-copy mode, select the cell where you want to paste the formula, and press Ctrl+V. Excel doesn't change the cell references when you copy your formula to another cell in this manner.

One quick way to change a cell reference from relative to absolute is to select the cell reference in the formula bar and then press F4. Pressing F4 cycles a cell reference through the four possible types of references:

- Relative columns and rows (for example, C4)

- Absolute columns and rows (for example, $C$4)

- Relative columns and absolute rows (for example, C$4)

- Absolute columns and relative rows (for example, $C4)

To copy a formula without changing its cell references

1. Select the cell that contains the formula you want to copy.

2. In the formula bar, select the formula text.

3. Press **Ctrl+C**.

4. Select the cell in which you want to paste the formula.

5. Press **Ctrl+V**.

6. Press **Enter**.

To move a formula without changing its cell references

1. Select the cell that contains the formula you want to copy.

2. Point to the edge of the selected cell until the pointer changes to a black four-headed arrow.

3. Drag the outline to the cell where you want to move the formula.

6

To copy a formula and change its cell references

1. Select the cell that contains the formula you want to copy.

2. Press **Ctrl+C**.

3. Select the cell in which you want to paste the formula.

4. Press **Ctrl+V**.

To create relative and absolute cell references

1. Enter a cell reference into a formula.

2. Do either of the following:

   - Enter a $ in front of a row or column reference you want to make absolute.

   - Select within the cell reference, and then press **F4** to advance through the four possible combinations of relative and absolute row and column references.

Create array formulas

Most Excel formulas calculate values to be displayed in a single cell. For example, you could add the formulas =B1*B4, =B1*B5, and =B1*B6 to consecutive worksheet cells to calculate shipping insurance costs based on the value of a package's contents.

	A	B	C	D
1	Insurance Rate:	2.25%		
2				
3	PackageID	Value	Premium	
4	PK101352	$ 591.00		
5	PK101353	$1,713.00		
6	PK101354	$3,039.00		
7				

A worksheet with data to be summarized by an array formula

Instead of entering the same formula in multiple cells one cell at a time, you can enter a formula in every cell in the target range at the same time by creating an *array formula*. To calculate package insurance rates by multiplying the values in the cell range B4:B6 by the insurance rate in cell B1, you select the target cells (C4:C6) and enter the formula =B1*B4:B6. Note that you must select a range of the same shape as the values you're using in the calculation. (For example, if the value range is three columns wide by one row high, the target range must also be three columns wide by one row high.) If you enter the array formula into a range of the wrong shape, Excel displays duplicate results, incomplete results, or error messages, depending on how the target range differs from the value range.

When you press Ctrl+Shift+Enter, Excel creates an array formula in the selected cells. The formula appears within a pair of braces to indicate that it is an array formula.

C4		✗ ✓ *fx*	{=B1*B4:B6}	
	A	B	C	D
1	Insurance Rate:	2.25%		
2				
3	PackageID	Value	Premium	
4	PK101352	$ 591.00	13.2975	
5	PK101353	$1,713.00	38.5425	
6	PK101354	$3,039.00	68.3775	
7				

An array formula calculates multiple results

> ⚠ **IMPORTANT** You can't add braces to a formula to make it an array formula. You must press Ctrl+Shift+Enter to create it.

To create an array formula

1. Select the cells in which you want to display the formula results.
2. In the formula bar, enter the array formula.
3. Press **Ctrl+Shift+Enter.**

To edit an array formula

1. Select every cell that contains the array formula.
2. In the formula bar, edit the array formula.
3. Press **Ctrl+Shift+Enter** to re-enter the formula as an array formula.

Find and correct errors in calculations

Including calculations in a worksheet gives you valuable answers to questions about your data. As is always true, however, it's possible for errors to creep into your formulas. With Excel, you can find the source of errors in your formulas by identifying the cells used in a specific calculation and describing any errors that have occurred. The process of examining a worksheet for errors is referred to as *auditing*.

Excel identifies errors in several ways. The first way is to display an error code in the cell that contains the formula generating the error.

19	Build Total			$18,326.00	
20	Labor Percentage		⚠ ▾	#DIV/0!	
21		Divide by Zero Error			
22					
23		Help on this Error			
24		Show Calculation Steps			
25		Ignore Error			
26		Edit in Formula Bar			
27		Error Checking Options...			
28					

A warning triangle and pound sign indicate an error

When the active cell generates an error, Excel displays an Error button next to it. Pointing to the button displays information about the error, and selecting the button displays a menu of options for handling the error.

The following table explains the most common error codes.

Error code	Description
#####	The column isn't wide enough to display the value.
#VALUE!	The formula has the wrong type of argument, such as text in a cell where a numerical value is required.
#NAME?	The formula contains text that Excel doesn't recognize, such as an unknown named range.
#REF!	The formula refers to a cell that doesn't exist, which can happen whenever cells are deleted.
#DIV/0!	The formula attempts to divide by zero.

Another technique you can use to find the source of formula errors is to ensure that the appropriate cells are providing values for the formula. You can identify the source of an error by having Excel trace a cell's *precedents*, which are the cells with values used in the active cell's formula. You can also audit your worksheet by identifying cells with formulas that use a value from a particular cell. Cells that use another cell's value in their calculations are known as *dependents*, meaning that they depend on the value in the other cell to derive their own value. They are identified in Excel by tracer arrows. If the cells identified by the tracer arrows aren't the correct cells, you can hide the arrows and correct the formula.

9	**Loading Dock**		
10	Concrete	$ 2,169.00	
11	Labor	$ 4,500.00	
12	Posts	$ 300.00	
13	Excavation	$ 2,500.00	
14	Drain	$ 1,800.00	
15	Rails	$ 495.00	
16	Stairs	$ 1,295.00	
17	*Subtotal*		$13,059.00
18			
19	**Build Total**		$31,385.00
20	**Labor Percentage**		34%

Tracing a cell's dependents

If you prefer to have the elements of a formula error presented as text in a dialog, you can use the Error Checking tool to locate errors one after the other. You can choose to ignore the selected error or move to the next or the previous error.

Error Checking   ?   ✕

Error in cell C20
=B11/C17

Divide by Zero Error
The formula or function used is dividing by zero or empty cells.

[Help on this Error]
[Show Calculation Steps]
[Ignore Error]
[Edit in Formula Bar]

[Options...]   [Previous]   [Next]

Identify and manage errors from the Error Checking window

✓ **TIP** You can have the Error Checking tool ignore formulas that don't use every cell in a region (such as a row or column). To do so, on the Formulas tab of the Excel Options dialog, clear the Formulas Which Omit Cells In A Region checkbox. Excel will no longer mark these cells as an error.

When you just want to display the results of each step of a formula and don't need the full power of the Error Checking tool, you can use the Evaluate Formula dialog to move through each element of the formula. The Evaluate Formula dialog is particularly useful for examining formulas that don't produce an error but aren't generating the result you expect.

Step through formulas in the Evaluate Formula window

Finally, you can monitor the value in a cell regardless of where you are in your workbook by opening a Watch Window that displays the value in the cell. For example, if one of your formulas uses values from cells in other worksheets or even other workbooks, you can set a watch on the cell that contains the formula, and then change the values in the other cells. As you change the precedent values, the formula result changes in the Watch Window. When you're done watching the formula, you can delete the watch and close the Watch Window.

Monitor formula results in the Watch Window

To display information about a formula error

1. Select the cell that contains the error.

2. Point to the error indicator next to the cell to display information about the error.

3. Select the error indicator to display options for correcting or learning more about the error.

To identify the cells that a formula references

1. Select the cell that contains the formula.

2. On the **Formulas** tab, in the **Formula Auditing** group, select **Trace Precedents**.

To identify formulas that reference a specific cell

1. Select the cell.

2. In the **Formula Auditing** group, select **Trace Dependents**.

To remove tracer arrows

- In the **Formula Auditing** group, do one of the following:

  - To remove all the arrows, select the **Remove Arrows** button (not its arrow).

  - To remove only precedent or dependent arrows, select the **Remove Arrows** arrow, and then select **Remove Precedent Arrows** or **Remove Dependent Arrows**.

To evaluate a formula one calculation at a time

1. Select the cell that contains the formula you want to evaluate.

2. In the **Formula Auditing** group, select **Evaluate Formula**.

3. In the **Evaluate Formula** dialog, select **Evaluate**. Excel replaces the underlined calculation with its result.

4. Do either of the following:

   - Select **Step In** to move forward by one calculation.

   - Select **Step Out** to move backward by one calculation.

5. When you finish, select **Close**.

To change error display options

1. Display the **Formulas** page of the **Excel Options** dialog.

2. In the **Error Checking** section, select or clear the **Enable background error checking** checkbox.

3. Select the **Indicate errors using this color** button and select a color.

4. Select **Reset Ignored Errors** to return Excel to its default error indicators.

5. In the **Error checking rules** section, select or clear the checkboxes next to errors you want to indicate or ignore, respectively.

To watch the values in a cell range

1. Select the cell range you want to watch.

2. In the **Formula Auditing** group, select the **Watch Window** button.

3. In the **Watch Window** dialog, select **Add Watch**.

4. In the **Add Watch** dialog, confirm the cell range, and then select **Add**.

To delete a watch

1. Select the **Watch Window** button.

2. In the **Watch Window** dialog, select the watch you want to delete.

3. Select **Delete Watch**.

Configure automatic and iterative calculation options

Excel formulas use values in other cells to calculate their results. If you create a formula that refers to the cell that contains the formula, the result is a circular reference.

Under most circumstances, Excel treats a circular reference as a mistake for two reasons. First, most Excel formulas don't refer to their own cell, so a circular reference is unusual enough to be identified as an error. The second, more serious consideration is that a formula with a circular reference can slow down your workbook. Because Excel repeats, or iterates, the calculation, you must set limits on how many times the app repeats the operation.

You can control how often Excel recalculates formulas. Three calculation options are available from the Formulas tab and from the Formulas page of the Excel Options dialog.

You can modify the iterative calculation options Excel uses

The calculation options work as follows:

- **Automatic** recalculates a worksheet whenever a value that affects a formula changes. This is the default setting.

- **Automatic Except for Data Tables** recalculates a worksheet whenever a value changes but doesn't recalculate data tables.

- **Manual** recalculates formulas only when you tell Excel to do so.

You can also use options in the Calculation Options section to allow or disallow iterative calculations (repeating calculations of formulas that contain circular references). The default values (a maximum of 100 iterations and a maximum change per iteration of 0.001) are appropriate for all but the most unusual circumstances.

To manually recalculate the active workbook

- On the **Formulas** tab, in the **Calculation** group, select **Calculate Now**.

- Press **F9**.

To manually recalculate the active worksheet

- In the **Calculation** group, select the **Calculate Sheet** button.

To set worksheet calculation options

- Display the worksheet whose calculation options you want to set.

- On the **Formulas** tab, in the **Calculation** group, select **Calculation Options**, and then select **Automatic, Automatic Except for Data Tables,** or **Manual.**

To enable iterative calculations

1. Open the **Excel Options** dialog and display the **Formulas** page.

2. In the **Calculation options** section, select the **Enable iterative calculation** checkbox.

3. In the **Maximum Iterations** box, enter the maximum iterations allowed for a calculation.

4. In the **Maximum Change** box, enter the maximum change allowed for each iteration.

5. Select **OK.**

Key points

- You can assign names to cell ranges to make it easier to reference them in formulas or move to them from other places in a workbook.

- Formulas calculate values based on other data that you provide directly in the formula or reference elsewhere in the workbook or another data source. Every formula begins with an equal sign (=). Simple formulas perform mathematic calculations. Other formulas include Excel functions that require specific input, known as *arguments*.

- Using a conditional function such as IF, AVERAGEIF, COUNTIF, IFERROR, or SUMIF in a formula summarizes only the data that meets specific conditions.

- A formula can include absolute references (indicated by a $ preceding row letters and/or column numbers) or relative references to unnamed cells or data ranges. When you copy or move a formula to another location, relative references update to reflect the move. Absolute references continue to reference the original cell or data range.

- An array formula is a formula that performs multiple calculations within a data array at one time, so you don't have to copy the formula.

- Excel displays various error messages when it finds fault with a formula. A yellow warning triangle and a # indicate an error message. You can manually identify and correct the error or use the Error Checking tool.

- If you're working with a very large amount of data, you can speed up Excel's response time by configuring it to recalculate formulas less frequently. You also have the option of allowing Excel to perform calculations that contain circular references, which is usually marked as an error but is necessary and appropriate in some circumstances.

> **SEE ALSO** This chapter is from the full-length book *Microsoft Excel Step by Step (Office 2021 and Microsoft 365)* (Microsoft Press, 2021). Please consult that book for information about features of Excel that aren't discussed in this book.

6

Practice tasks

Before you can complete these tasks, you must copy the book's practice files to your computer. The practice files for these tasks are in the **Office365SBS\Ch06** folder. You can save the results of the tasks in the same folder.

The introduction includes a complete list of practice files and download instructions.

Name data ranges

Open the **NameRanges** workbook in Excel, and then perform the following tasks:

1. Create a named range named Monday for the V_101 through V_109 values (found in cells **C4:C12**) for that weekday.

2. Edit the **Monday** named range to include the V_110 value for that column.

3. Select cells **B4:H13** and create a batch of named ranges for V_101 through V_110, using the row headings as the range names.

4. Delete the **Monday** named range.

Create formulas to calculate values

Open the **BuildFormulas** workbook in Excel, and then perform the following tasks:

1. On the **Summary** worksheet, in cell **F9**, create a formula that displays the value from cell **C4**.

2. Edit the formula in cell **F9** so it uses the SUM function to find the total of values in cells **C3:C8**.

3. In cell **F10**, create a formula that finds the total expenses for desktop software and server software.

4. Edit the formula in **F10** so the cell references are absolute references.

5. On the **JuneLabor** worksheet, in cell **F13**, create a SUM formula that finds the total of values in the **JuneSummary** table's **Labor Expense** column.

Summarize data that meets specific conditions

Open the **CreateConditionalFormulas** workbook in Excel, and then perform the following tasks:

1. In cell **G3**, create an IF formula that tests whether the value in **F3** is greater than or equal to 35,000. If it is, display **Request discount**; if not, display No discount available.

2. Copy the formula from cell **G3** to the range **G4:G14**.

3. In cell **I3**, create a formula that finds the average cost of all expenses in cells **F3:F14** where the **Type** column contains the value *Box*.

4. In cell **I6**, create a formula that finds the sum of all expenses in cells **F3:F14** where the **Type** column contains the value *Envelope,* and the **Destination** column contains the value *International*.

Create array formulas

Open the **CreateArrayFormulas** workbook in Excel, and then perform the following tasks:

1. On the **Fuel** worksheet, in cells **C11:F11**, enter the array formula =C3*C9:F9.

2. Edit the array formula you just created to read =C3*C10:F10.

3. On the **Volume** worksheet, in cells **D4:D7**, create the array formula =B4:B7*C4:C7.

Find and correct errors in calculations

Open the **AuditFormulas** workbook in Excel, and then perform the following tasks:

1. Set a watch on the value in cell **C19**.

2. Display the precedents for the formula in cell **C7**.

3. Hide the tracer arrows.

4. Use the **Error Checking** dialog to identify the error in cell **C20**.

5. Show the tracer arrows for the error.

6. Hide the arrows, and then change the formula in cell **C20** to =C12/D20.

7. Use the **Evaluate Formula** dialog to step through the formula in cell **C20**.

8. Delete the watch you created in step 1.

Configure automatic and iterative calculation options

Open the **SetIterativeOptions** workbook in Excel, and then perform the following tasks:

1. On the **Formulas** tab, in the **Calculation** group, select the **Calculation Options** button, and then select **Manual**.

2. In cell **B6**, enter the formula =B7*B9, and then press **Enter**.

3. Note that this result is incorrect because the Gross Savings value minus the Savings Incentive value should equal the Net Savings value, which it does not.

4. Press **F9** to recalculate the workbook and read the message box indicating that you have created a circular reference.

5. Select **OK**.

6. Use options in the **Excel Options** dialog to enable iterative calculation.

7. Close the **Excel Options** dialog and recalculate the worksheet.

8. Change the workbook's calculation options back to **Automatic**.

Manage worksheet data

You can manage vast amounts of data in an Excel workbook, but it's difficult to make business decisions based on that data unless you can focus on the specific information required for each decision.

By working with filtered data, you can more easily discover information such as the percentage of monthly revenue earned in the 10 best days of the month, the average revenue earned on a specific weekday, or the slowest business day of each month.

Just as you can limit the data that a worksheet displays, you can also create validation rules that limit the data entered in them. When you set rules for data entry, you can prevent many common data-entry errors, such as entering values that are too small or too large or attempting to enter a word in a cell that requires a number.

This chapter guides you through procedures related to filtering and summarizing data and creating validation rules that restrict data entry.

In this chapter

- Filter data ranges and tables
- Summarize filtered data
- Enforce data entry criteria

Filter data ranges and tables

An Excel worksheet can hold as much as 1,048,576 rows and 16,384 columns of data. You aren't likely to store that amount of data in a worksheet, but even so, there will be times when you want to display or work with only some of the worksheet data. For example, you might want to see your company's sales revenue for a specific week of the year, only values greater than 10,000, only sales by a specific person, or a combination of these criteria. You can choose to display and work with only the data you want, without disturbing the rest of the data, by creating filters: rules that specify the rows of a table or data range to display. Filtering is turned on by default for Excel tables, but you can also turn it on for data ranges.

> ⚠ **IMPORTANT** When you turn on filtering, Excel treats the cells in the active cell's column as a range. To ensure that the filtering works properly, you should always have a heading at the top of the column you want to filter. If you don't, Excel still treats the first value in the list as the heading and doesn't include it in the list of values by which you can filter the data.

When you turn on filtering, a filter arrow appears to the right of each column label in the list of data. Selecting the filter arrow displays a menu of filtering options and a list of the unique values in the column. Each value has a checkbox next to it, which you can use to create a selection filter.

Use filters to limit the data that appears in a worksheet

If the selection filters are too specific for your needs, you can create a custom text, number, or date filter. The specific filtering options vary based on the column data.

When you select a custom filtering option, Excel displays a dialog in which you can define the filter's criteria. For example, you could create a filter that displays only records that were created on or after a specific date. When a column is filtered, the filter arrow changes to a Filter icon, which looks like a small arrow next to a funnel. When you no longer need the filter, you can clear it, or turn off filtering, which hides the filter arrows.

A funnel symbol on a Filter button indicates a filtered column

If you want to display the highest or lowest values in a column of numbers, you can create a Top 10 filter. You can choose whether to show values from the top or bottom of the list and define the number or percentage of items you want to display.

If you know some of the data you're looking for, you can quickly create a search filter in which you enter a search string that Excel uses to identify the items to display. This is particularly useful when you're looking for multiple types of entries.

Applying a search filter limits the items that appear in the selection list

To narrow down the displayed data even further, you can apply filters to multiple columns at one time. You can clear individual filters or clear all filters at the same time.

Summarizing numerical values can provide valuable information to help you run your business. It can also be helpful to know how many different values appear within a column. For example, you might want to display all the countries and regions in which your company has customers. If you want to display a list of the unique values in a column, you can do so by creating an advanced filter.

Use the Advanced Filter dialog to find unique records in a list

All you need to do is identify the rows that contain the values you want to filter and indicate that you want to display unique records so that you get only the information you want.

To turn filtering on or off

1. Select any cell in the data range or table.

2. Do either of the following:

   - On the **Home** tab, in the **Editing** group, select **Sort & Filter**, and then select **Filter**.

   - Press **Ctrl+Shift+L**.

To create a selection filter

1. Turn on filtering.

2. Select the filter arrow for the column by which you want to filter the data range or table.

3. Do either of the following:

   - Clear the checkboxes next to the items you want to hide.

   - Clear the **Select All** checkbox and then select the checkboxes next to the items you want to display.

4. Select **OK** to apply the filter.

To create a filter rule

1. With filtering turned on, select the filter arrow for the column by which you want to filter the data range or table.

2. Select *Type* **Filters** to display the available filters for the column's data type.

3. Select the filter you want to create.

4. Enter the arguments required to define the rule, and then select **OK** to apply the filter.

To display the highest or lowest numeric values in a column

1. With filtering turned on, select the filter arrow for a column that contains numeric values, select **Number Filters**, and then select **Top 10**.

2. In the **Top 10 AutoFilter** dialog, do the following:

   a. In the first **Show** list, select **Top** or **Bottom**.

   b. In the second list, enter or select the number or percentage of items you want to display.

   c. In the third list, select **Items** to display the selected number of items or **Percent** to display the selected percentage of items.

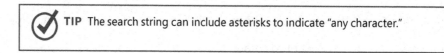

Applying a search filter limits the items that appear in the selection list

3. Select **OK** to apply the filter.

To create a search filter

1. With filtering turned on, select the filter arrow for the column by which you want to filter the data range or table.

2. In the **Search** box, enter the character string that should appear in the values you want to display in the filter list.

> ✓ **TIP** The search string can include asterisks to indicate "any character."

3. Select **OK** to apply the filter.

To reapply a filter

- Select the **Filter** button of the filtered column, and then press **Enter** or select **OK**.

To clear a filter

- Select the **Filter** button of the filtered column, and then select **Clear Filter** from *"Field."*

To find unique values within a data range

1. Select any cell in the range for which you want to find unique values.

2. On the **Data** tab, in the **Sort & Filter** group, select **Advanced**.

3. In the **Advanced Filter** dialog, do either of the following:

   - To display the unique values within the cell range, select **Filter the list, in place**.

   - To make a separate list of the unique values, select **Copy to another location**.

4. Verify that the correct data range appears in the **List range** box.

 TIP If you want to display the unique values from only one column, the List Range box should reference only that column.

5. If you chose the Copy To Another Location option, enter the location where you want to insert the separate list in the **Copy to** box.

6. Select the **Unique records only** checkbox, and then select **OK**.

Summarize filtered data

Excel includes a wide range of tools you can use to summarize worksheet data. This section describes how to summarize filtered data by using the Auto Calculate feature and the SUBTOTAL and AGGREGATE functions.

It's important to be able to analyze the data that's most relevant to your current needs, but there are some limitations when working with filtered data. One important limitation is that formulas that use the SUM or AVERAGE function make calculations based on all the data in a range rather than only the data displayed by the filter.

Excel provides two ways to summarize only the visible cells in a filtered data list. The simplest method is to use the AutoCalculate function, which displays calculation results in the Excel status bar. The more difficult method is to create a formula that uses the SUBTOTAL or AGGREGATE function.

The default AutoCalculate options include SUM, AVERAGE, and COUNT, but you can change the displayed calculations to suit your needs.

7

▲	A	B	C	D	E	F	G	H	I	J
1										
2			5:00 PM	6:00 PM	7:00 PM	8:00 PM	9:00 PM	10:00 PM	11:00 PM	
3		Northeast	53,587	41,438	36,599	43,023	37,664	44,030	36,930	
4		Atlantic	8,896	14,467	9,209	10,767	11,277	10,786	14,838	
5		Southeast	7,207	13,475	13,589	14,702	7,769	10,979	10,919	
6		North Central	9,829	9,959	10,367	8,962	14,847	12,085	8,015	
7		Midwest	7,397	7,811	10,292	7,776	14,805	8,777	14,480	
8		Southwest	7,735	11,352	7,222	11,412	14,948	10,686	14,741	
9		Mountain West	9,721	8,404	11,944	8,162	14,531	11,348	8,559	
10		Northwest	9,240	10,995	7,836	9,702	9,265	14,240	9,798	
11		Central	11,810	13,625	8,921	13,593	11,042	10,223	13,338	
12										

HourlySales

Ready   Average: 14,317   Count: 63   Sum: 901,946

The status bar displays summary values when you select more than one cell that contains numeric data

AutoCalculate is great for finding a quick total or average for filtered cells, but it doesn't enter the result into the worksheet for you. Formulas such as =SUM(C3:C26) always consider every cell in the range, regardless of whether a row is hidden. To calculate the sum of only the visible values, use either the SUBTOTAL function or the AGGREGATE function. The SUBTOTAL function lets you choose whether to summarize every value in a range or only those values in visible rows. When creating a formula that uses the SUBTOTAL function, you must enter the number of the operation you want to perform.

> ⚠ **IMPORTANT** Be sure to place your SUBTOTAL formula in a row that is even with or above the headers in the range you're filtering. If you don't, your filter might hide the formula's result!

The following table lists the summary operations available for the SUBTOTAL formula. Excel displays the available summary operations as part of the Formula AutoComplete functionality, so you don't need to remember the operation numbers or look them up in the Help system.

All values	Visible values	Function	Description
1	101	AVERAGE	Returns the average of the values in the range
2	102	COUNT	Counts the cells in the range that contain a number
3	103	COUNTA	Counts the nonblank cells in the range
4	104	MAX	Returns the largest (maximum) value in the range
5	105	MIN	Returns the smallest (minimum) value in the range
6	106	PRODUCT	Returns the result of multiplying all numbers in the range
7	107	STDEV.S	Calculates the standard deviation of values in the range by examining a sample of the values
8	108	STDEV.P	Calculates the standard deviation of the values in the range by using all the values
9	109	SUM	Returns the result of adding together all numbers in the range
10	110	VAR.S	Calculates the variance of values in the range by examining a sample of the values
11	111	VAR.P	Calculates the variance of the values in the range by using all the values

7

As the preceding table shows, the SUBTOTAL function has two sets of operations. The first set (operations 1–11) represents operations that include hidden values in their summary, and the second set (operations 101–111) represents operations that summarize only values visible in the worksheet. Operations 1–11 summarize all cells in a range, regardless of whether the range contains any manually hidden rows. By contrast, operations 101–111 ignore any values in manually hidden rows. What the SUBTOTAL function doesn't do, however, is change its result to reflect rows hidden by using a filter.

> ⚠ **IMPORTANT** Excel treats the first cell in the data range as a header cell, so it doesn't consider the cell as it builds the list of unique values. Be sure to include the header cell in your data range!

The AGGREGATE function extends the capabilities of the SUBTOTAL function. With it, you can select from a broader range of functions and use another argument to determine which, if any, values to ignore in the calculation. AGGREGATE has two possible syntaxes, depending on the summary operation you select. The first syntax is =AGGREGATE(*function_num*, *options*, *ref1*...), which is similar to the syntax of the SUBTOTAL function. The other possible syntax, =AGGREGATE(*function_num*, *options*, *array*, [*k*]), is used to create AGGREGATE functions that use the LARGE, SMALL, PERCENTILE.INC, QUARTILE.INC, PERCENTILE.EXC, and QUARTILE.EXC operations.

The following table describes the functions available for use in the AGGREGATE function and notes their function numbers.

Number	Function	Description
1	AVERAGE	Returns the average of the values in the range.
2	COUNT	Returns the number of cells in the range that contain numbers.
3	COUNTA	Returns the number of cells in the range that aren't empty.
4	MAX	Returns the largest (maximum) value in the range.
5	MIN	Returns the smallest (minimum) value in the range.
6	PRODUCT	Returns the result of multiplying all numbers in the range.
7	STDEV.S	Calculates the standard deviation of values in the range by examining a sample of the values.
8	STDEV.P	Calculates the standard deviation of the values in the range by using all the values.
9	SUM	Returns the result of adding together all numbers in the range.
10	VAR.S	Calculates the variance of values in the range by examining a sample of the values.
11	VAR.P	Calculates the variance of the values in the range by using all the values.
12	MEDIAN	Returns the value in the middle of a group of values.
13	MODE.SNGL	Returns the most frequently occurring number in the range.

Number	Function	Description
14	LARGE	Returns the kth largest value in a data set. k is specified by using the last function argument. If k is left blank, Excel returns the largest value.
15	SMALL	Returns the kth smallest value in a data set. k is specified by using the last function argument. If k is left blank, Excel returns the smallest value.
16	PERCENTILE.INC	Returns the kth percentile of values in a range, where k is a value from 0 to 1 (inclusive).
17	QUARTILE.INC	Returns the quartile value of a range, based on a percentage from 0 to 1 (inclusive).
18	PERCENTILE.EXC	Returns the kth percentile of values in a range, where k is a value from 0 to 1 (exclusive).
19	QUARTILE.EXC	Returns the quartile value of a range, based on a percentage from 0 to 1 (exclusive).

You use the second argument, *options*, to select which items the AGGREGATE function should ignore. These items can include hidden rows, errors, and SUBTOTAL and AGGREGATE functions. The following table summarizes the values available for the *options* argument and the effect they have on the function's results.

Option	Description
0	Ignore nested SUBTOTAL and AGGREGATE functions.
1	Ignore hidden rows and nested SUBTOTAL and AGGREGATE functions.
2	Ignore error values and nested SUBTOTAL and AGGREGATE functions.
3	Ignore hidden rows, error values, and nested SUBTOTAL and AGGREGATE functions.
4	Ignore nothing.
5	Ignore hidden rows.
6	Ignore error values.
7	Ignore hidden rows and error values.

To summarize values by using AutoCalculate

- Select the cells you want to summarize to display the calculations on the status bar.

To change the AutoCalculate summaries displayed on the status bar

1. Right-click a blank area of the status bar to display the Customize Status Bar context menu. The calculation options are near the bottom of the menu.

> **TIP** To display a context menu, right-click or long-press (tap and hold) the element.

> **TIP** If you're running Excel on a computer with a low screen resolution, it might be necessary to scroll the menu to see all the options.

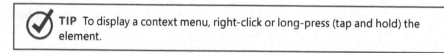

✓	Page Number	
✓	Average	14,317
✓	Count	63
	Numerical Count	
	Minimum	
	Maximum	
✓	Sum	901,946
✓	Upload Status	
✓	View Shortcuts	
✓	Zoom Slider	
✓	Zoom	100%

———— Calculation options

A check mark preceding a calculation indicates that it appears on the status bar

2. Select any calculation option to turn it on or off.

Randomly select list rows

Excel has a function that can randomly choose rows (records) from a data range or table instead of filtering by specific criteria. This is useful for choosing which customers will receive a special offer, deciding which days of the month to audit, or picking prize winners at an employee party.

To choose rows randomly, you use the RAND function—which generates a random decimal value between 0 and 1—and compare the value it returns with a test value included in a formula.

To use RAND to select a row, create an IF formula that tests the random values. If you want to check 30 percent of the rows, a formula such as =IF(cell_address<0.3, "TRUE", "FALSE") would display TRUE in the formula cells for any value of 0.3 or less and FALSE otherwise.

Because the RAND function is a *volatile function* that recalculates its results every time you update the worksheet, when you're ready to freeze the selection, you should copy the cells that use the RAND function and then paste the formula values (instead of the formula) back into the cells.

TIP The RANDBETWEEN function generates a random whole number within a defined range. For example, the formula =RANDBETWEEN(1,100) generates a random integer value in the range from 1 to 100 (inclusive). This function is very useful for creating sample data collections.

7

To create a SUBTOTAL formula

- Use the syntax =SUBTOTAL(*function_num, ref1, ref2, ...*) where:

  - *function_num* is the reference number of the function you want to use.

  - *ref1, ref2*, and subsequent *ref* arguments refer to cell ranges.

To create an AGGREGATE formula

- Use the syntax =AGGREGATE(*function_num, options, ref1...*) where:

  - *function_num* is the reference number of the function you want to use.

  - *ref1, ref2*, and subsequent *ref* arguments refer to cell ranges.

- Use the syntax =AGGREGATE(*function_num*, *options*, *array*, [*k*]) where:

  - *function_num* is the reference number of the function you want to use.

  - *options* is the reference number of the options you want to use.

  - *array* is the cell range that provides data for the formula.

  - The optional *k* argument, used with LARGE, SMALL, PERCENTILE.INC, QUARTILE.INC, PERCENTILE.EXC, or QUARTILE.EXC, indicates which value, percentile, or quartile to return.

Enforce data entry criteria

When multiple people will enter information into a worksheet, you can help ensure the accuracy of the information by creating *validation rules* that govern the information that specific cells can contain. Excel doesn't allow the entry of data that doesn't meet the criteria you define

Data-validation rules ensure that users can enter only data that meets your requirements

Data validation includes three components:

- **Validation criteria** The type of data, the range of acceptable values, and whether blank cells are allowed

- **Input message** An optional message that appears when a workbook user selects the cell

- **Error alert** An optional message that appears when a workbook user enters data that doesn't conform to the validation criteria

The following table describes the validation criteria you can configure.

Type	Criteria
Whole number	Between minimum and maximum values
Decimal	Not between minimum and maximum values
Date	Equal to a specific value
Time	Not equal to a specific value
Text length	Greater than a minimum value
	Greater than or equal to a minimum value
	Less than a maximum value
	Less than or equal to a maximum value
List	You specify the list of acceptable text or numeric entries, which can optionally be displayed as an in-cell list.
Custom	You specify a formula.

When you restrict the data that can be entered into a cell, it's nice to include an input message that lets people know what the validation criteria are so they don't become frustrated. The input message appears in a small yellow box adjacent to the cell when it is selected. The message can include a bold title or only the message.

If someone tries to enter invalid data, Excel displays a standard warning message that the value doesn't match the data-validation restrictions for the cell. You can replace the standard message with a custom error alert that displays a Stop, Warning, or Information icon and provides additional information. A Warning alert gives the user the choice to complete the entry. Stop and Information alerts only allow the user to return to the cell.

When you apply validation restrictions to cells that already contain data, Excel doesn't automatically notify you if the existing data conforms to the validation restrictions. You can find out by having Excel circle any cells that contain invalid data. If you want to retain the data that violates the restrictions, you can turn off data validation for those cells.

	A	B	C	D	E	F	G
1	CustomerName	Address	City	State	PostalCode	CreditLimit	
2	Adventure Works Cycles	1 Wheel Way	San Francisco	CA	31975	$ 12,000.00	
3	Contoso Suites	1 Contoso Way	Seattle	WA	12345	$ 26,000.00	
4	Fabrikam, Inc.	1 Fabrikam Circle	San Diego	CA	32165	$ 7,500.00	
5	Graphic Design Institute	1 Artistry Plaza	Portland	OR	24680	$ 18,000.00	
6	Lamna Healthcare Company	1 Lamna Court	Vancouver	WA	14703	$ 6,000.00	
7	Northwind Traders	1 Gale Street	Spokane	WA	13579	$ 15,000.00	

Validation circles flag data that violates data-validation rules

To limit data to a range of values or lengths

1. Select the cells to which you want to apply the validation rule.

2. On the **Data** tab, in the **Data Tools** group, select **Data Validation**.

3. In the **Data Validation** dialog, on the **Settings** tab, select the **Allow** arrow, and then select **Whole number**, **Decimal**, **Date**, **Time**, or **Text length**.

4. Define the criteria in the list(s) specific to the rule.

5. If you want to require that users enter a value in the cell, clear the **Ignore blank** checkbox. (This option is selected by default to allow users to navigate away from the cell without entering a value.)

Defining a rule to permit only whole numbers within a specific range

6. If you want to, create an input message and/or error alert.

7. Select **OK** to implement the data-validation rule.

To limit data to a specific list

1. On any worksheet in the workbook, create the list of acceptable entries, with one entry in each cell of a column.

	A	B
1	Meal Options	
2	Beef	
3	Chicken	
4	Fish	
5	Vegan	
6	Vegetarian	
7		

A column heading is optional

2. Select the cells to which you want to apply the validation rule.

3. On the **Data** tab, in the **Data Tools** group, select **Data Validation**.

4. In the **Data Validation** dialog, on the **Settings** tab, select the **Allow** arrow, and then select **List**.

5. In the **Source** box, do either of the following:

   - Enter the cell range (and worksheet, if other than the one you're on).

   - Select the **Collapse** button (the upward-pointing arrow) to hide the rest of the dialog, and then select the list of acceptable entries. (If the list has a heading, don't select the heading.) Excel will enter the cell reference into the box. Then select the **Expand** button (the downward-pointing arrow) to return to the full dialog.

The list can be on any worksheet, even a hidden one

7

6. If you don't want the list to be available within the cells, clear the **In-cell drop-down** checkbox.

7. If you want to require users to enter a value in the cell, clear the **Ignore blank** checkbox.

8. If you want to, create an input message and/or error alert.

9. Select **OK** to implement the data-validation rule.

To display a message when a user selects the cell

1. In the **Data Validation** dialog, on the **Input Message** tab, ensure that the **Show input message when cell is selected** checkbox is selected.

2. In the **Title** box, enter any text you want to appear in bold at the top of the message.

3. In the **Input message** box, enter the message text.

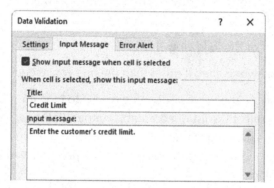

The input message can be up to 255 characters

 TIP The on-screen input message box has a fixed width and dynamic length. Shorter words will fill the message box more neatly.

4. Select **OK** to implement the input message.

To configure an error alert

1. In the **Data Validation** dialog, on the **Error Alert** tab, ensure that the **Show error alert after invalid data is entered** checkbox is selected.

2. In the **Style** list, select one of the following:

    *   **Stop** to display a stop icon in the alert box and prevent the data entry.

    *   **Warning** to require the user to confirm that they want to enter the data.

    *   **Information** to display an information icon in the alert box and prevent the data entry.

3. In the **Title** box, enter the text you want to appear in the alert box title bar.

4. In the **Error message** box, enter the alert text, and then select **OK** to implement the error alert.

7

The error alert can be up to 224 characters

To edit a validation rule

1. Select one or more cells that contain the validation rule.

2. On the **Data** tab, in the **Data Tools** group, select **Data Validation**.

3. On the **Settings** tab, do either of the following:

    *   To implement the change for all cells in the data-validation range, select the **Apply these changes to all other cells with the same settings** checkbox.

    *   To change the data-validation rule in only the selected cells, clear the **Apply these changes to all other cells with the same settings** checkbox.

4. Use the controls in the dialog to edit the rule, input message, and error alert.

5. Select **OK**.

To circle invalid data in a worksheet

- On the **Data** tab, in the **Data Tools** group, select the **Data Validation** arrow, and then select **Circle Invalid Data**.

To remove validation circles

- On the **Data** tab, in the **Data Tools** group, select the **Data Validation** arrow, and then select **Clear Validation Circles**.

Key points

- You can easily filter a data range or table to display only rows that meet specific criteria such as value, cell color, or font color. When filtering by value, you can specify part of or all the data you want to match, or a range of values. Before filtering data, ensure that each column of the data range or table has a heading.

- The Excel status bar displays simple statistics—the sum, average, and count—of filtered data. To perform more-complex calculations that include only filter results, you can use the SUBTOTAL or AGGREGATE function.

- Validation rules help to guide worksheet users in entering the correct types of data in specific cells. You can create validation rules that limit the data to a range of acceptable values or to a specific list of entries. You can optionally display an input message when a user selects a cell and an error alert when a user enters data that doesn't meet the validation rule.

> **SEE ALSO** This chapter is from the full-length book *Microsoft Excel Step by Step (Office 2021 and Microsoft 365)* (Microsoft Press, 2021). Please consult that book for information about features of Excel that aren't discussed in this book.

Practice tasks

Before you can complete these tasks, you must copy the book's practice files to your computer. The practice files for these tasks are in the **Office365SBS\Ch07** folder. You can save the results of the tasks in the same folder.

The introduction includes a complete list of practice files and download instructions.

Filter data ranges and tables

Open the **FilterData** workbook in Excel, and then perform the following tasks:

1. Create a filter that displays only those package exceptions that happened on *RT189*.

2. Clear the previous filter, and then create a filter that shows exceptions for the *Northeast* and *Northwest* centers.

3. With the filter still in place, create a second filter that displays only those exceptions that occurred in the month of April.

4. Clear the filter that shows values related to the *Northeast* and *Northwest* centers.

5. Turn off filtering for the list of data.

Summarize filtered data

Open the **SummarizeValues** workbook in Excel, and then perform the following tasks:

1. Combine the IF and RAND functions into formulas in cells **H3:H27** that display TRUE if the value is less than 0.3 and FALSE otherwise.

2. Use AutoCalculate to find the SUM, AVERAGE, and COUNT of cells **G12:G16**.

3. Remove the COUNT summary from the status bar and add the MINIMUM summary.

4. Create a SUBTOTAL formula that finds the average of the values in cells **G3:G27**.

5. Create an AGGREGATE formula that finds the maximum of values in cells **G3:G27**.

6. Create an advanced filter that finds the unique values in cells **F3:F27**.

Enforce data entry criteria

Open the **ValidateData** workbook in Excel, and then perform the following tasks:

1. Create a data-validation rule in cells **J4:J9** that requires values entered into those cells to be no greater than $25,000.

2. Attempt to type the value 30000 in cell **J7**, observe the message that appears, and then cancel data entry.

3. Edit the rule you created so it includes an input message and an error alert.

4. Display validation circles to highlight data that violates the rule you created, and then hide the circles.

Reorder and summarize data

One of the most important uses of business information is to keep a record of when something happens. Whether you ship a package to a client or pay a supplier, tracking when you took those actions, and in what order, helps you analyze your performance. Sorting your information based on the values in one or more columns helps you discover useful trends, such as whether your sales are generally increasing or decreasing, whether you do more business on specific days of the week, or whether you sell products to lots of customers from certain regions of the world.

Excel includes capabilities you might expect to find only in a database program: the ability to organize your data into levels of detail you can show or hide and formulas that let you look up values in a list of data. Organizing data by detail level lets you focus on specific aspects of the data, and looking up values in a worksheet helps you find specific data. If a customer calls to ask about an order, you can use the order number or customer number to discover the information that customer needs.

This chapter guides you through procedures related to sorting your data by using one or more criteria, sorting data against custom lists, outlining data, and calculating subtotals.

In this chapter

- Sort worksheet data
- Sort data by using custom lists
- Outline and subtotal data

Sort worksheet data

Although Excel makes it easy to enter your business data and to manage it after you've saved it in a worksheet, unsorted data will rarely answer every question you want to ask. For example, you might want to discover which of your services generates the most profits or which service costs the most for you to provide. You can discover that information by sorting your data.

When you sort data in a worksheet, you rearrange the rows that contain the data based on the contents of cells in a specific column or set of columns. The first step in sorting a range of data is to identify the column or columns that contain the values by which you want to sort. You can sort by as many of the columns as you want to.

	A	B	C
1	**Customer**	**Service**	**Revenue**
2	Contoso	2-Day	$ 246,811
3	Fabrikam	2-Day	$1,152,558
4	Tailspin Toys	2-Day	$ 851,922
5	Contoso	3-Day	$ 318,710
6	Fabrikam	3-Day	$ 658,371
7	Tailspin Toys	3-Day	$1,026,163
8	Contoso	Ground	$ 941,717
9	Fabrikam	Ground	$ 964,280
10	Tailspin Toys	Ground	$1,147,078
11	Contoso	Overnight	$ 675,122
12	Fabrikam	Overnight	$ 801,656
13	Tailspin Toys	Overnight	$ 35,456
14	Contoso	Priority Overnight	$ 955,755
15	Fabrikam	Priority Overnight	$ 175,699
16	Tailspin Toys	Priority Overnight	$ 161,061

A data range sorted by Service and then Customer

If you want to sort data by only one column that contains words, numbers, or dates, you can quickly do so from the Home tab of the ribbon.

A simple sort from the ribbon

The options on the Sort & Filter menu vary depending on whether you're sorting a column of words, numbers, or dates. Excel sorts words from A to Z or Z to A, numbers from smallest to largest or largest to smallest, and dates from newest to oldest or oldest to newest.

You perform multiple-column sort operations from the Sort dialog, in which you can specify the columns to sort by, the order in which to sort each column, and the order in which to perform the sort operations. When creating similar rules, you can save time by copying one rule and changing only the field name.

If cell values within the data range have font or fill colors applied to them, either manually or though conditional formatting, you can sort the data to place a specific color at the beginning or end of the column.

Sort by multiple columns and properties

You can easily change the order in which rules are applied, as well as edit and delete rules, in the Sort dialog.

To display the Sort & Filter menu

- On the **Home** tab, in the **Editing** group, select **Sort & Filter**.

To sort a data range alphanumerically by a single column

1. Select a cell in the column by which you want to sort the data range.

2. Display the **Sort & Filter** menu.

3. Do either of the following:

   - Select **Sort A to Z**, **Sort Smallest to Largest**, or **Sort Oldest to Newest** to sort the data in ascending order.

   - Select **Sort Z to A**, **Sort Largest to Smallest**, or **Sort Newest to Oldest** to sort the data in descending order.

Or

1. Select the data range you want to sort or a cell in the range.

2. Display the **Sort & Filter** menu and then select **Custom Sort**.

3. If appropriate, select the **My data has headers** checkbox.

4. In the **Sort by** list, select the field by which you want to sort.

5. In the **Sort On** list, select **Cell Values**.

6. In the **Order** list, do either of the following:

   - Select **A to Z** or **Smallest to Largest** to sort the data in ascending order.

   - Select **Z to A** or **Largest to Smallest** to sort the data in descending order.

To sort a data range by cell color, font color, or icon

1. Select the data range you want to sort or a cell in the range.

2. Display the **Sort & Filter** menu, and then select **Custom Sort**.

3. If appropriate, select the **My data has headers** checkbox.

4. In the **Sort by** list, select the field by which you want to sort.

5. In the **Sort On** list, select **Cell Color**, **Font Color**, or **Conditional Formatting Icon**.

6. In the **Order** list, select the cell or font color or icon that you want to isolate. Then, in the last list box, do either of the following:

   - Select **On Top** to sort that color or icon to the beginning of the list.

   - Select **On Bottom** to sort that color or icon to the end of the list.

Sort lists of data using cell fill color as a criterion

7. Select **OK** to sort the values.

Or

1. In the data range, right-click the cell that has the color or icon you want to isolate, and then on the context menu, select **Sort**.

> **TIP** To display a context menu, right-click or long-press (tap and hold) the element.

2. On the **Sort** submenu, select **Put Selected *Attribute* On Top**.

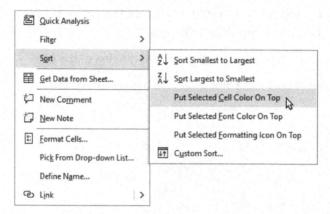

Sort by multiple columns and properties

To sort a data range based on values in multiple columns

1. Select the data range you want to sort or a cell in the range.

2. On the **Home** tab, in the **Editing** group, select **Sort & Filter**.

3. On the **Sort & Filter** menu, select **Custom Sort**.

4. If appropriate, select the **My data has headers** checkbox.

5. In the **Sort by** list, select the first field by which you want to sort.

6. In the **Sort On** list, select the option by which you want to sort the data (**Cell Values**, **Cell Color**, **Font Color**, or **Conditional Formatting Icon**).

Create sorting rules in the Sort dialog

7. In the **Order** list, select an order for the sort operation.

8. For each additional column by which you want to sort, do the following:

   a. Select **Add Level**.

   b. In the **Then by** list, select the column.

   c. Select values in the **Sort On** and **Order** lists.

9. Select **OK** to sort the values.

	A	B	C
1	**Customer**	**Season**	**Revenue**
2	Contoso	Summer	$114,452.00
3	Contoso	Fall	$118,299.00
4	Contoso	Winter	$183,651.00
5	Contoso	Spring	$201,438.00
6	Fabrikam	Winter	$100,508.00
7	Fabrikam	Spring	$139,170.00
8	Fabrikam	Summer	$183,632.00
9	Fabrikam	Fall	$255,599.00
10	Northwind Traders	Spring	$120,666.00
11	Northwind Traders	Summer	$129,732.00
12	Northwind Traders	Winter	$174,336.00
13	Northwind Traders	Fall	$188,851.00

A data range sorted by Customer and then by Revenue

To copy a sorting level

1. In the **Sort** dialog, select the sorting level you want to copy.

2. Select the **Copy Level** button.

To move a sorting rule up or down in priority

1. In the **Sort** dialog, select the sorting rule you want to move.

2. Do either of the following:

   • Select the **Move Up** (^) button to move the rule earlier in the order.

   • Select the **Move Down** (v) button to move the rule later in the order.

To delete a sorting rule

1. In the **Sort** dialog, select the sorting level you want to delete.

2. Select **Delete Level**.

Sort data by using custom lists

By default, Excel sorts words in alphabetical order and numbers in numeric order. But that pattern doesn't work for some sets of values. For example, if you're sorting a series of months, alphabetical order begins with April and ends with September.

Fortunately, Excel recognizes days of the week and months of the year as special lists that it uses for sorting and when filling series. You can add custom series to Excel for the same purposes, either by entering the list values or copying them from a worksheet.

To define a custom list by entering its values

1. Display the **Advanced** page of the **Excel Options** dialog.

2. Scroll to the **General** section, and then select **Edit Custom Lists**.

3. In the **Custom Lists** dialog, with *NEW LIST* active, activate the **List entries** box.

4. Enter the custom list items in order, pressing **Enter** between items.

Manage lists in the Custom Lists dialog

5. After you enter all the list items, select **Add** to move them to the Custom Lists pane.

6. Select **OK**, and then select **OK** again to close the **Excel Options** dialog.

To define a custom list by copying values from a worksheet

1. Enter the custom list values in a column, in the correct sort order (first to last, from top to bottom), and then select the cells that contain the list values.

2. Open the **Custom Lists** dialog.

3. Verify that the **Import list from cells** box contains the correct cells, and then select **Import**.

Sort and fill series from any list

4. Select **OK**, and then select **OK** again to close the **Excel Options** dialog.

To sort worksheet data by using a custom list

1. Select a cell in the list of data you want to sort.

2. On the **Home** tab, select the **Sort & Filter** button, and then select **Custom Sort**.

3. If necessary, select the **My data has headers** checkbox.

4. In the **Sort by** list, select the field that contains the data by which you want to sort.

5. If necessary, in the **Sort On** list, select **Values**.

6. In the **Order** list, select **Custom List**.

7. In the **Custom Lists** dialog, select the list you want to use. Then select **OK**.

8. In the **Sort** dialog, select **OK** to close the dialog and sort the data.

Outline and subtotal data

When your data range is sorted into the order you want, you can use the Subtotal feature to have Excel outline the data by specific categories and summarize the categories. The available summary functions are SUM, COUNT, AVERAGE, MAX, MIN, PRODUCT, COUNT NUMBERS, STDDEV, STDDEVP, VAR, and VARP.

> ⚠️ **IMPORTANT** You can outline, group, and summarize data ranges by using the SUBTOTAL feature; it does not work on data in Excel tables. To subtotal table data, you must first convert it to a range.

In a subtotal operation, you choose the column by which to group the data, the summary calculation you want to perform, and the values to be summarized. After you define the subtotals, Excel displays them in your worksheet.

	Year	Quarter	Month	Package Volume
1	**Year**	**Quarter**	**Month**	**Package Volume**
2	2019	1	January	5,213,292
3	2019	1	February	2,038,516
4	2019	1	March	2,489,601
5	2019	2	April	9,051,231
6	2019	2	May	5,225,156
7	2019	2	June	3,266,644
8	2019	3	July	2,078,794
9	2019	3	August	1,591,434
10	2019	3	September	8,518,985
11	2019	4	October	1,973,050
12	2019	4	November	7,599,195
13	2019	4	December	9,757,876
14	**2019 Total**			58,803,774
15	2020	1	January	5,304,039
16	2020	1	February	5,465,096

A data range with subtotal outlining applied

Excel also defines groups based on the subtotal calculation. The groups form an out-line of the data based on the criteria you used to create the subtotals. For example, all the rows representing months in the year 2019 could be in one group, rows represent-ing months in 2020 in another, and so on. You can use the controls in the outline area on the left side of the worksheet to hide or display groups of data.

	Year	Quarter	Month	Package Volume
1	**Year**	**Quarter**	**Month**	**Package Volume**
14	**2019 Total**			58,803,774
15	2020	1	January	5,304,039
16	2020	1	February	5,465,096
17	2020	1	March	1,007,799
18	2020	2	April	4,010,287
19	2020	2	May	4,817,070
20	2020	2	June	8,155,717
21	2020	3	July	6,552,370
22	2020	3	August	2,295,635
23	2020	3	September	7,115,883
24	2020	4	October	1,362,767
25	2020	4	November	8,935,488
26	2020	4	December	9,537,077
27	**2020 Total**			64,559,228
28	**Grand Total**			123,363,002

The data range with details for the year 2019 hidden

The numbers above the outline controls are the level buttons. Each represents a level of data organization. Selecting a level button hides all levels of detail below that of the button you selected.

8

The following table describes the data contained at each level of a worksheet with three levels of organization.

Level	Description
1	Grand total
2	Subtotals for each group
3	Individual rows in the worksheet

	A	B	C	D
1	Year	Quarter	Month	Package Volume
14	2019 Total			58,803,774
27	2020 Total			64,559,228
28	Grand Total			123,363,002

The data range with details hidden at level 2

You can add custom levels of detail to the outline that Excel creates by grouping specific rows. (For example, you can hide revenues from specific months.) You can also delete groups you don't need and remove the subtotals and outlining entirely.

To organize data into levels

1. Sort the data range, ensuring that the top-level sort is on the column by which you want to group the data.

2. Select the data range you want to sort or a cell in the range.

3. On the **Data** tab, in the **Outline** group, select the **Subtotal** button.

4. In the **Subtotal** dialog, in the **At each change in** list, select the field by which you want to group the data.

> ⚠ **IMPORTANT** You must first sort the data by the field that you plan to summarize by selecting the Subtotal button.

5. In the **Use function** list, select the summary function you want to use for each subtotal.

6. In the **Add subtotal to** group, select the checkbox next to any field you want to summarize. Then select **OK**.

Apply subtotals to data from the Subtotal dialog

To show or hide detail in an outlined range

- To hide or show one group, select its **Hide Detail** (+) or **Show Detail** (–) control.

- To hide or show one level, select the level button.

To create a custom group in an outlined range

1. Select the rows you want to include in the group.

2. On the **Data** tab, in the **Outline** group, select the **Group** button (not the arrow).

	Year	Quarter	Month	Package Volume
1	**Year**	**Quarter**	**Month**	**Package Volume**
2	2019	1	January	5,213,292
3	2019	1	February	2,038,516
4	2019	1	March	2,489,601
5	2019	2	April	9,051,231

A custom group within an outline

To remove a custom group from an outlined range

1. Select the rows you want to remove from the group.

2. On the **Data** tab, in the **Outline** group, select the **Ungroup** button (not the arrow).

To remove subtotals from a data range

1. Select any cell in the range.

2. On the **Data** tab, in the **Outline** group, select **Subtotal**.

3. In the **Subtotal** dialog, select **Remove All**.

Key points

- You can sort the data in a range or table by the values in one or multiple columns. Excel discerns the basic sort order (A to Z, small to large, old to new) based on the data in the column. You can also sort data to bring a single cell color, font color, or icon to the top.

- If the default sort orders don't meet your needs, you can provide Excel with a list by which it should sort. Custom lists with the days of the week and months of the year in order of occurrence are built in to Excel, but you can make up your own.

- You can outline, group, and subtotal data by using the Subtotal feature (which is different from the SUBTOTAL function). To successfully subtotal data, you must first sort it by the column that will define the data groups.

> **SEE ALSO** This chapter is from the full-length book *Microsoft Excel Step by Step (Office 2021 and Microsoft 365)* (Microsoft Press, 2021). Please consult that book for information about features of Excel that aren't discussed in this book.

Practice tasks

Before you can complete these tasks, you must copy the book's practice files to your computer. The practice files for these tasks are in the **Office365SBS\Ch08** folder. You can save the results of the tasks in the same folder.

The introduction includes a complete list of practice files and download instructions.

Sort worksheet data

Open the **SortData** workbook in Excel, and then perform the following tasks:

1. Sort the data in the cell range **B3:D14** in ascending order by the values in the Revenue column.

2. Sort the data range in descending order by the values in the Revenue column.

3. Perform a two-level sort of the data range:

   a. In ascending order by Customer.

   b. In ascending order by Season.

   Review the effect of the multiple-column sort. Be sure that you understand the effect of the sort operation order.

4. Reverse the order of the fields in the Sort dialog to sort first by Season and then by Customer.

5. Sort the data range by the Revenue column so that the cells that have a red fill color are at the top of the list.

6. Save and close the file.

Sort data by using custom lists

Open the **CustomSortData** workbook in Excel, and then perform the following tasks:

1. Create a custom list by using the values in cells **G4:G7**.

2. Sort the data in the cell range **B2:D14** by the Season column based on the custom list you just created.

Chapter 8

3. Perform a two-level sort of the data range:

   a. By Customer in ascending order.

   b. By Season in the custom list order.

4. Save and close the file.

Outline and subtotal data

Open the **OutlineData** workbook in Excel, and then perform the following tasks:

1. Outline the data list in cells **A1:D25** to find the subtotal for each year.

2. Hide the details of rows for the year 2020.

3. Create a new group consisting of the rows showing data for June and July 2019.

4. Hide the details of the group you just created.

5. Show the details of all months for the year 2020.

6. Remove the subtotal outline from the entire data list.

7. Save and close the file.

Analyze alternative data sets

9

When you store data in an Excel workbook, you can use that data, either by itself or as part of a calculation, to discover important information about your organization.

The data in your worksheets is great for answering "what-if" questions, such as "How much money would we save if we reduced our labor to 20 percent of our total costs?" You can always save an alternative version of a workbook and create formulas that calculate the effects of your changes, but you can do the same thing in your existing workbooks by defining one or more alternative data sets. You can also create a data table that calculates the effects of changing one or two variables in a formula, find the input values required to generate the result you want, and describe your data statistically.

This chapter guides you through procedures related to defining scenarios that result in alternative data sets, forecasting data by using data tables, and using Goal Seek to identify the input necessary to achieve a specific result.

In this chapter

- Define and display alternative data sets
- Forecast data by using data tables
- Identify the input necessary to achieve a specific result

Define and display alternative data sets

When you save data in an Excel worksheet, you create a record that reflects the characteristics of an event or object. For example, that data could represent the number of deliveries in an hour on a specific day, the price of a new delivery option, the percentage of total revenue accounted for by a delivery option—the possibilities are endless. After the data is in place, you can create formulas to generate totals, find averages, and sort the rows in a worksheet based on the contents of one or more columns. However, if you want to perform a what-if analysis or explore the impact that changes in the data would have on any of the calculations in your workbooks, you must change the data. By doing so, you run the risk of losing the original data. If you only want to make temporary changes for forecasting purposes, you can safely do so by applying a scenario—a set of alternative values—to the original data set to create an alternative data set.

A scenario changes data in specific cells

Applying a scenario creates an alternative data set by replacing the values in the original data set with the alternative values defined in the scenario and recalculating any formulas that depend on those values. After you apply the scenario, you can return to the original data set by undoing the scenario.

> ⚠ **IMPORTANT** It's important to revert to the original data set before you save and close the workbook, because the original data isn't stored anywhere. To avoid accidentally losing the original data, create a scenario that contains the original values or create a scenario summary.

Each scenario can change a maximum of 32 cells, so if you want to modify a lot of data, you will need to create multiple scenarios. You can create and apply as many scenarios as you want. (If multiple scenarios affect the same cell, the cell displays the value created by the most recently applied scenario.)

If you want to keep a record of the effect of various scenarios within a workbook, you can create a scenario summary worksheet that displays the effect of the scenarios on specific cells.

	Current Values:	2022_RateIncreases	2022_VolumeForecast
Scenario Summary			
Changing Cells:			
$C$3	$ 8.15	$ 8.50	$ 8.15
$C$4	$ 10.25	$ 10.50	$ 10.25
$C$5	$ 12.35	$ 12.35	$ 12.35
$C$6	$ 17.50	$ 17.50	$ 17.50
$C$7	$ 24.75	$ 24.75	$ 24.75
$D$3	14,000,000	14,000,000	14,000,000
$D$4	9,000,000	9,000,000	9,000,000
$D$5	9,000,000	9,000,000	9,000,000
$D$6	23,000,000	23,000,000	23,000,000
$D$7	800,000	800,000	800,000
Result Cells:			
$E$3	$ 114,100,000.00	$ 119,000,000.00	$ 114,100,000.00
$E$4	$ 92,250,000.00	$ 94,500,000.00	$ 92,250,000.00
$E$5	$ 111,150,000.00	$ 111,150,000.00	$ 111,150,000.00
$E$6	$ 402,500,000.00	$ 402,500,000.00	$ 402,500,000.00
$E$7	$ 19,800,000.00	$ 19,800,000.00	$ 19,800,000.00
$E$8	$ 739,800,000.00	$ 746,950,000.00	$ 739,800,000.00

Notes: Current Values column represents values of changing cells at time Scenario Summary Report was created. Changing cells for each scenario are highlighted in gray.

A scenario summary worksheet tracks the effects of all scenarios

As with other Excel tools, you can edit and delete the scenarios you create. Deleting a scenario does not undo the effects of the scenario on the worksheet data; it only removes the scenario from the Scenario Manager dialog.

To open the Scenario Manager dialog

- On the **Data** tab, in the **Forecast** group, select **What-If Analysis**, and then select **Scenario Manager**.

Manage and summarize scenarios

To define a scenario

1. Open the **Scenario Manager** dialog.

2. Select **Add**.

3. In the **Add Scenario** dialog, enter a name for the scenario in the **Scenario name** box.

4. Do either of the following:

   - In the **Changing cells** box, enter the cell references of the cell values you want to change.

   - Activate the **Changing cells** box and then, on the worksheet, select the cells in which you want to change the values.

   > **TIP** When you select the cells on the worksheet, the dialog name changes from Add Scenario to Edit Scenario.

5. In the **Comment** box that contains your name and the date, append any notes that you might find useful later.

6. In the **Add Scenario** dialog, select **OK**.

7. In the **Scenario Values** dialog, replace the original values of each of the changing cells, and then select **OK**.

Scenario Values	? ✕
Enter values for each of the changing cells.	
1: $C$3	8.15
2: $C$4	10.25
3: $C$5	12.35
4: $C$6	17.5
5: $C$7	24.75
Add	OK Cancel

Enter alternative data in the Scenario Values dialog

To display an alternative data set

1. In the **Scenario Manager** dialog, select the scenario you want to apply, and then select **Show**.

2. To apply additional scenarios, repeat step 1.

To revert to the original data set

- Close the **Scenario Manager** dialog, and then do either of the following:

  - On the Quick Access Toolbar, select the **Undo** button.

  - Press **Ctrl+Z**.

To edit a scenario

1. In the **Scenario Manager** dialog, select the scenario you want to edit, and then select **Edit**.

2. In the **Edit Scenario** dialog, change any values in the **Scenario name**, **Changing cells**, or **Comment** boxes, and then select **OK**.

3. In the **Scenario Values** dialog, modify the new values for the changing cells, and then select **OK**.

9

To delete a scenario

- In the **Scenario Manager** dialog, select the scenario you want to delete, and then select **Delete**.

To create a scenario summary worksheet

1. Revert any scenarios that have been applied to the original data set.

> ⚠ **IMPORTANT** Make sure there are no scenarios applied to the workbook when you create the summary worksheet. If a scenario is active, Excel will record the alternative data set as the original values, and the summary will be inaccurate.

2. In the **Scenario Manager** dialog, select **Summary**.

3. In the **Scenario Summary** dialog, select **Scenario summary**.

4. Do either of the following:

   - In the **Result cells** box, enter the cell references of the cell changes you want to summarize.

   - Activate the **Result cells** box and then, on the worksheet, select the cells whose changes you want to summarize.

Summarize scenarios by using the Scenario Summary dialog

5. In the **Scenario Summary** dialog, select **OK**.

Forecast data by using data tables

Data tables are another useful data-forecasting tool in Excel. They let you clearly see the result of applying different patterns to existing data

	A	B	C	D
1	Revenue Forecast			
2				
3	Factor	Current	Increase	Revenue
4	Year	2021		$ 2,102,600.70
5	Increase	0%	2%	$ 2,144,652.71
6	Package Count	237,582	5%	$ 2,207,730.74
7	Average Rate	$ 8.85	8%	$ 2,270,808.76

Projecting different rates of increase on the current data

A data table can forecast changes to either one or two formula inputs. These are called the *variables*. To create a data table with one variable, you arrange the formula inputs—including the changing value, the variable values, and a summary formula—on a worksheet, leaving an area for the data table in the lower-right corner of the cell range. The variable values can be in a column (as shown here) or in a row.

D4			fx	=(1+B5)*(B6*B7)
	A	B	C	D
1	Revenue Forecast			
2				
3	Factor	Current	Increase	Revenue
4	Year	2021		$ 2,102,600.70
5	Increase	0%	2%	
6	Package Count	237,582	5%	
7	Average Rate	$ 8.85	8%	

Excel substitutes the variables for the changing value

In the example shown above, the formula inputs are in B5:B7, with the changing value in B5, the variables in C5:C7, and the summary formula (shown in the formula bar) in cell D4. Excel builds the data table in D5:D7 to reflect the effect of the variables on the summary formula.

9

To create a two-variable data table, arrange the formula inputs, including the two changing values, in the same way as for the one-variable table. Place one set of variable values in a column and another in a row, again leaving an area for the data table in the lower-right corner. Place the summary formula at the junction of the column and the row.

D4			X ✓ fx	=((1+B5)*B7)*B6		
	A	B	C	D	E	F
1	Revenue Forecast					
2						
3	Factor	Current		Revenue		
4	Year	2021		$ 2,102,600.70	260,000	280,000
5	Increase	0%		2%	$2,347,020.00	$2,527,560.00
6	Package Count	237,582		5%	$2,416,050.00	$2,601,900.00
7	Average Rate	$ 8.85		8%	$2,485,080.00	$2,676,240.00
8				10%	$2,531,100.00	$2,725,800.00

Two-variable data tables generate multiple outcomes

In this example, the variables in D5:D8 represent the rate increase and the variables in E4:F4 represent the package count increase.

To create a one-variable data table

1. On a worksheet, enter the following information, and arrange it as shown and described above:

   - A summary formula

   - The input values for the summary formula

   - A column (or row) of alternative values for one of the input values

2. Select the cells representing the variables and the summary formula, and the cells in which the data table displaying the alternative formula results should appear.

	A	B	C	D
1	Revenue Forecast			
2				
3	Factor	Current	Increase	Revenue
4	Year	2021		$ 2,102,600.70
5	Increase	0%	2%	
6	Package Count	237,582	5%	
7	Average Rate	$ 8.85	8%	

Identify the input and output cells for the data table

3. On the **Data** tab, in the **Forecast** group, select **What-If Analysis**, and then select **Data Table**.

4. In the **Data Table** dialog, do either of the following:

   - If the variables are in a row, enter the cell reference of the changing value in the **Row input cell** box.

   - If the variables are in a column, enter the cell reference of the changing value in the **Column input cell** box.

| Data Table | ? | × |

Row input cell: _____ ↑
Column input cell: B5 ↑

OK   Cancel

Identify the changing value

5. Select **OK**.

To create a two-variable data table

1. On a worksheet, enter the following information, and arrange it as shown and described above:

   - A summary formula

   - The input values for the summary formula

   - A column of alternative values for one input value

   - A row of alternative values for another input value

2. Select the cells representing the variables and the summary formula, and the cells in which the data table displaying the alternative formula results should appear.

3. On the **What-If Analysis** menu, select **Data Table**.

4. In the **Data Table** dialog, in the **Row input cell** box, enter the cell reference of the cell whose alternative values are in a row.

5. In the **Column input cell** box, enter the cell reference of the cell whose alternative values are in a column.

9

Identify both changing values

6. Select **OK**.

Identify the input necessary to achieve a specific result

When you run an organization, you must track how every element performs, both in absolute terms and in relation to other parts of the organization. There are many ways to measure your operations, but one useful technique is to limit the percentage of total costs contributed by a specific item.

As an example, consider a worksheet that displays the actual costs and percentage of total costs for several production input values.

A worksheet that contains formulas that calculate the percentage of total costs for each of four categories

Under the current pricing structure, transportation represents 44.3 percent of the total cost of creating the product. If you want to get the transportation costs below 35 percent of the total, you can manually change the cost until you find the number you want. Alternatively, you can use Excel's Goal Seek feature to find the solution for you. You simply tell Goal Seek your target value for the cell and the value you want to change to get there.

	A	B	C	D	E	F	G	H
1						**Goal Seek**		? X
2			Facilities	Labor	Transportation			
3		Cost	$19,000,000	$18,000,382	$ 35,000,000	Set cell:	E4	⬆
4		Share	24.05%	22.79%	44.30%	To value:	35%	
5						By changing cell:	E3	⬆
6								
7						OK		Cancel
8								

Identify the cell that contains the formula you want to use to generate a target value

Goal Seek finds the closest solution it can without exceeding the target you set and provides a suggested value. You can accept the suggestion to replace the original value or reject it to revert to the original value.

	A	B	C	D	E	F	G	H	I
1						**Goal Seek Status**		? X	
2			Facilities	Labor	Transportation				
3		Cost	$19,000,000	$18,000,382	$ 23,642,114	Goal Seeking with Cell E4 found a solution.		Step	
4		Share	28.09%	26.61%	34.95%			Pause	
5						Target value: 0.35			
6						Current value: 34.95%			
7						OK		Cancel	
8									

A worksheet in which Goal Seek found a solution to a problem

9

To find a target value by using Goal Seek

1. On the **Data** tab, in the **Forecast** group, select **What-If Analysis**, and then select **Goal Seek**.

2. In the **Goal Seek** dialog, in the **Set cell** box, enter the cell whose value you want to change.

3. In the **To value** box, enter the target value for the cell.

4. In the **By changing cell** box, enter the cell that contains the value you want to vary to produce the result you want.

5. Select **OK**.

> ⚠ **IMPORTANT** Saving a workbook with the results of a Goal Seek calculation in place overwrites the original workbook values. Consider running Goal Seek calculations on copies of the original data or reverting calculations immediately so you don't accidentally save or autosave them.

Key points

- In the Scenario Manager, you can forecast the effect of changing data within a data range or table without actually making the changes and possibly losing track of your original data. You can save the results of various scenarios in a scenario summary worksheet.

- Another way to forecast data is in a data table, which shows the effect on a formula of changing either one or two variables.

- If you know the specific result that you need to achieve with a formula, you can use the Goal Seek feature to identify the necessary input values.

SEE ALSO This chapter is from the full-length book *Microsoft Excel Step by Step (Office 2021 and Microsoft 365)* (Microsoft Press, 2021). Please consult that book for information about features of Excel that aren't discussed in this book.

Practice tasks

Before you can complete these tasks, you must copy the book's practice files to your computer. The practice files for these tasks are in the **Office365SBS\Ch09** folder. You can save the results of the tasks in the same folder.

The introduction includes a complete list of practice files and download instructions.

Define and display alternative data sets

Open the **CreateScenarios** workbook in Excel, and then perform the following tasks:

1. Create a scenario named Overnight that changes the Base Rate value for Overnight and Priority Overnight packages (in cells C6 and C7) to $18.75 and $25.50.

2. Apply the Overnight scenario and note its effects on the data.

3. Press **Ctrl+Z** to revert to the original data.

4. Create a scenario named HighVolume that increases the number of Ground packages to 17,000,000 and 3-Day packages to 14,000,000.

5. Create a scenario named NewRates that increases the Ground rate to $9.45 and the 3-Day rate to $12.

6. Create a scenario summary worksheet that displays the effects of the three scenarios.

7. Apply the HighVolume scenario and note its effects on the data.

8. Apply the NewRates scenario and note the additional changes.

Forecast data by using data tables

Open the **DefineDataTables** workbook in Excel, and then perform the following tasks:

1. On the **RateIncreases** worksheet, select cells **C4:D7**.

2. Perform the steps to create a data table in cells D5:D7, entering B5 as the **Column input cell**. Review the resulting data.

3. On the **RateAndVolume** worksheet, select cells **D4:F8**.

4. Perform the steps to create a data table in cells E5:F8, entering **B6** as the **Row input cell** and **B5** as the **Column input cell**. Review the resulting data.

Identify the input necessary to achieve a specific result

Open the **PerformGoalSeekAnalysis** workbook in Excel, and then perform the following tasks:

1. Select cell **C4**.

2. Open the **Goal Seek** dialog.

3. Verify that **C4** appears in the **Set cell** box.

4. In the **To value** box, enter 20%.

5. In the **By changing cell** box, enter C3.

6. Select **OK**.

Part 4

PowerPoint

CHAPTER 10
Create and manage slides 291

CHAPTER 11
Insert and manage simple graphics 323

CHAPTER 12
Add sound and movement to slides. 361

Create and manage slides

Most newly created PowerPoint presentations contain only a title slide, to which you add more slides. You can create slides based on slide templates designed to hold specific types of content, or you can copy existing slides from other presentations.

You can change the appearance of a presentation or individual slides by applying a different theme or theme variant or by changing one or more slide backgrounds.

When the presentation you're developing includes a lot of slides, it can be useful to organize them into sections. Sections are not visible to the audience, but they make it easier to work with slide content in logical segments. A logical presentation and an overall consistent look, punctuated by variations that add weight exactly where it's needed, can enhance the likelihood that your intended audience will receive the message you want to convey.

This chapter guides you through procedures related to adding, copying, and importing slides; importing slide content; hiding and deleting slides; applying themes; changing slide backgrounds; dividing presentations into sections; and rearranging slides and sections.

> **✓ TIP** The content in this chapter is about slides rather than slide content. Chapter 11, "Insert and manage simple graphics" and Chapter 12, "Add sound and movement to slides" are about working with various types of slide content.

In this chapter

- Add and remove slides
- Apply themes
- Change slide backgrounds
- Divide presentations into sections
- Rearrange slides and sections

Add and remove slides

The appearance and structure of slides is defined by the slide layouts associated with the design template. Slide layouts define the elements on specific types of slides, such as:

- Slide backgrounds and incorporated graphics.

- Text box locations, sizes, and formats.

- Default paragraph and character formats for each text box location.

- Standard headers or footers.

> ✓ **TIP** Text boxes can contain static content that can't be changed by the presentation author (for example, a company logo), or they can serve as placeholders that define the default formatting of content entered within the text box.

A template could have only one slide layout, but most have unique slide layouts for slides that display the presentation title, section titles, various combinations of slide titles and content, and a blank slide that contains only the background. Each slide layout is named; the name suggests the primary application of the slide layout, but you aren't limited to that suggestion; you can enter any type of content in any slide layout and modify the layout of any slide. The slide layouts available in a presentation are displayed on the New Slide menu.

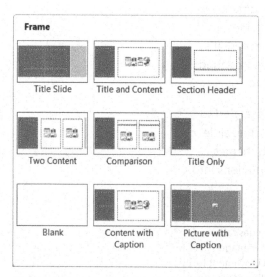

The New Slide menu displaying thumbnails of each available slide layout

You can modify the built-in slide layouts, create your own slide layouts, or create entirely new sets of slide layouts called *slide masters*, and you can reset slides to match their slide layouts or apply different slide layouts to existing slides.

Insert new slides

When you create a new slide, PowerPoint inserts it after the currently active slide. In a new presentation based on a standard PowerPoint template, a slide you add after the title slide has the Title And Content layout, and a slide added after a slide other than the title slide has the layout of the preceding slide.

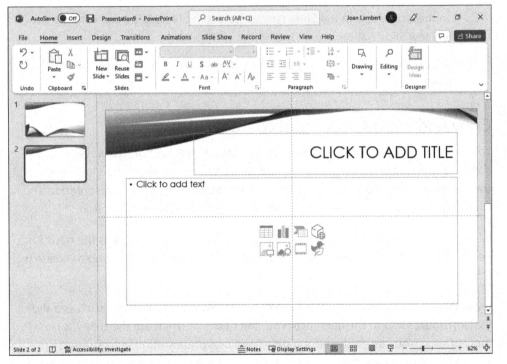

The Title And Content layout accommodates a title and either text or graphic content—a table, chart, diagram, picture, clip art image, or media clip

If you want to add a slide that has a different layout, you can select the layout when you insert the slide, or you can change the slide layout at any time after you create the slide.

10

To add a slide based on the default slide layout

1. Select the slide after which you want to add the new slide.

2. Do either of the following:

   - On the **Home** tab, in the **Slides** group, select the **New Slide** button (not its arrow).

   - Press **Ctrl+M**.

To add a slide based on any slide layout

1. Select the slide after which you want to add the new slide.

2. On the **Home** tab, in the **Slides** group, select the **New Slide** arrow to display the **New Slide** gallery and menu.

3. In the gallery, select a slide layout thumbnail to add a slide based on that slide layout.

Copy and import slides and content

You can reuse slides from one presentation in another, in one of two ways: you can copy the slides from the original presentation to the new presentation, or you can use the Reuse Slides tool, which displays the content of an original presentation and allows you to choose the slides you want to insert in the new presentation.

Within a presentation, you can duplicate an existing slide to reuse it as the basis for a new slide. You can then customize the duplicated slide instead of having to create it from scratch.

If you frequently include a certain type of slide in your presentations, such as a slide that introduces you to the audience, you don't have to re-create the slide for each presentation. You can easily reuse a slide from one presentation in a different presentation. (You can use the same techniques to reuse a slide from someone else's presentation to standardize the appearance or structure of slide content with other members of your organization.) Depending on the technique you use, the reused slide might automatically take on the destination theme.

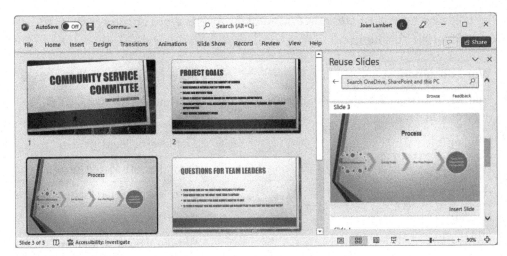

Reuse slides from existing presentations

If the content of your presentation exists in a document, you can configure that content in outline format and then import the outline into PowerPoint. For the import process to work smoothly, format as headings the document content that you want to import to the presentation. PowerPoint converts some styles into slide headings, converts some styles into bullet points, and ignores other styles.

10

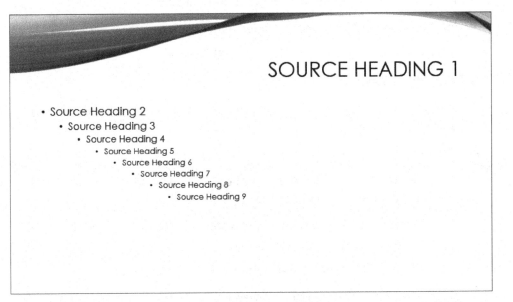

A slide created from an imported outline, showing document headings translated into PowerPoint content

The following table illustrates how PowerPoint converts Word document styles to PowerPoint slide elements.

Word document style	PowerPoint presentation style
Title, Subtitle, Heading 1, any bulleted list level, or any numbered list level	Slide title
Heading 2	First-level bulleted list item
Heading 3	Second-level bulleted list item
Heading 4	Third-level bulleted list item
Heading 5	Fourth-level bulleted list item
Heading 6	Fifth-level bulleted list item
Heading 7	Sixth-level bulleted list item
Heading 8	Seventh-level bulleted list item
Heading 9	Eighth-level bulleted list item

To select a single slide

- In Normal view, select the slide in the **Thumbnails** pane.

- In Outline view, select the slide header in the **Outline** pane.

- In Slide Sorter view, select the slide in the **Slide** pane.

To select multiple slides

1. In Normal view, Outline view, or Slide Sorter view, click the first slide you want to select.

2. Do either of the following:

   - To select a contiguous series of slides, press and hold the **Shift** key and then click the last slide you want to select.

   - To select noncontiguous slides, press and hold the **Ctrl** key and then click each additional slide you want to select.

To insert a copy of a slide immediately following the original slide

1. Display the presentation in Normal view.

2. In the **Thumbnails** pane, right-click or long-press (tap and hold) the slide that you want to copy, and then select **Duplicate Slide**.

To insert a copy of one or more slides anywhere in a presentation

1. Display the source and destination presentations in Normal view or Slide Sorter view.

2. Do either of the following:

   - Select the thumbnail or thumbnails of the slide or slides you want to copy, and then press **Ctrl+C** or, on the **Home** tab, in the **Clipboard** group, select the **Copy** button.

   - Right-click the thumbnail of the slide that you want to copy, and then select **Copy**.

3. Do either of the following:

   - Select the thumbnail that you want to insert the slide copy or copies after, or select the empty space after the thumbnail. Then press **Ctrl+V** or, on the **Home** tab, in the **Clipboard** group, select **Paste**.

   - Right-click after an existing thumbnail where you want to insert the slide copy or copies, and then, in the **Paste Options** section of the shortcut menu, select the **Use Destination Theme** button or the **Keep Source Formatting** button.

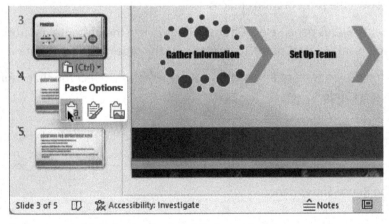

You can match the destination theme, retain the source theme, or paste as a picture

> ✓ **TIP** When PowerPoint displays the paste options, press **H** to use the destination style or **K** to use the source style.

To insert a slide from another presentation

1. Open the source and destination presentations in PowerPoint. Display each presentation in Normal view or Slide Sorter view.

2. Display the two PowerPoint windows side by side.

3. In the source presentation, select the slide or slides you want to copy.

4. Drag the selection to the destination presentation. A horizontal line between slide thumbnails in Normal view or a vertical line between thumbnails in Slide Sorter view indicates the location at which PowerPoint will insert the slides.

   PowerPoint creates copies of the slides and applies the destination theme to the copies.

Or

1. Display the destination presentation in Normal view.

2. On the **Home** tab or **Insert** tab, in the **Slides** group, select **Reuse Slides** to open the **Reuse Slides** pane on the right side of the screen.

3. The Reuse Slides pane displays thumbnails of the available presentations.

4. If necessary, enter search text in the Search PowerPoint Files for Slides box to narrow down the presentation choices.

5. In the **Reuse Slides** pane, select **Choose Slides** below the presentation from which you want to insert slides, to display only the slides in that presentation.

6. For each slide you want to insert into your presentation, select the slide thumb-nail or **Insert Slide**.

 TIP Use the Paste Options button to specify whether the inserted slide matches the source or destination formatting.

7. Close the **Reuse Slides** pane.

To prepare a source document to import as a presentation

1. Enter the content that you want to appear on the slides (and any other content) in a document.

2. Review the styles applied to the content you want to include in the presentation.

   - Title, Subtitle, Heading 1, and any list items will convert to slide titles.

   - Heading 2 through Heading 8 will convert to bulleted list items.

3. Save and close the document.

To create a presentation by importing a Word document

1. On the **Open** page of the Backstage view, select **Browse**.

2. In the file type list, select **All Files (*.*)**.

3. Browse to the folder that contains the Word document that contains the slide title and bullet point information.

4. Double-click the document to create a new presentation.

5. Select all the slides in the new presentation, and then on the **Home** tab, in the **Slides** group, select the **Reset** button.

6. Apply the design template you want.

To create slides in an existing presentation by importing a Word document

1. Select the slide after which you want to insert the new slides.

2. On the **Home** tab or **Insert** tab, in the **Slides** group, select the **New Slide** arrow.

3. On the **New Slide** menu, below the gallery, select **Slides from Outline** to open the **Insert Outline** dialog, which resembles the **Open** dialog.

4. Use standard Windows techniques to browse to the folder that contains the Word document you want to use for the slide titles and content.

5. Double-click the document to insert slides based on its content.

10

Hide and delete slides

If you create a slide and then later realize that you don't need it, you can delete it. If you don't need the slide for a presentation to a specific audience but might need it later, you can hide the slide instead. Hidden slides aren't presented in slideshows. They remain available from the Thumbnails pane, but their thumbnails are dimmed, and their slide numbers are crossed through with a backslash.

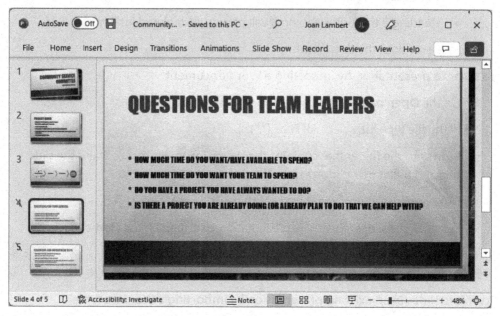

You can edit the content of hidden slides

When you select a hidden slide, the Hide Slide button on the Slide Show tab is shaded to indicate that the command is in effect. You can edit a hidden slide in the Slide pane just as you can any other, so you might use this feature to keep a slide that you're still working on hidden until it's final. You can unhide a slide to include it in the slideshow.

To hide or unhide slides

■ Right-click a single slide, and then select **Hide Slide**.

Or

1. Select the slide or slides you want to hide or unhide.

2. Do either of the following:

   - Right-click the selection, and then select **Hide Slide**.

   - On the **Slide Show** tab, in the **Set Up** group, select **Hide Slide**.

> ✓ **TIP** The name of the Hide Slide command and button doesn't change; when a hidden slide is active, the command and button are shaded.

To delete slides

- Right-click a single slide, and then select **Delete Slide**.

Or

1. Select the slide or slides you want to delete.

2. Do any of the following:

   - Right-click the selection, and then select **Delete Slide**.

   - On the **Home** tab, in the **Clipboard** group, select **Cut**.

   - Press the **Delete** key.

> ✓ **TIP** When you add or delete slides, PowerPoint renumbers all the subsequent slides.

10

Apply themes

The appearance of every presentation that you create is governed by a theme—a combination of colors, fonts, effect styles, and background graphics or formatting that coordinates the appearance of all the presentation elements. Even a blank presentation has a theme: the Office theme, which has a white slide background, a standard set of text and accent colors, and the Office font set, which uses Calibri Light for headings and Calibri for body text.

PowerPoint and the other Microsoft 365 apps (Office apps) share a common set of themes and theme elements. This enables you to easily produce coordinated print and presentation materials. Approximately 30 of these themes are available to you from the PowerPoint Themes gallery. Many of the themes come with predefined variants, which have a different color scheme or background graphic.

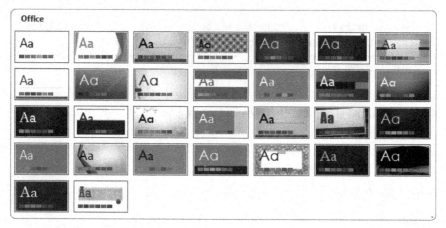

The built-in Office themes for PowerPoint

Each thumbnail in the PowerPoint Themes gallery displays a sample of the font set in the form of an uppercase and lowercase letter A (*Aa*) and the color scheme in the form of colored blocks over the default title slide. Title slides frequently have background graphics that set the tone for the presentation. The standard slides associated with the theme will often have a more subtle background graphic that coordinates with the title slide background. You can choose to hide the background graphic and use only a colored background if you want.

You can change the theme applied to an entire presentation or to only one section of the presentation. If you like the colors of one theme, the fonts of another, and the effects of another, you can mix and match theme elements. You can also create your own themes.

When working in Normal view, you can use the Live Preview feature to see how your presentation would look with a different theme applied. Simply point to any theme and pause. PowerPoint temporarily applies the selected formatting to the slide in the Slide pane. This makes it easy to try different themes and theme elements until you find the ones you want.

To apply a standard theme to a presentation

1. Display the presentation in Normal view.

2. On the **Design** tab, in the **Themes** group, select the **More** button (below the scroll arrows) to display the menu that includes the **Office** theme gallery.

> ✓ **TIP** The menu displays the currently applied template and any custom Office templates on your computer above the Office themes.

3. Point to thumbnails in the gallery to display the theme names in tooltips and preview the effect of applying the themes to your presentation.

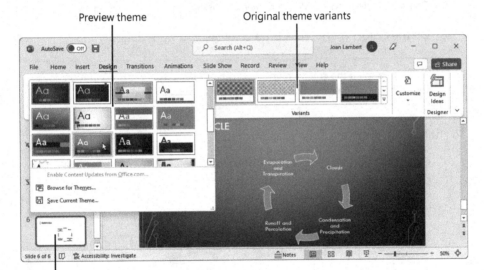

Choose a theme that enhances the content of your presentation

4. Select a theme thumbnail to apply that theme to the entire presentation.

To change the color scheme of the presentation

- On the **Design** tab, in the **Variants** group, select a variant thumbnail.

Or

1. On the **Design** tab, in the **Variants** group, select the **More** button (below the scroll arrows) to expand the **Variants** menu.

2. On the **Variants** menu, select **Colors**.

10

Choose from the dozens of standard color schemes

3. On the **Colors** menu, select the color set you want to apply.

> **TIP** Changing the color scheme, font set, or effect style of a presentation doesn't change the theme that is applied to the presentation.

To change the font set of the presentation

1. On the **Design** tab, in the **Variants** group, select the **More** button (below the scroll arrows) to expand the **Variants** menu.

2. On the **Variants** menu, select **Fonts**.

Choose from same-font or complementary-font heading/body font combinations

3. On the **Fonts** menu, select the font set you want to apply.

To change the effect style of the presentation

1. On the **Design** tab, in the **Variants** group, select the **More** button (below the scroll arrows) to expand the **Variants** menu.

2. On the **Variants** menu, select **Effects**.

The effect style preview color coordinates with the current color scheme

3. On the **Effects** menu, select the effect style you want to apply.

To apply a theme or theme variant to only part of a presentation

1. Create a section that contains the slides you want to have a different theme.

2. Click the section header to select the section.

3. Apply the theme or theme element.

Change slide backgrounds

The presentation theme includes a standard background. The background might be a color or range of colors and might include image elements.

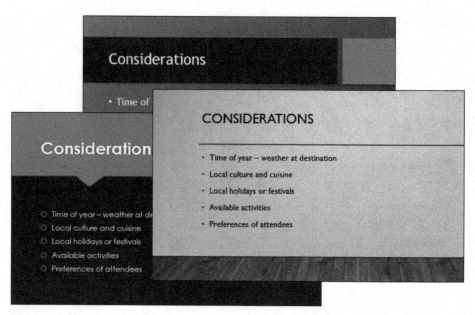

A variety of thematic background graphics

You can customize slide backgrounds by removing the background graphic and filling the slide background with a solid color, a color gradient, a texture, a pattern, or a picture of your choice. You make these changes in the Format Background pane.

You can control the color, texture, pattern, or picture in the background of one or all slides

Each of the options in the Format Background pane has specific settings that appear when you select the option.

A solid color background is a good choice for readability, but if you want to add some interest without a lot of distraction, you can use a color gradient in which a solid color gradually changes to another. PowerPoint offers several light-to-dark and dark-to-light gradient patterns based on the color scheme. You can also create custom gradients of two, three, or more colors. Each change in color within a gradient is controlled by a gradient stop. For each gradient stop, you can specify the location and specific color (including the transparency and brightness of the color). A color gradient can have from 2 to 10 gradient stops.

A gradient can include up to 10 color changes

10

If you want something fancier than a solid color or a color gradient, you can give the slide background a texture or pattern. PowerPoint comes with several built-in textures that you can easily apply to the background of slides.

Choose a background that doesn't overpower your presentation

If none of these meets your needs, you might want to use a picture of a textured surface. For a dramatic effect, you can even incorporate a picture of your own, although these are best reserved for small areas of the slide rather than the entire background.

If you prefer to use a simple pattern rather than a texture, you can choose from 48 patterns and set the background and foreground color to your liking.

Click any pattern to preview it on the slide

To display the Format Background pane

- On the **Design** tab, in the **Customize** group, select **Format Background**.

To close the Format Background pane

- In the upper-right corner of the pane, select the **Close** button (the X).

- To the right of the pane name, click the down arrow, and then select **Close**.

To apply a background change to all slides

1. In the **Format Background** pane, configure the slide background formatting you want.

2. At the bottom of the pane, select **Apply to All**.

To remove the slide background graphic applied by a theme

1. Display the **Format Background** pane.

2. In the **Format Background** pane, select the **Hide background graphics** checkbox.

To apply a solid background color to one or more slides

1. In the **Format Background** pane, select **Solid fill**.

2. Select the **Color** button to display the color palette.

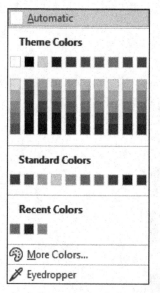

The color palette displays theme colors, standard colors, and recently used custom colors

> **SEE ALSO** For information about the colors you can use, see the sidebar "Non-theme colors" later in this topic.

3. Select a theme color variant, a solid color, or a recent color, or select **More Colors** and select a custom color.

4. Move the **Transparency** slider to adjust the background color transparency, or set a specific transparency percentage.

To apply a gradient background color to one or more slides

1. In the **Format Background** pane, select **Gradient fill**.

2. Select the **Preset gradients** button, and then select a gradient option based on the current color palette.

Preset color gradients offer linear and radial variants of the theme accent color

Or

1. In the **Type** list, select **Linear**, **Radial**, **Rectangular**, **Path**, or **Shade from title**.

2. In the **Direction** list, select the direction you want the gradient to flow.

3. If you chose the **Linear** type, you can specify the angle you want the gradient to move along. Enter the angle in the **Angle** box.

4. If you want to add gradient stops, do either of the following in the **Gradient Stops** area:

   • Select the **Add gradient stop** button, and then reposition the marker that appears on the slider.

   • Click the slider in the approximate location where you want to insert the gradient stop.

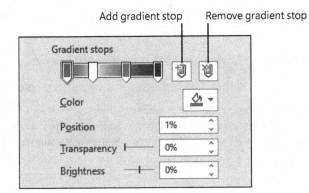

You can precisely control a color by adjusting the transparency and brightness

10

5. If you want to remove gradient stops, do either of the following in the **Gradient stops** area:

    - On the slider, select the marker for the gradient stop you want to remove. Then select the **Remove gradient stop** button.

    - Drag the gradient stop marker off the slider.

6. In the **Gradient stops** area, set the color, position, transparency, and brightness for each color in the gradient. Note the following:

    - You can select a color swatch or match an existing color by using the Eyedropper tool to select a color.

    - You can change the transparency and brightness by moving the markers on the sliders, by entering specific percentages, or by scrolling the dials.

To apply a textured background to one or more slides

1. In the **Format Background** pane, select **Picture or texture fill**.

2. Select the **Texture** button to display the texture gallery. You can select from a variety of textures, including fabric, marble, granite, wood grain, and Formica-like textures in various colors.

3. In the texture gallery, select the texture you want to apply.

4. Move the **Transparency** slider to adjust the background color transparency, or set a specific transparency percentage.

To apply a patterned background to one or more slides

1. In the **Format Background** pane, select **Pattern fill**.

2. In the **Pattern** palette, select one of the 48 pattern swatches.

3. Select the **Foreground** button, and then select the primary pattern color.

4. Select the **Background** button, and then select the secondary pattern color.

> **TIP** If you want to add a watermark, such as the word *Draft* or *Confidential*, to the background of all your slides, you can do so by adding the text to the background of the slide master.

Non-theme colors

Although using themes enables you to create presentations with a color-coordinated design, you can also use colors that aren't part of the theme. Whenever you apply a color to any presentation element, you can choose from among these options:

- Six shades of each of the 10 theme colors.

- Ten standard colors available in all Office documents, regardless of the theme.

- Non-standard colors that you've used recently.

- The Standard color palette that offers permutations of primary, secondary, and tertiary colors in a hexagonal color wheel.

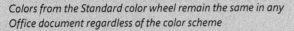

Colors from the Standard color wheel remain the same in any Office document regardless of the color scheme

- A custom color model on which you can select from permutations of primary and secondary colors or specify colors by RGB (Red, Green, and Blue) or HSL (Hue, Saturation, and Luminescence) values.

If you want to make a selected element the same color as another element on the same slide, display the color menu, select the Eyedropper, and then select the color you want.

Divide presentations into sections

To make it easier to organize and format a longer presentation, you can divide it into sections. In both Normal view and Slide Sorter view, sections are designated by titles above their slides. The titles do not appear in other views, and they do not create slides or otherwise interrupt the flow of the presentation.

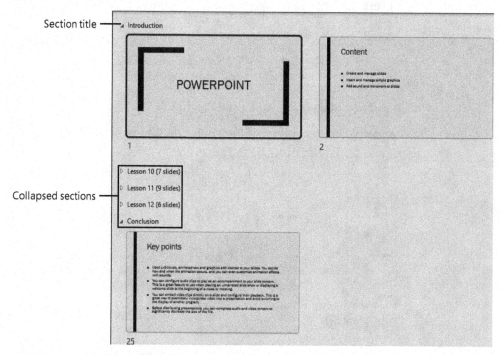

You can rename, remove, move, collapse, and expand sections

Because you can collapse entire sections to leave only the section titles visible, the sections make it easier to focus on one part of a presentation at a time.

You can collapse sections to provide an "outline" of long presentations, with the number of slides in each section displayed in parentheses

> **TIP** If you're collaborating with other people on the development of a presentation, sections provide a convenient way of assigning slides to different people.

Some templates include a slide layout, similar to the title slide layout, that is specifically designed for section divider slides. If you divide a long presentation into sections based on topic, you might want to transfer your section titles to these slides to provide guidance to the audience or to mark logical points in the presentation to take breaks or answer questions.

To create a section

1. In Normal view or Slide Sorter view, select the slide that you want to be first in the new section.

2. On the **Home** tab, in the **Slides** group, select the **Section** button, and then select **Add Section** to insert a section title named *Untitled Section* before the selected slide.

To rename a section

1. In Normal view or Slide Sorter view, do either of the following to open the **Rename Section** dialog:

   • Right-click the section title you want to change, and then select **Rename Section**.

   • On the **Home** tab, in the **Slides** group, select the **Section** button, and then select **Rename Section**.

10

| Rename Section | ? | X |

Section name:

Chapter Review

Rename | Cancel

The current section name is selected so that you can easily replace it

2. In the **Section name** box, replace or edit the existing section name, and then press Enter or select **Rename**.

To collapse or expand one slide section

- In Normal view or Slide Sorter view, click the arrow that precedes the section title.

> ✓ **TIP** A right-pointing arrow indicates a collapsed section; an arrow that points to the lower-right corner indicates an expanded section.

To collapse or expand all slide sections

- On the **Home** tab, in the **Slides** group, select the **Section** button, and then select **Collapse All** or **Expand All**.

- Right-click any section name, and then select **Expand All** or **Collapse All**.

Rearrange slides and sections

After you've added several slides to a presentation, you might want to rearrange their order so that they more effectively communicate your message.

You can rearrange a presentation by moving individual slides or entire sections of slides.

To move a slide within a presentation

- In Normal view or Slide Sorter view, drag the slide thumbnail to its new position. Notice as you drag that the other thumbnails move to indicate where the selected slide will appear when you release the mouse button.

Or

1. Select the slide thumbnail, and then press **Ctrl+X** or, on the **Home** tab, in the **Clipboard** group, select **Cut**.

2. Do either of the following:

   - Select the slide thumbnail that you want to insert the cut slide after, and then press **Ctrl+V** or, in the **Clipboard** group, select **Paste**.

   - Click between the other slide thumbnails to insert a thin red marker (horizontal in Normal view or vertical in Slide Sorter view) where you want to move the slide. Then press **Ctrl+V** or, in the **Clipboard** group, select **Paste**.

Or

1. Right-click the slide thumbnail, and then select **Cut**.

2. Right-click between the other slide thumbnails where you want to move the slide.

 TIP The thin red destination marker appears only when you click between thumbnails, not when you right-click between thumbnails.

3. In the **Paste Options** section of the shortcut menu, select the **Use Destination Theme** button or the **Keep Source Formatting** button.

 TIP When PowerPoint displays the paste options, press H to use the destination style or K to use the source style.

To move a section within a presentation

1. Click the title of the section of slides you want to move, to select all the slides in the section.

2. Drag the section to its new location.

Or

- Right-click the section title, and then select **Move Section Up** or **Move Section Down** to move the section and all its slides before the preceding section or after the following section.

 TIP The Move Section commands aren't available on the Section menu; they are available only on the shortcut menu that appears when you right-click a section title.

10

To merge a section into the preceding section by removing the section divider

1. Select the title of the section of slides you want to ungroup.

2. On the **Home** tab, in the **Slides** group, select the **Section** button, and then select **Remove Section**.

Or

- Right-click the section title, and then select **Remove Section**.

To merge all sections by removing all section dividers

- On the **Home** tab, in the **Slides** group, select the **Section** button, and then select **Remove All Sections**.

To delete a section of slides

1. Select the title of the section of slides you want to delete, to select all the slides in the section.

2. Press the **Delete** key.

Or

1. Right-click the section title, and then select **Remove Section & Slides**.

If the selected section is collapsed, PowerPoint prompts you to confirm the deletion

2. If PowerPoint prompts you to confirm the deletion, select **Yes** to delete the section title and all the slides in the section.

> **TIP** The Remove Section & Slides command isn't available on the Section menu; it is available only on the shortcut menu that appears when you right-click a section title.

Key points

- You can add as many slides as you want to a presentation. Most templates provide a variety of readymade slide layouts to choose from. If you change your mind about a slide layout, you can easily switch to a different layout.

- Grouping slides into sections makes it easy to focus on and format specific parts of a presentation.

- If you need to change the order of slides or sections, you can rearrange them in Slide Sorter view or in the Thumbnails pane in Normal view.

- Switching to another predefined theme or theme variant is an easy way to change the look of a presentation. Applying a different theme variant is a simple way to signal a topic change within a presentation.

- To dress up the background of a slide or all the slides in a presentation, you can apply a solid color, color gradient, texture, pattern, or picture to the slide background.

10

Practice tasks

Before you can complete these tasks, you must copy the book's practice files to your computer. The practice files for these tasks are in the **Office365SBS\Ch10** folder. You can save the results of the tasks in the same folder.

The introduction includes a complete list of practice files and download instructions.

Add and remove slides

Open the **AddRemoveSlides** presentation in PowerPoint, and then perform the following tasks:

1. Add two slides after the title slide. First, add a slide that has the default **Title and Content** layout. Then add a slide that has the **Two Content** layout.

2. Add 7 more slides, so you have a total of 10 slides. Use each slide layout at least once.

3. In Normal view, delete slide **3**.

4. Switch to Slide Sorter view, and then delete slides **5** through **8**. The presentation now contains five slides.

5. Add seven slides to the end of the presentation by inserting the content of the **ImportOutline** document.

6. Use the **Reuse Slides** feature to insert the first slide from the **ReuseSlides** presentation as slide **2** in the **AddRemoveSlides** presentation. Then close the **Reuse Slides** pane.

7. Insert a duplicate copy of slide **2** as slide **3**.

8. Hide slide **2**, and then delete slide **8**.

9. Save and close the presentation.

Apply themes

Open the **ApplyThemes** presentation in Normal view, and then perform the following tasks:

1. On slide **1**, click the slide title. On the **Home** tab, in the **Font** group, notice that the title font is blue-gray, 44-point, Times New Roman.

2. Apply the **Ion** theme to the presentation. On the **Home** tab, in the **Font** group, notice that the title font is now white, 72-point, Century Gothic.

3. Switch to **Slide Sorter** view and adjust the magnification to display all the slides.

4. Apply the **Circuit** theme to the presentation. Notice that the slide background is blue.

5. Apply the **gray** variant of the Circuit theme to the **Past** section of the presentation.

6. Apply the **red** variant of the Circuit theme to the **Present** section of the presentation.

7. Apply the **green** variant of the Circuit theme to the **Future** section of the presentation.

8. Review the effects of your changes on the individual slides. Then save and close the presentation.

Change slide backgrounds

Open the **ChangeBackgrounds** presentation, and then perform the following tasks:

1. Apply a gradient fill background to slide **1**.

2. Change the gradient type to **Rectangular** and set the direction to **From Top Left Corner**.

3. Configure the gradient to have the following four gradient stops:

Stop	Color	Position	Transparency	Brightness
1	Light Green	5%	0%	−10%
2	White	45%	0%	90%
3	Light Blue	75%	0%	0%
4	Purple	100%	20%	0%

4. Apply the custom gradient fill to all slides in the presentation.

5. For only slide 1, change the slide background to the **Water droplets** texture, and set the **Transparency** of the texture to **25%**.

6. Review the effects of your changes on the individual slides. Then save and close the presentation.

Divide presentations into sections

Open the **CreateSections** presentation in Normal view, and then perform the following tasks:

1. Divide the presentation into two sections:

   - A section that contains slides 1 through 3

   - A section that contains slides 4 through 12

2. Change the name of the first section to Introduction.

3. Switch to **Slide Sorter** view, and then change the name of the second section to Process.

4. Collapse both sections, and then expand only the **Process** section.

5. Save and close the presentation.

Rearrange slides and sections

Open the **RearrangeSlides** presentation in Normal view, and then perform the following tasks:

1. Move the first slide in the **Step 1** section so that it is the third slide in the Introduction section. Then delete the last slide in the Introduction section.

2. Switch to **Slide Sorter** view and scroll through the presentation, noticing the sections.

3. Collapse the sections, and then rearrange them so that the sections for steps 1 through 7 are in order and the End section is at the end of the presentation.

4. Merge the **End** section into the **Step 7** section.

5. Save and close the presentation.

Insert and manage simple graphics

With the ready availability of professionally designed templates, presentations have become more visually sophisticated and appealing. Gone (ideally) are the days of presenters reading a list of bullet points to the audience; successful presentations are likely to have fewer words and more graphic elements. You can use images, diagrams, animations, charts, tables, and other visual elements to graphically reinforce your spoken message (which can be conveniently documented in the speaker notes attached to the slides).

The term *graphics* generally refers to several kinds of visual objects, including photos, clip art images, diagrams, charts, and shapes. You can insert all these types of graphics as objects on a slide and then size, move, and copy them. Because elements on a PowerPoint slide float independently, it's simpler to creatively present information on PowerPoint slides than in Word documents.

This chapter guides you through procedures related to inserting, moving, and resizing pictures; editing and formatting pictures; working with picture attributions and alt text; creating a PowerPoint photo album; inserting and formatting icons, and drawing and modifying shapes.

In this chapter

- Insert, move, and resize pictures
- Edit and format pictures
- Provide additional information about pictures
- Create a photo album
- Insert and format icons
- Draw and modify shapes

Insert, move, and resize pictures

You can place digital photographs and images created and saved in other programs on slides in your PowerPoint presentations. Collectively, these types of images are referred to as *pictures*. You can use pictures to make slides more visually interesting, but in a PowerPoint presentation, you're more likely to use pictures to convey information in a way that words cannot.

Pictures can help illustrate a concept

You can insert a picture onto a slide either from your computer or from an online source, such as the internet or your cloud storage drive. PowerPoint also provides access to a variety of online content and to a library of professional "stock images" that you can use without additional license fees.

> ⚠ **IMPORTANT** Pictures you acquire from the web are often copyrighted, meaning that you cannot use them without the permission of the image's owner. Sometimes owners will grant permission if you give them credit. Professional photographers usually charge a fee to use their work. Always assume that pictures are copyrighted unless the source clearly indicates that they are license free.

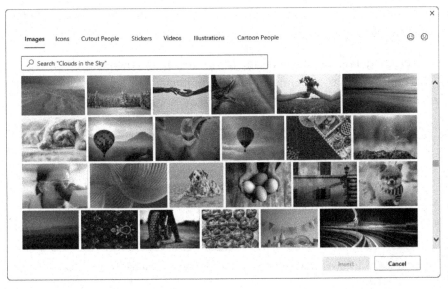

Photos in the stock image library

Many PowerPoint slide templates include a content placeholder that provides shortcuts for inserting various types of media from the slide instead of from the ribbon. The content placeholder icons have been updated to reflect the current media options.

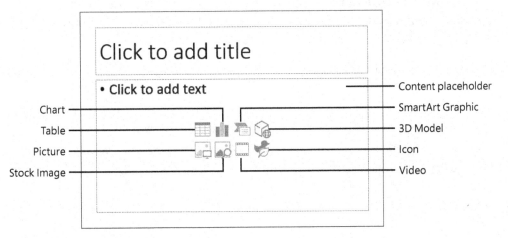

A Title and Content slide template

11

325

After you insert a picture, you can change its size and location on the slide and apply a variety of frames and effects.

Inserting or selecting a picture activates its sizing handles and the Picture Format tool tab. This tab contains commands for formatting the appearance of a picture and controlling its position relative to text, images, and other page elements.

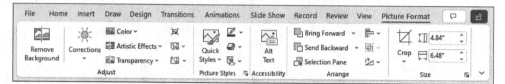

The Picture Format tool tab

> ✓ **TIP** You can save PowerPoint slides as pictures that you can insert in other types of documents.

Graphic formats

Many common graphic formats store graphics as a series of dots, or *pixels*. Each pixel is made up of bits. The number of bits per pixel (bpp) determines the number of distinct colors that can be represented by a pixel.

The mapping of bits to colors isn't 1:1; it's 2^{bpp}. In other words:

1 bpp = 2 colors	16 bpp = 65,536 colors
2 bpp = 4 colors	32 bpp = 4,294,967,296 colors
4 bpp = 16 colors	64 bpp = 18,446,744,073,709,551,616 colors
8 bpp = 256 colors	

Image files that you will use in a PowerPoint presentation are usually in one of the following file formats:

- **BMP (bitmap)** There are different qualities of BMPs.

- **GIF (Graphics Interchange Format)** This format is common for images that appear on webpages because the images can be compressed with no loss of information, and groups of them can be animated. GIFs store at most 8 bits per pixel, so they are limited to 256 colors.

- **JPEG (Joint Photographic Experts Group)** This compressed format works well for complex graphics such as scanned photographs. Some information is lost in the compression process, but often the loss is imperceptible to the human eye. Color JPEGs store 24 bits per pixel. Grayscale JPEGs store 8 bits per pixel.

- **PNG (Portable Network Graphic)** This format has the advantages of the GIF format but can store colors with 24, 32, 48, or 64 bits per pixel and grayscales with 1, 2, 4, 8, or 16 bits per pixel. A PNG file can also specify whether each pixel blends with its background color and can contain color correction information so that images look accurate on a broad range of display devices. Graphics saved in this format are smaller, so they display faster.

- **SVG (Scalable Vector Graphic)** This format, a recent addition to those supported by PowerPoint, stores image data in XML format rather than in pixels. For more information about SVG images, see "Insert and format icons" later in this chapter.

Of the commonly available file formats, PNG images are often the best choice for images other than photographs, because they provide high-quality images with a small file size and support transparency.

11

To insert a picture from your computer

1. Do either of the following to open the Insert Picture dialog:

   - If the slide has a content placeholder, select the **Pictures** button in the placeholder.

   - If the slide doesn't have a content placeholder, on the **Insert** tab, in the **Images** group, select the **Pictures** button and then select **This Device**.

Picture source options

2. In the **Insert Picture** dialog, browse to and select the picture (or pictures) you want to insert. Then select **Insert**.

> ✅ **TIP** If a picture might change, you can ensure that the slide is always up to date by selecting the Insert arrow and then selecting Link To File to insert a link to the picture, or by selecting Insert And Link to insert the picture and link it to its graphic file.

The inserted picture is surrounded by a frame to indicate that it is selected. You can use the handles around the frame to size and rotate the picture.

To insert a picture from an online source

1. Do either of the following to open the Insert Pictures window:

   - If the slide has a content placeholder, select the **Online Pictures** button in the placeholder.

   - If the slide doesn't have a content placeholder, on the **Insert** tab, in the **Images** group, select the **Online Pictures** button.

2. In the **Online Pictures** window, select the source you want to use (such as OneDrive) or enter a search term in the search box.

3. Browse to and select the picture or pictures you want to insert. Then select **Insert**.

To select a picture for editing

- Click or tap the picture once.

To move a picture

- Point to the image. When the cursor changes to a four-headed arrow, drag the picture to its new location.

> ✓ **TIP** As you drag, red dotted lines, called *smart guides*, might appear on the slide to help you align the picture with other elements.

To resize a picture

- Select the picture, and then do any of the following:

  - To change only the width of the picture, drag the left or right size handle.

  - To change only the height of the picture, drag the top or bottom size handle.

  - To change both the height and the width of the picture without changing its aspect ratio, drag a corner size handle or set the **Height** or **Width** measurement in the **Size** group on the **Picture Format** tool tab, and then press **Enter**.

Edit and format pictures

From time to time in this book, we have alluded to the modern trend away from slides with bullet points and toward presentations that include more graphics. Successful presenters have learned that most people can't listen to a presentation while they are reading slides. So these presenters make sure most of their slides display graphics that represent the point they are making, giving the audience something to look at while they focus on what is being said. PowerPoint gives you the tools you need to create graphic-intensive rather than text-intensive presentations.

After you insert any picture into a presentation, you can modify it by using the commands on the Picture Format tool tab. For example, you can do the following:

- Remove the background by designating either the areas you want to keep or those you want to remove.

- Sharpen or soften the picture, or change its brightness or contrast.

- Enhance the picture's color.

- Make one of the picture's colors transparent.

- Choose an effect, such as Pencil Sketch or Paint Strokes.

- Apply effects such as shadows, reflections, and borders; or apply combinations of these effects.

- Add a border consisting of one or more solid or dashed lines of whatever width and color you choose.

- Rotate the picture to any angle, either by dragging the rotating handle or by choosing a rotating or flipping option.

- Crop away the parts of the picture that you don't want to show on the slide. (The picture itself is not altered; parts of it are simply covered up.)

- Minimize the presentation's file size by specifying the optimum resolution for where or how the presentation will be viewed—for example, on a webpage or printed page. You can also delete cropped areas of a picture to reduce file size.

All these changes are made to the representation of the picture on the slide and do not affect the original picture.

To crop a picture

1. Select the picture. On the **Picture Format** tool tab, in the **Size** group, select **Crop** to display thick black handles on the sides and in the corners of the picture.

2. Drag the handles to define the area you want to crop to. The areas that will be excluded from the cropped picture are shaded.

Cropping a photo

> ⚠️ **IMPORTANT** When you select a crop handle, be careful not to drag the picture sizing handles instead—they're very close to each other.

3. When you finish defining the area, click away from the picture, or select **Crop** again to apply the crop effect.

> ✅ **TIP** To redisplay the uncropped picture at any time, select it and select the Crop button.

Or

- Select the picture. On the **Picture Format** tool tab, in the **Size** group, select the **Crop** arrow, and then do either of the following:

    - Select **Crop to Shape**, and then select a shape.

    - Select **Aspect Ratio**, and then select an aspect ratio.

    PowerPoint crops the picture to meet your specifications.

Cropping a photo to a shape

11

To frame a picture

1. Select the picture. On the **Picture Format** tool tab, in the **Picture Styles** group, select the **More** button to display the Picture Styles gallery.

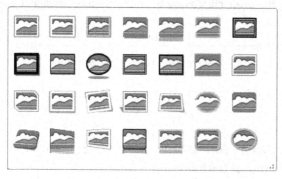

Quick styles can add frames, shadows, reflections, and more

2. Point to each picture style in turn to display a live preview of the frame applied to your picture. Then select the picture style you want to apply.

Experiment with the picture styles to identify those you like

To remove a background from a picture

1. Select the picture. On the **Picture Format** tool tab, in the **Adjust** group, select **Remove Background** to display the Background Removal tool tab and apply purple shading to the areas of the picture that the tool thinks you want to remove.

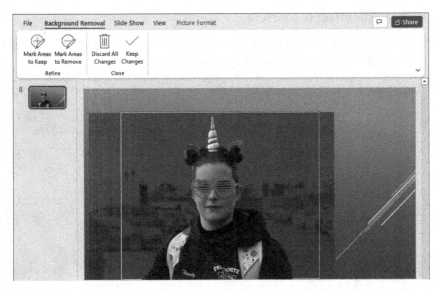

The accuracy of the estimate depends on the intricacy of the background

2. On the **Background Removal** tool tab, select **Mark Areas to Keep**, and then with the pencil tool, select any shaded areas of the photo that you'd like to expose and keep.

3. On the **Background Removal** tool tab, select **Mark Areas to Remove**, and then select any areas of the photo that aren't shaded that you'd like to remove.

4. Depending on the simplicity of the picture, you might need to make a lot of adjustments or only a few. When you finish, select **Keep Changes** to display the results. You can return to the Background Removal tool tab at any time to make adjustments.

11

Select elements of photos to decorate your slides

To apply an artistic effect to a picture

1. Select the picture. On the **Picture Format** tool tab, in the **Adjust** group, select **Artistic Effects** to display the Artistic Effects gallery.

2. Point to each effect to display a live preview of the effect on the selected photo.

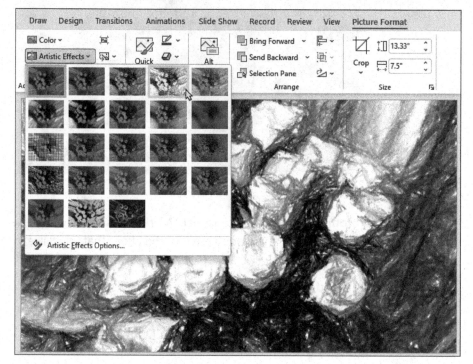

A color photo with the pencil sketch applied

3. Select the effect that you want to apply.

Provide additional information about pictures

PowerPoint has two features that make it easy to provide additional information about images that you insert in your presentations.

You can provide information—in the form of an *attribution*—about the image: the photographer, artist, or copyright holder, and the image licensing. PowerPoint automatically inserts image attributions when you insert an image by using the Online Pictures feature. You can manually insert attributions for pictures that you insert from your computer.

An automatic attribution for an online image with Creative Commons licensing

The attribution provided for online pictures includes two important hyperlinks. The first is to the picture in its online location so that it can be seen in context. The second is to the applicable licensing information.

Attributions are provided as normal text within floating text boxes. You can modify the attribution text and move or rotate the text box; when you do, the attribution remains linked to, and part of, the picture object.

11

A vertical attribution can save space and be less distracting

An important accessibility feature, *alt text* provides an alternative text description for images. This is useful for people using screen readers, when the content of an image is unclear, or when the image doesn't render. PowerPoint automatically generates alt text when you insert a picture from your computer or will generate it when you request it.

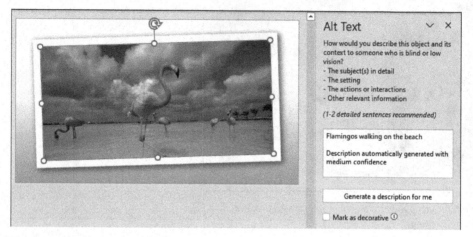

Auto-generated alt text provides a starting point

You might use images in your presentations that accompany and enhance text but don't provide additional information—for example, a decorative image in the slide footer. You can mark these images as decorative to indicate to screen-reading software that it should skip over the image and its alt text.

To select an attribution for editing

- Select the picture. Point to the top of the attribution area (the bottom of the picture), and when the pointer changes to a four-headed arrow, click to select the attribution text box.

To modify the attribution for an online picture

- Select the attribution text box. Then select within the text and edit it.

To move an online picture attribution

- Select the attribution text box, and then drag it to the new location.

To rotate an online picture attribution

1. Select the attribution text box, and then drag the rotation handle.

2. Drag the text box size handle to match the text box width to the side of the picture you're aligning it with.

To add or edit alt text for a picture

1. Do either of the following:

    *   Select the picture. On the **Format** tools tab, in the **Accessibility** group, select **Alt Text**.

    *   Right-click or long-press (tap and hold) the picture, and then select **Edit Alt Text**.

2. In the **Alt Text** pane, if PowerPoint doesn't generate alt text automatically or accurately, do either of the following:

    *   In the text box, enter text that describes the image and gives it context.

    *   Select **Generate a description for me**, and then edit the alt text in the text box if you want.

3. If the image is not important in context, select the **Mark as decorative** checkbox.

Create a photo album

When you want to display a dynamic array of pictures in a presentation, you can use a photo album template to do the initial layout and then customize the album by adding frames of different shapes, in addition to captions, or by applying layouts from the Design Ideas pane.

11

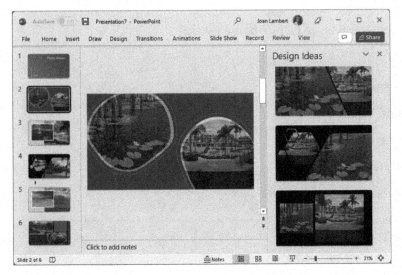

A PowerPoint photo album

The first step in creating a photo album is to choose the pictures you want to include. After you know the album contents, you can configure the album options.

When creating a photo album, you have several choices. The primary choice is the slide layout. You can choose from seven layouts that display one, two, or four pictures per slide. The pictures can optionally have titles. The default layout is Fit To Slide, which creates one slide per photo. The photo album uses the layout you select on all pages of the album.

A basic preview of the selected layout is available in the Photo Album dialog while you're creating the album. When you choose a layout, a slide number appears next to the first picture that will be on that slide. If you want to group pictures differently, you can reorder the photos before creating the album.

You can insert a text box on a photo album page, where it takes the place of a picture. You can use the text boxes to display comments about the pictures on that page, or you can leave them blank to control the layout. The total number of text boxes and pictures on a slide is the same as the layout that you choose. (In other words, if you choose a four-picture layout, the slide can display any combination of pictures and text boxes for a total of four objects.)

When you choose any layout other than Fit To Slide, you can opt to display captions below all the pictures. It isn't necessary to specify the captions when you select the photos for the album; if you choose the option to have captions, PowerPoint creates placeholders for them.

You can choose from these seven picture frame styles:

- Rectangle
- Rounded Rectangle
- Simple Frame, White
- Simple Frame, Black
- Compound Frame, Black
- Center Shadow Rectangle
- Soft Edge Rectangle

PowerPoint applies the same frame to all the pictures in the album.

You can choose a theme for the album when you're creating it, but it's easier to create the album and then apply the theme separately, because you can't preview the theme in the Photo Album dialog.

You can also choose to render all the pictures in the album in black and white rather than their native colors.

You can make these changes when creating the album, or you can create an album and then edit its settings to make changes.

> **TIP** To integrate the slide layouts from a photo album template into a more traditional presentation, create the photo album and then import its slides into the other presentation by selecting Reuse Slides at the bottom of the New Slide gallery. For information about reusing slides, see "Copy and import slides and content" in Chapter 10, "Create and manage slides."

To create a photo album

1. Start PowerPoint and display any blank or existing presentation. (PowerPoint creates the photo album as an entirely separate file.)

2. On the **Insert** tab, in the **Images** group, select **Photo Album** to open the Photo Album dialog.

3. In the **Insert picture from** area, select **File/Disk** to open the Insert New Pictures dialog.

4. Browse to the folder that contains the pictures you want to use, and select the photos. Then select **Insert** to add the selected files to the Pictures In Album list in the Photo Album dialog.

> **TIP** If you want to include all the pictures in a folder in your photo album, browse to the folder, select one picture, and press Ctrl+A to select all the folder contents. Then select Insert to add all the files to the photo album.

11

5. Review the images in the Preview window. Select any image that you want to rotate or recolor, and then use the commands beneath the Preview window to do so.

Default photo album settings

6. Next, configure the album layout. In the **Picture layout** list, select the layout you want to use. A generic preview of the layout appears to the right of the list. The numbers preceding the photo file names change to reflect the slide number the photo appears on.

7. Now confirm the picture order and slide content. Do any of the following in the **Pictures in album** list:

   - To preview a picture, select its file name (not its checkbox).

   - To move a picture to an earlier position, select its checkbox, and then select the **Move Up** button.

   - To move a picture to a later position, select its checkbox, and then select the **Move Down** button.

   - To rotate a picture or adjust its coloring, select its checkbox, and then select the buttons below the preview to rotate it, or to increase or decrease the contrast or brightness.

   - To insert a blank text box in a picture position, select the picture that you want to precede the text box, and then select **New Text Box**.

   - To remove a photo from the album, select its checkbox, and then select **Remove**.

8. Next, if the picture layout is set to something other than Fit To Slide, choose the picture frame. In the **Frame shape** list, select the frame you want to use.

The generic preview updates to reflect your frame choice

9. Finally, do any of the following:

   - If you want to display captions below the photos, select the **Captions below ALL pictures** checkbox.

   - If you want to display grayscale versions of the photos, select the **ALL pictures black and white** checkbox.

   - If you know the theme you want to apply to the photo album, select the **Browse** button to the right of the **Theme** box, and then double-click the theme you want to use.

10. Select **Create** to create the photo album.

11. Review the photo album, and do any of the following:

    - Change the photo album title from the generic *Photo Album* to something more meaningful.

    - If you added titles, captions, or text boxes, insert appropriate content in the placeholders.

    - If you didn't choose a theme, or don't like the theme you chose, choose an appropriate theme from the **Themes** gallery on the **Design** tab.

12. Save the photo album.

To edit photo album settings

1. On the **Insert** tab, in the **Images** group, select the **Photo Album** arrow, and then select **Edit Photo Album** to open the Photo Album dialog with all the current settings.

2. Add, remove, and modify photos; change the photo order; insert or remove text boxes; change the picture layout or frame; add or remove captions; or make any other changes you want.

3. When you finish, select the **Update** button to apply your changes.

Insert and format icons

A terrifically useful feature that was introduced in Office 365 and has now been made available in Word, Excel, PowerPoint, and Outlook is an extensive icon library. The icon library originally consisted of only simple icons but now also includes "cutout people" against transparent backgrounds, stickers, illustrations, and cartoon people, giving you access to thousands of creative resources that you can insert into your PowerPoint presentations.

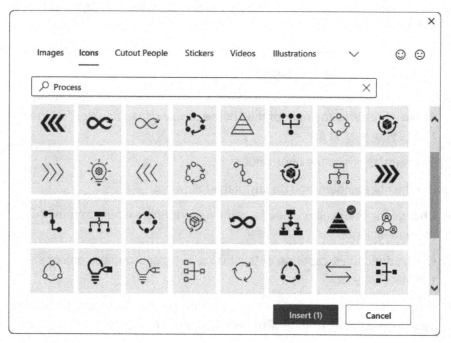

The icon library

The icon library is stored online—which is good because Microsoft can easily add new icons to it, but not perfect, because it requires an internet connection to access it. Provided that you're online, the icon library is easy to access and use. The library is not searchable but is divided into categories that make it a bit easier to find what you're looking for. Because the library is updated from time to time, it's worth looking there for simple image formats before you look online, for these reasons:

- There are no rights or permission issues when using icons from the icon library.

- The icons provide clear and consistent representations of the image subjects.

- You can smoothly scale the icons to whatever size you need without worrying about them developing jagged edges.

- You can easily recolor the icons to fit the color scheme of your presentation.

- You can convert the icons to shapes, which allows you to ungroup the icon elements and recolor or otherwise modify them individually.

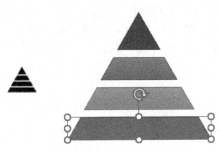

An icon converted to shapes that have been individually recolored

To insert an icon

1. Position the cursor where you want to insert the icon.

2. On the **Insert** tab, in the **Illustrations** group, select **Icons**.

3. Scroll the icon library or select any category in the left pane to move to that section of the library.

4. Select each icon that you want to insert. A check mark appears in the corner of each selected icon. Then select **Insert** to insert the icon or icons as individual drawings.

11

Work with scalable vector graphics

PowerPoint supports scalable vector graphics (SVG images), which sound fancy (and in fact, are) but can be used quite easily within PowerPoint and other Microsoft 365 apps by people who aren't professional graphic artists.

The icons provided with PowerPoint and other Microsoft 365 apps are scalable vector graphics. *Vector graphics* are graphics composed of shapes, rather than pixels, which means that as you increase or decrease their size (scale them) their edges remain smooth rather than becoming pixelated, as the edges of the more commonly used GIF, JPG, and PNG image types do. In other words, they look just as good at 1000 percent as they do at 100 percent.

Scalability is only one cool feature of SVG images—rather than being simply "a picture," the content of an SVG image is defined in XML format within the file and can be transformed, animated, and otherwise modified by using scripts and cascading style sheets (CSS files) or simply by selecting the image and recoloring it within PowerPoint or another Microsoft 365 app.

To convert an icon to an Office shape

1. Do either of the following:

   - Select the icon. On the **Graphics Format** tool tab, in the **Change** group, select **Convert to Shape**.

   - Right-click the icon, and then select **Convert to Shape**.

2. In the **Microsoft PowerPoint** message box prompting you to confirm that you want to convert the icon to a Microsoft Office drawing object, select **Yes**.

To resize, recolor, rotate, or otherwise modify an icon

- Select the icon, and then use the standard tools on the **Graphics Format** tool tab to modify it as you would any other image object.

Draw and modify shapes

An extensive library of shapes is available in PowerPoint. Shapes can be simple, such as lines, circles, or squares; or more complex, such as stars, hearts, and arrows. Some shapes are three-dimensional (although most are two-dimensional). Some of the shapes have innate meanings or connotations, and others are simply shapes.

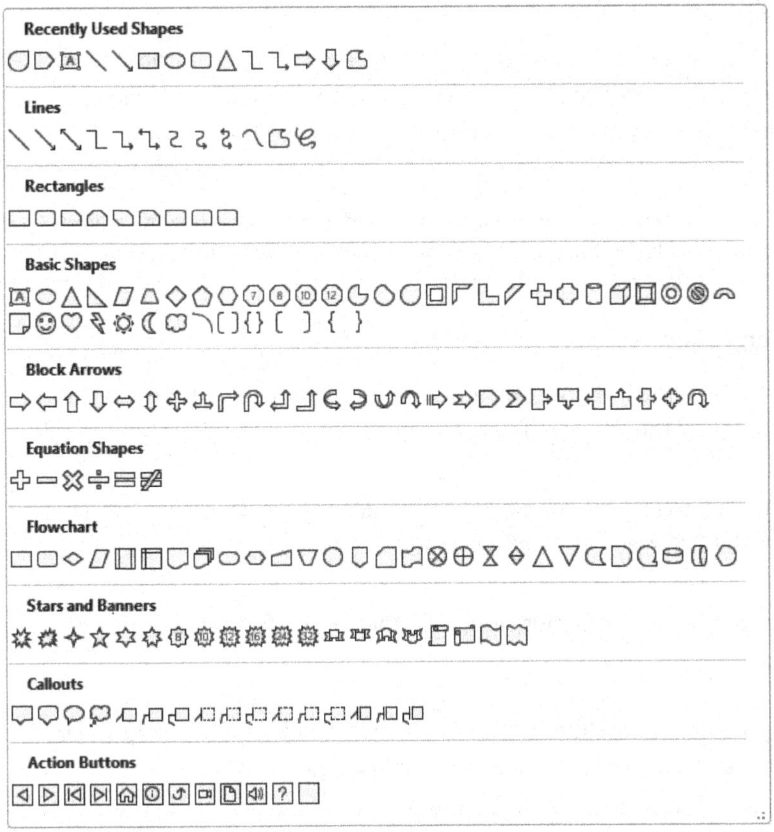

Recently Used Shapes

Lines

Rectangles

Basic Shapes

Block Arrows

Equation Shapes

Flowchart

Stars and Banners

Callouts

Action Buttons

Simple representations of the shapes you can insert and modify

Pointing to any shape in the gallery displays a ScreenTip that contains the shape name.

Draw and add text to shapes

After you select a shape that you want to add to your slide, you drag to draw it on the slide. Shapes are also text boxes, and you can enter text directly into them. You can format the text in shapes just as you would regular text.

11

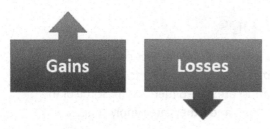

Shapes can help to visually reinforce a concept

With a little imagination, you'll soon discover ways to create images by combining shapes. You can use these images to illustrate a concept on a slide, or you can animate the drawings to convey actions or draw attention to specific elements.

 SEE ALSO For information about animating shapes and text on slides, see "Animate text and pictures on slides" in Chapter 12, "Add sound and movement to slides."

To create a shape on a slide

1. On the **Insert** tab, in the **Illustrations** group, select **Shapes** and then, on the **Shapes** menu, select the shape you want to insert.

   TIP If you select a shape button and then change your mind about drawing the shape, you can release the shape by pressing the Esc key.

2. When the cursor changes to a plus sign, do either of the following:

   - Click on the slide to create a shape of the default size.

   - Drag diagonally on the slide to specify the upper-left and lower-right corners of the rectangle that surrounds the shape (the drawing canvas).

   TIP To draw a shape that has the same height and width (such as a circle or square), hold down the Shift key while you drag.

To add text to a shape

- Select the shape, and then enter the text you want to display on the shape. There is no cursor to indicate the location of the text; simply start typing and it appears on the shape.

Locate additional formatting commands

You control the area of the shape available for text by formatting the Text Box margins of the shape. This setting is gathered with many others in the Format Shape pane, which you can display by selecting the dialog launcher (the small diagonal arrow) in the lower-right corner of the Shape Styles, WordArt Styles, or Size group on the Shape Format tool tab.

You can display different pages of
settings by selecting the text and icons
at the top of the pane

In Microsoft 365 apps, including PowerPoint, the most frequently used formatting commands are located on the ribbon. If additional commands are available, the ribbon group includes a dialog launcher. Selecting the dialog launcher displays either a dialog or a control pane.

Move and modify shapes

You can change the size, angles, outline and fill colors, and effects applied to the shape. You can apply different colors to the outline and inside (fill) of a shape.

When you first draw a shape, and anytime you select it thereafter, PowerPoint displays a set of handles.

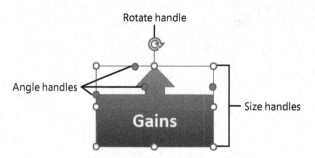

You can easily modify the shape, size, and angle of an image

You can use the handles to manipulate the shape in the following ways:

- Drag the side or corner handles (hollow circles) to change the size or aspect ratio of the shape.

- Drag the angle handles (yellow circles) to change the angles or curves of the text within the shape. Not all shapes have angle handles.

- Drag the rotate handle (circling arrow) to rotate the shape on the slide.

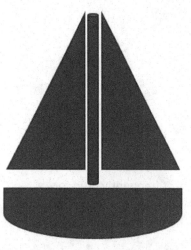

Four shapes arranged to create a sailboat

To select a shape for editing

- Select the shape once.

To select multiple shapes

- Select a shape, hold down the **Shift** or **Ctrl** key, and select each other shape.

- Drag to encompass all the shapes you want to select. If you don't want all the shapes within the selection area, hold down the **Shift** or **Ctrl** key and then click or tap individual shapes to deselect them.

To resize a shape

- Select the shape, and then do any of the following:

  - To change only the width of the shape, drag the left or right size handle.

  - To change only the height of the shape, drag the top or bottom size handle.

  - To change both the height and the width of the shape, drag a corner size handle.

  - To resize a shape without changing its aspect ratio, hold down the **Shift** key and drag a corner size handle or press an arrow key.

To move a shape on a slide

1. Select the shape that you want to move.

2. Drag the shape or press the arrow keys to move it to the new location.

To rotate or flip a shape

1. Select the shape.

2. On the **Shape Format** tool tab, in the **Arrange** group, select the **Rotate Objects** button.

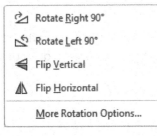

The menu illustrates the rotate and flip options

11

3. On the **Rotate Objects** menu, select the Rotate or Flip option you want.

> **TIP** You can rotate or flip any type of image. Rotating turns a shape 90 degrees to the right or left; flipping turns a shape 180 degrees horizontally or vertically.

Or

1. Select the shape.

2. Drag the **Rotate** handle in a clockwise or counterclockwise direction until the shape is at the angle of rotation you want.

To change a shape to another shape

1. Select the shape you want to change.

2. On the **Shape Format** tool tab, in the **Insert Shapes** group, select the **Edit Shape** button, select **Change Shape**, and then select the new shape.

   Changing the shape doesn't affect the shape formatting or text.

Format shapes

When a shape is selected, the Shape Format tool tab in the Drawing Tools tab group appears on the ribbon. You can use the commands on the Shape Format tool tab to do the following:

- Replace the shape with another without changing the formatting.

- Change the fill and outline colors of the shape, and the effects applied to the shape.

- Separately, change the fill and outline colors and effects of any text that you add to the shape.

- Arrange, layer, and group multiple shapes on a slide.

Having made changes to one shape, you can easily apply the same attributes to another shape, or you can apply the attributes to all future shapes you draw on the slides of the active presentation.

A happy fan cheering her team to victory!

When you have multiple shapes on a slide, you can group them so that you can copy, move, and format them as a unit. You can change the attributes of an individual shape—for example, its color, size, or location—without ungrouping the shapes.

To format a shape

1. Select the shape that you want to format.

2. On the **Shape Format** tool tab, in the **Shape Styles** group, select the **More** button to display the Shape Styles gallery.

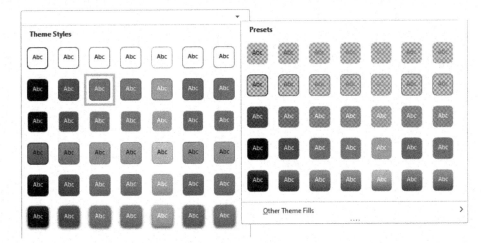

The color options reflect the current color scheme

3. Point to thumbnails to display live previews of their effects, and then select a style thumbnail to apply the selected style.

To format text on a shape

1. Select the shape.

2. On the **Shape Format** tool tab, in the **WordArt Styles** group, modify the style, text fill, text outline, or text effects.

Or

1. Select the text on the shape.

2. Do either of the following:

   - On the **Shape Format** tool tab, in the **WordArt Styles** group, modify the style, text fill, text outline, or text effects.

   - On the **Home** tab, in the **Font** and **Paragraph** groups, use the standard text formatting commands.

To copy formatting from one shape to another

1. Select the shape from which you want to copy the formatting

2. On the **Home** tab, in the **Clipboard** group, select the **Format Painter** button.

3. Select the shape to which you want to copy the formatting.

To set formatting as the default for the active presentation

- Right-click the shape from which you want to set the default formatting, and then select **Set as Default Shape**.

> **TIP** The Set As Default Shape command doesn't actually set a default shape; it sets only the default shape formatting.

To group shapes together as one object

1. Select all the shapes on a slide that you want grouped together.

2. On the **Shape Format** tool tab, in the **Arrange** group, select the **Group** button (when you point to this button, the ScreenTip that appears says Group Objects) and then, in the list, select **Group**.

Grouped objects have a common set of handles

To move an entire group

1. Point to any shape in the group.

2. When the pointer changes to a four-headed arrow, drag the group to the new location.

To ungroup shapes

1. Select the group.

2. On the **Shape Format** tool tab, in the **Arrange** group, select the **Group** button, and then select **Ungroup**.

To regroup shapes

1. Select any one shape from the former group.

2. On the **Shape Format** tool tab, in the **Arrange** group, on the **Group** menu, select **Regroup**.

11

Connect shapes

If you want to show a relationship between two shapes, you can connect them with a line by joining special handles called *connection points*.

To connect shapes, follow these steps:

1. On the **Insert** tab, in the **Illustrations** group, select **Shapes**. In the **Lines** area of the **Shapes** gallery, select a **Connector** shape.

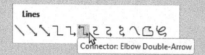

Identify connectors by their tooltips

2. Point to the first shape you want to connect.

3. When a set of small gray connection points appears, point to a connection point, press and hold the mouse button, and then drag to the other shape (don't release the mouse button).

4. When connection points appear on the other shape, point to a connection point, and release the mouse button.

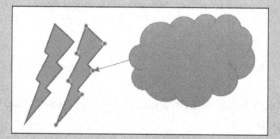

When you move a shape, the connector line adapts to the change

TROUBLESHOOTING The connector has green handles when the shapes are connected. If a handle is white, drag it to a connection point.

After you draw a connector, you can adjust its shape by dragging a yellow handle and format it by changing its color and weight. If you move a connected shape, the connector moves with it, maintaining the relationship between the shapes.

Key points

- PowerPoint makes it easy to use images of your own or from online sources to provide information and decoration within a presentation. You can modify the appearance of images in many ways.

- Shapes can add interest to a slide and draw attention to key concepts. However, they can become tiresome and produce an amateurish effect if overused.

- The icon library provides thousands of professional, scalable images that you can easily match to your presentation theme.

- You can easily create a photo album of images within a PowerPoint presentation without having to individually import and place the images.

11

Practice tasks

Before you can complete these tasks, you must copy the book's practice files to your computer. The practice files for these tasks are in the **Office365SBS\Ch11** folder. You can save the results of the tasks in the same folder.

The introduction includes a complete list of practice files and download instructions.

Insert, move, and resize pictures

Open the **InsertPictures** presentation, and then perform the following tasks:

1. Display slide **5**.

2. In the content placeholder, insert the **Flowers01** picture from the practice file folder.

3. Resize the picture to a width of **4"**. Ensure that the aspect ratio doesn't change.

4. Move the picture on the slide to identify locations in which the smart guides appear—for example, the edges of the content space and below the slide title. Align the picture with the upper-right corner of the content area as defined by the smart guides.

5. From the **Insert** tab, open the **Online Pictures** window and search for pictures related to flowers.

6. Review the search results and locate a picture that you like. Insert the picture onto the slide.

7. Resize the picture to a width of **4"** and align it with the right side of the content area, near the bottom of the slide (a smart guide might not appear at the bottom of the slide). Note that the pictures overlap near the center of the slide.

8. Close the presentation, saving your changes if you want to.

Edit and format pictures

Open the **EditPictures** presentation, and then perform the following tasks:

1. Display slide **5**.

2. Select the picture located on the right side of the slide.

3. On the **Picture Format** tool tab, in the **Adjust** group, select **Corrections**, and then point to the thumbnails to identify one that will brighten the picture to make it similar to the picture on the left. Select that thumbnail to apply the correction.

4. Select the **Crop** arrow, point to **Aspect Ratio**, and then select **1:1**. Adjust the picture so the flowers are in the center, and then complete the cropping process.

5. Display the **Picture Styles** gallery, and point to the thumbnails in the gallery to find one that you like. Select the thumbnail to apply the picture style.

6. Select the picture located on the left side of the slide.

7. Remove the neutral background from the selected picture.

8. Close the presentation, saving your changes if you want to.

Provide additional information about pictures

Open the **AccreditPictures** presentation, and then perform the following tasks:

1. Display slide **2**.

2. Select the picture located on the right side of the slide.

3. From the **Picture Format** tool tab, open the **Alt Text** pane.

4. Have PowerPoint generate a description of the photograph for you.

5. Edit the description to read Sunset over the Aegean Sea.

6. Display slide **5**.

7. From the **Insert** tab, open the **Online Pictures** window and search for Greece.

8. Select and insert a search result that you like. (You can choose a layout from the **Design Ideas** pane if it opens.)

9. Close any open panes and zoom in on the slide as necessary to read the attribution inserted with the image.

10. Close the presentation, saving your changes if you want to.

Create a photo album

Start PowerPoint, and then perform the following tasks:

1. From the **Insert** tab, create a new photo album. Select photos from the practice file folder or select your own photos.

2. While creating the album, do the following:

   - Experiment with the different picture layouts and frame shapes.

   - Change the order of the pictures in the album.

   - Insert text boxes to make spaces between photos.

   - Apply a theme.

3. After you create the album, experiment with the changes you can make from within PowerPoint. For example:

   - Replace placeholder text.

   - Change the theme.

   - Resize pictures.

4. If you want to, select the **Edit photo album** command to return to the Photo Album dialog and make additional changes.

5. Save your photo album as MyPhotoAlbum, and then close it.

Insert and format icons

Open the **InsertIcons** presentation, and then perform the following tasks:

1. Slide 1 provides a neutral outdoor background. Consider what sort of story you could tell on this slide.

2. From the **Insert** tab, open the **Insert Icons** window. Scroll through the window and look for icons you could use to tell a story on the slide.

3. Find and select the following icons:

   - An icon that depicts a person.

   - An icon that depicts the sun coming out from behind a cloud.

   - An icon that depicts an umbrella.

4. Insert the three selected icons. (Close the **Design Ideas** pane if it opens.)

5. Click anywhere on the slide away from the icons to release the selection, and then drag the icons to the following positions:

   - Position the sun and cloud in the upper-right corner.

   - Position the person at the edge of the street.

   - Position the umbrella above the person.

6. Resize the three icons as you like.

7. Select the sun and cloud icon and, from the **Graphics Format** tool tab, fill the image with the gold color.

8. Ungroup the parts of the icon, converting it as you do so.

9. Select only the cloud portion of the icon and fill the shape with a gray color.

10. Experiment with resizing and recoloring the other icons you inserted. Insert more icons if you want to!

11. Close the presentation, saving your changes if you want to.

Draw and modify shapes

Open the **DrawShapes** presentation, and then perform the following tasks:

1. Display slide **5**.

2. Draw a **5-Point Star** shape (in the **Stars and Banners** category of the **Shapes** gallery) near the center of the slide.

3. Draw a small arrow (in the **Block Arrows** category of the **Shapes** gallery) to the right of the star.

4. Drag a copy of the arrow to the left of the star and align it with the right arrow. Then flip the left arrow so that it points away from the star.

5. Adjacent to the left arrow, add a scroll shape, and then adjacent to the right arrow, add a heart shape.

6. Paste a copy of the heart shape on top of the original and make the second heart smaller than the first.

7. In the star, enter the word ME. Then increase the font size to make it prominent.

8. Repeat step 7 to add the word Education to the scroll shape and Family to the heart shape. Then resize the shapes as necessary to make all the words fit on one line.

9. Select the scroll, star, and heart shapes (don't select the text), and apply the style **Intense Effect – Light Blue, Accent 6**.

10. Suppose you have completed your education and entered the workforce. Change the scroll shape to the **Up Arrow** (in the **Block Arrows** category) to reflect your new status.

11. In the upward-pointing arrow shape, change the word *Education* to Job. Then adjust the size and position of the shape so that it balances with the other shapes on the slide, using the smart guides to help align the shapes.

12. Group all the shapes together as one object and apply a purple outline.

13. Move the entire group until the shapes are centered and balanced with the slide title.

14. Change the fill color of the left and right arrows to **Purple**.

15. Close the presentation, saving your changes if you want to.

Add sound and movement to slides

A PowerPoint presentation might be designed to provide ancillary information for a live presentation or to stand alone as an information source. Regardless of the method of delivery, a presentation has no value if it doesn't keep the attention of the audience. An element that can make the difference between an adequate presentation and a great presentation is the judicious use of animated content, sound, and videos. By incorporating these dynamic effects, you can grab and keep the attention of your audience. You can emphasize key points, control the focus of the discussion, and entertain in ways that will make your message memorable.

PowerPoint provides so many opportunities to add pizzazz to your slides that it's easy to end up with a presentation that looks more like an amateur experiment than a professional slideshow. When you first start adding animations, sound, and videos to your slides, it's best to err on the conservative side. As you gain more experience, you'll learn how to mix and match effects to get the results you want for a particular audience.

This chapter guides you through procedures related to animating text and pictures on slides, customizing animation effects, adding audio content to slides, adding video content to slides, and optimizing and compressing media.

In this chapter

- Animate text and pictures on slides
- Customize animation effects
- Add audio content to slides
- Add video content to slides
- Compress media to decrease file size

Animate text and pictures on slides

In the context of PowerPoint, *animation* refers to the movement of an element on a slide. When used appropriately, animated slide elements can both capture the audience's attention and effectively convey information. You can animate individual objects on a slide, including text containers, pictures, and shapes. (You can't animate objects that are part of the slide background or slide master, other than as part of the transition between slides.)

Thoughtfully designed animations can be very informative, particularly for audience members who are more receptive to visual input than to auditory input. Animations have the added benefit of providing a consistent message with or without a presenter to discuss or externally illustrate a process.

Elements of a multipart animation

You can configure four types of animations: the appearance, movement, emphasis, and disappearance of objects on the slide. There are multiple options within these four categories. The options are categorized as Basic, Subtle, Moderate, and Exciting (although you might have a different concept of "exciting" than the PowerPoint developer who categorized the effects). A few more animation effects are available for text than for other slide objects.

Here's a breakdown of the animation effects available in PowerPoint:

- **Entrance animations** An object with an animated entrance is not visible when the slide first appears. (It is visible during the development process but not when you present the slideshow.) It then appears on the slide in the manner specified by the entrance effect. Some entrance effects are available in the Animation gallery. They're illustrated in green, and their icons provide some idea of the movement associated with the effect.

Have fun experimenting with the different effects

Selecting More Entrance Effects at the bottom of the Animation menu opens a dialog that displays all the available entrance animations by category to help you choose an appropriate effect.

The entrance animation effects available for text

- **Emphasis animations** These effects animate an object that is already visible on the slide to draw attention to it, without changing its location. The emphasis effects available in the Animation gallery are illustrated in yellow.

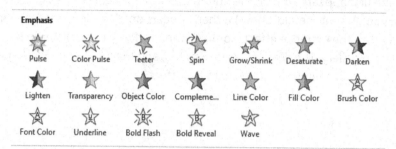

Extra emphasis effects are available for text

Selecting More Emphasis Effects at the bottom of the Animation menu opens a dialog that displays all the available emphasis animations by category.

Basic	
Fill Color	Font Color
Grow/Shrink	Line Color
Spin	Transparency

Subtle	
Bold Flash	Brush Color
Complementary Color	Complementary Color 2
Contrasting Color	Darken
Desaturate	Lighten
Object Color	Pulse
Underline	

Moderate	
Color Pulse	Grow With Color
Shimmer	Teeter

Exciting	
Blink	Bold Reveal
Wave	

The emphasis animations available for text and images

- **Motion Path animations** These effects move an object along a path that you specify, over a period of time that you specify. A few simple motion paths are available from the Animation gallery, but a surprisingly large variety is available from the dialog that opens when you select More Motion Paths at the bottom of the Animation menu.

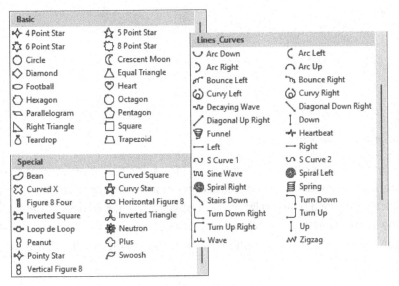

The motion path animations available for text

- **Exit animations** These effects take an existing object through a process that results in the object no longer being visible on the slide. The exit effects available in the Animation gallery are illustrated in red.

Choose an effect that suits the style of your presentation

12

Additional exit effects are available from the Change Exit Effect dialog.

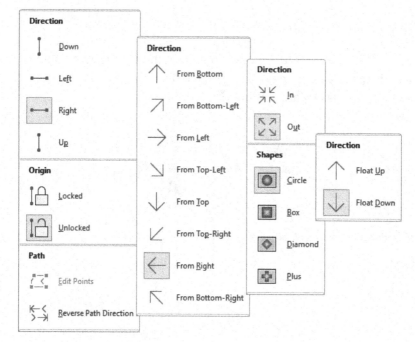

The exit animations available for text

Animations can be very simple or very complex. Many animations have options that you can configure, such as the direction, speed, size, or color. For example, when you configure an entrance effect for a bulleted list, you can specify whether to have the entire list enter the slide at the same time, or to have only one bulleted item enter at a time. After you choose an effect, the applicable options are available on the Effect Options menu.

Different animations have different options

You can apply multiple animation effects (for example, an entrance effect and an emphasis effect) to a single object. As you assign animations to slide objects, numbers appear on the objects to specify the order of the animation effects. The numbers are visible only when the Animation tab is active.

Each number represents one animation event

As you build an animated slide, you can add and animate individual elements, or you can first add all the elements to the slide and then animate them. Regardless of the process you choose, position the objects on the slide as follows:

- **Entrance effects** Position the object where you want it to end up after it enters the slide.

- **Emphasis effects** Position the object where it will be before and after the effect.

- **Exit effects** Position the object where it will be before it leaves the slide.

After all the elements are in place, animate them in the order you want the animations to occur. (If you're animating multiple objects, it might be helpful to write out a description of the process before starting.) If you animate something out of order, don't worry; you can reorder the animations from within the Animation Pane.

12

Animate this

Animations can greatly enrich presentation content. However, incorporating a "dazzling" array of animation effects into a presentation can be distracting or confusing to the audience. Ensure that the time you put into creating an animation has value to you and to your audience.

Consider using animations to provide subliminal information—for example, in a multipart presentation, use one consistent entrance effect for the part opener titles to draw the attention of the audience and cue them to a change of subject.

An excellent use of animation is to create "build slides" that add information in layers and essentially culminate in a review slide. Simple examples of build slides include:

- A bulleted list that adds one item to the list at a time. For greater impact, display an image related to the current list item, and replace the image as each new list item appears.

- A pie chart that displays each chart wedge individually, and finishes with the complete pie. Make this even more informative by displaying a detailed breakdown of the chart data for each category as you display its chart wedge.

You could achieve these effects by creating series of separate slides, but it's much simpler to animate the list or chart object.

A more difficult but often worthwhile use of slide object animation is to provide a visual image of a process as you describe it. You can narrate the animation in person or, if you're going to distribute the presentation electronically, you can record the narration and synchronize the animations with the relevant wording.

To animate an object on a slide

1. Display the slide in the **Slide** pane, and select the object that you want to animate, or its container. (For example, if you want to animate the entrance of a bulleted list, select the text box that contains the bulleted list.)

2. On the **Animations** tab, in the **Animation** group, select the **More** button to display the **Animation** menu and gallery.

> **TIP** If the menu expands to cover the slide content, you can drag the handle in the lower-right corner of the menu to resize it.

The Animation gallery and menu

3. Do either of the following:

- In the **Entrance**, **Emphasis**, **Exit**, or **Motion Path** section, select the icon that represents the animation you want to apply.

- At the bottom of the **Animation** menu, select the **More** command for the type of animation you want to apply, and then in the **Change** *Type* **Effect** dialog, select the animation you want.

PowerPoint displays a live preview of the selected animation effect and adds an animation number adjacent to the object. A star appears next to the slide thumbnail to indicate that the slide contains either an animation or a transition.

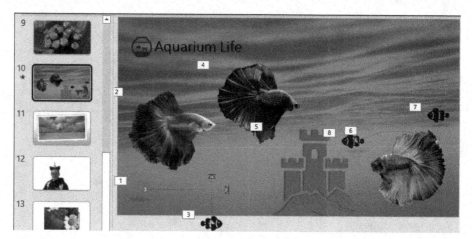

In the Thumbnails pane, the star below the slide number indicates the presence of movement on the slide

> **TIP** When you apply an animation, PowerPoint automatically previews (plays) the animation. If this is distracting to you, you can turn off this feature by selecting the Preview arrow (in the Preview group on the Animations tab) and then selecting AutoPreview to remove the check mark that indicates the option is turned on.

To select an applied animation

- On the slide or in the **Animation Pane**, select the animation number.

To display or hide the Animation Pane

- On the **Animations** tab, in the **Advanced Animation** group, select **Animation Pane**.

> **TIP** You can expand and collapse sets of animation effects in the Animation Pane to help you focus on those you want to work with.

To configure animation options

1. Apply the animation, or select a previously applied animation.

2. On the **Animations** tab, in the **Animation** group, select **Effect Options**. (If the button is unavailable, the animation has no configurable options.)

   The Effect Options menu has one titled section for each option that you can configure.

3. On the **Effect Options** menu, select one option in each section.

To apply multiple animation effects to one object

1. Apply the first animation effect and configure any options.

2. Select the object (not the animation). The existing animation information is highlighted on the Animations tab and in the Animation Pane.

3. On the **Animations** tab, in the **Advanced Animation** group, select **Add Animation**. In the **Add Animation** gallery, select the additional animation you want to apply.

To copy a set of animation effects from one object to another object

1. Select the source object.

2. On the **Animations** tab, in the **Advanced Animation** group, select **Animation Painter**.

3. Point to the object you want to format. When a paintbrush appears to the right of the cursor, select the object to apply the formatting.

> **TIP** The Animation Painter is similar to the Format Painter. If you select Animation Painter one time, you can copy the formatting to one other object. If you double-click the Animation Painter button, you can copy the formatting to many other objects, until you select the button again or press Esc to deactivate it.

12

To preview animations

- To preview all animations on a slide in order, on the **Animations** tab, in the **Preview** group, select **Preview**.

- To preview a specific animation and those that follow, in the **Animation Pane**, select the first animation, and then select **Play From**.

- To preview one animation, select the animation on the slide and then, in the **Animation Pane**, select **Play From**.

To remove animation effects from slide objects

- Do either of the following in the **Animation Pane**:

    - To remove one animation, right-click or long-press (tap and hold) the animation, and then select **Remove**.

    - To remove all animations, select any animation, press **Ctrl+A** to select all the animations, and then press **Delete**.

Morphing slide content into new forms

Morphing is the process of changing from one form to another. The new Morph feature (available only to Office 365 users) smoothly transitions the content of one slide into the content of another, in a way that appears as though the change is taking effect directly on the slide. It's a cool effect, and it's easy to use. Morph is technically a transition rather than an animation, but it creates an animation-like effect and is definitely fun to play with. If you create slideshows that show before-and-after effects or ongoing processes, give this feature a try!

Customize animation effects

Many presentations don't require much in the way of animation, and you might find that transitions and ready-made animation effects will meet all your animation needs. However, for those occasions when you want a presentation with pizzazz, you can customize the animation effects.

 TIP Animations can be useful for self-running presentations, where there is no presenter to lead the audience from one concept to another.

After you apply an animation effect, you can fine-tune its action in the following ways:

- Specify the direction, shape, or sequence of the animation. (The options vary depending on the type of animation you apply.)

- Specify what action will trigger the animation. For example, you can specify that selecting a different object on the slide will animate the selected object.

- As an alternative to clicking the mouse button to build animated slides, have PowerPoint build the slide for you.

- Control the implementation speed (duration) of each animation, or delay an animation effect.

- Change the order of the animation effects.

Entrance and exit effects cause objects to appear and disappear when you're previewing or presenting a slide. However, all the objects are visible while you're working in the Slide pane. The Animation Pane is a very helpful tool when managing multiple animated objects on a slide. Each numbered animation on the slide has a corresponding entry in the Animation Pane that provides information and options for managing the animations.

Manage all aspects of animations from the Animation Pane

The color coding of the Entrance, Emphasis, and Exit effects is visible in the Animation Pane, and a timeline is available at the bottom of the pane. The visual indicators to the right of each object name represent the type, starting point, and duration of each animation event, as follows:

- The indicator color represents the animation type (green for Entrance, yellow for Emphasis, blue for Motion Path, and red for Exit).

- The left side of the indicator aligns with the animation starting point. If the left sides of two indicators align, those animations start at the same time. If the left side of an indicator aligns with the right side of the previous indicator, the animations run in order.

- The width of the indicator is the animation duration as it relates to the timeline at the bottom of the Animation Pane.

- The right side of the indicator is either triangular or square. A square indicates that the animation has a fixed duration; a triangular edge indicates that the duration is set to Auto.

Each animation is an individual event. By default, each animation starts immediately "on click," meaning when you switch to the slide, click the mouse button, tap the screen, or press an arrow key—any action that would otherwise move to the next slide. You can change the animation "trigger" to run with or after another event, to run it after a certain length of time, or to run it when you select a specific screen element or reach a bookmark in an audio or video clip. You control these settings either from the Advanced Animation and Timing groups on the Animations tab, or from the Animation Pane.

Selecting an animation in the Animation Pane selects the animation and displays an arrow to the right of the animation timing indicators. Selecting the arrow displays a menu of actions. Some of these actions are available from the Animations tab, but the effect options available from this menu are more complex than those on the Effect Options menu in the Animation group.

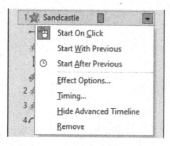

You can configure these actions from the Animation Pane to customize an animation

Selecting Effect Options on the shortcut menu provides access to an effect-specific dialog where you can refine that type of animation in the following ways:

- Specify whether the animation should be accompanied by a sound effect.

- Dim or hide the element after the animation, or have it change to a specific color.

- If the animation is applied to text, animate all the text at once or animate it word by word or letter by letter.

- Repeat an animation and specify what triggers its action.

- If a slide has more than one level of bullet points, animate different levels separately.

- If an object has text, animate the object and the text together (the default) or separately, or animate one but not the other.

The dialog title is the animation type, and the options available in the dialog are specific to that type of animation.

Some of the settings available through the Animation Pane Effect Options menu

To open the effect-specific dialog for an animation

- Do either of the following in the **Animation Pane**:

  - Point to the animation, select the arrow, and then select **Effect Options**.

  - Double-click the animation.

To change the order of animation effects on a slide

1. On the slide or in the **Animation Pane**, select the animation you want to reorder.

2. On the **Animations** tab, in the **Timing** group, select **Move Earlier** or **Move Later**.

Or

1. In the **Animation Pane**, select the animation or animations that you want to move.

2. Drag the selection to the new position in the **Animation Pane**. The animation numbers change to reflect the new positions.

 TIP After reordering animations, it's a good idea to preview the animations to ensure that the actions happen in a logical order.

To set the trigger for a selected animation

 TIP Many of the following settings can be configured on the Animations tab, in the Animation Pane, or in the effect-specific options dialog. We've provided one path to the setting, but use the interface that you're most comfortable with.

- Do any of the following in the **Timing** group on the **Animations** tab:

  - To start the animation manually, select the **Start** list, and then select **On Click**.

  - To start the animation based on the previous animation, select the **Start** list, and then select **With Previous** or **After Previous**.

  - To start the animation a specific period of time after the trigger, specify the **Delay** in seconds.

Or

- Do either of the following in the **Advanced Animation** group on the **Animations** tab:

  - To start the animation when you select an object on the slide, select the **Trigger** button, select **On Click of**, and then select a trigger object on the slide.

  - To start the animation at a specific point during the playback of an audio clip or video clip, in the **Trigger** list, select **On Bookmark**, and then select a bookmark that you've set in an audio or video clip.

    > **SEE ALSO** For information about setting bookmarks, see the sidebar "Bookmark points of interest in media clips" later in this chapter.

Or

- In the **Animation Pane**, drag the colored indicator bar to the starting point you want.

To set the duration of a selected animation

- On the **Animations** tab, in the **Timing** group, specify the **Duration** in seconds.

- In the **Animation Pane**, drag the right side of the colored indicator bar to set the duration in accordance with the timeline at the bottom of the pane.

To add a sound effect to an animation

1. In the **Animation Pane**, double-click the animation to open the animation-specific effect options dialog.

2. On the **Effect** tab, select the **Sound** list, and then select the sound effect you want to assign to the animation.

3. Select the speaker icon to the right of the **Sound** list to display the volume slider. Then set the volume level of the sound effect.

4. Select **OK** to close the dialog.

12

Bookmark points of interest in media clips

Bookmarks are a useful feature for PowerPoint users who incorporate audio, video, and animation into presentations. You can insert bookmarks into audio and video clips to identify locations either that you want to quickly get to or that you want to use as triggers for other events.

For example, you could create an animation that visually describes a process and record a narration that verbally describes the process. Instead of setting up a series of timing points to synchronize the narration and animation, you could insert bookmarks at key points in the narrative audio clip that trigger specific segments of the animation to play.

As another example, you could embed a video on a slide, and record audio comments about certain parts of the video. Then you can insert bookmarks at those points of the video to trigger the playback of the relevant audio comments.

When you insert bookmarks in audio and video clips within PowerPoint, those bookmarks exist only in PowerPoint and don't affect the original recording.

To insert a bookmark in an audio or video clip, follow these steps:

1. Display the slide in Normal view and select the audio or video clip to display the Audio Tools or Video Tools tab group.

2. Play the clip by selecting the **Play/Pause** button on the playback toolbar or in the **Preview** group on the **Playback** tool tab.

3. At the point that you want to insert a bookmark, select **Add Bookmark** in the **Bookmarks** group on the **Playback** tool tab.

4. To insert additional bookmarks, repeat steps 2 and 3.

Bookmarks in audio or video clips are indicated by circles on the playback tool-bar. Pointing to a bookmark on the toolbar displays a ScreenTip that includes the bookmark name. You can select a bookmark as the starting point for an anima-tion from the Trigger list on the Animations tab.

Adding a bookmark to a media clip makes it available as a trigger

If you create a bookmark but then don't need it, you can remove it by selecting it and then selecting Remove Bookmark in the Bookmarks group on the Playback tool tab.

Add audio content to slides

You can enhance presentations by adding sound to slide transitions, to animated content, to an individual slide, or to the presentation as a whole. For example, you could run a presentation that provides basic information and icebreakers during the time leading up to your actual presentation. You can add a pleasant royalty-free soundtrack that loops while the presentation plays, to avoid the discomfort of a room full of people who don't want to break the silence.

If you plan to distribute a presentation electronically for people to watch on their own, you might want to add audio narration to an animation or provide narration for the entire presentation.

> **SEE ALSO** For information about adding sound effects to animations, see "Customize animation effects" earlier in this chapter.

You can add prerecorded audio content to a presentation or record your own content directly within PowerPoint. PowerPoint supports the most common audio formats—MP3, MP4, WAV, and WMA—and more specialized formats such as ADTS, AIFF, AU, FLAC, MIDI, and MKA audio.

> **TIP** The Insert Online Audio feature that was present in earlier versions of PowerPoint is no longer available. However, you can download royalty-free audio music and sound effects from many online sources. Some of these require that you credit the website as the source, so be sure to read the website's fine print. When you locate an audio clip that you want to use, you can download it to your computer and follow the instructions in this topic to use it in a PowerPoint presentation.

When you add audio to a slide (rather than to an animation or transition), the audio icon (shaped like a speaker) appears on the slide, and the audio trigger event appears in the Animation Pane.

When the audio icon is selected, the Audio Tools tab group, which includes the Audio Format and Playback tool tabs, appears on the ribbon, and audio playback controls appear on the slide.

The playback controls are simple but provide sufficient options

You can start audio content on a slide automatically or from the playback controls. The playback controls are visible only when the audio icon is active. The icon isn't obtrusive, but you can disguise or hide it if you want to.

The audio controls are visible only when the icon is active

You can customize the audio content by using commands on the Playback tool tab as follows:

- Edit the audio content so that only part of it plays.

- Make the sound gradually increase and decrease in volume.

- Adjust the volume or mute the sound.

- Specify whether the audio content plays:

  - Automatically when the slide appears.

  - Only if you select its icon.

- Make the audio object invisible while the presentation is displayed in Reading view or Slide Show view.

- Specify that the audio content should play continuously until you stop it.

- Ensure that the audio content starts from the beginning each time it is played.

To insert a local audio clip onto a slide

1. Save the audio clip on your computer or on a network-connected location.

2. On the **Insert** tab, in the **Media** group, select **Audio**, and then select **Audio on My PC** to open the Insert Audio dialog.

3. In the **Insert Audio** dialog, browse to and select the audio file, and then select **Insert**.

Or

1. In File Explorer, open the folder that contains the audio file.

2. Arrange the File Explorer and PowerPoint windows on your screen so that both are visible.

3. Drag the audio file from File Explorer to the slide.

To record audio directly onto a slide

1. On the **Insert** tab, in the **Media** group, select **Audio**, and then select **Record Audio** to open the Record Sound dialog.

2. In the **Name** box, enter a name to uniquely identify the recording. Then select the **Record** button (labeled with a circle).

The Record Sound dialog

3. Speak or otherwise provide the audio that you want to record. When you finish, select the **Stop** button (labeled with a square). The audio icon and an accompanying trigger icon appear in the center of the slide, and the trigger event appears in the Animation Pane.

> ✓ **TIP** If you record multiple clips, the audio icons stack up in the same location on the slide. It might be necessary to move one or more out of the way to get to an earlier clip.

To restrict the playback of an audio clip to a specific segment

1. Select the audio icon. On the **Playback** tool tab, in the **Editing** group, select **Trim Audio** to open the Trim Audio dialog.

You can trim unwanted audio from the beginning and end of a clip

2. In the **Trim Audio** dialog, do any of the following:

    -   Select the **Play** button to play the clip, and then select the **Pause** button to pause when you locate a point that you want to mark.

    -   Drag the green **Start** marker to specify a playback starting point other than the beginning of the clip. (If you drag the marker near the point at which you paused the playback, the marker snaps to that location.)

    -   Drag the red **End** marker to specify a playback end point other than the end of the clip.

    -   Select the **Start** or **End** marker, and then select the **Previous Frame** or **Next Frame** button to move the selected marker back or forward 0.1 seconds (one-tenth of a second).

12

3. When you finish, select **OK** to close the Trim Audio dialog.

> ✓ **TIP** Trimming the audio affects only the playback of the audio on the slide, not the original audio clip. You can re-trim or restore the audio clip at any time. For information about discarding trimmed content, see "Compress media to decrease file size" later in this chapter.

To fade into or out of an audio clip

- Select the audio icon. On the **Playback** tool tab, in the **Editing** group, do the following:

  - In the **Fade In** box, specify the length of time over which you want to increase the audio to full volume.

  - In the **Fade Out** box, specify the number of seconds at the end of the audio clip over which you want to decrease the audio volume.

> ✓ **TIP** The Fade In and Fade Out times can be specified precisely down to a hundredth of a second.

To modify or hide the audio icon

- Select the audio icon, and then do any of the following:

  - Drag the sizing handles to make the icon larger or smaller.

  - Drag the icon to a different location on the slide, or to a location slightly off the slide but still on the development canvas.

  - Use the commands on the **Graphics Format** tool tab to change the icon's appearance.

  - Replace the default icon with a different image (such as a picture or logo).

To manually start audio playback

- In Normal view, Reading view, or Slide Show view, point to the audio icon. When the playback controls appear, select the **Play** button.

- In Normal view, select the audio icon, and then select the **Play** button on the playback toolbar or in the **Preview** group on the **Playback** tool tab.

- In Slide Show view, after the audio icon has had focus, press **Alt+P.**

> **TIP** To play sounds and other audio content, you must have a sound card and speakers installed.

To automatically start audio playback

- On the **Playback** tool tab, in the **Audio Options** group, in the **Start** list, select **Automatically**. Then select the **Loop until Stopped** checkbox.

> **TIP** If your presentation might be viewed by people using assistive technologies such as screen readers or text-to-speech tools, you should avoid starting audio clips or files automatically. Instead, allow the user to play the audio content after the tool has finished communicating the slide content.

To prevent an audio clip from stopping when the slide changes

- On the **Playback** tool tab, do either of the following:

  - To play to the end of the audio and then stop, in the **Audio Options** group, select the **Play Across Slides** checkbox.

  - To loop the audio until the end of the slideshow regardless of other audio tracks, in the **Audio Styles** group, select **Play in Background**.

To loop (repeat) an audio clip

- On the **Playback** tool tab, in the **Audio Options** group, select the **Loop until Stopped** checkbox.

> **TIP** To automatically start and continuously play an audio clip through an entire slideshow, configure the settings as follows: on the Playback tool tab, in the Audio Options group, change the Start setting to Automatically. Then select the Play Across Slides, Loop Until Stopped, and Hide During Show checkboxes.

12

Add video content to slides

Sometimes the best way to ensure that your audience understands your message is to show a video. For example, if your company has developed a short advertising video, it makes more sense to include the video in a presentation about marketing plans than to try to describe it by using bullet points or even pictures. To save yourself the trouble of switching between PowerPoint and a video player, you can embed a video recording directly onto a slide, and then play the video as part of presenting the slideshow. This is a much smoother way of presenting information from multiple sources than switching between them.

You can insert a video onto a slide from your computer or a connected local storage device, from your Facebook account, from YouTube, or from a website that provides an "embed code" (basically, an address that you can link to).

> **TIP** If a publicly posted video clip has an "embed code" available, you can link to the online video rather than embedding it in the slideshow. PowerPoint uses the embed code to locate and play the video. As long as the video remains available in its original location (and you have an active internet connection), you'll be able to access and play the video from the slide at any time.

After you insert the video, you can format its representation on the slide in all the ways that you can other imagery. You can move and resize it, display it in a frame of your choice, and even adjust the brightness or color contrast.

You can resize the video frame

> **TIP** The changes that you make to an image on a slide also affect the video playback. So, for example, if you change the aspect ratio of the video representation on the slide, imagery in the video might appear to be skewed.

When working with local videos that you embed rather than online videos that you link to, you can fade into and out from the video playback, and manage the content of the video by trimming it to play only a specific portion. You can insert bookmarks to use as triggers for other events (for example, you might display a list of selling points as each is presented in the advertising video).

Set your start and end times to focus on the specific content you want to highlight

When you're previewing or presenting a slideshow, you can play (and pause) embedded audio or video, move around within the recording, and control the volume by using the controls that appear when the audio icon or video placeholder image is active. When playing back a video, you can display it at the embedded size or full screen.

12

Many of the processes for managing video clips are the same as those for managing audio clips:

- Restricting the playback of a video clip to a specific segment
- Fading into or out of a video clip
- Manually or automatically starting video playback
- Preventing a video clip from stopping when the slide changes
- Looping a video clip

> (Q) **SEE ALSO** For additional information related to the preceding processes, see "Add audio content to slides" earlier in this chapter.

To insert a video clip from your computer

1. Do either of the following to open the Insert Video dialog:
   - If the slide has a content placeholder, select the **Insert Video** button in the placeholder.
   - If the slide doesn't have a content placeholder, on the **Insert** tab, in the **Media** group, select the **Video** button and then select **This Device**.
2. In the **Insert Video** dialog, browse to and select the video you want to insert. Then select **Insert** or press **Enter**.

To insert a stock video clip

1. On the **Insert** tab, in the **Media** group, select **Video**, and then select **Stock Videos** to display the Videos tab of the stock image library.
2. Enter a search term to locate the video you want to insert.
3. Select the video to display the check mark, and then select **Insert**.

To insert a video clip from an online provider

1. On the **Insert** tab, in the **Media** group, select **Video**, and then select **Online Videos**.
2. In the window that opens, paste the address of a video that is hosted on YouTube, SlideShare, Vimeo, Stream, or Flipgrid.

3. Verify that the video preview displays the video you want to insert, and then select **Insert**.

To select an embedded video

- Select the video image one time. Selection handles appear around the video image, the playback toolbar appears below it, and the Video Tools tab group appears on the ribbon.

To move the video image on the slide

- Select the video, and then do either of the following:

  - Drag the video to the new location. Smart guides might appear on the slide to help you align the video with other objects.

  - Press the arrow keys to move the video by small amounts.

To resize the video image on the slide and retain its aspect ratio

- Drag any corner handle. Smart guides appear on the slide to help you align the video with other objects.

- On the **Video Format** tool tab, in the **Size** group, set a specific **Video Height** or **Video Width**, and then press **Enter** to change both settings.

To format the video image on the slide

- Select the video, and then apply formatting from the **Video Format** tool tab just as you would for a picture.

> **SEE ALSO** For information about formatting pictures, see "Edit and format pictures" in Chapter 11, "Insert and manage simple graphics."

To configure an embedded video to play back at full screen size

1. Select the video.

2. On the **Playback** tool tab, in the **Video Options** group, select the **Play Full Screen** checkbox.

To set the relative volume of a video soundtrack

1. Select the video.

2. On the **Playback** tool tab, in the **Video Options** group, select **Volume**.

3. In the **Volume** list, select **Low**, **Medium**, **High**, or **Mute**.

12

Compress media to decrease file size

Trimming an audio or video clip affects only the playback of the media on the slide, not the original media clip. The original media clip is stored in its entirety as part of the presentation, and you can re-trim or restore the media clip at any time.

You can decrease the size of a PowerPoint file that contains trimmed media clips by discarding the unused portions of the clips. PowerPoint offers three compression configurations designed to balance size and quality.

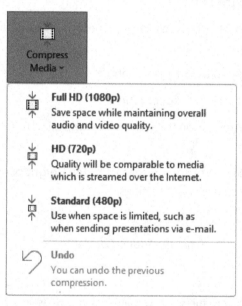

Choose the size and quality that best fits your needs

When you save and close the file after compressing the media, the trimmed portions of the videos are discarded and no longer available. You can reverse the compression operation until you save and close the file.

To compress media files

1. Save the PowerPoint presentation, and then display the **Info** page of the Backstage view.

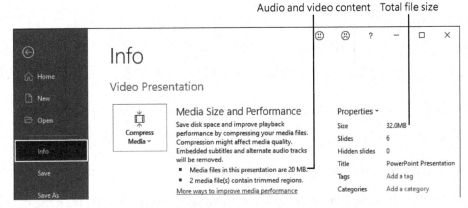

The Info page displays file properties and information

2. Note the total size of the presentation, the size of the media files in the presentation, and the number of files that have been trimmed.

3. On the **Info** page, select **Compress Media**, and then select the level of compression you want. In the Compress Media window, PowerPoint itemizes the media elements and their compression levels, and reports the total space savings.

Slide	Name	Initial Size (MB)	Status
4	Video 9	4.4	Unsupported
5	Recorded Sound	0.8	Already Compressed
6	Narration	6.4	Complete - 3.7 MB Saved
6	Video 4	8.8	Unsupported

Some files could not be compressed. You saved 3.7 MB.

Compressing media files can make a big difference in file size

12

4. In the **Compress Media** window, select the **Close** button. In the Media Size And Performance area of the Info page, the Compress Media button is active to indicate that media has been compressed, and specifics about the compression are available.

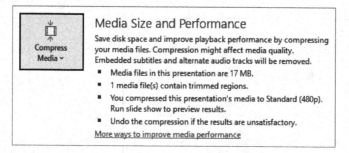

Media Size and Performance

Save disk space and improve playback performance by compressing your media files. Compression might affect media quality. Embedded subtitles and alternate audio tracks will be removed.

- Media files in this presentation are 17 MB.
- 1 media file(s) contain trimmed regions.
- You compressed this presentation's media to Standard (480p). Run slide show to preview results.
- Undo the compression if the results are unsatisfactory.

More ways to improve media performance

You can undo the compression if you don't like the results

5. Play the presentation to assess the quality, and then save the file if the quality is acceptable.

To reverse the compression of media files

- On the **Info** page, select **Compress Media**, and then select **Undo**. PowerPoint immediately reverts to the uncompressed files.

Hyperlink to additional resources

Presentations often include URLs of websites that provide additional information related to the presentation topic. When a presentation will be viewed electronically, the URLs can be formatted as hyperlinks so that the websites can be accessed directly from the presentation. Hyperlinks can also provide access to information that might be on a hidden slide in the presentation, or in a separate file.

TIP If you use Microsoft Outlook, you can also use a hyperlink to open an email message window so that people viewing the presentation can easily contact you.

Hyperlinks are most frequently in text format, but you can attach a hyperlink to any object—for example, an image such as a shape, logo, or picture. Selecting the hyperlinked object then takes you directly to the linked location. Editing the object does not disrupt the hyperlink; however, deleting the object also deletes the hyperlink.

The simplest method of creating a hyperlink is to enter a URL in a text box and then press the Enter key. PowerPoint automatically inserts the hyperlink and formats the URL so that people recognize it as a hyperlink.

If you want the same hyperlink to appear on every slide in a presentation, attach the hyperlink to text or an object on the presentation's primary slide master.

To attach a hyperlink to an object, follow these steps:

1. Select the object from which you want to hyperlink.

2. Open the **Insert Hyperlink** box by doing either of the following:

    - On the **Insert** tab, in the **Links** group, select **Hyperlink**.

    - Press **Ctrl+K**.

3. In the **Link to** list, select the type of target you're linking to. Often this is a webpage or another place in the file.

4. If you're linking to a webpage, enter the URL in the **Address** box. If you're linking to a slide or heading in the current file, select it in the **Select a place in this document** pane. Then select **OK**.

12

Key points

- Used judiciously, animated text and graphics add interest to your slides. You decide how and when the animation occurs, and you can even customize animation effects with sounds.

- You can configure audio clips to play as an accompaniment to your slide content. This is a great feature to use when playing an unnarrated slideshow or displaying a welcome slide at the beginning of a class or meeting.

- You can embed video clips directly on a slide and configure their playback. This is a great way to seamlessly incorporate video into a presentation and avoid switching to the display of another program.

- Before distributing presentations, you can compress audio and video content to significantly decrease the size of the file.

Practice tasks

Before you can complete these tasks, you must copy the book's practice files to your computer. The practice files for these tasks are in located the **Office365SBS\Ch12** folder. You can save the results of the tasks in the same folder.

The introduction includes a complete list of practice files and download instructions.

Animate text and pictures on slides

Open the **AnimateSlides** presentation, and then perform the following tasks:

1. On slide **1**, apply the **Shape** entrance animation to the slide title and then to the subtitle. Notice that the animation numbers 1 and 2 appear to the left of the animated objects.

2. Display slide **2**, and apply the **Shape** entrance animation to the left content placeholder. Notice that boxes containing the numbers 1 through 3 appear to the left of the bullet points to indicate the order of their animations.

3. Repeat task 2 for the placeholder on the right.

4. Preview all the animations on slide **2**.

5. Display slide **3**. Apply the **Shape** entrance animation to the frog photo, and then add the **Pulse** emphasis animation.

6. Copy the animations from the frog photo to the crow photo and to the cat photo.

7. Preview the animations on the slide, and then preview the entire presentation.

8. Return to Normal view.

9. Save and close the presentation.

Customize animation effects

Open the **CustomizeAnimation** presentation, and then perform the following tasks:

1. On slide **1**, apply the **Diamond** entrance effect to the slide title. Set the direction to **Out**.

2. Copy the animation from the slide title to the subtitle. Then change the timing of the subtitle animation to **After Previous**.

3. Switch to Reading view and preview the animation effects on slide **1**.

4. Switch back to Normal view, display slide **2**, and then select anywhere in the bulleted list on the left.

5. Display the **Animation Pane**. Right-click animation 1, and then select **Effect Options** to open the Circle dialog.

6. In the **Circle** dialog, do the following:

   • Apply the **Chime** sound.

   • Dim the text color to **Red** after the animation.

   • Animate the text by letter.

   • Set the duration to **3 seconds (Slow)**.

7. Watch the effects of your changes to the animation effects. The Shape animation doesn't work very well with the selected effect options, so let's adjust them.

8. On the slide, select the left content placeholder. Notice that in the Animation Pane, all the animations for the bullet points in the placeholder are selected.

9. Apply the **Float Up** entrance animation to the entire placeholder, and then display the effect options.

10. In the **Float Up** dialog, do the following:

    • Apply the **Chime** sound.

    • Dim the text color to **Red** after the animation.

    • Animate text by letter.

    • Set the duration to **1 seconds (Fast)**.

11. Preview the animations and make any additional adjustments you want to your custom animation effects.

12. Copy the animation effects of the bullet points on the left to those on the right.

13. Switch to Reading view, and then select **Next** to display the animated bullet points on slide 2.

14. When all the bullet points are visible and dimmed to red, press the **Esc** key to return to Normal view.

15. Save and close the presentation.

Add audio content to slides

Open the **AddAudio** presentation, display slide 1, and then perform the following tasks:

1. On the **Insert** tab, in the **Media** group, select **Audio**, and then select **Audio on My PC** to open the Insert Audio dialog.

2. In the **Insert Audio** dialog, browse to the practice file folder, and double-click the **SoundTrack** file to insert the audio clip on the slide.

3. On the **Playback** tool tab, in the **Audio Options** group, change the **Start** setting to **Automatically**. Then select the **Play Across Slides**, **Loop until Stopped**, and **Hide During Show** checkboxes.

4. Switch to Reading view, and listen to the audio file as the presentation moves from slide to slide.

5. Press **Esc** to stop the presentation and return to Normal view.

6. Save and close the presentation.

Add video content to slides

Open the **AddVideo** presentation, and then perform the following tasks:

1. In the left content placeholder, insert the **Butterfly** video from the practice file folder.

2. On the playback toolbar, select the **Play/Pause** button, and then watch the video.

3. Insert the **Wildlife** video from the practice file folder into the content placeholder on the right, and then play the video.

4. With the **Wildlife** video selected, open the **Trim Video** dialog, and drag the green start marker until it sits at about the **00:17.020** mark. Then, frame by frame, adjust the starting point until the first marmot frame comes into view at about the **00:17.292** mark.

5. Drag the red stop marker until it sits at about the **00:20.900** mark. Then, frame by frame, adjust the ending point until the last marmot frame comes into view at about the **00:20.790** mark.

6. Play the trimmed video, and then select **OK** to close the Trim Video dialog.

7. Change the height of the **Butterfly** video representation to **3"**.

8. Change the height of the **Wildlife** video representation to **3"**, and then crop it to a width of **4"**.

9. Drag the video representations until they are evenly spaced on the slide and center-aligned with each other.

10. Apply the **Reflected Bevel, Black** (in the **Intense** area of the **Video Styles** gallery) video style to both video objects.

11. Set up the **Butterfly** video to play back on mute, to start automatically, and to loop until stopped.

12. Set up the **Wildlife** video to play back on mute, to start on click, and to loop until stopped.

13. Preview and pause the **Butterfly** video. Then preview and pause the **Wildlife** video.

14. Return to Normal view.

15. Save and close the presentation.

Compress media to decrease file size

There are no practice tasks for this topic.

Part 5

Microsoft Outlook

CHAPTER 13
Send and receive email messages........................ 401

CHAPTER 14
Organize your Inbox 447

CHAPTER 15
Manage scheduling..................................... 475

Send and receive email messages

Although Microsoft Outlook is an excellent tool for managing your schedule, contact records, and task lists, the primary reason most people use Outlook is to send and receive email messages. Over the past decade, email has become an important method of communication for both business and personal purposes. Outlook provides all the tools you need to send, respond to, organize, find, filter, sort, and otherwise manage email messages for one or more email accounts.

When creating email messages in Outlook, you can format the text, include images, attach files, and set message options such as importance, sensitivity, and reminders. You can also include voting buttons and request receipts when messages are delivered or read.

Outlook has many features that make it easy to display and track information about the people you correspond with, particularly if your organization uses technologies that interact with Outlook, such as Microsoft Exchange, Teams, and SharePoint. These features include presence icons that indicate whether a person is online and available, and information cards that provide a convenient starting point for many kinds of contact.

This chapter guides you through procedures related to creating, sending, and displaying messages and message attachments; displaying message participant information; and responding to messages.

In this chapter

- Create and send messages

- Attach files and Outlook items to messages

- Display messages and message attachments

- Display message participant information

- Respond to messages

Create and send messages

If you have an internet connection, you can send email messages to people within your organization and around the world by using Outlook, regardless of the type of email account you have. Outlook can send and receive email messages in three message formats:

- **HTML** Supports paragraph styles (including numbered and bulleted lists), character styles (such as fonts, sizes, colors, weight), and backgrounds (such as colors and pictures). Most (but not all) email programs support the HTML format. Programs that don't support HTML display these messages as Plain Text.

- **Rich Text** Supports more paragraph formatting options than HTML, including borders and shading, but is compatible only with Outlook and Exchange Server. Outlook converts Rich Text messages to HTML when sending them outside of an Exchange network.

- **Plain Text** Does not support the formatting features available in HTML and Rich Text messages but is supported by all email programs.

Email message content isn't limited to simple text. You can create almost any type of content in an email message that you can in a Microsoft Word document. Because Outlook and Word share similar commands, you might already be familiar with many processes for formatting content.

You can personalize your messages by using an individual font style or color and add a professional touch by inserting your contact information in the form of an email signature. (You can apply other formatting, such as themes and page backgrounds, but these won't always appear to email recipients as you intend them to, and they can make your communications appear less professional.)

> **TIP** You can specify different email signatures for new messages and for replies and forwarded messages. For example, you might want to include your full name and contact information in the signature that appears in new messages, but only your first name in the signature that appears in replies and forwarded messages.

You can format the text of your message to make it more readable by including headings, lists, or tables, and you can represent information graphically by including charts, pictures, and other types of graphics. You can attach files to your message and link to other information, such as files or webpages.

You can format content in the message composition window just as you can in Word

> **SEE ALSO** For information about attaching files and other content to email messages, see "Attach files and Outlook items to messages" later in this chapter.

For the purposes of this book, we assume that you know how to enter, edit, and format content by using standard Word techniques, including typing and dictation.

13

> **SEE ALSO** For extensive information about entering and editing content and about formatting content by using character and paragraph styles, Quick Styles, and themes, refer to *Microsoft Word Step by Step (Word 2021 and Microsoft 365)*, by Joan Lambert (Microsoft Press, 2022).

Create messages

Creating an email message is a relatively simple process. You will usually provide three types of information:

- **Recipient** Addressing an email message is easy: just insert the intended recipient's email address (or name, if he or she is in your address book) into an address box in the message header of a message composition window. You can enter email recipients into any of three address boxes:

  - **To** Use for primary message recipients. Usually, these are the people you want to respond to the message. Each message must have at least one address in the To box.

  - **Cc** Use for "courtesy copy" recipients. These are usually people you want to keep informed about the subject of the email message but from whom you don't require a response.

  - **Bcc** Use for "blind courtesy copy" recipients. These are people you want to keep informed, but whom you want to keep hidden from other message recipients. Bcc recipients are not visible to any other message recipients and therefore aren't included in message responses unless specifically added to one of the address boxes in the response message.

> **TIP** As an added level of security for Bcc recipients, Outlook warns you if you respond to all the recipients of a message that you were Bcc'd on.

The To and Cc address boxes are always displayed in the message header. The Bcc address box is not displayed by default. You can display it in the message header by selecting the Bcc button, located in the Show Fields group on the Options tab of the message composition window.

> **TIP** Replying to or forwarding a received message automatically fills in one or more of the address boxes in the new message window. For information, see "Respond to messages" later in this chapter.

- **Subject** Enter a brief description of the message contents or purpose in this field. The subject is not required, but it's important to provide information in this field, both so that you and the recipient can identify the message and so that the message isn't blocked as suspected junk mail by a recipient's email program. Outlook will warn you if you try to send a message with no subject.

- **Message body** Enter your message to the recipient in this field, which is a large text box. You can include many types of information, including formatted text, hyperlinks, and graphics, in the message body.

> **TIP** In this chapter and throughout this book, for expediency's sake, we sometimes refer to email messages simply as *messages*. When referring to other types of messages we use full descriptions such as *instant messages* or *text messages* to avoid confusion.

If your email account is part of a Microsoft Exchange network, you can send messages to another person on the same network by entering only his or her *email alias*— for example, *joan.lambert*; the at symbol (@) and domain name aren't required. If you enter only the name of a person whose email address is in your address book, Outlook associates the name with the corresponding email address—a process called *resolving the address*—before sending the message.

Depending on the method you use to enter a message recipient's name or email address into an address box, Outlook either resolves the name or address immediately (if you chose it from a list of known names) or resolves it when you send the message.

The resolution process for each name or address has one of two results:

- If Outlook successfully resolves the name or address, an underline appears below it. If the name or address matches one stored in an address book, Outlook replaces your original entry with the content of the Display As field in the contact record, and then underlines it.

- If Outlook is unable to resolve the name or address, the Check Names dialog opens, asking you to select the address you want to use.

A cool message-addressing feature supported by Outlook is *@mentioning*. You can use this feature to add someone to a conversation or draw someone's attention to specific message content.

13

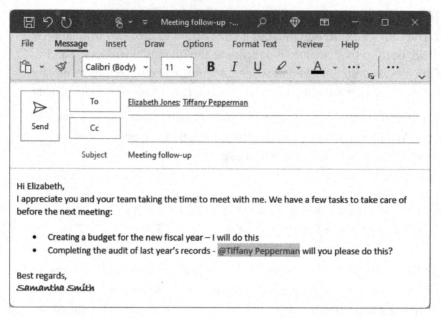

@mentioning someone adds them to the To field and inserts a special reference in the message body

You can format message content by using commands on the message window ribbon. By default, Outlook displays the Simplified Ribbon that shows unlabeled formatting commands. The visible command buttons vary depending on the width of the message window. An ellipsis indicates that additional commands are available. Selecting the ellipsis displays a list of the hidden commands.

Simplified Ribbon   Switch Ribbons

Access additional commands from the More menus

You can easily switch from the Simplified Ribbon to the Classic Ribbon that shows more commands. The visible command buttons and their shape, size, and labels vary depending on the width of the message window.

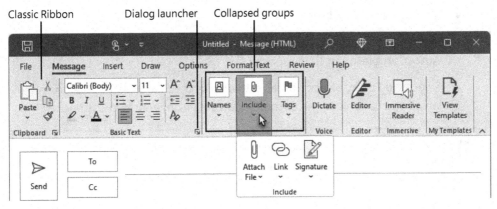

Expand collapsed groups of commands

> ⚠ **IMPORTANT** This book includes images that show both the Simplified Ribbon and the Classic Ribbon. The commands available to you on the Classic Ribbon might vary based on the type of email account—business or personal—to which Outlook is connected.

To open an email message composition window

- In the Mail module:
    - With the ribbon minimized, select the **New Email** button at the top of the **Folder Pane**.
    - On the **Home** tab of the ribbon, in the **New** group, select **New Email**.
- In any module, on the **Home** tab, in the **New** group, select **New Items**, and then select **E-mail Message**.

13

To enter an email address into an address box

- In the message composition window, click in the **To**, **Cc**, or **Bcc** box, and then do any of the following:

  - Enter the entire address.

  - Enter part of a previously used address and then select the address from the **Auto-Complete List** that appears.

  - Select the **To**, **Cc**, or **Bcc** box label to display the Select Names dialog, in which you can select one or more addresses from your address book(s).

> **SEE ALSO** For information about the Auto-Complete List, see "Troubleshoot message addressing" later in this topic.

To enter a subject for an email message

- In the message composition window, in the **Subject** box, enter the subject of the email message.

To enter content for an email message

- In the message composition window, in the message body field, enter the content of the email message.

To @mention someone in an email message

- In the message composition window, enter @ and then the name or email address of a person in your address book.

To switch between the Simplified and Classic Ribbons

1. In the lower-right corner of the ribbon, select the **Switch Ribbons** button.

2. In the **Ribbon Layout** section, select **Classic Ribbon** or **Simplified Ribbon**.

To format the content of an email message

1. In the message composition window, in the message body field, select the content you want to format.

2. Do any of the following from the Classic Ribbon:

   - Apply basic font and paragraph formatting from the **Mini Toolbar** that appears when you select the content, or from the **Basic Text** group on the **Message** tab.

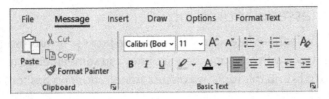

The Basic Text group includes commonly used formatting options

- Apply an extended range of font and paragraph formats from the **Format Text** tab.

The Format Text tab provides additional formatting options for the message body

- On the **Message** tab, select the **Basic Text** dialog launcher, or on the **Format Text** tab, select the **Font** dialog launcher to open the Font dialog. Apply the full range of font formatting, including character spacing, from this dialog.

The Font dialog provides the same options as in Word

13

Troubleshoot message addressing

Outlook includes many features intended to simplify the process of addressing messages to recipients. As with any tool, these features can sometimes be more difficult to use than you'd like. In this topic, we discuss troubleshooting tips for some common problems.

Troubleshoot the Auto-Complete List

As you enter a name or an email address into the To, Cc, or Bcc box, Outlook displays matching addresses in a list. You can insert a name or address from the list into the address box by selecting it or by pressing the arrow keys to select it and then pressing Tab or Enter.

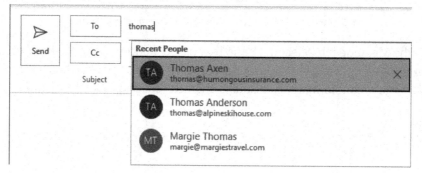

You can insert a recipient from the Auto-Complete List

Sometimes the Auto-Complete List might contain incorrect or outdated addresses—for example, if you have previously sent a message to an incorrect email address, or if a person changes his or her email address. The list might also contain people with whom you no longer correspond. If you don't remove incorrect or outdated addresses from the list, it can be easy to mistakenly accept Outlook's suggestion and send a message to the wrong address.

You can modify the Auto-Complete List settings in the Outlook Options dialog.

Troubleshoot address lists

When resolving email addresses, Outlook first searches your Global Address List (the corporate directory provided with an Exchange account, if you're working with one), and then searches the contact records stored in the People module of your default account.

If you have multiple address lists, such as those in custom contact folders that you create or associated with additional email accounts configured in Outlook, you can specify the order in which Outlook searches for names and addresses, or you can exclude an address list from the search if you don't want to accidentally resolve to an email address from that list.

Troubleshoot multiple recipients

By default, Outlook requires that you separate multiple email addresses with semi-colons. If you find it easier, you can separate multiple addresses by pressing the Enter key. Outlook will pull all the addresses onto one line and insert the semicolons for you before sending the message. If you separate multiple addresses by using a comma (which might seem to be the more natural action), Outlook treats the addresses as one address and displays an error message when you try to send the message.

You can instruct Outlook to accept commas as address separators in the Outlook Options dialog.

To remove a name or email address from the Auto-Complete List

1. In the **To**, **Cc**, or **Bcc** box, enter the first letter or letters of a name or email address to display the Auto-Complete List of matching names and addresses.

2. In the list, point to the name or address you want to remove.

3. Select the **Delete** button (the X) that appears to the right of the name or address.

To open the Outlook Options dialog

- In any module or message window, select the **File** tab to display the Backstage view, and then select **Options**.

To change the Auto-Complete List settings

1. Open the **Outlook Options** dialog, and then select the **Mail** tab.

2. On the **Mail** page, scroll to the **Send messages** section.

13

3. Do either of the following:

- To prevent the Auto-Complete List from appearing when you enter an address, clear the **Use Auto-Complete List to suggest names...** checkbox.

- To remove all entries from the Auto-Complete List (and start the list from scratch), select the **Empty Auto-Complete List** button, and then select **Yes** in the dialog that appears.

4. Select **OK** to apply the changes and close the dialog.

Recipient address options

You can customize how Outlook resolves addresses

To use commas as a separator between email addresses

1. Open the **Outlook Options** dialog, and then select the **Mail** tab.

2. On the **Mail** page, scroll to the **Send messages** section.

3. Select the **Commas can be used to separate multiple message recipients** checkbox.

4. Select **OK** to apply the changes and close the dialog.

To change the order in which Outlook searches the address books

1. On the **Home** tab of any module, in the **Find** group, select **Address Book** to open the Address Book displaying your default address list.

2. In the **Address Book** window, on the **Tools** menu, select **Options**.

You can designate the order in which Outlook searches address books for contacts

3. In the **Addressing** dialog, do one of the following:

    • Select **Start with Global Address List** to have Outlook search first in your default Exchange account directory.

    • Select **Start with contact folders** to have Outlook search first in the contact records in the People module of your default account.

    • Select **Custom**, and then reorder address lists by selecting the list and then selecting the **Move Up** or **Move Down** button, to specify a custom search order.

4. In the **Addressing** dialog, select **OK**. Then close the **Address Book** window.

To modify the address lists that Outlook searches

1. On the **Home** tab of any module, in the **Find** group, select **Address Book**.

2. In the **Address Book** window, on the **Tools** menu, select **Options**.

3. In the **Addressing** dialog, select **Custom** to activate the buttons below the list. Then do any of the following:

    • To search additional address lists, select **Add**. In the **Add Address List** dialog, select the address list you want to add, select **Add**, and then select **Close**.

    • To prevent Outlook from searching an address list, select the address list, and then select **Remove**.

    • If you're uncertain of the source of an address list, select the address list, and then select **Properties** to display the server address or account name and folder name of the address list.

4. In the **Addressing** dialog, select **OK**. Then close the **Address Book** window.

13

Save and send messages

At regular intervals while you're composing a message (every three minutes, by default), Outlook saves a copy of the message in the Drafts folder. This is intended to protect you from losing messages that are in progress. If you close a message that hasn't yet had a draft saved, Outlook gives you the option of saving one. You can manually save a message draft at any time, and you can resume working on it later, either in its own window or directly in the Reading Pane. When you save a draft, the number in the unread message counter to the right of the Drafts folder in the Folder Pane increases. If the draft is in response to a received message, [Draft] appears in the message header of the received message.

Draft indicators

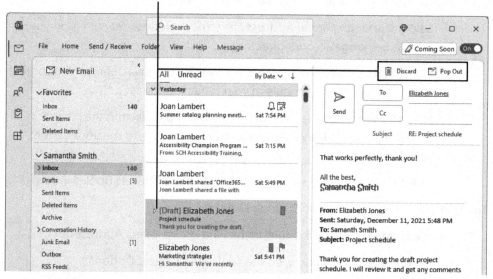

Locate a message draft in the Drafts folder or message list

When you send a message, Outlook deletes the message draft, if one exists, and moves the message temporarily to the Outbox. After successfully transmitting the message, Outlook moves it from the Outbox to the Sent Items folder. If a connectivity issue prevents Outlook from transmitting the message, it remains in your Outbox.

> ✓ **TIP** Each account you access from Outlook has its own Drafts folder and its own Sent Items folder. Outlook automatically saves draft messages and sent messages in the folders associated with the email account in which you compose or send the message. You can change the location in which Outlook saves message drafts from the Mail page of the Outlook Options dialog.

Send from a specific account

If you configure Outlook to connect to multiple email accounts, a From button appears in the header area of the message composition window, with your active account to the right of it.

In a multiple-account configuration, Outlook assumes that you intend to send a message from the account you're currently working in. If you begin composing a message while viewing the Inbox of your work account, for example, Outlook selects the work account as the message-sending account. If you reply to a message received by your personal account, Outlook selects the personal account as the message-sending account.

To change the active account when you're composing a message, select From, and then select the account from which you want to send the message.

The From list displays all types of email accounts

TIP If Outlook is configured to connect to only one account, you can display the From button by selecting From in the Show Fields group on the Options tab of a message composition window.

If you have permission to send messages from an account that you haven't configured in Outlook—for example, a generic Customer Service email account for your company—you can select Other Email Address in the From list, enter the email address you want to send the message from, and select OK.

Selecting From displays the Address Book window in which you can choose a sending address

13

To save a draft of an email message

- In the message composition window, do either of the following to save a draft without closing the message:

  - On the **Quick Access Toolbar**, select the **Save** button.

  - Press **Ctrl+S**.

Or

1. At the right end of the title bar, select the **Close** button.

If you close a message before sending it, Outlook prompts you to save a draft

2. In the **Microsoft Outlook** message box, select **Yes** to save a draft and close the message window.

To change how often Outlook automatically saves email message drafts

1. Open the **Outlook Options** dialog, and then select the **Mail** tab.

2. On the **Mail** page, scroll to the **Save messages** section.

You can customize how often and where Outlook saves message drafts

3. Do either of the following:

- In the **Automatically save items that have not been sent after this many minutes** box, change the number of minutes.

- Clear the **Automatically save items that have not been sent after this many minutes** checkbox to turn off automatic saving of message drafts.

4. Select **OK** to apply the changes and close the dialog.

To modify an email message draft

1. Do either of the following in the Mail module to display the message draft in the Reading Pane:

- In the **Folder Pane**, select the **Drafts** folder, and then select the message you want to continue composing.

- If the draft is a response, select the received message in the **Inbox**. If you are displaying messages in Conversation view and have received additional messages in the same thread since beginning the draft, expand the conversation.

> **TIP** If you have a lot of message drafts in your Drafts folder, this can be the simplest method of locating a specific draft.

When you select the message in either message list, the message becomes active for editing in the Reading Pane, and a Message tool tab appears on the ribbon.

2. Do any of the following:

- Edit the message in the **Reading Pane**. The Message tool tab contains the most frequently used commands from the message composition window ribbon.

- In the upper-left corner of the **Reading Pane**, select **Pop Out** to open the message in a message composition window (with the full ribbon).

- In the message list, double-click the message header to open the message in a message composition window.

3. After you edit the message, you can send it or close it. If you close the message, it remains in the Drafts folder.

13

To send an email message

1. In the message composition window, do either of the following:

   - In the message header, select **Send**.

   - Press **Ctrl+Enter**. (The first time you press this key combination, Outlook asks whether you want to designate this as the keyboard shortcut for sending messages.)

2. The message window closes and the message is sent. If the message was saved in the Drafts folder, sending it removes it from the Drafts folder.

To verify that an email message was sent

1. In the **Folder Pane** of the Mail module, select the **Sent Items** folder to verify that the message is in the folder.

2. If the message is not in the Sent Items folder, check the **Outbox** folder.

> ✓ **TIP** If you want to send personalized copies of the same email message to several people, you can use the mail merge feature of Word. For more information, refer to *Microsoft Word Step by Step (Word 2021 and Microsoft 365)*, by Joan Lambert (Microsoft Press, 2022).

Attach files and Outlook items to messages

A convenient way to distribute a file (such as a Microsoft PowerPoint presentation, Excel workbook, Word document, or picture) is by attaching the file to an email message. Message recipients can preview or open the file from the Reading Pane, open it from the message window, forward it to other people, or save it to their computers.

When Outlook is set as your default email app, you can email files by using several different methods:

- **From Outlook** You can create a message, and then attach the file to the message. If the file you attach is stored in a shared location such as a OneDrive folder or SharePoint library, you have the option of sending a link rather than a copy of the file.

- **From an Office app** You can send a document from Word, a workbook from Excel, or a presentation from PowerPoint while you're working in the file. You have the option of sending a copy of the file as a message attachment or, if the file is stored in a shared location, you can send a link to the file.

- **From File Explorer** You can send any file as an attachment directly from File Explorer. When sending pictures from File Explorer, you have the option of resizing the pictures to reduce the file size.

After you attach a file to an email message by using any of these methods, and before you send the message, you can modify or remove the attachments. When you attach files from shared locations, a cloud symbol on the file icon indicates that the attachment is a link, rather than a copy of the file. If you want to send a copy of the online file, you can easily do so.

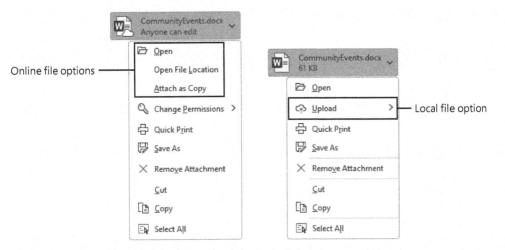

The options for online files are different from those for local files

13

In addition to sending files, you can send Outlook items, such as email messages or contact records.

To attach a file to an outgoing email message

1. In the message composition window, do either of the following to display the Attach File menu:

   - On the **Message** tab, in the **Include** group, select **Attach File**.

   - On the **Insert** tab, in the **Include** group, select **Attach File**.

The Attach File menu includes a list of local and online files you've worked with recently that are stored in locations Outlook can connect to.

Cloud overlays indicate files stored online

2. On the **Attach File** menu, do any of the following:

- If the file you want to attach is in the list, select the file.

- At the bottom of the menu, select **Browse Web Locations**, and then select a connected online storage location to open the Insert File dialog displaying the storage structure of that location. Browse to the file you want to attach, select it, and then select **Insert**.

- At the bottom of the menu, select **Browse This PC** to open the Insert File dialog displaying your local storage structure. Browse to the file you want to attach, select it, and then select **Insert**.

The attached file or files appear at the bottom of the message header. If the file that you attached is stored online, the file icon includes a cloud.

Information about file attachments is visible to the sender and to the recipient

To insert a link to an online business file in an email message

1. Position the insertion point in the message body where you want to insert the link.

2. In the message composition window, on the **Message** tab, in the **Include** group, select the **Link** arrow (not the button) to display the Link menu.

   The Link menu includes a list of files you've worked with recently that are stored in business SharePoint and OneDrive sites.

Specify the access level when sending business documents

13

3. On the **Link** menu, do either of the following:

- In the **Recent Items** list, select the file you want to link to.

- Select **Insert Link**. In the **Insert Hyperlink** dialog, browse to and select the file you want to link to, and then select **OK**.

To create an email message with an attachment from within an Office file

1. In the document, workbook, or presentation, select the **File** tab to display the Backstage view.

2. On the **Share** page of the Backstage view, select **Email** to display the email options.

Share any Office document through an Outlook email message

3. In the **Email** pane, select **Send as Attachment**, **Send a Link**, **Send as PDF**, or **Send as XPS** to create an email message and attach the specified version of the file.

> **TIP** If you have an account with a fax service provider that permits the transmission of fax messages by email, you can select the Send As Internet Fax option and provide the fax number to address the message in the format required by the fax service. For example, if your fax service provider is Contoso and the fax number is (425) 555-0199, the email might be addressed to 14255550199@contoso.com. The fax service relays the message electronically to the recipient's fax number.

To create an email message with an attachment from File Explorer

1. Select the file or files you want to send.

2. Right-click or long-press (tap and hold) the selected file or files you want to email, and then do either of the following on the context menu:

   - On a Windows 11 computer, select **Show more options**, **Send to**, and then **Mail recipient**.

   - On a Windows 10 computer, select **Send to** and then **Mail recipient**.

3. If the files are pictures, the Attach Files dialog opens and provides the opportunity to reduce the file size. In the **Picture size** list, select a size to display an estimate of the total file size of the pictures at those maximum dimensions.

Reducing picture size can significantly reduce the attachment size

4. Select **Attach** to create the message.

To attach a copy of an online file

1. Attach the file to the email message.

2. In the **Attached** area, select the arrow on the right side of the file attachment, and then select **Attach as Copy** to download a temporary copy of the file to your computer and attach that copy to the message.

To remove an attachment from an outgoing email message

- In the **Attached** area, select the arrow on the right side of the file attachment, and then select **Remove Attachment**.

- Select the file attachment (not the arrow), and then press the **Delete** key.

To attach an Outlook item to an outgoing email message

1. In the message composition window, do either of the following to display the Attach File menu:

    - On the **Message** tab, in the **Include** group, select **Attach File**.

    - On the **Insert** tab, in the **Include** group, select **Attach File**.

2. On the **Attach File** menu, select **Attach Item**, and then select **Outlook Item** to open the Insert Item dialog.

The Look In area displays the folder list

3. In the **Look in** area, select the folder that contains the item you want to attach.

Insert Item			✕
Look in:			OK
> ▦ Calendar			
⌄ ᴁ≡ Contacts			Cancel
ᴁ≡ Customers			Insert as
ᴁ≡ School			○ Text only
> ▢ Conversation History			● Attachment
▦ Journal			
✉ **Junk Email** [1]			
▢ Notes			

Items:					
▯	◍	Filed As ⁄	Job Title	Company	▲
	ᴁ≡	Anderson, Thomas			
	ᴁ≡	Axen, Thomas			
	ᴁ≡	Jones, Elizabeth	Marketing Manager	Tailspin Toys	
	ᴁ≡	Lambert, Joan			
	ᴁ≡	Pepperman, Tiffany			
	ᴁ≡	Smith, Samantha			
	ᴁ≡	Thomas, Margie	Owner	Margie's Travel	▼

You can insert any type of Outlook item

4. Locate and select the message, calendar item, contact record, note, or task you want to send.

> ✓ **TIP** There is no Find or Search feature in the Insert Item dialog. To locate an item, you can scroll the list or sort the list by any field by clicking that field header.

5. If you want to insert the item content into the message body instead of attaching the item to the message, select **Text only** in the **Insert as** area.

6. Select **OK** to attach the item to the message.

Or

1. In the Outlook program window, locate the item you want to send.

2. Right-click the item, and then select **Forward** to create a message that contains the item.

13

New mail notifications

When new messages, meeting requests, or task assignments arrive in your Inbox, Outlook alerts you in several ways so that you can be aware of email activity if you're using another application or you've been away from your computer.

These are the default notifications:

- A chime sounds.

- A desktop alert appears on your screen for a few seconds, displaying the sender's information, the message subject, and the first few words of the message.

You can open the message by selecting the desktop alert

- A closed envelope icon appears on the Outlook taskbar button and in the notification area of the Windows taskbar.

- In Windows 10, the Action Center icon in the notification area changes from hollow to white, and the new message is available in the Action Center.

You can configure the notification options from the Mail page of the Outlook Options dialog. The only optional notification that isn't turned on by default is for Outlook to briefly change the shape of the mouse pointer to an envelope.

Display messages and message attachments

Each time you start Outlook and connect to your email server, any new messages received since the last time you connected appear in your Inbox. Depending on your settings, Outlook downloads either the entire message to your computer or only the message header, which provides basic information about the message, such as:

- The item type (message, meeting request, task assignment, and so on)
- Who sent it
- When you received it
- The subject

Icons displayed in the message header indicate optional information such as:

- The most recent response action taken
- Whether files are attached
- If the message has been digitally signed or encrypted
- If the sender marked the message as being of high or low importance

The message list displays the message header information. You can open messages from the message list or display message content in the Reading Pane.

Display message content

You can display the content of a message by opening it in a message window. However, you can save time by reading and working with messages (and other Outlook items) in the Reading Pane. You can display the Reading Pane to the right of or below the module content pane.

If a message contains external content, which many marketing email messages do, the external content will be automatically downloaded only if your security settings are configured to permit this. Otherwise, you must give permission to download the external content.

13

> **TIP** If you find it difficult to read the text in the Reading Pane at its default size, you can change the magnification level of the Reading Pane content by using the Zoom controls located at the right end of the program window status bar. Changing the Zoom level is temporary and lasts only until you switch to a different message. The Zoom controls are available only for message content; they're unavailable when you preview an attachment in the Reading Pane.

To display the content of a message

- In the Mail module, do any of the following:

  - Open a message in its own window by double-clicking its header in the message list.

  - Read a message without opening it by selecting its header once in the message list to display the message in the Reading Pane.

  - Display the first three lines of each unread message under the message header by using the Message Preview feature.

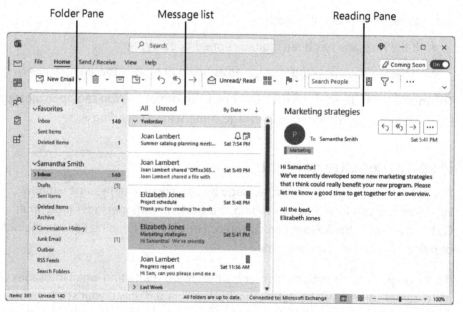

The Reading Pane displays the message content

To move through message content in the Reading Pane

- In the Reading Pane, do any of the following:

  - Scroll at your own pace by dragging the vertical scroll bar that appears at the right side of the Reading Pane.

  - Move up or down one line at a time by selecting the scroll arrows.

  - Move up or down one page at a time by selecting above or below the scroll box.

  - Move up or down one page at a time by pressing the Spacebar. When you reach the end of a message by using this feature, called *Single Key Reading*, pressing the Spacebar again displays the first page of the next message. This option is very convenient if you want to read through several consecutive messages in the Reading Pane, or if you find it easier to press the Spacebar than to use the mouse.

Display attachment content

If a message has attachments, you can open or download them from the message window or Reading Pane. Outlook can also display interactive previews of many types of attachments, including Word documents, Excel workbooks, PowerPoint presentations, Visio diagrams, text files, XPS files, and image files.

If a preview app for a file type hasn't been installed, Outlook won't be able to preview a file of that type in the Reading Pane. You can display the apps Outlook uses to preview files from the Attachment Handling page of the Trust Center, which you open from the Outlook Options dialog.

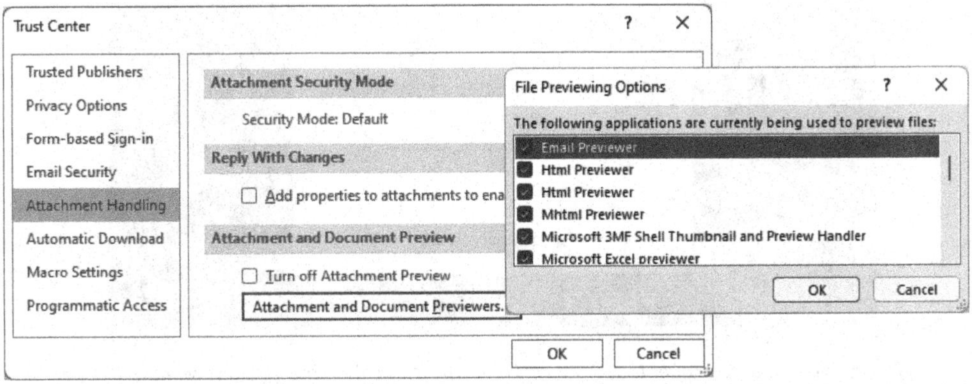

13

You can select the apps used to preview files in the Reading Pane, or turn off the Attachment Preview feature

Selecting certain types of attachments displays a warning message asking you to confirm that the content comes from a trusted source. You can approve the content on a case-by-case basis or give Outlook permission to skip the warning message for files of this type.

Previewing a file can save you a great deal of time. You can interact with the preview in many ways, to the point that you might not have to take the time to open the file at all.

> ✓ **TIP** If you suspect that an attachment might contain a virus, and you have a reputable anti-malware program installed, you might want to download the file and scan it for viruses before you open it.

To preview the content of a message attachment

- In the open message window or **Reading Pane**, select the attachment once. The **Attachments** tool tab appears on the ribbon, and a preview of the attachment appears in the message content pane or Reading Pane.

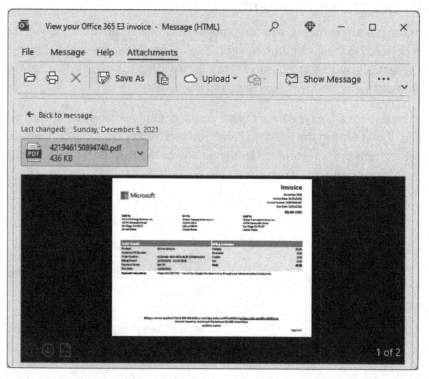

You use the same techniques to preview and open attachments in the message window and Reading Pane

To work with attachment content in the preview

- Display the attachment preview, and then do any of the following:

  - Scroll vertically or horizontally through content.

  - Point to comment markup in a Word document to display the full comment.

  - Select worksheet tabs at the bottom of the preview area to switch between worksheets in an Excel workbook.

  - Scroll vertically or select the **Next** button to move through slides in a PowerPoint presentation. Transitions and animations function in the preview area.

  - When previewing a PowerPoint presentation, select the slides in the preview area to advance through the presentation, including all transitions and animations; or select the **Next** button (the arrow) at the bottom of the vertical scroll bar to advance through the presentation without displaying the animated elements.

  - Select **hyperlinks** to open the target webpages or files, or select **mailto links** to create email messages.

To return from the attachment preview to the message content

- In the upper-left corner of the message header, select **Back to message**.

- On the **Attachments** tool tab, in the **Message** group, select the **Show Message** button. (The ScreenTip that appears when you point to the button says *Return to Message*.)

To open an attachment in the default app for that file type

- In the message window or **Reading Pane**, do either of the following:

  - In the message header, double-click the attachment.

  - In the message header, select the attachment to display a preview. Then on the **Attachments** tool tab, in the **Actions** group, select **Open**.

To save an attachment to a storage drive

1. From the message window or **Reading Pane**, do either of the following:

   - Select the arrow on the right side of the file attachment, and then select **Save As**.

13

- On the **Attachments** tool tab, in the **Save to Computer** group, select **Save As**.

2. In the **Save As** dialog, browse to the folder in which you want to save the file, and then select **Save**.

To save multiple attachments to a storage drive

1. From the message window or **Reading Pane**, do either of the following to display a list of all the files attached to the message:

   - Select the arrow on the right side of any file attachment, and then select **Save All Attachments**.

   - On the **Attachments** tool tab, in the **Save to Computer** group, select **Save All Attachments**.

2. In the **Save All Attachments** list, all the attached files are selected by default. If you want to save only some of the files, select one file that you want to save, and then do either of the following:

   - Press **Shift+click** to select contiguous files.

   - Press **Ctrl+click** to select noncontiguous files.

You can choose which attached files you want to save

3. When the files you want to save are selected in the list, select **OK**.

4. In the **Save All Attachments** dialog, browse to the folder in which you want to save the files, and then select **OK**.

Display message participant information

After you receive a message (or after Outlook validates a recipient's name in a message that you're sending), you have access to contact information and a history of your communications with that person. In a message window, presence icons and contact cards provide additional information about the message recipients.

Outlook uses presence information provided by central administration server programs such as Office 365. If presence information is available, a round presence icon appears in the Reading Pane or message window to the left of each message participant's name, and a round icon appears to the left of each contact picture when shown in a message.

The presence icon (casually referred to as a *jelly bean* or *chiclet*) is color-coded to indicate the availability or online status of the message participant as follows:

- **Green** The person is online and available.
- **Red** The person is busy, in a conference call, or in a meeting.
- **Dark red with a white bar** The person does not want to be disturbed.
- **Yellow** The person is away or has not been active online for a certain length of time (usually five minutes).
- **Gray** The person is offline.
- **White** The person's presence information is not known.

> **TIP** This same set of presence icons is used in all Microsoft Office apps and on Microsoft SharePoint sites, to provide a consistent user experience. We don't display the presence icons in all the graphics in this book, but we do display some in this topic.

13

Pointing to a message participant's name displays an interactive contact card of information that includes options for contacting the person by email, instant message, or phone; for scheduling a meeting; and for working with the person's contact record.

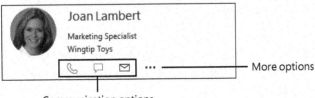

Communication options — More options

You can initiate many types of communication from the contact card

Pointing to the contact card for a short time expands it to display more contact information, more interaction options, and links to additional information. From the expanded contact card, you can access the contact's manager, direct reports, and position within the organization and learn which distribution lists they belong to.

Pin Contact Card

Pinning the contact card keeps it open even if you send or close the email message

> **TIP** A distribution list is a membership group created through Exchange and available from an organization's Global Address List. You can't create distribution lists, but you can create contact groups, which are membership groups saved in the Outlook Contacts module.

Selecting any of the blue links initiates contact with the person through the stored phone number or email address, initiates a meeting request, or, if the person is in your address book, opens his or her contact record.

The Organization section displays information about the person's manager and direct reports. The Membership section displays information about distribution lists the contact is a member of. This information is available only for Exchange accounts.

The All Items tab of the detailed view displays all your recent Outlook interactions with the selected person. If you're looking for a specific item, such as a meeting request or a document attached to a message, you can filter the item list.

To display a message participant's contact information

1. Point to the person's name to display a simple contact card.

2. In the contact card, select the **Open Contact Card** button (the arrow) to display a more extensive range of information and interaction options.

To initiate contact from a contact card

1. In the basic contact card, do any of the following:

   - Select the **Instant Message** icon to initiate a Teams message.

   - Select a **Phone** number to initiate a voice call through Teams or your con-nected enterprise phone system.

   - Select the **Email** icon to create a preaddressed email message form.

2. In the expanded contact card, select any blue link.

To filter the All Items list

- Select the **Mail**, **Attachments**, or **Meetings** tab to display only interactions of that type.

To enable Cached Exchange Mode

1. On the **Info** page of the Backstage view of the Outlook program window, select **Account Settings**, and then in the list that appears, select **Account Settings**.

2. On the **Email** tab of the **Account Settings** dialog, select your Exchange account, and then select **Change**.

3. On the **Server Settings** page of the **Change Account** wizard, select the **Use Cached Exchange Mode** checkbox, select **Next**, and then on the wizard's final page, select **Finish**.

4. Exit and restart Outlook to implement the change.

13

Respond to messages

You can respond to most email messages that you receive by selecting a response button either in the Reading Pane, in the message window, or in the Respond group on the Message tab. You can respond to a message by replying to the sender, by replying to all the message participants, by replying with a meeting request, by replying with an instant message, or by forwarding the message.

When you choose one of the following options, Outlook creates a new message based on the original message and fills in one or more of the address boxes for you:

- **Reply** Creates an email message, addressed only to the original message sender, that contains the original message text.

- **Reply All** Creates an email message, addressed to the message sender and all recipients listed in the To and Cc boxes, that contains the original message text. The message is not addressed to recipients of blind courtesy copies (Bcc recipients).

- **Reply with Meeting** Creates a meeting invitation addressed to the message sender and all recipients listed in the To and Cc boxes. The message text is included in the meeting window content pane. Outlook suggests the current date and an upcoming half-hour time slot for the meeting.

> **SEE ALSO** For information about meeting invitations, see Chapter 15, "Manage scheduling."

Message replies include the original message header and text, preceded by a space in which you can respond. Replies do not include any attachments from the original message.

You can add, change, and delete recipients from any reply email before sending it.

> **TIP** When responding to an email message, take care to use good email etiquette. For example, if your response is not pertinent to all the original recipients of a message, don't reply to the entire recipient list, especially if the message was addressed to a distribution list that might include hundreds of members. You can prevent other people from replying to all recipients of a message you send by addressing the message to yourself and entering other recipients in the Bcc box. Then the recipient list will not be visible any recipients.

You can forward a received message to any email address (regardless of whether the recipient uses Outlook) provided the message was not sent with restricted permissions. Outlook has the following message-forwarding options:

- **Forward** Creates a new message that contains the text of the original and retains any attachments from the original message.

- **Forward as Attachment** Creates a blank message that contains no text but includes the original message as an attachment. The original message text and any attachments are available to the new recipient when he or she opens the attached message.

Both types of forwarded messages include the original message header and text, preceded by a space in which you can add information. Forwarded messages include attachments from the original message.

When you forward a message, Outlook does not fill in the recipient boxes for you.

If you reply to or forward a received message from within the message window, the original message remains open after you send your response. You can instruct Outlook to close original messages after you respond to them, because you'll probably be finished working with the message at that point.

If your organization has the necessary unified communications infrastructure, you may also have these additional response options:

- **Call or Call All** Initiates a VoIP (Voice over Internet Protocol) call from your computer to the phone number of the original message sender or to those of the sender and the other message recipients.

- **Reply with IM or Reply All with IM** Opens an instant messaging window with the message sender or with the sender and the other recipients as the chat participants. You must enter and send the first message to start the IM session.

> **TIP** The response options available in your Outlook installation might vary from those described here. The available response options for your installation are available from the Respond group that is on the Message tab of the message window and on the Home tab of the program window.

13

Nonstandard messages have alternative response options, such as the following:

- A meeting request includes options for responding to the request.

- A task assignment includes options for accepting or declining the assignment.

- If a message contains voting buttons, you can respond by opening the message, selecting the Vote button in the Respond group on the Message tab, and then selecting the response you want to send. Or you can select the InfoBar (labeled *Click here to vote*) in the Reading Pane and then select the response you want.

> **SEE ALSO** For information about meeting requests, see "Respond to meeting requests" in Chapter 15."

To reply to an email message

1. At the top of the **Reading Pane** or in the **Respond** group on the **Message** tab, do either of the following:

   - Select **Reply** to create a response already addressed to the original sender. If the message had been sent to any other people, the reply would not include them.

   - Select **Reply All** to create a response already addressed to the original sender. If the message had been sent to any other people, the reply also includes them.

   The *RE:* prefix appears at the beginning of the message subject to indicate that this is a response to an earlier message. The original message, including its header information, appears in the content pane, separated from the new content by a horizontal line.

   > **TIP** Note that a Reply or Reply All response does not include attachments, even if there were attachments in the original message. (In fact, there is no indication that the original message had any.)

2. At the top of the content pane, enter the text of your reply.

3. In the response header, select the **Send** button to send the reply. The original message remains open on your screen.

To forward an email message

1. At the top of the **Reading Pane** or in the **Respond** group on the **Message** tab, select **Forward** to create a new version of the message that is not addressed to any recipient. The *FW:* prefix at the beginning of the message subject indicates that this is a forwarded message.

> ✅ **TIP** Any files that were attached to the original message appear in the Attached box. The message is otherwise identical to the earlier response. You address and send a forwarded message as you would any other.

2. At the top of the content pane, enter the text of your reply.

3. In the response header, select **Send** to send the reply. The original message remains open on your screen.

To have Outlook close messages after responding

1. Open the **Outlook Options** dialog, and then select the **Mail** tab.

2. On the **Mail** page, scroll to the **Replies and forwards** section.

You can customize how Outlook opens, closes, and formats replies and forwards

3. Select the **Close original message window when replying or forwarding** checkbox.

4. Select **OK** to apply the changes and close the dialog.

Resending and recalling messages

If you want to send a new version of a message you've already sent—for example, a status report in which you update details each week—you can *resend* the message. Resending a message creates a new version of the message with none of the extra information that might be attached to a forwarded message. To resend a message, follow these steps:

1. From your **Sent Items** folder, open the message you want to resend. (Or, if you copied yourself on the message, you can open it from your **Inbox**.)

2. On the **Message** tab, in the **Move** group, select the **Actions** button (the ScreenTip that appears when you point to it says *More Move Actions*), and then in the list, select **Resend This Message**.

Outlook creates a new message identical to the original. You can change the message recipients, subject, attachments, or content before sending the new version of the message.

If, after sending a message, you realize that you shouldn't have sent it—for example, if the message contained an error or was sent to the wrong people—you can *recall* it by instructing Outlook to delete or replace any unread copies of the message. If a recipient has already opened a message, it can't be recalled.

The message recall operation works only for recipients with Exchange accounts. Recipients with internet email accounts or those who have already opened the original message will end up with both the original message and the recall notification or replacement message.

IMPORTANT You might want to test the message recall functionality within your organization before you have occasion to need it so that you can feel confident about the way it works.

To recall a message, follow these steps:

1. From your **Sent Items** folder, open the message you want to recall.

2. On the **Message** tab, in the **Move** group, select the **Actions** button, and then select **Recall This Message**. The Recall This Message dialog offers options for handling the recalled message.

Recall This Message	✕
Some recipients may have already read this message.	

Message recall can delete or replace copies of this message in recipient Inboxes, if they have not yet read this message.

Are you sure you want to

- ● Delete unread copies of this message
- ○ Delete unread copies and replace with a new message

☑ Tell me if recall succeeds or fails for each recipient

    [OK]   [Cancel]

You can delete or replace a message you've sent if it hasn't been read yet

3. In the **Recall This Message** dialog, select an option to indicate whether you want to delete or replace the sent message, and whether you want to receive an email notification of the success or failure of each recall. Then select **OK**.

4. If you choose to replace the message, a new message window opens. Enter the content that you want to include in the replacement message, and then send it.

13

Key points

- You can easily create email messages and attach files or other Outlook items to the messages.

- You can add message recipients by entering their email addresses, selecting them from an address book or list of recent contacts, or @mentioning them in a message.

- By default, messages you receive appear in the message list in your Inbox.

- You can display the first few lines of each message in Preview view, open a message in its own window, or preview messages in the Reading Pane. You can also preview message attachments in the Reading Pane.

- You can reply to the message sender only or to the sender and all other recipients. You can also forward a message and its attachments to other people.

Practice tasks

Before you can complete these tasks, you must copy the book's practice files to your computer. The practice files for these tasks are in located the **Office365SBS\Ch13** folder. You can save the results of the tasks in the same folder.

The introduction includes a complete list of practice files and download instructions.

> ⚠ **IMPORTANT** As you work through the practice tasks in this book, you will create Outlook items that might be used as practice files for tasks in later chapters. If you haven't created specific items referenced in later chapters, you can substitute items of your own.

Create and send messages

Start Outlook, and then perform the following tasks:

1. Start a new email message. Begin entering your name or address in the **To** box and notice the results that the Auto-Complete List provides. If you want to, remove one or more names or addresses from the list. (They'll be added to the list again the next time you send messages to them.)

2. Create a new email message, and do the following:

   - Address the message to yourself.

   - In the **Subject** box, enter SBS Test.

   - In the content pane, enter Welcome to Outlook!

   - Format the word *Welcome* in bold font and the word *Outlook* in blue font.

3. Close the message window, and have Outlook save a draft copy of the message.

4. Open the **Outlook Options** dialog. Locate the Auto-Complete List, comma separator, and AutoSave settings discussed in this chapter and make any changes that you want to the standard configuration. Then close the dialog.

5. Display the **Drafts** folder and edit your draft in the **Reading Pane**. Append Sincerely, and your name on separate lines at the end of the message. Then send the message.

6. Display the Address Book and find out what contact lists are available to you. If you want to, follow the procedures described in this chapter to change the order in which Outlook searches the address books. Then close the Address Book.

7. Display the **Sent Items** folder and verify that the *SBS Test* message was sent.

Attach files and Outlook items to messages

Start File Explorer, browse to the practice file folder, and then perform the following tasks:

1. From the practice file folder, open the **AttachFiles** document in Word. Enter your name in the **Contact Information** section and save the file. Then save a copy of the file in the same folder with the name AttachCopy.

2. In the **AttachCopy** document, display the **Share** page of the Backstage view. Send a PDF copy of the document to yourself. Then close the document.

3. Display your Outlook Inbox. Create a new email message, and do the following:

   • Address the message to yourself.

   • In the **Subject** box, enter SBS Attachment from Outlook.

4. In the message window, display the **Attach File** menu. Notice that the two files you worked with in Word are at the top of the list. Attach the **AttachFiles** document to your message. Then send the message to yourself.

5. Display the contents of the practice file folder in File Explorer. Select the **AttachFiles** and **AttachCopy** messages. Right-click the selection, select **Send to**, and then select **Mail recipient** to create a new message.

6. Address the message to yourself and enter SBS Attachments from Explorer as the message subject. Then send the message.

Display messages and message attachments

Display your Inbox, and then perform the following tasks:

1. In your Inbox, locate the **SBS Test** message that you sent to yourself in an earlier practice task.

2. Display the message content in the **Reading Pane** and magnify the Reading Pane content.

3. In your Inbox, locate the **SBS Attachments from Explorer** message.

4. Select the **AttachFiles** attachment to preview its content in the **Reading Pane**. Scroll through the document by using the tools available in the **Reading Pane**, and by pressing keyboard keys.

5. Return from the attachment preview to the message content.

6. Save the **AttachFiles** attachment from the message to the practice files folder with the name AttachCopy2.

Display message participant information

Display your Inbox, and then perform the following tasks:

1. In your Inbox, locate an email message from another person (preferably someone in your organization or who you have saved contact information for). Display the message in the **Reading Pane**.

2. In the **Reading Pane**, point to the sender's name or email address. Notice the information displayed in the contact card. Then expand the contact card to display more information.

3. From the contact card, initiate an email message to the person. Then close the message window without sending it.

4. In the **Microsoft Outlook** message box asking whether you want to save your changes, select **No**.

Respond to messages

Display your Inbox, and then perform the following tasks:

1. In your Inbox, locate the **SBS Attachment from Outlook** message that you sent to yourself in an earlier set of practice tasks. Using this email message, do both of the following:

   - Reply to the message. Enter Test of replying in the message content, and then send it.

   - Forward the message to yourself. Enter Test of forwarding in the message content, and then send it.

2. Open each of the received messages from your Inbox. Notice the difference between the message subjects, and that only the forwarded message contains the original attachment.

3. If you want to, follow the procedures in this chapter to change the way that Outlook handles received messages after you respond to them.

Organize
your Inbox

14

You can use Outlook to manage multiple email accounts, including multiple Microsoft Exchange Server or Office 365 accounts and their associated contacts, calendars, and other elements. Even if you use Outlook only for sending and receiving email messages, it can be challenging to keep track of them and to locate specific information that you're looking for. Fortunately, Outlook provides many simple yet useful features that you can use to organize messages and other Outlook items and to quickly find information you need.

By default, the message list displays the email messages you receive in order by time and date of receipt (from newest to oldest). You can arrange, group, and sort messages in Outlook to keep conversation threads together and to help you quickly determine which are the most important, decide which can be deleted, and locate any that need an immediate response.

You can simplify the process of organizing Outlook items of all kinds by assigning categories to related items. You can then arrange, sort, filter, and search for Outlook items by category.

This chapter guides you through procedures related to working with Conversation view, arranging messages by specific attributes, organizing items by using color categories, organizing messages in folders, and printing messages.

In this chapter

- Display and manage messages
- Arrange messages by specific attributes
- Categorize items
- Organize messages in folders
- Print messages

Display and manage messages

You might receive dozens or hundreds of email messages each day. The developers of Outlook have experimented with many ways of presenting messages to users, with the goal of putting the messages you want at your fingertips and keeping the messages you don't want out of your way. In this topic, we'll look at the Focused Inbox and the Conversation view of your messages. Both tools help you more easily locate and respond to important current conversations.

Select the primary Inbox content

The Junk Mail filter is a useful tool that has filtered out likely spam messages for many years. Outlook 2016 displayed all the messages that survived the Junk Mail filter on the default All tab of the Inbox and also provided an Unread tab on which you could view only those messages you hadn't yet interacted with. For Exchange Server accounts, Outlook goes one step further with the Focused Inbox, which displays the messages you're likely to want to read on the Focused tab and messages of the type that you've previously ignored or deleted on the Other tab. This is somewhat like the Clutter feature, which moved random, and often important, messages to a separate folder, but it's easier to find the messages now.

The Focused Inbox is the default setting for Exchange Server accounts, but you can easily switch between the Focused/Other and All/Unread views.

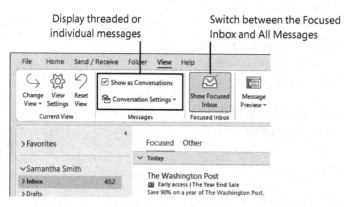

Primary settings for managing the display of messages in the Inbox

> ⚠️ **IMPORTANT** This book includes images that show both the Simplified Ribbon and the Classic Ribbon. The commands available to you on the Classic Ribbon might vary based on the type of email account—business or personal—to which Outlook is connected.

To hide or show the Focused Inbox (Exchange Server accounts only)

1. In the **Mail** module, display the **View** tab.

2. In the **Focused Inbox** group, select **Show Focused Inbox**.

Display and manage conversations

When a recipient replies to an email message, the exchange of multiple messages creates a *conversation*. Conversations that involve multiple recipients and responses can contain many messages. Conversation view is an alternative arrangement of messages grouped by subject. All the messages with the same subject appear together in your Inbox (or other message folder) under one conversation header.

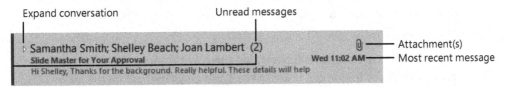

Until you expand the conversation header, the entire conversation takes up only as much space in your Inbox as a single message would

The conversation header provides information about the messages within the conversation, including the number of unread messages and whether one or more messages includes an attachment, is categorized, or is flagged for follow-up.

Select the conversation header or the Expand button to display the most recent message in the Reading Pane and to display all the unique messages in the conversation (the most recent message in each thread) in the message list. Reading only these messages will give you all the information that exists in the conversation.

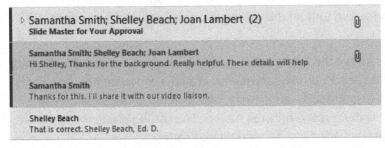

When a conversation is expanded to display unique messages, the conversation header displays recent participants and subjects

14

> ✓ **TIP** When an email conversation involves more than two people, particularly if the email was addressed to a large distribution list, often more than one person responds to the same message, and other people respond to each of those messages. Multiple conversations that emerge from the primary conversation are referred to as *branches*.

Benefits of displaying messages as conversations include the following:

- When you receive a message that is part of a conversation, the entire conversation moves to the top of your Inbox and the new message appears when you select the conversation header.

  A blue vertical line and bold blue subject indicate that a conversation includes unread messages. If there are multiple unread messages, the number is indicated in parentheses following the subject. The senders of the unread messages are listed below the subject.

- Sent messages are available from within the conversation. (They remain stored in the Sent Items folder, but you can read and open them from the Inbox.) This is particularly convenient when you need to access sent attachments that aren't available in the replies.

- You can manage all the messages that are part of a conversation as a group. Selecting the conversation headers selects all the messages in the conversation. You can move or categorize all the messages as a unit.

You can modify the way Conversation view displays messages to suit the way you work by turning the following display settings on or off:

- **Show Messages from Other Folders** By default, Conversation view displays messages stored in any folder, including sent messages stored in the Sent Items folder. (Within an expanded conversation, sent messages are indicated by an italic font.) You can turn off this setting to display only messages from the current folder.

- **Show Senders Above the Subject** By default, when a conversation is collapsed, the conversation header displays the names of all the conversation participants above the conversation subject; when the conversation is fully expanded, the conversation header displays only the subject. This setting places the conversation subject first in the collapsed conversation header.

- **Always Expand Selected Conversation** This setting causes Outlook to display all messages in a conversation when you select the Expand Conversation button or conversation header once.

- **Use Classic Indented View** This setting causes Outlook to indent older messages within individual message threads to show the progression of the thread. This setting is not as effective as the default setting for displaying split conversations, because a message might be at the root of multiple branches but can appear only once in the message list.

Outlook tracks conversations by subject regardless of whether you display the messages in Conversation view. You can use the following features to manage conversations:

- **Ignore Conversation** This command moves the selected conversation and any related messages you receive in the future directly to the Deleted Items folder.

> ⚠️ **IMPORTANT** Be cautious when using the Ignore Conversation command. Outlook identifies conversations based on message subjects. If you receive unrelated messages in the future that have the same message subject as a conversation that you've chosen to ignore, you won't receive those messages.

- **Clean Up Conversation** This command deletes redundant messages—messages whose text is wholly contained within later messages—from a conversation or folder. By default, Outlook doesn't clean up categorized, flagged, or digitally signed messages. You can modify conversation clean-up settings when you start a clean-up process and on the Mail page of the Outlook Options dialog.

> ✓ **TIP** Because Conversation view displays only unique messages until you fully expand the conversation, a specific message that you're looking for might not be immediately visible. If this happens, you can temporarily disable Conversation view by choosing a different message arrangement. For more information, see "Arrange messages by specific attributes" later in this chapter.

14

To turn Conversation view on or off for one or all folders

> ⚠️ **IMPORTANT** Conversation view is available only when messages are arranged by date.

1. On the **View** tab, in the **Messages** group, select or clear the **Show as Conversations** checkbox.

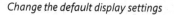

Specify the scope of the change

2. In the **Microsoft Outlook** message box, indicate the scope of the change by selecting **This folder** or **All mailboxes**.

> ✓ **TIP** When you arrange a folder by an attribute other than date, Conversation view is temporarily disabled. For more information, see "Arrange messages by specific attributes" later in this chapter.

To display the messages within a conversation

1. Select the conversation header or the **Expand** button once to display the unique messages in the conversation.

2. Select the **Expand** button again to display all messages in the conversation.

To select all the messages in a conversation

■   Select the conversation header once. Any action you take on the selected header applies to all messages in the conversation.

To change the way conversations are displayed in the message list

1. On the **View** tab, in the **Messages** group, select **Conversation Settings**. On the Conversation Settings menu, a check mark indicates that an option is turned on.

Change the default display settings

2. On the **Conversation Settings** menu, select a setting to turn it on or off.

To remove redundant messages from a conversation

1. Select any message in the conversation.

2. On the **Home** tab, in the **Delete** group, select the **Clean Up** button, and then on the menu, select **Clean Up Conversation**.

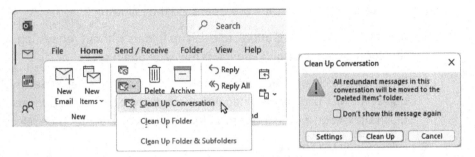

You can change the location to which Outlook moves the messages it cleans up

3. If the **Clean Up Conversation** message box opens, do the following:

    a. If you want to instruct Outlook to clean up conversations without requesting confirmation, select the **Don't show this message again** checkbox.

    b. If you want to change the conversation clean-up settings, select **Settings** to display the Mail page of the Outlook Options dialog. Scroll to the **Conversation Clean Up** section and change any of the settings you want to. Then select **OK**.

You can retain specific categories of messages

    c. Select **Clean Up**.

To remove redundant messages from a folder

1. Select any message in the folder.

2. On the **Home** tab, in the **Delete** group, select **Clean Up**, and then on the menu, select **Clean Up Folder** or **Clean Up Folder & Subfolders**.

3. If the Clean Up Folder message box opens, do the following:

   a. If you want to instruct Outlook to clean up folders without requesting con-firmation, select the **Don't show this message again** checkbox.

   b. If you want to change the conversation clean-up settings, select **Settings** to display the Mail page of the Outlook Options dialog. Scroll to the **Conversation Clean Up** section and change any of the settings you want to. Then select **OK**.

   c. Select **Clean Up Folder**.

To ignore a conversation

1. Select any message in the conversation, and then do either of the following:

   - On the **Home** tab, in the **Delete** group, select the **Ignore Conversation** button.

   - Press **Ctrl+Del**.

Automatically delete future messages in the conversation

2. If the Ignore Conversation message box opens, do the following:

   a. If you want to instruct Outlook to ignore conversations without requesting confirmation, select the **Don't show this message again** checkbox.

   b. Select **Ignore Conversation**.

To stop ignoring a conversation

1. Display the **Deleted Items** folder.

2. Locate and select any item in the ignored conversation.

3. On the **Home** tab, in the **Delete** group, the Ignore button is active for a conver-sation that is being ignored. Select the **Ignore** button to turn it off.

Arrange messages by specific attributes

By default, Outlook displays messages arranged by date, from newest to oldest. Alternatively, you can arrange items by any of the following attributes:

- **Account** Messages are grouped by the email account to which they were sent. This is useful if you receive messages for more than one email account in your Inbox (for example, if you receive messages sent to your POP3 account within your Exchange account mailbox).

- **Attachments** Messages are grouped by whether they have attachments and secondarily by date received.

- **Categories** Messages are arranged by the category you assign to them. Messages without a category appear first. Messages with multiple categories assigned to them appear in each of those category groups.

- **Flag: Start Date or Due Date** Unflagged messages and messages without specific schedules appear first. Messages that you've added to your task list with specific start or due dates are grouped by date.

- **From** Messages appear in alphabetical order by the message sender's display name. If you receive messages from a person who uses two different email accounts, or who sends messages from two different email clients (for example, from Outlook and from Windows Mail), the messages will not necessarily be grouped together.

- **Importance** Messages are grouped by priority: High (indicated by a red exclamation point), Normal (the default), or Low (indicated by a blue downward-pointing arrow).

- **To** Messages are grouped alphabetically by the primary recipients (the addresses or names on the To line). The group name exactly reflects the order in which addresses appear on the To line. Therefore, a message addressed to *Bart Duncan; Lukas Keller* is not grouped with a message addressed to *Lukas Keller; Bart Duncan.*

- **Size** Messages are grouped by message size, including any attachments. Groups include Very Large (5–10 MB), Large (1–5 MB), Medium (25 KB–1 MB), Small (10–25 KB), and Tiny (less than 10 KB). This feature is useful if you work for an organization that limits the size of your Inbox, because you can easily locate large messages and delete them or move them to a personal folder.

14

- **Subject** Messages are arranged alphabetically by their subjects and then by date. This is similar to arranging by conversation except that the messages aren't threaded.

- **Type** Items in your Inbox (or other folder) are grouped by the type of item— for example, messages, encrypted messages, message receipts, meeting requests and meeting request responses, tasks, Microsoft InfoPath forms, and server notifications.

After arranging the items in your message list, you can change the sort order of the arrangement. The message list header displays the current sort order and arrangement of the message list.

Select arrangement and sort order from the header or from the ribbon

By default, the messages within each arrangement are in groups specific to that category. For example, when messages are arranged by date, they are grouped by date; groups include each day of the current week, Last Week, Two Weeks Ago, Three Weeks Ago, Last Month, and Older. Each group has a header. You can collapse a group so that only the header is visible, or select and process messages by group.

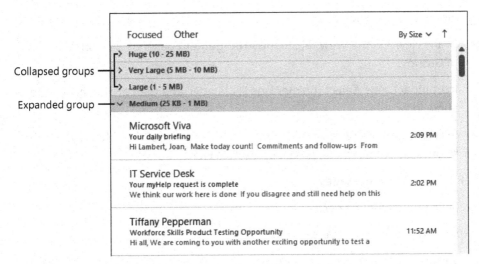

Collapsing groups of messages displays only the group headers

In Single view or Preview view, you can sort messages by any visible column. If you want to sort by an attribute that isn't shown, you can add that column to the view.

To arrange messages by a specific attribute

- In any view: On the **View** tab, in the **Arrangement** gallery, select the message attribute.

- In Compact view: In the message list header, select the current arrangement, and then select the message attribute.

- In Single view or Preview view: Right-click or long-press (tap and hold) any column header, select **Arrange By**, and then select the message attribute.

To reverse the default sort order of the message list arrangement

- In any view: On the **View** tab, in the **Arrangement** group, select **Reverse Sort**.

- In Compact view: In the message list header, select the current sort order.

- In Single view or Preview view: Right-click any column header, and then select **Reverse Sort**.

> **TIP** In a list view, you can sort by any column by selecting the column header, and reverse the sort order by selecting the column header again.

14

To group or ungroup messages

- In any view: On the **View** tab, in the **Arrangement** gallery, select **Show in Groups**.

- In Compact view: Select the message list header, and then on the menu, select **Show in Groups**.

- In Single view or Preview view: Right-click the header of the column you want to group by, and then select **Group By This Field**.

To select a group of messages

- Select the group header.

To expand the current message group

- Select the arrow at the left end of the group header.

- Press the **Right Arrow** key.

- On the **View** tab, in the **Arrangement** group, select **Expand/Collapse**, and then select **Expand This Group**.

To collapse the current message group

- Select the arrow at the left end of the group header.

- Press the **Left Arrow** key.

- On the **View** tab, in the **Arrangement** group, select **Expand/Collapse**, and then select **Collapse This Group**.

To expand or collapse all message groups

- On the **View** tab, in the **Arrangement** group, select **Expand/Collapse**, and then select **Expand All Groups** or **Collapse All Groups**.

- Press **Ctrl+Plus sign** to expand all groups, or **Ctrl+Minus sign** to collapse all groups.

To reset the message arrangement (and other view settings)

1. On the **View** tab, in the **Current View** group, select **Reset View**.

2. In the **Microsoft Outlook** dialog, select **Yes**.

Categorize items

To help you more easily locate Outlook items associated with a specific subject, project, person, or other common factor, you can create a category specific to that attribute and assign the category to any related items. You can assign a category to any type of Outlook item, such as a message, an appointment, or a contact record. For example, you might have categories for different people, clients, interest groups, or occasions.

Each category has an associated color, which provides a visual indicator in the item windows and in the module content views. More importantly, you can use the category property to search, sort, and filter items within or across all the Outlook modules.

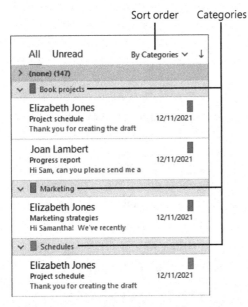

Messages that have multiple categories assigned appear in multiple category groups

14

Outlook comes with six starter categories named for their associated colors. You can rename these six categories to suit your needs. If you don't rename a standard color category before assigning it for the first time, Outlook gives you the option of renaming the category the first time you use it.

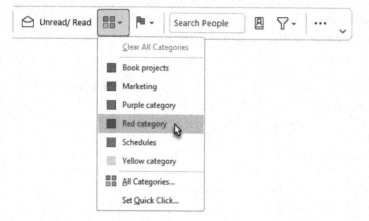

You can rename a category multiple times

You can create new categories as you need them. Each category can have the following elements:

- **Name** The category name can be one simple word or a long, descriptive phrase. The first 32 characters of the category name are visible in the Color Categories dialog, but pointing to a truncated name displays the entire name in a ScreenTip.

- **Shortcut key** You can assign any of the 11 available keyboard shortcut combinations (Ctrl+F2 through Ctrl+F12) to the individual color categories.

- **Color** You can assign any of the 25 available colors to a category, or you can choose not to assign a color and to rely only on the name to distinguish between categories. When you assign a category that doesn't have an associated color to an Outlook item, the color block or color bar is shown as white. You can assign a color to multiple color categories.

Categories that you assign are represented by color blocks in a content list view, and by color bars in the open item window and the Reading Pane.

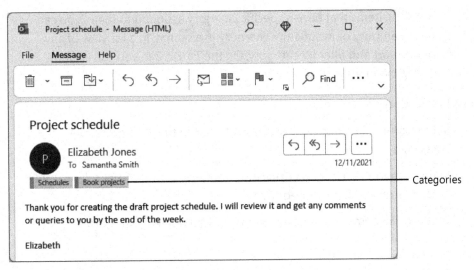

You can assign multiple categories to a message or other item

When Conversation view is on, the conversation header displays all the color category blocks assigned to the individual messages in the conversation.

You can designate one category as the Quick Click category. When displaying items in a view that includes a Categories column—such as Single view or Preview view—selecting the Categories column assigns the Quick Click category.

> **TIP** You can instruct Outlook to automatically assign a category to an incoming message that meets specific criteria by creating a *rule*.

You can apply a category with one click or by using a keyboard shortcut

14

To quickly view the items that have a specific category assigned to them, you can group items by category or include the category in a search. In a list view of any module, you can sort and filter by category. On the To-Do Bar, you can arrange flagged messages and tasks by category.

To display the Categorize menu

- On the **Home** tab of any mail or contact folder, in the **Tags** group, select **Categorize**.

- On the item tool tab (such as **Appointment** or **Meeting**) of any calendar item, in the **Tags** group, select **Categorize**.

- Right-click an item or selection of items, and then select **Categorize**.

The Categorize menu displays recently assigned categories

To open the Color Categories dialog

■ Display the **Categorize** menu, and then select **All Categories**.

You can manage all aspects of categories in the Color Categories dialog

To assign a category to a message or other item

1. Select the item or items that you want to categorize.

2. Display the **Categorize** menu, and then do either of the following:

   • If the menu includes the category you want to assign, select the category.

   • If the menu doesn't include the category you want to assign, select **All Categories**. In the **Color Categories** dialog that opens, select the checkbox of the category you want to assign, and then select **OK**.

To set or change the Quick Click category

1. Display the **Categorize** menu, and then select **Set Quick Click**.

2. In the **Set Quick Click** dialog, select the list, select the category that you want to set as the default, and then select **OK**.

Or

1. Open the **Outlook Options** dialog and display the **Advanced** page.

2. Scroll down on the Advanced page to display the **Other** section, and then select the **Quick Click** button.

3. In the **Set Quick Click** dialog, select the list, select the category that you want to set as the default, and then select **OK**.

14

To assign or remove the Quick Click category

- In Single view or any other module content list view, click or tap in the **Categories** column for the item.

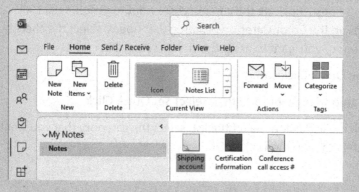

From	Subject	Received ▼	Size	Categories		Mention	▽
Joan Lambert	Summer catalog planning meeting	Sat 12/11/202...	50 KB				
Joan Lambert	Joan Lambert shared "Office365SBS_Outlook" with you.	Sat 12/11/202...	85 KB				⚑ 🗑
Joan Lambert shared a file with you Joan Lambert shared "Office365SBS_Outlook" with you.							
Elizabeth Jones	Project schedule	Sat 12/11/202...	32 KB	Toggle Quick Click category			
Thank you for creating the draft project schedule. I will review it and get any comments or queries to				Right-click for all options			
Elizabeth Jones	Marketing strategies	Sat 12/11/202...	33 KB	Marketing			
Hi Samantha! We've recently developed some new marketing strategies that I think could really benefit your new program.							
Joan Lambert	Progress report	Sat 12/11/202...	32 KB	Book projects			
Hi Sam, can you please send me a high-level overview of where you are with the current set of books? All the best, Joan							
Microsoft	FW: View your Office 365 E3 invoice	Sun 12/5/202...	524 ...				
From: Microsoft <microsoft-noreply@microsoft.com>							

Clicking or tapping in the column turns the category on or off

Store information in Outlook notes

You can store miscellaneous information such as reminders, passwords, account numbers, and processes by saving them in electronic notes. Because your notes are available to you from wherever you access Outlook, this can be a very convenient way of retaining information you might need later. And because you're less likely to accidentally delete a note than a message, it's safer than sending information to yourself in an email message.

You can categorize notes to easily find them

You can enter only text into a note; you can't format the text or include graphic elements. Notes do support hyperlinks; if you enter a website address and then press Enter, the website address will change to blue underlined text to indicate that it is a hyperlink. You can select the hyperlink to open the website or page in your default web browser.

Although notes are a type of Outlook item, they don't appear in the same type of windows as messages, appointments, contact records, and tasks. Instead, they appear in the form of "sticky notes." By default, note icons and sticky note representations are a pale yellow color, like the color of standard paper sticky notes. When you assign a category to a note, the note color changes to the category color.

You can view, sort, and organize notes in the same way you do other Outlook items. The standard views include Icons, Notes List, and Last 7 Days.

As with other Outlook items, if you're looking for a specific piece of information in a note, you can quickly locate it by entering a search word or phrase in the Search Notes box at the top of the content area.

To store information in a note:

1. At the end of the Navigation Bar, select the **More Apps** button and then **Notes**.

2. Do one of the following to create a note:

   - With the ribbon minimized, select the **New Note** button at the top of the **Folder Pane**.

   - On the **Home** tab of the ribbon, in the **New** group, select **New Note**.

   - Press **Ctrl+N**.

   The current date and time appear in the note's lower-left corner.

3. Enter the note title, press **Enter**, and then enter the information you want to store in the note.

4. To save and close the note, select the **Close** button in its upper-right corner. In the note list, only the title is visible. You can access the stored information by opening the note.

14

To remove a category from an item

1. Open the item, and then right-click the colored category bar.

2. On the shortcut menu, select **Clear "*Category*,"** **Clear All Categories**, or the name of the category that you want to clear.

Or

1. Select or open the item, and then display the **Categorize** menu.

2. On the **Categorize** menu, select **Clear All Categories**, or select the category that you want to clear.

To create a category

1. Open the **Color Categories** dialog, and then select **New**.

2. In the **Add New Category** dialog, do the following, and then select **OK**:

   - In the **Name** box, enter the category name.

   - In the **Color** list, select the color you want to assign to the category.

   - If you want to assign a keyboard shortcut, select it in the **Shortcut Key** list.

Choose from 25 category colors

To rename a category

1. Open the **Color Categories** dialog.

2. Do either of the following to activate the category name for editing:

   - Select the category name or checkbox, and then select **Rename**.

   - Slowly double-click the category name.

3. Change or replace the category name, and then press **Enter** or click away from the active name box.

> **TIP** The category order doesn't immediately change, but the next time you display the categories in a list or dialog, they will be in alphabetical order.

To delete a category

1. Open the **Color Categories** dialog.

2. Select the name or the checkbox of the category, and then select **Delete** or press **Alt+D**.

3. In the **Microsoft Outlook** message box asking you to confirm the deletion, select **Yes**.

Organize messages in folders

After you read and respond to messages, you might want to keep some for future reference. You can certainly choose to retain them all in your Inbox if you want, but as the number of messages in your Inbox increases to the thousands and even tens of thousands, it might quickly become overwhelming. (Yes, faithful reader, it happens to the best of us!) To minimize your Inbox contents and avoid an accumulation of unrelated messages, you can organize messages into folders. For example, you can keep messages that require action on your part in your Inbox and move messages that you want to retain for future reference into other folders.

> **TIP** Because the Outlook search function provides the option of searching within all folders containing items of a particular type, you can easily locate a message that's been moved to a folder without having to remember which folder it's in.

Popular personal-organization experts advocate various folder structures (for paper folders and email message folders) as an important part of an organizational system. You can apply any of these ideas when you create folders in Outlook, or you can use any other structure that works for you. For example, you might create folders that designate the level of action required, create a folder for each project you're working on, or create a folder to store all messages from a specific person, such as your manager, regardless of the message subject.

14

⌄Samantha Smith	⌄Samantha Smith	
⌄ **Inbox**	⌄ ✉ **Inbox**	148
Orders	▢ Orders	
References	▢ References	
Save for Later	▢ Save for Later	
Drafts	▧ Drafts	[5]
Sent Items	▢ Sent Items	
Deleted Items	🗑 Deleted Items	
Archive	▢ Archive	
˃ Conversation History	˃ 📅 Calendar	
Junk Email	˃ ᴀ≡ Contacts	
Outbox	˃ ▢ Conversation History	
RSS Feeds	📖 Journal	
Search Folders	🗷 Junk Email	[2]
	▢ Notes	
	📤 Outbox	
	📰 RSS Feeds	
	˃ ▢ Sync Issues	
	📋 Tasks	
	🔍 Search Folders	

Inbox subfolders

Expand the Inbox in the Folders pane to display subfolders

When you create a folder, you specify the location of the folder within your existing Outlook folder structure and the type of items you want the folder to contain. You can create folders to contain the following types of items:

- Calendar items
- Contact items
- InfoPath Form items
- Journal items
- Mail and Post items
- Note items
- Task items

The selection you make governs the folder icon that precedes its name in the Folder Pane, the folder window layout, the ribbon tabs and commands available in the folder, and the content of the Folder Pane when displaying the folder.

You can move messages to folders manually, or if your organization is running Exchange, you can have the email system move them for you. You can automatically move messages to another folder by creating a rule—for example, you can automatically move all messages received from your manager to a separate folder. You can also set up different rules that go into effect when you're away from the office.

To create a message folder

1. Do either of the following to open the **Create New Folder** dialog:

    -   On the **Folder** tab, in the **New** group, select **New Folder**.

    -   Press **Ctrl+Shift+E**.

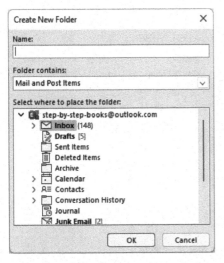

The default settings in the Create New Folder dialog match the module you open it from

2. In the **Name** box, enter a name for the new folder.

3. In the **Folder contains** list, select **Mail and Post Items**.

14

4. In the **Select where to place the folder** box, do either of the following:

   - Select your mailbox (at the top of the list) to create the folder at the same level as the Inbox.

   - Select your **Inbox** to create a subfolder of the Inbox.

5. Select **OK**.

To move a message to a folder

- Drag the message from the message list to the destination folder in the **Folder Pane**.

Or

1. In the message list, select the message you want to move.

2. Do either of the following to display the **Move** menu:

   - On the **Home** tab, in the **Move** group, select **Move**.

   - Right-click the message, and then select **Move**.

The Move menu automatically includes folders that you create

3. On the **Move** menu, do either of the following:

   - Select the folder you want to move the message to.

   - Select **Other Folder**. In the **Move Items** dialog displaying the full Folders list, select the folder you want to move the message to, and then select **OK**.

> ✓ **TIP** When Conversation view is turned on, moving the last message of a conversation from a folder removes the conversation from that folder.

Saving Messages Externally

If you want to store email messages independently of Outlook, you can save them to your hard drive or other file storage location in the Outlook Message file format. In my organization, we do this so that we can attach messages to Azure Dev Ops tickets for evidentiary purposes. Some people prefer to archive messages with other project-related files on a storage drive.

The Outlook Message file type varies depending on whether Outlook is installed on the computer you're displaying it on. Saving the message from Outlook creates a .msg file. On a computer that doesn't have Outlook configured, the file is recognized as a more generic .eml file and can be opened as a message in other desktop email programs such as Microsoft Mail.

Print messages

Although electronic communications certainly have less of an environmental impact than paper-based communications, you might at times want or need to print an email message—for example, if you want to take a hard copy of it to a meeting for reference, or if you keep a physical file of important messages or complimentary feedback. You can print the message exactly as it appears in your Inbox or embellish it with page headers and footers. Outlook prints messages in Memo style, which prints your name, the message header information, and then the message content as shown on the screen, including font and paragraph formats.

14

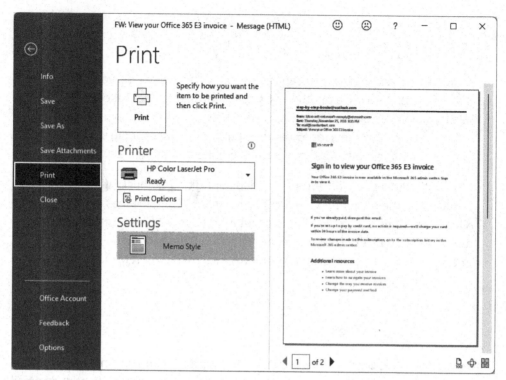

You can preview the message and modify the print settings

To preview and print a message:

1. In an open message window, display the **Print** page of the Backstage view. The right pane displays the message as it will appear when printed. In the **Printer** list, select the printer you want to use.

2. Do either of the following:

   - To print one copy of the message with the default settings, select **Print**.

   - To print only specific pages, print multiple copies, or print attachments, select **Print Options**, change the settings in the **Print** dialog, and then select **Print**.

To print a message with the default settings without first previewing it, right-click the message in the message list and then select **Quick Print**.

Key points

- You can display messages in your Inbox individually or as threaded conversations to keep your Inbox cleaner.

- You can group and sort messages by sender, time, subject, size, category, or any other field.

- You can assign color-coded categories to messages and then group and sort items by using color categories. You can use the default Outlook categories or tailor them to fit your needs.

- You can create folders to organize your mail, and move items to folders manually or automatically.

14

Practice tasks

No practice files are necessary to complete the practice tasks in this chapter.

> ⚠️ **IMPORTANT** As you work through the practice tasks in this book, you will create Outlook items that might be used as practice files in later chapters. If you haven't created specific items referenced in later chapters, you can substitute items of your own.

Display and manage messages

Start Outlook, display your Inbox in Compact view, and then complete the following tasks:

1. Display the messages in your Inbox as conversations. Notice the changes in the appearance and grouping of the messages in the message list.

2. Change the conversation settings so that the senders are shown below the subject in the message list instead of above it. Consider the benefits of the two options.

3. Select one conversation that has several messages, display the unique messages in the conversation, and then display all the messages in the conversation.

4. Remove redundant messages from the conversation.

5. Select any message in the conversation and open the **Ignore Conversation** dialog. Read the message in the dialog, and then select **Cancel**.

6. Configure the conversation settings to suit your preferences.

Arrange messages by specific attributes

Display your Inbox in Preview view and then complete the following tasks:

1. Use any method described in this chapter to arrange messages by sender (*From*).

2. Use any method described in this chapter to reverse the default sort order of the message list arrangement.

3. Switch to Compact view. Notice that the messages are no longer arranged by sender; the arrangement is applied only to the view in which you set it.

4. Use any method described in this chapter to group the messages in your Inbox.

5. Collapse a group of messages so that only the group header is displayed, and then expand the group again.

6. Collapse all message groups, and then expand them all.

7. Configure the view and arrangement settings to suit your preferences.

Categorize items

Display your Inbox in Compact view and then complete the following tasks:

1. Create a new email message addressed to yourself. Enter Work with categories as the subject, and send the message.

2. When the message appears in your Inbox, select it.

3. Create a new color category, and do the following:

    - Name the category StepByStep.

    - Assign the **Dark Maroon** color to the category.

    - Assign the **Ctrl+F10** keyboard shortcut to the category.

4. Finish creating the category and close any open dialogs. Notice that the selected message now has the StepByStep category assigned to it.

5. Set the **StepByStep** category as the Quick Click category.

6. Switch to Single view. In the message list, point to an unassigned category block in the **Categories** column to display the ScreenTip.

7. Select the block to assign the Quick Click category to the message. Then select again to remove the category.

Organize messages in folders

Display your Inbox and then complete the following tasks:

1. Create a new folder, and do the following:

    - Name the folder StepByStep.

    - Configure the folder to contain messages.

    - Save the folder as a subfolder of your Inbox.

2. Finish creating the folder. Then move the **Work with categories** message that you created in an earlier set of practice tasks to the **StepByStep** folder.

3. Retain the folder, message, and category for use in practice tasks in later chapters.

Print messages

In Outlook, complete the following tasks:

1. Display the Step by Step folder you created in the preceding task.

2. Open the Work with categories message.

3. Print the message in Memo style.

Manage scheduling

You can use the Outlook calendar to organize your daily activities and to remind you of important tasks and events. If you're a busy person and you use the Outlook calendar to its fullest potential, it might at times seem as though the calendar runs your life—but that isn't necessarily a bad thing! Using the calendar effectively can help you stay organized, on time, and on task. You can schedule and track appointments, meetings, and events, and block time as a reminder to yourself to take care of tasks. And because you can also set up Outlook on your mobile device, you can be assured of having up-to-date schedule information available wherever and whenever you need it.

If you have a Microsoft Exchange Server account, a calendar is part of that account. Some internet email accounts also have associated calendars. When you configure Outlook to connect to a different type of account, Outlook also connects to the associated calendar. If you don't have a calendar as part of your account, Outlook creates a blank calendar for you. You can easily schedule appointments, events, and meetings on any Outlook calendar.

This chapter guides you through procedures related to displaying different views of a calendar; scheduling and changing appointments, events, and meetings; and responding to meeting requests.

In this chapter

- Display different views of a calendar
- Schedule appointments and events
- Convert calendar items
- Configure calendar item options
- Schedule and change meetings
- Respond to meeting requests

Display different views of a calendar

Just as you can with other Outlook modules, you can specify the way that Outlook displays calendar information (the view) and the attribute by which that information is arranged (the arrangement).

The Calendar module has these four content views:

- **Calendar** This is the standard view in which you display your Outlook calendar. In the Day, Work Week, or Week arrangement, Calendar view displays the subject, location, and organizer (if space allows) of each appointment, meeting, or event, in addition to the availability bar and any special icons, such as Private or Recurrence.

- **Preview** In the Day, Work Week, or Week arrangement, Preview view displays more information, including information from the notes area of the appointment window, as space allows.

- **List** This list view displays all appointments, meetings, and events on your calendar.

- **Active** This list view displays only future appointments, meetings, and events.

When working in a list view, you can group calendar items by selecting a field from the Arrangement gallery on the View tab.

> ⚠ **IMPORTANT** In this book, we assume that you're working in Calendar view, and refer to the standard Calendar view arrangements as *Day view*, *Work Week view*, *Week view*, *Month view*, and *Schedule view*.

The available arrangements vary based on the view. In Calendar view and Preview view, the arrangements are based on the time span, and include the following:

- **Day** Displays one day at a time separated into half-hour increments.

- **Work Week** Displays only the days of your work week. The default work week is Monday through Friday from 8:00 AM to 5:00 PM. Time slots that fall within the work week are white on the calendar; time slots outside of the work week are colored.

- **Week** Displays one calendar week (Sunday through Saturday) at a time.

- **Month** Displays one calendar month at a time, in addition to any preceding or following days that fall into the displayed weeks.

- **Schedule view** Displays a horizontal view of the calendar for a selected time period. You can add other people's calendars as rows in this view, so that you can easily compare multiple calendars for specific time periods.

Schedule view for a group of coworkers

This arrangement is very useful for comparing limited time periods for multiple calendars, such as those of the members of a calendar group.

You switch among arrangements by selecting the buttons in the Arrangement group on the View tab of the Calendar module ribbon.

15

> ✓ **TIP** If you've made changes to any view (such as the order in which information appears) and you want to return to the default settings, select Reset View in the Current View group on the View tab. If the Reset View button is unavailable, the view already displays the default settings.

Display your entire work week at one time

You can use these additional tools to change the time period shown in the calendar:

- Display the previous or next time period by selecting the Back button or the Forward button next to the date or date range in the calendar header.

- Display the current day by selecting the Today button in the Go To group on the Home tab.

- Display a seven-day period starting with the current day by selecting Next 7 Days in the Go To group on the Home tab.

- Display week numbers to the left of each week in Month view and in the Date Navigator. If you implement this option, you can select the week tab to display that week.

> ✓ **TIP** Specific weeks are referred to in some locations and industries by number to simplify the communication of dates. (For example, you can say you'll be out of the office "Week 24" rather than "June 7–11.") Week 1 is the calendar week in which January 1 falls, Week 2 is the following week, and so on through to the end of the year. Because of the way the weeks are numbered, a year can end in Week 52 or (more commonly) in Week 53. To display week numbers in the Date Navigator and in the Month view of the calendar, select the Show Week Numbers checkbox on the Calendar page of the Outlook Options dialog.

To display your calendar for a month

- On the **Home** tab, in the **Arrange** group, select **Month** to display your calendar for the month.

- Press **Ctrl+Alt+4**.

To navigate in Month view

- To the left of the date range in the calendar header, select the **Forward** button to move the calendar forward one month or the **Back** button to move the calendar back one month.

- On the **View** tab, in the **Current View** group, select **Change View** and then, in the gallery, select **Preview** to display additional details on the monthly calendar.

To display a seven-day week in the calendar

1. In the **Date Navigator** at the top of the **Folder Pane**, point to the left edge of a calendar row that contains one or more bold dates.

2. When the cursor changes from pointing left to pointing right toward the calendar, click once to display the selected seven-day week in the calendar.

To display your work week schedule

- On the **Home** tab, in the **Arrange** group, select **Work Week**.

- Press **Ctrl+Alt+2**.

  The first time slot of your defined work day appears at the top of the pane. Time slots within your work day are white; time slots outside of your work day are shaded.

15

Use the Date Navigator

By default, the Outlook Calendar module displays the current month and next month in the Date Navigator at the top of the Folder Pane. These compact monthly calendars provide quick indicators of the current date, the time period that is displayed in the content pane, days that you are free, and days that you are busy.

<	**December 2021**					>
SU	MO	TU	WE	TH	FR	SA
28	29	30	1	2	3	4
5	6	7	8	9	10	11
12	13	14	15	16	17	18
19	20	21	22	23	24	25
26	27	28	29	30	31	

The Date Navigator is a convenient and useful tool

The current date is indicated by a blue square. The date or dates currently displayed in the calendar are indicated by light blue highlighting. Bold dates indicate days with scheduled appointments, meetings, or events. Days of the preceding and following months appear on the two default calendars in gray.

You can display more or fewer months by changing the width or height of the area allocated to the Date Navigator. To change the size of the Date Navigator area, do either of the following:

- Drag the right edge of the Folder Pane to the right to increase the width, or to the left to decrease the width.

- Drag the horizontal border below the Date Navigator calendars down to increase the height, or up to decrease the height.

The Date Navigator displays each month in seven-day weeks. The first day of the week shown in the Date Navigator is controlled by the First Day Of Week setting on the Calendar page of the Outlook Options dialog. When the Date Navigator displays more than one month, each month shows either five or six weeks at a time—whichever is necessary to show all the days of the currently selected month.

You can display a specific day, week, month, or range of days in the calendar by selecting it in the Date Navigator. When you're displaying the Calendar in the Week arrangement, selecting a day displays the week that contains it. Otherwise, the Calendar arrangement changes to show the time period that you select.

Use these techniques to work with the Date Navigator:

- To display a day, select that date.

- To display a week, point to the left edge of the week; when the pointer direction changes from left to right, click to select the week. (You can configure the Calendar Options to display week numbers in the Date Navigator and Calendar. If you do, selecting the week number displays the week.)

- To display a range of days (from two days to a maximum of six weeks), point to the first date you want to display and then drag across the Date Navigator to the last date.

- To change the period displayed in the calendar one month at a time, select the Previous or Next arrow on either side of the month name, at the top of the Date Navigator.

- To move multiple months back or forward, press the month name, and then drag up or down on the list that appears.

15

To display your calendar for a day

- On the **View** tab, in the **Arrangement** group, select **Day** to display only the selected day's schedule.

To display today's schedule

- On the **Home** tab, in the **Go To** group, select **Today**. If the calendar wasn't previously displaying the current week, it does so now. The times displayed remain the same. The current day and the current time slot are highlighted.

To display your task list on the Calendar

> **TIP** The Daily Task List is available in the Day, Work Week, or Week arrangement of the Calendar. It is not available in Month view or Schedule view.

- On the **View** tab, in the **Layout** group, select **Daily Task List** and then do any of the following:

  - Select **Normal** to display the task list area below the calendar.

  - Select **Minimized** to display a single row below the calendar. The minimized Daily Task List displays a count of your total, active, and completed tasks for the day.

  - Select **Off** to hide the task list.

To return the calendar to its default settings

1. In the **Change View** gallery, select **Calendar** to return the calendar to its default settings.

2. In the **Current View** group, select **Reset View** to return to the default calendar state.

Schedule appointments and events

Appointments are blocks of time you schedule for only yourself (as opposed to meetings, to which you invite other Outlook users). An appointment has a specific start time and end time (as opposed to an event, which occurs for one or more full 24-hour period).

Events are day-long blocks of time that you schedule on your Outlook calendar, such as birthdays, payroll days, or anything else occurring on a specific day but not at a specific time. In all other respects, creating an event is identical to creating an appointment, in that you can specify a location, indicate recurrence, indicate your availability, and attach additional information to the event item.

You can schedule an appointment by entering, at minimum, a subject and time in an appointment window or directly on the calendar. The basic appointment window also includes a field for the appointment location and a notes area in which you can store general information, including formatted text, website links, and even file attachments so that they are readily available to you at the time of the appointment.

If your organization has Teams, that option is available on the Appointment tab

If you create an appointment that immediately follows or precedes another, the InfoBar at the top of the window indicates that the appointment is adjacent to another on your calendar. If you create an appointment that has a time overlap with an existing appointment, the InfoBar indicates that the appointment conflicts with another.

15

To schedule an event, you need to provide only the date. You can schedule an event in an appointment window or directly on the calendar.

> **TIP** You don't have to create appointments and events from scratch; you can also create them from email messages. For information, see the next topic, "Convert calendar items."

When the Calendar view is displayed, events are shown on the calendar in the date area; appointments are displayed in the time slots.

Display basic details in a ScreenTip by pointing to the appointment or event

> **SEE ALSO** For information about setting availability, see "Configure calendar item options" later in this chapter. For information about the calendar views, see "Display different views of a calendar" earlier in this chapter.

> **IMPORTANT** The procedures in this chapter assume that you're working with an Exchange account. Some functionality might be unavailable if you're working with a calendar that's part of another type of account.

To open a new appointment window

- In the Calendar module, do one of the following:

  - With the ribbon minimized, select the **New Appointment** button at the top of the **Folder Pane**.

  - On the **Home** tab of the ribbon, in the **New** group, select **New Appointment**.

  - Press **Ctrl+N**.

- In any module, do either of the following:

  - On the **Home** tab, in the **New** group, select **New Items**, and then select **Appointment**.

  - Press **Ctrl+Shift+A**.

To schedule an appointment

1. Open a new appointment window.

2. In the **Subject** field, enter an identifying name for the appointment.

3. In the **Location** field, enter the appointment location, if it's pertinent, or any other information that you want available in the appointment header.

4. In the **Start time** row, enter or select a date and time. Outlook automatically sets the End Time to a half hour after the start time.

5. In the **End time** row, enter or select a date and time. An appointment can span overnight or across multiple days.

6. On the **Appointment** tab, in the **Actions** group, select **Save & Close**.

Or

1. Display the calendar in the Day, Work Week, or Week arrangement of the Calendar view.

2. Do either of the following in the calendar pane:

   - In the calendar, select the time slot at the appointment start time on the day of the appointment.

   - Drag from the appointment start time through to the appointment end time.

15

When you release the mouse button, Outlook displays an editable bar that spans the selected time (or one time slot, as specified by the time scale of the calendar).

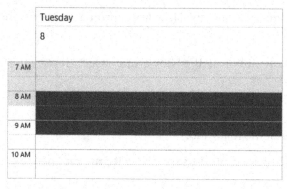

Schedule simple appointments directly on the calendar

> 🔍 **SEE ALSO** For information about setting the calendar time scale, see "Display different views of a calendar" earlier in this chapter.

3. In the editable bar, enter an identifying name for the appointment. When you begin typing, Outlook creates an appointment with the default availability and reminder time.

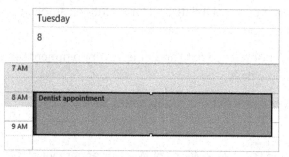

When an appointment is being edited on the calendar, it has sizing handles on the top and bottom

4. If you want to change the appointment time span, drag the top or bottom sizing handle.

5. Press **Enter** or click away from the bar to create the appointment.

To schedule an event

1. Open a new appointment window.

2. In the **Subject** field, enter an identifying name for the event.

3. In the **Location** field, enter the event location, if it's pertinent, or any other information that you want available in the event header.

4. In the **Start time** row, enter or select the event date. Then at the right end of the row, select the **All day event** checkbox.

5. Enter any additional information as you would for an appointment. Then save and close the event.

Or

1. Display the Calendar view of the calendar.

2. Do either of the following:

   - In the Day, Work Week, or Week arrangement of the calendar, on the day that you want to create the event, click or tap the space below the day and date and above the time slots. This is the event slot.

   - In the Month arrangement of the calendar, click or tap the day that you want to create the event.

3. Enter a title for the event, and then press **Enter**.

Convert calendar items

All Outlook calendar items are built from the same basic template. These two factors define a calendar item as an appointment, event, or meeting:

- Whether the item has specific start and end times or is all day

- Whether you invite other people through Outlook

You can easily convert an appointment into an event or meeting or convert an event into an appointment or an invited event.

If you want to schedule an appointment, event, or meeting based on the information in an email message that you receive, you can easily do so by dragging the message to the calendar. For example, if a friend or coworker sends you a message that contains the details of the grand opening for a local art gallery, you can add that information to your calendar. You can retain any or all of the message information as part of the calendar item so that you (or other meeting participants) have the information on hand when you need it. After creating the calendar item, you can delete the actual message from your Inbox.

15

Add holidays to your calendar

Holidays are a type of event, and it can be useful to have them on your calendar so you can plan around days that you might not be working or that businesses might be closed. Instead of creating events on your calendar for individual holidays, you can have Outlook add them for you.

When adding holidays to the calendar, you can choose from the national holidays of 111 countries or regions, and four sets of observed religious holidays (Christian, Shia, Sunni, and Jewish). You can add multiple sets of holidays to your calendar, so if you work with clients or colleagues in another location, you can add those holidays to your calendar so you can anticipate scheduling issues.

To add holidays to your Outlook calendar, follow these steps:

1. Open the **Outlook Options** dialog and display the **Calendar** page.

2. In the **Calendar options** section, select the **Add Holidays** button to open the **Add Holidays to Calendar** dialog.

You can add holidays from a specific location or religion to your calendar

3. Select the checkboxes of the locations and/or religions whose holidays you want to add to your calendar, and then select **OK**.

4. After Outlook adds the selected holidays to your calendar, select **OK** to close the **Outlook Options** dialog.

TIP If you try to install the holidays of the same location or religion twice, Outlook notifies you of this and asks whether you want to import them again. If you inadvertently add the same set of holidays to the calendar twice, the easiest way to rectify the situation is to remove all occurrences of that location's holidays and then add them again.

Outlook adds the holiday occurrences from 2012 through 2026 to your calendar, and assigns a color category named *Holiday* to them. The Holiday category has the same color as the calendar and can't be changed.

SEE ALSO For information about color categories, see "Categorize items" in Chapter 14, "Organize your Inbox."

To remove a set of holidays from your calendar, follow these steps:

1. Display a list view of the calendar.

2. Search the calendar for categories:holiday. If necessary, narrow the search to a specific location, religion, or year by adding search criteria to locate the holidays you want to remove.

		Subject	Location	Start ▲	End	Categories
		(none): 371 item(s)				
		New Year's Day (Observed)	Thailand	Tue 1/3/2012 12:00 AM	Wed 1/4/2012 12:00 AM	Holiday
		Children's Day	Thailand	Sat 1/14/2012 12:00 AM	Sun 1/15/2012 12:00 AM	Holiday
		Chinese New Year (1st Day)	Thailand	Mon 1/23/2012 12:00 AM	Tue 1/24/2012 12:00 AM	Holiday
		Makha Bucha Day	Thailand	Wed 3/7/2012 12:00 AM	Thu 3/8/2012 12:00 AM	Holiday
		Songkran Festival (Observed)	Thailand	Mon 4/16/2012 12:00 AM	Tue 4/17/2012 12:00 AM	Holiday
		Songkran Festival (Observed)	Thailand	Tue 4/17/2012 12:00 AM	Wed 4/18/2012 12:00 AM	Holiday
		Coronation Day	Thailand	Sat 5/5/2012 12:00 AM	Sun 5/6/2012 12:00 AM	Holiday
		Coronation Day (Observed)	Thailand	Mon 5/7/2012 12:00 AM	Tue 5/8/2012 12:00 AM	Holiday
		Visakha Bucha Day	Thailand	Mon 6/4/2012 12:00 AM	Tue 6/5/2012 12:00 AM	Holiday

Outlook highlights the search terms in the results

3. Select individual holidays you want to remove, or select any holiday in the list to activate the list, and then press **Ctrl+A** to select all the holidays in the search results. Then press the **Delete** key.

15

To create an appointment from an email message

1. Display your Inbox.

2. Drag the message from the message list to the **Calendar** link or button on the **Navigation Bar**.

3. After the cursor changes to a plus sign, release the mouse button to create an appointment based on the message and open the appointment window for editing. The appointment has the subject and content of the original message. The start and end times are set to the next half-hour increment following the current time.

4. Set the date and times for the appointment, and do any of the following:

   • In the **Options** group, change the availability, reminder time, or recurrence.

   • In the **Tags** group, assign a category to the appointment, mark it as private, or change the priority.

   • In the content pane, edit the original message content to suit the requirements of the appointment.

5. In the appointment window, select **Save & Close** to save the appointment to your calendar.

To convert an appointment to an event

1. Open the appointment window.

2. At the right end of the **Start time** row, select the **All day event** checkbox.

3. Change the event date, options, or tags, and then save and close the event window.

To convert an appointment to a meeting

1. Open the appointment window.

2. On the **Appointment** tab in the **Attendees** group, select **Invite Attendees** to add Required and Optional fields to the header and display the meeting window features.

3. Enter contact information for the people you want to invite to the meeting.

4. Add a location if necessary, and then select **Send**.

To convert an event to an invited event

1. Open the event window.

2. On the **Event** tab, in the **Attendees** group, select **Invite Attendees** to add Required and Optional fields to the header and display the meeting window features.

3. Enter contact information for the people you want to invite to the event.

4. Add a location if necessary, and then select **Send**.

To convert an event to an appointment

1. Open the event window.

2. At the right end of the **Start time** row, clear the **All day event** checkbox.

3. Set the appointment start and end times, and change the options as necessary. Then save and close the appointment window.

Configure calendar item options

Appointments, events, and meetings share many common elements, and you use the same techniques to work with those options in all types of calendar items. The five options that you can configure for all items are:

- **Time zones** You can specify the time zone in which an appointment, event, or meeting occurs. This helps to ensure that the start and end times are clearly defined when you're traveling or inviting people in multiple time zones to an online meeting. You have the option of specifying different time zones for the start time and the finish time. This is useful when your "appointment" is an airplane flight with departure and arrival cities located in different time zones and you want the flight to show up correctly wherever you're currently located.

- **Availability** When creating an appointment or event, you indicate your availability (referred to as *Free/Busy time*) by marking it as Free, Working Elsewhere, Tentative, Busy, or Out Of Office. The appointment or event is color-coded on your calendar to match the availability you indicate. Your availability is visible to other Outlook users on your network and is also displayed when you share your calendar or send calendar information to other people.

  The default availability for new appointments and meetings is Busy, and for events is Free.

15

- **Reminder** By default, Outlook displays a reminder message 15 minutes before the start time of an appointment or meeting, or 12 hours before an event (at noon the preceding day). You can change the reminder to occur as far as two weeks in advance, or you can turn it off completely if you want to. If you synchronize your Outlook installation with a mobile device, reminders also appear on your mobile device. This is very convenient when you are away from your computer.

> **✓ TIP** Reminders can be indicated on the calendar by a bell icon. This option is turned off by default in Outlook. You can turn it on in the Calendar Options section of the Calendar page of the Outlook Options dialog.

- **Recurrence** If you have the same appointment, event, or meeting on a regular basis—for example, a weekly exercise class, a monthly team meeting, or an anniversary—you can set it up in your Outlook calendar as a recurring item. A recurring calendar item can happen at almost any regular interval, such as every Tuesday and Thursday, every other week, or the last weekday of every month.

  Configuring a recurrence creates multiple instances of the item on your calendar at the time interval you specify. You can set the item to recur until further notice, to end after a certain number of occurrences, or to end by a certain date. The individual occurrences of the recurring item are linked. When making changes to a recurring item, you can choose to update all occurrences or only an individual occurrence of the appointment.

  Recurring items are indicated on the calendar by circling arrows.

- **Privacy** You can tag a calendar item as Private if you want to ensure that the details aren't displayed when you share your calendar or send calendar information to other people.

  Private items are indicated on the calendar by a lock and are identified to other people as Private Appointment rather than by the subject.

You can specify time zones, your availability, the reminder time, and the recurrence, and mark an item as private, when you create the item. Alternatively, you can edit the item later and configure any of these options. The time zone can be specified only in the item window; the other options can be set on the item type–specific tab in the item window or the item type–specific tool tab that appears on the Outlook ribbon when you select an item on the calendar. In single-occurrence items, these tabs are labeled *Appointment*, *Event*, *Meeting*, or *Invited Event*. In recurring items, the tab names include *Occurrence* or *Series* to indicate that you're editing one or all occurrences of the item.

Outlook identifies conflicts with recurring item instances

You can assign categories and importance to appointments, events, and meetings in the same way that you do to messages and other Outlook items. In many ways, categories are more useful in the Calendar than in other modules.

Color categories provide information at a glance about your schedule.

15

To specify the time zone of an appointment or meeting

1. Open the item window.

2. On the **Appointment** or **Meeting** tab, in the **Options** group, select **Time Zones** to display the time zone controls in the Start Time and End Time rows. The time zone controls display the time zone your computer is currently set to.

3. Select the time zone control that you want to change, and then select the time zone.

Set the time zones to ensure that Outlook blocks the correct time

To hide the time zone controls

1. Select identical entries in the **Start time** and **End time** time zone controls.

2. On the **Appointment** or **Meeting** tab, in the **Options** group, select the **Time Zones** button to remove the controls.

To modify an appointment, event, or meeting

1. Display the calendar in the Day, Work Week, or Week arrangement of the Calendar view, with the appointment visible.

2. In the calendar pane, click or tap the item once to select it. Then do any of the following:

   • On the item type–specific tool tab, make any changes to the options or tags.

   • Drag the item from the current time slot to a new time slot.

   • Drag the top sizing handle to change an appointment start time.

   • Drag the bottom sizing handle to change an appointment end time.

3. To open the item window, in which you can make other changes, do either of the following:

- Press **Enter**.

- On the item type–specific tool tab, in the **Actions** group, select **Open**.

To indicate your availability during an appointment, event, or meeting

1. Open the item window or select the item on the calendar.

2. On the item-specific tab or tool tab, in the **Options** group, select the **Show As** list, and then select the availability.

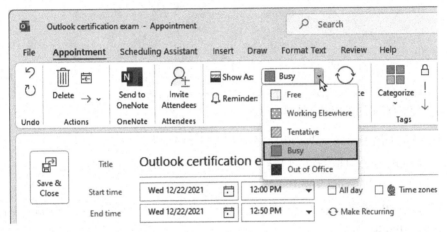

The default availability for appointments is Busy

To change the default reminder for an appointment, event, or meeting

1. Open the item window, or select the item on the calendar.

2. On the item-specific tab or tool tab, in the **Options** group, select the **Reminder** list, and then select the time (or select None to have no reminder).

To create recurrences of an appointment, event, or meeting

1. Open the item window, or select the item on the calendar.

2. On the item-specific tab or tool tab, in the **Options** group, select **Recurrence** to open the Appointment Recurrence, Event Recurrence, or Meeting Recurrence dialog. The default recurrence is weekly on the currently selected day of the week.

15

You can change the times, days, frequency, and quantity from the Appointment Recurrence dialog

3. In the **Recurrence** dialog, do any of the following:

   - In the **End** list, select the arrow and select an end time for the recurring meeting.

   - In the **Recurrence pattern** section, select how often you want the meeting to recur.

   - In the **Range of recurrence** section, select how many times you want the meeting to occur, or select the last date you want the meeting to recur.

4. Select **OK** in the **Recurrence** dialog to replace the Start Time and End Time fields in the appointment window with the recurrence details.

Schedule and change meetings

A primary difficulty when scheduling a meeting is finding a time that works for all the people who need to attend it. Scheduling meetings through Outlook is significantly simpler than other methods of scheduling meetings, particularly when you need to accommodate the schedules of several people. Outlook displays the individual and collective schedules of people within your own organization, and of people outside of your organization who have published their calendars to the internet. You can review attendees' schedules to locate a time when everyone is available or have Outlook find a convenient time for you.

You can send an Outlook meeting invitation (referred to as a *meeting request*) to anyone who has an email account—even to a person who doesn't use Outlook. You can send a meeting request from any type of email account (such as an Exchange account or an internet email account).

The meeting window has two pages: the Meeting page and the Scheduling Assistant or Scheduling page. The Meeting page is visible by default. You can enter all the required information directly on the Meeting page.

The Meeting page of a meeting window

If your email account is part of an Exchange Server network, the secondary page of the meeting window is the Scheduling Assistant page, which provides additional features that help you to identify meeting times that work for the invited participants.

15

You can view information about meeting attendees' schedules on the Scheduling Assistant page

> ✓ **TIP** The secondary page for non-Exchange accounts is the Scheduling page, which has features similar to those of the Scheduling Assistant page but is less helpful because it's unlikely that you have online access to calendar information for the other participants.

The Scheduling Assistant page includes a group schedule that shows the status of each attendee's time throughout your working day. Outlook indicates your suggested meeting time on the group schedule. If free/busy information is available for meeting attendees, the status is indicated by the standard free/busy colors and patterns that match the legend at the bottom of the page. If no information is available (either because Outlook can't connect to an attendee's calendar or because the proposed meeting is further out than the scheduling information stored on the server), Outlook shows the time with gray diagonal stripes. The row at the top of the schedule, to the right of the All Attendees heading, indicates the collective schedule of all the attendees.

> **✓ TIP** You can enter additional attendees in the Required and Optional fields on the Meeting page or in the All Attendees list on the Scheduling or Scheduling Assistant page. You can also add attendees by selecting the Required or Optional button on the Meeting page or the Add Attendees button on the Scheduling or Scheduling Assistant page, and then selecting attendees from an address box.

You can change the time and duration of the meeting to work with the displayed schedules by selecting a different time in the Start Time and End Time lists, by dragging the vertical start time and end time bars in the group schedule, or by selecting the time you want in the Suggested Times list.

The Scheduling Assistant page includes the Room Finder feature, which helps you identify dates and times that work for the greatest number of attendees, and available meeting rooms if your IT department has identified these within Exchange. The monthly calendar at the top of the Room Finder indicates the collective availability of the group on each day, as follows:

- Dates that occur in the past and nonworking days are unavailable (gray).

- Days when all attendees are available are Good (white).

- Days when most attendees are available are Fair (light blue).

- Days when most attendees are not available are Poor (medium blue).

> **✓ TIP** All the capabilities of the Room Finder are available for Exchange accounts, but functionality is limited for other types of accounts. You can display or hide the Room Finder pane by selecting Room Finder in the Attendees group on the Scheduling tab. The Room Finder button is available only after you invite at least one attendee.

Managed conference rooms that are available at the indicated meeting time are shown in the center of the Room Finder. At the bottom of the Room Finder pane, the Suggested Times list displays attendee availability for appointments of the length of time you have specified for the meeting.

Selecting a date in the calendar displays the suggested meeting times for just that day. (Scheduling suggestions are not provided for past or nonworking days.) Selecting a meeting time in the Suggested Times list updates the calendar and the meeting request.

15

People you invite to meetings are referred to as *attendees*. By default, the attendance of each attendee is indicated as Required. You can inform noncritical attendees of the meeting by marking their attendance as Optional. You can invite entire groups of people by using a contact group or distribution list. You can also invite managed resources, such as conference rooms and audio/visual equipment, that have been set up by your organization's Exchange administrator.

A meeting request should have at least one attendee other than you, and it must have a start time and an end time. It should also include a subject and a location, but Outlook will send the meeting request without this information if you specifically allow it. The body of a meeting request can include text and web links, and you can also attach files. This is a convenient way to distribute meeting information to attendees ahead of time.

> (O) **SEE ALSO** For information about creating a meeting request from an email message, see "Convert calendar items" earlier in this chapter.

Outlook tracks responses from attendees and those responsible for scheduling the resources you requested, so you always have an up-to-date report of how many people will attend your meeting. The number of attendees who have accepted, tentatively accepted, and declined the meeting request appears in the meeting header section when you open a meeting in its own window.

You might find it necessary to change the date, time, or location of a meeting after you send the meeting request, or to add or remove attendees. As the meeting organizer, you can change any information in a meeting request at any time, including adding or removing attendees or canceling the meeting. Meeting attendees receive updates. Changes to meeting details are tracked so that attendees can quickly identify them.

To open a new meeting window

- On the **Home** tab of the Calendar module, in the **New** group, select **New Meeting**.

- On the **Home** tab of any module, in the **New** group, select **New Items**, and then select **Meeting**.

- In any module, press **Ctrl+Shift+Q**.

To create a meeting request

1. Open a new meeting window.

2. In the **Title** field, enter an identifying name for the meeting.

3. In the **Required** and **Optional** fields, enter contact information for the attendees.

4. In the **Start time** row, enter or select a date and time. Outlook automatically sets the end time to a half hour after the start time.

5. In the **End time** row, enter or select a date and time. A meeting can span overnight or across multiple days.

6. In the **Location** field, enter the meeting location. If your organization uses Microsoft Teams, you can select the corresponding button on the Meeting toolbar to enter meeting information in the Location field and content pane.

7. Verify the meeting details, and then select **Send** to add the meeting to your calendar and send the meeting request to the attendees.

To identify times that colleagues are available for meetings

> ⚠ **IMPORTANT** This procedure is for Outlook users with Exchange email accounts. Free/busy time is available only for attendees in your organization or another connected organization, or attendees that share free/busy information through a web service.

1. On the **Meeting** tab, in the **Show** group, select **Scheduling Assistant**. The **All Attendees** list on the **Scheduling Assistant** page includes you and any attendees you entered in the **Required** and **Optional** fields. The icon next to your name (a magnifying glass in a black circle) indicates that you are the meeting organizer. The icon next to each attendee's name (an upward-pointing arrow in a red circle) indicates that he or she is a required attendee.

> ✓ **TIP** If you're inviting someone as a courtesy, you can indicate that he or she does not need to attend by selecting the Required Attendee icon to the left of the attendee's name and then, in the list, selecting Optional Attendee.

2. If necessary, scroll to the bottom of the **Room Finder** to display the **Suggested Times** list. The times shown are based on your schedule and the schedule information available for the attendees.

15

3. To add attendees, enter their email addresses in the **All Attendees** list, and then press **Tab** to update the Suggested Times list in the Room Finder.

4. If you need to change the meeting time or duration, you can do so by dragging the start time and end time bars on the group schedule or by entering times in the boxes below the group schedule.

5. Select **Appointment** in the **Show** group to return to the Meeting page, which reflects the current attendees and meeting times.

6. Verify the meeting details, and then select **Send** to add the meeting to your calendar and send the meeting request to the attendees.

To edit a meeting request

1. Open the meeting window for editing.

2. If the meeting is one of a series (a recurring meeting), Outlook prompts you to indicate whether you want to edit the meeting series or only the selected instance of the meeting. Select **Just this one** or **The entire series**.

3. Modify the date, time, notes, options, or attendees. Then select **Send Update**.

4. If you modified the attendees, Outlook prompts you to specify whether to send updates to all attendees or only to the changed attendees. Select either option to send an updated meeting request.

> ✅ **TIP** You don't need to cancel and reschedule a meeting to change the date or time, or to add or remove an attendee. You can edit the meeting request, remove the attendee, and then send a meeting update to the affected attendees.

To cancel a meeting or a meeting occurrence

1. Select the meeting on your calendar or open the meeting window.

2. Do either of the following:

    *   On the **Meeting** tool tab, in the **Actions** group, select **Cancel Meeting**.

    *   On the **Meeting Series** tool tab, in the **Actions** group, select **Cancel Meeting**, and then select **Cancel Occurrence** or **Cancel Series**.

> **TIP** The Cancel Meeting button is available only for meetings that you organize, not for meetings you're invited to.

A meeting window containing cancellation information opens.

Canceling a meeting removes it from attendees' calendars

3. Do either of the following:

   - In the meeting header, select **Send Cancellation**. Outlook sends an updated meeting request to the attendees and removes the meeting from their calendars.

   - If you change your mind about canceling the meeting, select the **Close** button (**X**) at the right end of the message window title bar. Outlook reminds you that you haven't sent the cancellation and provides options. In the message box that appears, select **No, don't cancel. Close the meeting.** Then select **OK**.

You can't cancel a meeting without notifying the attendees

Respond to meeting requests

When you receive a meeting request from another Outlook user, the meeting appears on your calendar with your time scheduled as Tentative. Until you respond to the meeting request, the organizer doesn't know whether you plan to attend.

A meeting request in the Reading Pane

The meeting request displays your current calendar information at the time of the meeting, so you are aware of any schedule conflicts at that time. You can respond to a meeting request in one of these four ways:

- **Accept the request** Outlook deletes the meeting request and adds the meeting to your calendar.

- **Tentatively accept the request** This option indicates that you might be able to attend the meeting but are undecided. Outlook deletes the meeting request and shows the meeting on your calendar as tentatively scheduled.

- **Propose a new meeting time** Outlook sends your request to the meeting organizer for confirmation and shows the meeting with the original time on your calendar as tentatively scheduled.

- **Decline the request** Outlook deletes the meeting request and removes the meeting from your calendar.

If you don't respond to a meeting request, the meeting remains on your calendar with your time shown as tentatively scheduled and the meeting details in gray font rather than black.

When accepting or declining a meeting, you can choose whether to send a response to the meeting organizer. If you don't send a response, your acceptance will not be tallied, and the organizer will not know whether you are planning to attend the meeting. If you do send a response, you can add a message to the meeting organizer before sending it.

To respond to a meeting request

1. In the meeting window, in the **Reading Pane**, or on the shortcut menu that appears when you right-click or long-press (tap and hold) the meeting request, select **Accept**, **Tentative**, or **Decline**.

2. Choose whether to send a standard response, a personalized response, or no response at all.

To propose a new time for a meeting

1. In the meeting window or in the **Reading Pane**, select **Propose New Time**, and then in the list, select **Tentative and Propose New Time** or **Decline and Propose New Time** to open the Propose New Time dialog.

You can respond to a meeting request by proposing a different meeting time

15

2. In the **Propose New Time** dialog, change the meeting start and end times to the times you want to propose, either by dragging the start time and end time bars or by changing the date and time in the lists, and then select **Propose Time**.

3. In the meeting response window that opens, enter a message to the meeting organizer if you want to, and then select **Send** to send your response and add the meeting to your calendar as tentatively scheduled for the original meeting time. If the meeting organizer approves the meeting time change, you and other attendees will receive updated meeting requests showing the new meeting time.

Key points

- You can create and manage appointments and all-day events in your calendar.

- Other people in your Exchange organization can find out whether you are free, busy, or out of the office by reviewing the appointments, events, and meetings scheduled in your calendar.

- You can personalize the display of your available working hours, and mark appointments as private to hide the details from other people.

- You can use Outlook to set up meetings, invite participants, and track their responses.

- Outlook can identify a meeting time based on participants' schedules.

- If your organization is running Exchange Server or you have an Exchange Online account through Office 365, you can use the Scheduling Assistant features to quickly identify meeting times of a specific duration during which your planned attendees are available.

- You can display many different views of your calendar. You can change the dates and date ranges displayed in the calendar by using the Date Navigator, by using navigational buttons located in the calendar header, or by using commands on the ribbon.

Practice tasks

You will use the SBS Test message that you sent to yourself in Chapter 13, "Send and receive email messages" to complete a practice task in this chapter. If you haven't already created that message, you can do so now or substitute another message.

Display different views of a calendar

Display your calendar in Calendar view, and then perform the following tasks:

1. Display your calendar for the current month.

2. In the **Date Navigator**, notice the shading that identifies the current day. Select a different day that shows no appointments, to display your calendar for only that day. Then select the **Next Appointment** bar on the right side of the day to display the day of the next appointment on your calendar.

3. Switch to the **Work Week** calendar arrangement and turn on the display of the **Daily Task List** below the calendar.

4. Change to the **Active** view of your calendar to display only your future appointments, events, and meetings.

5. If you want to, add the holidays from your country or region to the calendar. Notice the change in the calendar content displayed in the Active view.

6. Configure the calendar to display the view and arrangement that you like best.

Schedule appointments and events

Start Outlook, display your calendar, and then perform the following tasks:

1. Create a new appointment with the subject **SBS Study Session**, and configure it as follows:

   - Set the date to one week from today.

   - Set the time from 11:30 AM to 12:30 PM.

   - Specify the location as **Library Meeting Room**.

2. Save and close the appointment.

3. Create a new all-day event named National Dessert Day.

- Set the date to the next occurrence of **October 14**, and then save and close the event.

Convert calendar items

Display your Inbox, and then perform the following tasks:

1. Locate the **SBS Test** message that you sent to yourself in Chapter 13, "Send and receive email messages."

2. Create an appointment based on the message, and configure it as follows:

- Change the subject from *SBS Test* to SBS Rafting Trip.

- Set the date to next Saturday, and the time from 11:00 AM to 2:00 PM.

- Specify the location as **To Be Determined**.

3. Save and close the appointment.

4. Display your calendar.

5. Locate the **SBS Rafting Trip** appointment, and convert it to an all-day event.

6. Locate the **SBS Rafting Trip** event.

- Invite a friend to the event. In the content pane, enter I'm practicing my Outlook scheduling skills. Please accept this invitation. Then send the event invitation.

Configure calendar item options

Display your calendar, and then perform the following tasks:

1. Locate the **SBS Study Session** appointment that you created in the first set of practice tasks for this chapter.

2. Open the appointment window and display the time zone controls.

3. Change the **Start time** and **End time** to occur in a time zone that is one hour earlier than your own.

4. Set your availability during the appointment to **Out of Office**.

5. Set a reminder for **1 hour** before the appointment.

6. Configure the appointment to recur **Monthly**, on the **first Monday** of each month, and to end after 3 occurrences.

7. Save and close the appointment series.

Schedule and change meetings

This practice task is designed for Outlook users in Exchange environments.

Display your calendar, and then perform the following tasks:

1. Create a new meeting with the subject **SBS Project Review**, and configure it as follows:

   • Invite a colleague from your Exchange network.

   • Specify the location as **My Office**.

   • Set the date to next Thursday.

2. In the **Room Finder**, look at the **Date Navigator** and scroll the **Suggested Times** list for information about availability. In the **Suggested Times** list, select a half-hour time slot that shows *No conflicts*.

3. On the **Scheduling Assistant** page of the invitation, do the following:

   • Wait for the group calendar to display your colleague's availability. Notice the color blocks that identify the working hours and availability of each person and of the group.

   • Verify that the selected time is shown as available for both of you. If it isn't, change the time by dragging the start and end time markers.

4. Return to the **Meeting** page of the meeting invitation and verify the meeting information. In the content pane, enter I'm practicing scheduling meetings. Please accept this meeting request. Then send the meeting invitation.

5. On your calendar, locate the **SBS Project Review** meeting, and open the meeting window.

6. Display the **Scheduling Assistant** page of the meeting window, and do the following:

   - Add another colleague to the attendee list and wait for the group calendar to display his or her availability.

   - Scroll the group calendar backward and forward a few days to identify times that you and your colleagues are busy or out of the office.

   - If necessary, change the meeting time and date by selecting them in the area below the group calendar.

7. Return to the **Meeting** page of the meeting invitation and verify the meeting information. Then send the meeting update to all attendees.

Respond to meeting requests

This practice task is designed for Outlook users in Exchange environments.

Display your Inbox, and then perform the following tasks:

1. Ask a colleague to send you a meeting request.

2. When you receive the meeting request, review the information in the Reading Pane, and then open the meeting request.

3. From the meeting request window, display your calendar. Notice the colors and patterns that represent the unaccepted meeting request and your availability during that time.

4. Return to the meeting request. Respond as **Tentative** and propose a new time for the meeting.

Keyboard shortcuts

Throughout this book, we provide information about how to perform tasks quickly and efficiently by using keyboard shortcuts. The following keyboard shortcuts are available in all the primary Microsoft 365 apps. You can use these keyboard shortcuts to:

- Display and use windows
- Work in dialogs
- Use the Backstage view
- Navigate the ribbon
- Change the keyboard focus without using the mouse
- Move around in and work in tables
- Access and use panes and galleries
- Access and use available actions
- Find and replace content
- Get help

> **TIP** In the keyboard shortcut tables, keys you press at the same time are separated by a plus sign (+), and keys you press sequentially are separated by a comma (,).

Display and use windows

Action	Keyboard shortcut
Switch to the next window	Alt+Tab
Switch to the previous window	Alt+Shift+Tab
Close the active window	Ctrl+W or Ctrl+F4
Restore the size of the active window after you maximize it	Alt+F5
Move to a pane from another pane in the app window (clockwise direction) If pressing F6 does not display the pane that you want, press Alt to put the focus on the ribbon, and then press Ctrl+Tab to move to the pane	F6 or Shift+F6
Switch to the next open window	Ctrl+F6
Switch to the previous window	Ctrl+Shift+F6
Maximize or restore a selected window	Ctrl+F10
Copy a picture of the screen to the clipboard	Print Screen
Copy a picture of the selected window to the clipboard	Alt+Print Screen

Work in dialogs

Action	Keyboard shortcut
Move to the next option or option group	Tab
Move to the previous option or option group	Shift+Tab
Switch to the next tab in a dialog	Ctrl+Tab
Switch to the previous tab in a dialog	Ctrl+Shift+Tab
Move between options in an open dropdown list, or between options in a group of options	Arrow keys
Perform the action assigned to the selected button; select or clear the selected checkbox	Spacebar

Action	Keyboard shortcut
Select an option; select or clear a checkbox	Alt+the underlined letter
Open a selected dropdown list	Alt+Down Arrow
Select an option from a dropdown list	First letter of the list option
Close a selected dropdown list; cancel a command and close a dialog	Esc
Run the selected command	Enter

Use edit boxes within dialogs

An edit box is a blank box in which you enter or paste an entry.

Action	Keyboard shortcut
Move to the beginning of the entry	Home
Move to the end of the entry	End
Move one character to the left or right	Left Arrow or Right Arrow
Move one word to the left	Ctrl+Left Arrow
Move one word to the right	Ctrl+Right Arrow
Select or unselect one character to the left	Shift+Left Arrow
Select or unselect one character to the right	Shift+Right Arrow
Select or unselect one word to the left	Ctrl+Shift+Left Arrow
Select or unselect one word to the right	Ctrl+Shift+Right Arrow
Select from the insertion point to the beginning of the entry	Shift+Home
Select from the insertion point to the end of the entry	Shift+End

Use the Open and Save As dialogs

Action	Keyboard shortcut
Open the Open dialog	Ctrl+F12 or Ctrl+O
Open the Save As dialog	F12
Open the selected folder or file	Enter
Open the folder one level above the selected folder	Backspace
Delete the selected folder or file	Delete
Display a shortcut menu for a selected item such as a folder or file	Shift+F10
Move forward through options	Tab
Move back through options	Shift+Tab
Open the Look In list	F4 or Alt+I
Refresh the file list	F5

Use the Backstage view

Action	Keyboard shortcut
Display the Open page of the Backstage view	Ctrl+O
Display the Save As page of the Backstage view (when saving a file for the first time)	Ctrl+S
Continue saving a Microsoft 365 file (after giving the file a name and location)	Ctrl+S
Display the Save As or Save A Copy page of the Backstage view (after initially saving a file)	Alt+F+A
Close the Backstage view	Esc

> **TIP** You can use dialogs instead of Backstage view pages by selecting the Don't Show The Backstage When Opening Or Saving Files With Keyboard Shortcuts checkbox on the Save page of the Options dialog. Set this option in any Office app to enable it in all Office apps.

Navigate the ribbon

Follow these steps:

1. Press **Alt** to display the KeyTips of each feature in the current view.

2. Press the letter shown in the KeyTip for the feature that you want to use.

> ⊘ **TIP** To cancel the action and hide the KeyTips, press Alt.

Change the keyboard focus without using the mouse

Action	Keyboard shortcut
Select the active tab of the ribbon and activate the access keys	Alt or F10; press either of these keys again to move back to the document and cancel the access keys
Move to another tab of the ribbon	F10 to select the active tab, and then Left Arrow or Right Arrow
Expand or collapse the ribbon	Ctrl+F1
Display the shortcut menu for the selected item	Shift+F10
Move the focus among the following areas of an app window: ■ Active tab of the ribbon ■ Any open panes ■ Status bar at the bottom of the window ■ Your file content	F6
Move the focus to each command on the ribbon, forward or backward, respectively	Tab or Shift+Tab
Move among the items on the ribbon	Arrow keys

Action	Keyboard shortcut
Activate the selected command or control on the ribbon	Spacebar or Enter
Display the selected menu or gallery on the ribbon	Spacebar or Enter
Activate a command or control on the ribbon so that you can modify a value	Enter
Finish modifying a value in a control on the ribbon, and move focus back to the document	Enter
Get help on the selected command or control on the ribbon	F1

Move around in and work in tables

Action	Keyboard shortcut
Move to the next cell	Tab
Move to the preceding cell	Shift+Tab
Move to the next row	Down Arrow
Move to the preceding row	Up Arrow
Insert a tab in a cell	Ctrl+Tab
Start a new paragraph	Enter
Add a new row at the bottom of the table	Tab at the end of the last row

Access and use panes and galleries

Action	Keyboard shortcut
Move to a pane from another pane in the app window	F6
When a menu is active, move to a pane	Ctrl+Tab
When a pane is active, select the next or previous option in the pane	Tab or Shift+Tab

Action	Keyboard shortcut
Display the full set of commands on the pane menu	Ctrl+Spacebar
Perform the action assigned to the selected button	Spacebar or Enter
Open a dropdown menu for the selected gallery item	Shift+F10
Select the first or last item in a gallery	Home or End
Scroll up or down in the selected gallery list	Page Up or Page Down
Close a pane	Ctrl+Spacebar, C
Open the clipboard	Alt+H, F, O

Access and use available actions

Action	Keyboard shortcut
Display the shortcut menu for the selected item	Shift+F10
Display the menu or message for an available action or for the AutoCorrect Options button or the Paste Options button	Alt+Shift+F10
Move between options in a menu of available actions	Arrow keys
Perform the action for the selected item on a menu of available actions	Enter
Close the available actions menu or message	Esc

Find and replace content

Action	Keyboard shortcut
Open the Find dialog	Ctrl+F
Open the Replace dialog	Ctrl+H
Repeat the last Find action	Shift+F4

Get help

Action	Keyboard shortcut
Open the Help pane	F1
Select the next item in the Help pane	Tab
Select the previous item in the Help pane	Shift+Tab
Perform the action for the selected item	Enter
Select the next hidden text or hyperlink, including Show All or Hide All at the top of a Help topic	Tab
Select the previous hidden text or hyperlink	Shift+Tab
Perform the action for the selected Show All, Hide All, hidden text, or hyperlink	Enter
Move back to the previous Help topic (Back button)	Alt+Left Arrow or Backspace
Move forward to the next Help topic (Forward button)	Alt+Right Arrow
Scroll small amounts up or down, respectively, within the currently displayed Help topic	Up Arrow, Down Arrow
Scroll larger amounts up or down, respectively, within the currently displayed Help topic	Page Up, Page Down

Index

SYMBOLS

+ (addition) operator, Excel, 210–212
[] (brackets), using in Excel formulas, 215–216
& (concatenation) operator, Excel, 210–212
/ (division) operator, Excel, 210, 212
= (equal) sign, Excel formulas, 210
^ (exponentiation) operator, Excel, 210, 212
* (multiplication) operator, Excel, 210–212
- (negation) operator, Excel, 210, 212
% (percentage) operator, Excel, 210
– (subtraction) operator, Excel, 210–212
error, Excel, 226

A

absolute references, Excel, 223–224
accepting and rejecting tracked changes, 141–142
accessibility features, 20
account information, managing, 21–25
actions, keyboard shortcuts, 519
addition (+) operator, Excel, 210–212
Address Block merge field, 187–189
address books, searching in Outlook, 412–413
address box, entering addresses in, 408
address lists
    modifying in searches, 413
    troubleshooting in Outlook, 411
addresses, commas as separators, 412
AGGREGATE function, Excel, 243, 246–250
alignment, configuring, 81–82
Alt key. See keyboard shortcuts
Analyze Data tool, Excel, 21
animating
    "build slides," 368
    objects on slides, 369–370
    text and pictures on slides, 362–372
animation effects. See also PowerPoint
    adding sound effects, 377
    applying, 371
    configuring options, 371
    copying, 371
    customizing, 372–377, 396–397
        dialogs, 375
        emphasis, 364
        entrance, 363, 373
        exit, 365–367, 373
        motion path, 365
        previewing, 372
        removing from slides, 372
        reordering, 376
        selecting, 370
        setting durations for, 377
        setting triggers for, 376–377
Animation Painter, 371
Animation pane, displaying, 371, 373–375
app options
    changing, 21–29, 45
    managing, 25–29
app windows
    changing, 24
    elements of, 5
    keyboard shortcuts, 514
    maximizing, 12, 16
    opening files n, 61
    personalizing appearance of, 23
    splitting, 61–62
appointments
    creating from messages, 492
    events, 509–510
    modifying, 496–497
    Outlook, 484–489
    scheduling, 509–510
apps, suggesting changes to, 42
array formulas, Excel, 224–225. See also formulas
artistic effects
    applying to pictures, 334
    applying to text, 93
asterisks, overriding in bulleted lists, 102
attaching files to messages, 418–425, 444
attachment content, displaying, 429–432.
        See also Outlook
Attachment Preview feature, 429
attachments
    displaying, 445
    grouping messages by, 455
    saving to storage drives, 431–432

attributes. *See* file properties
attributions, applying to pictures, 334–337
audio clips
    fading into or out of, 384
    inserting onto slides, 382
    looping, 385
    preventing from stopping, 385
    recording onto slides, 382–383
    restricting playback, 383–384
audio content, adding to slides, 380–385, 397
audio icon, modifying or hiding, 384
audio playback, starting, 384
AutoCalculate options, Excel, 243–244, 248
Auto-Complete list, troubleshooting in Outlook,
    410–412
AutoCorrect dialog, 106
AutoFormat As You Type page, 106
AutoRecover feature, 68
AutoSum list, Excel, 212
availability, configuring for calendar, 493, 497
AVERAGE functions, Excel, 212, 218–221, 243,
    245–246

B

backgrounds
    changing for slides, 305–312, 321–322
    choosing for Office, 23
    removing from pictures, 334
    of themes, 115
Backstage view. *See also* commands
    commands, 9–10
    keyboard shortcuts, 516
    Open page, 54
balloons, displaying markup in, 136
Bar tab
    identifying, 98
    setting, 100
Bcc "blind courtesy copy" recipients, 404
bits, mapping to colors, 326
blank documents, creating, 52
BMP (bitmap) files, PowerPoint, 327
bold text, formatting, 92
bookmarking media clips, 378–379
Border Lines option, 106
borders and shading, configuring for
    paragraphs, 88–89
brackets ([]), using in Excel formulas, 215–216

Browse Button, locating, 67
"build slides," animating, 368
bullet symbol, changing, 104
bulleted lists
    adjusting space in, 103
    converting paragraphs to, 102
    formatting, 102
    overriding asterisks, 102
    sorting, 104
button labels, visibility of, 12
buttons and arrows, 8

C

Cached Exchange Mode, Outlook, 435
calculating values, Excel, 210–216, 234
calculation options, Excel, 236
Calendar. *See also* Outlook
    adding holidays, 490–491
    categories, 495
    configuring item options, 493–498
    Date Navigator, 482–483
    task list, 484–489
    views, 478–481, 484, 509
calendar items, converting and configuring,
    489–493, 510–511
Call options for messages, 437
Capitalize Each Word, applying to text, 93
case of text, changing, 93–94
categories, Outlook, 459–467, 475, 495
Cc "courtesy copy" recipients, 404
cells, moving to, 518
Center alignment, configuring, 81
Center tab
    identifying, 98
    setting, 100
change tracking, locking and unlocking, 131–132.
    See also content changes
changes to documents
    recommending against, 154
    tracking, 128–132
character formatting. *See also* fonts; text effects
    applying, 89–97, 120
    case considerations, 94
    removing, 95
character spacing, changing, 97. *See also* spacing
characters
    hiding and showing, 99
    nonprinting and hidden, 61–62

circular references, Excel, 230
Classic versus Simplified ribbon, 407–408
Clear All Formatting button, locating, 95
Clipboard group, locating, 95
closing
    Comments pane, 138
    files, 67–72, 76
    Revisions pane, 138
cloud storage, connecting to, 6, 19, 24, 69
coauthoring
    defined, 125
    documents, 158–161, 166
collaboration
    commands, 127
    overview, 125
    tools, 10–11
color models, 313
color schemes, presentations, 303–305
color sets and themes, 115
colors
    applying to presentation elements, 313
    assigning to categories in Outlook, 460
    mapping bits to, 326
    specifying for Track Changes, 131
commands. See also Backstage view
    adding to Quick Access Toolbar, 30–32
    increasing space between, 19
    in ribbon, 6–9
comments
    activating for editing, 139
    button, 10–11
    deleting, 140
    displaying, 134–137
    inserting, 126–128
    marking as Resolved, 140
    moving among, 139
    reviewing and responding to, 138–140
    specifying user name and initials, 27, 29
Comments pane
    closing, 138
    relocating and resizing, 138
comparing and combining documents, 143–147,
        165–166
Compatibility Mode, 65
compressing media, 390–392
concatenation (&) operator, Excel, 210–212
conditional formulas, Excel, 217–221, 235.
        See also formulas

connecting cloud storage locations, 24
contact cards, Outlook, 434–435
contact list, data source, 178–179
content, structuring manually, 97–101, 121
content changes. See also change tracking
    controlling, 166
    protecting, 147
    restricting access, 148
content pane, 5
content templates, 50. See also design templates;
    templates
conversations, displaying and managing,
        449–454. See also messages
copying
    animation effects, 371
    formatting to text, 95
    and importing slides, 294–299
    and moving formulas in Excel, 221–224
    sorting levels in Excel, 265
COUNT functions, Excel, 212, 218–221, 245–246
cropping pictures, 330–331
Ctrl key. See keyboard shortcuts
cursor, moving around documents, 55
custom lists, sorting in Excel, 266–267, 273–274.
        See also lists

D

data
    refreshing in mail merge, 186
    summarizing in Excel, 217–221
data entry criteria, Excel, 250–256, 258
data ranges
    filtering in Excel, 238–243, 257
    sorting, 260
data sets, Excel, 276–280, 287
data sources. See also mail merge
    choosing and refining, 200
    creating, 180–181
    mail merge process, 168
    refining records, 181–185
    selecting, 177–180
    sorting records in, 184–185
data tables, using to forecast data, 281–284,
        287–288
data validation, Excel, 250
Date Navigator, Outlook Calendar, 482–483
Day view, Calendar, 478

Decimal tab
identifying, 98
setting, 100
deleting
categories in Outlook, 467
comments, 140
custom themes, 118
and hiding slides, 300–301
named ranges, 209
scenarios in Excel, 280
sections of slides, 318
sorting rules in Excel, 265
design templates, previewing, 52–53. *See also* templates
dialog launcher in ribbon, 6
dialogs
keyboard shortcuts, 514–516
and panes, 8
Dictate feature, 19
Display For Review options, Word, 132–133
display settings, differences in, 14–15
#DIV/0! error, Excel, 226
division (/) operator, Excel, 210, 212
docking panes, 19
.docm file type, 64
Document Formatting gallery, 108
document markup
displaying and reviewing, 164–165
inserting comments, 126–128, 163–164
tracking changes, 128–132, 163–164
document themes, changing, 114–118, 124. *See also* themes
documents. *See also* files; merged documents
basing on templates, 53
closing, 72
coauthoring, 158–161, 166
comparing and combining, 143–147, 165–166
converting styles to slides, 296
creating, 52
creating presentations from, 299
displaying, 62
displaying versions of, 147
marking up, 126–132, 163–164
opening, 57
saving, 69
tracking changes to, 128–132
viewing, 54–55
.docx file type, 64
.dotm file type, 64

.dotx file type, 64
double lines, drawing, 106
Down Arrow, using, 55
Download Center, 65
downloading practice files, xxi–xxiv
Draft view, Word, 59
Drafts folder, messages in, 414
drop caps, formatting, 96

E

edit boxes, dialogs, 515
Editor tool, locating, 142
effect styles, presentations, 305
email addresses. *See* addresses
email messages. *See* messages
emphasis animations, 364, 367
Encrypted password protection, 153, 156
End key, using, 55
entrance animations, 363, 367, 373
envelopes, generating, 192–195, 201–202
equal (=) sign, Excel formulas, 210
error alerts, Excel, 250, 255
Error Checking window, Excel, 227
errors
checking for, 142
finding and correcting in Excel, 235–236
Evaluate Formula window, Excel, 228
events
converting appointments to, 492
converting to appointments, 493
modifying, 496–497
Outlook, 484–489
scheduling, 509–510
Excel. *See also* workbooks
absolute references, 223–224
achieving specific results, 284–285
AGGREGATE function, 243, 246–247, 249
array formulas, 224–225
AutoCalculate options, 243–244, 248
AutoSum list, 212
AVERAGE functions, 212, 218–221, 243, 245–246
calculating values, 234
calculation options, 230–232, 236
circular references, 230
conditional formulas, 217–221, 235
content templates, 50
copying and moving formulas, 221–224

COUNT functions, 212, 218–221, 245–246
creating formulas, 215–216
data entry criteria, 250–256, 258
data sets, 276–280, 287
data validation, 250
dependents of cells, 227
error alerts, 250, 255
Error Checking window, 227
error codes, 226
Evaluate Formula window, 228
file types, 64
filtering data ranges and tables, 238–243, 257
finding and correcting errors, 226–230, 235–236
finding target values, 285
forecasting with data tables, 281–284, 287–288
Formula AutoComplete feature, 212–213
formula errors, 229
formulas, 210–216, 234
Function Arguments dialog, 215
funnel symbol, 239
Goal Seek, 284–285, 288
IF function, 217–221
IFERROR function, 218–221
Insert Function dialog, 214
LARGE function, 247
mathematical operations, 212
MAX function, 212, 245–246
MEDIAN function, 246
MIN function, 212, 245–246
mixed references, 223
MODE.SNGL function, 246
name data ranges, 206–209
Name Manager, 208–209
named data ranges, 234
new features, 21
Normal view, 59
numeric values in columns, 242
operators and precedence, 210–211
Options dialog, 27
organizing data into levels, 270–271
outlining data, 268–272, 274
Page Break Preview view, 59
Page Layout view, 59
PERCENTILE.EXC function, 247
PERCENTILE.INC function, 247
precedents of cells, 227
PRODUCT function, 245–246

QUARTILE functions, 247
RAND function, 249
relative references, 221–222, 224
Scenario Manager dialog, 278
scenarios, 276–280
selecting list rows, 249
SMALL function, 247
Sort & Filter menu, 262
sorting data using custom lists, 266–267, 273–274
sorting worksheet data, 273
STDEV functions, 245–246
SUBTOTAL function, 243–244, 247, 249
subtotaling data, 268–272, 274
SUM function, 212, 243, 245–246
SUM functions, 218–221
summarizing data, 217–221, 235
summarizing filtered data, 243–250, 257
summary function, 268
validation circles, 256
validation criteria, 250
validation rules, 255
VAR functions, 245–246
Watch Window, 228
Exchange Online email, 178
exit animations, 365–366, 373
exponentiation (^) operator, Excel, 210, 212
Eyedropper, using with color menu, 313

F

feedback, providing, 38–42, 48
fields. *See* merge fields
File Explorer, messages with attachments, 423
file name, locating, 6
file properties, displaying and editing, 49, 63–68, 75. *See also* settings
file storage folder, navigating to, 58
file types, 64–65
files. *See also* documents; open files
    cloud storage, 19
    creating, 50–53, 73
    displaying views of, 59–62
    managing, 9
    moving around in, 54–58, 73–74
    opening, 54–58, 73–74
    opening in second windows, 61
    saving and closing, 67–72, 76
filtered data, summarizing in Excel, 243–250, 257

filtering data ranges and tables, 262
filters, using in Excel, 238–243
finding and replacing content, keyboard
    shortcuts, 519
First Line Indent, configuring, 86
Focused Inbox, Outlook, 448–449
folders
    moving messages to, 470
    organizing messages in, 467–470, 475–476
    removing messages from, 454
    saving files in, 67
font color, changing, 93
Font dialog, opening, 95
font formats, messages, 409
font sets, presentations, 304–305
fonts. *See also* character formatting; text effects
    changing, 89–92
    and themes, 115
forecasting with data tables, 287–288
Format Background pane, PowerPoint, 309
Format Shape pane, PowerPoint, 347
formatting
    copying to text, 95
    drop caps, 96
    messages, 403
    options, 8
    removing, 95
    repeating, 95
    text while typing, 106
formatting marks, displaying, 62
Formula AutoComplete feature, Excel, 212–213
formula errors, Excel, 229
formulas. *See also* array formulas; conditional
    formulas
    calculating values in Excel, 234
    copying and moving, 221–224
    creating in Excel, 215–216
    evaluating in Excel, 228
Forward options for messages, 430, 437
Function Arguments dialog, Excel, 215
functions, inserting in Excel, 214
funnel symbol, Excel, 239

G

galleries, keyboard shortcuts, 518–519
gallery content, scrolling, 8
GIF (Graphics Interchange Format) files,
    PowerPoint, 327

Goal Seek, Excel, 284–285, 288
gradient background, applying to slides, 310–312
graphic formats, 326
Greeting Line merge field, 187, 189
gridlines and rulers, displaying and hiding, 61–62
Groups in ribbon, 6
guides, displaying and hiding, 62

H

Hanging Indent marker, using with bulleted lists, 103
hanging indents, 86–88
help
    Excel, 21
    getting, 38–42, 48
    keyboard shortcuts, 519
hidden characters, 61, 97
hiding ribbon, 17
highlighting text, 94
holidays, adding to Calendar, 490–491
Home key, using, 55
Home page
    displaying and suppressing, 4–5, 27, 29
    suppressing, 52
HSL (Hue, Saturation, Luminescence) values, 313
HTML message format, 402
hyperlinks, attaching to objects, 393. *See also* links

I

icons, inserting and formatting, 342–344,
    358–359
IF function, Excel, 217–221
IFERROR function, Excel, 218–221
image library, PowerPoint, 325
images
    animating on slides, 362–372, 395
    artistic effects, 334
    attributions, 334–337
    cropping, 330–331
    editing and formatting, 329–334, 357
    framing, 332
    inserting, 328, 356
    managing in presentations, 324–329
    moving, 329, 356
    providing information about, 357
    removing backgrounds, 332–333
    resizing, 329, 356
    selecting, 329

Inbox, managing display of messages, 448.
    See also messages
indenting and outdenting paragraphs, 86–87, 89
indents, configuring, 85–89
Insert Function dialog, Excel, 214, 216
italic text, formatting, 92

J

JPEG (Joint Photographic Experts Group) files,
    PowerPoint, 327
Junk Mail filter, Outlook, 448–449
Justify alignment, configuring, 82

K

keyboard focus, changing, 517–518
keyboard shortcuts, 513–520
    actions, 519
    appointment windows, 487
    array formulas, 225
    Backstage view, 516
    bold text, 92
    Calendar views, 481
    case options, 93
    categories in Outlook, 460
    copying and pasting, 223–224
    cursor movement, 55
    dialogs, 514–516
    filtering in Excel, 241
    finding and replacing content, 519
    folders in Outlook, 469
    Font dialog, 95
    formatting commands, 95
    galleries, 518–519
    help, 519
    hiding and showing characters, 99
    hyperlinking to resources, 393
    Insert Function dialog, 216
    italic text, 92
    line breaks, 99
    panes, 518–519
    saving files, 72
    Search feature, 40
    tables, 518
    Track Changes feature, 130
    underlined text, 92
    windows, 514
KeyTips, displaying, 517

L

labels, mail merge, 171–174. *See also* mailing
    labels
Labels function, mail merge, 195–198
LARGE function, Excel, 247
Left alignment, configuring, 81
Left Arrow, using, 55
Left Indent, configuring, 86
Left tab
    identifying, 98
    setting, 100
letter mail merge, starting, 170–171
Levels of outlines, 112–114
line break character
    identifying, 97
    inserting, 99
line spacing, configuring, 82–83
Line Spacing Options, 82
lines, drawing, 106
links, including in messages, 421–422. *See also*
    hyperlinks
list rows, selecting in Excel, 249
lists. *See also* custom lists
    creating and modifying, 101–105, 122
    creating levels of, 103
    modifying indentation of, 103
    starting at predefined numbers, 105
Live Preview feature, 8, 27–28, 302
locations, displaying with Places list, 57
"lorem ipsum" text, displaying, 53
lowercase, applying to text, 93

M

magnification, changing, 13, 16, 61–62
mail. *See* messages
mail merge. *See also* data sources; merge
    attaching files to email, 175
    email messages, 174–176
    envelopes, 192–195
    labels, 171–174
    letters, 170–171
    mailing labels, 195–198
    process of, 167–169, 199
    refreshing data, 186
    starting, 169
Mail Merge Recipients list, displaying, 182
Mail Merge wizard, using, 169, 180–181

Mail module, composing messages in, 407
mailing labels. *See also* labels
    generating, 195–198, 201–202
    printing, 198
marking up documents
    inserting comments, 126–128, 163–164
    tracking changes, 128–132, 163–164
markup, displaying and hiding, 132–138
mathematical operations, performing, 212
MAX function, Excel, 212, 245–246
maximizing
    app windows, 16
    slides on canvas, 62
media clips
    bookmarking, 378–379
    compressing, 390–392
MEDIAN function, Excel, 246
meeting requests, responding to, 506–508, 512
meetings
    converting appointments to, 492
    modifying, 496–497
    scheduling and changing, 498–505, 511–512
@*mentioning* feature, Outlook, 405–406
merge, previewing and completing, 189–191, 201.
    See also mail merge
merge fields, inserting, 168, 186–189, 200–201
merged documents, previewing, 190. *See also*
    documents
merging data. *See* mail merge
message addressing, troubleshooting, 410–413
message content, displaying, 427–429
message window, commands in, 406
messages. *See also* conversations; Inbox;
    Outlook
    address box, 408
    arranging by attributes, 455–458, 474–475
    attachments, 418–425, 444
    Call options, 437
    categories, 459
    closing, 439
    collapsing groups, 457
    creating, 404–409
    creating and sending, 443–444
    creating appointments from, 492
    displaying, 445
    displaying and managing, 474
    in Drafts folder, 414
    font formats, 409
    formats, 402
    formatting, 403, 408–409
    Forward options, 437, 439
    grouping and ungrouping, 458
    mail merge, 174–176
    modifying drafts, 417
    moving to folders, 470
    organizing in folders, 467–470, 475–476
    paragraph formatting, 409
    participant information, 433–435, 445
    previewing, 472
    printing, 471–472, 476
    rearranging, 458
    receiving notifications, 426
    removing from folders, 454
    Reply, 437–438
    resending and recalling, 440–441
    resolving addresses, 405
    responding to, 436–439, 446
    reversing sort order, 457
    saving and sending, 414, 416–418
    saving externally, 471
    selecting groups of, 458
    sending from accounts, 415
    verifying Sent Items, 418
    VoIP (Voice over Internet Protocol), 437
Microsoft Download Center, 65
Microsoft Exchange, 178, 405
Microsoft Office, new features, 19–21, 44–45
Microsoft Search, 5–6, 19, 40
MIN function, Excel, 212, 245–246
Mini Toolbar, enabling and disabling, 27–28.
    See also tool tabs
mixed references, Excel, 223
MODE.SNGL function, Excel, 246
Month view, Calendar, 479, 481
motion path animations, 365
Mouse mode, switching with Touch mode, 16
multiplication (*) operator, Excel, 210–212

N

#NAME? error, Excel, 226
Name Manager, Excel, 208–209
named ranges
    creating in Excel, 206–209, 234
    referencing in formulas, 216
Navigation pane, using, 21, 55–56, 58
negation (-) operator, Excel, 210, 212
New page, 4–5

nonprinting characters, displaying, 61–62
Normal template, 107
Normal view
Excel, 59
and Live Preview, 302
PowerPoint, 60
and Slide Sorter view, 314
Notes, storing Outlook information in, 464–465
Notes Page view, PowerPoint, 60
notifications, receiving for messages, 426
number style, changing and customizing, 104
numbered lists
converting paragraphs to, 102
formatting, 102
overriding numbers, 102
starting at predefined numbers, 105

O

Office 365 subscription, managing, 25
Office apps, suggesting changes to, 42
Office background, choosing, 23
Office themes. *See also* document themes
adding to presentations, 321
applying to presentations, 301–305
Office updates, managing, 25
OneDrive, saving files to, 70–71
online templates, using, 53
Open dialog, 516
open files, displaying, 62. *See also* files
Open page, Backstage view, 4–5, 54
opening files, 57
operators and precedence, Excel, 210–211
options
changing, 21–29, 45
managing, 25–29
outdenting and indenting paragraphs, 86–87, 89
outline levels, managing, 112–114
Outline view
PowerPoint, 60
Word, 59
outlining data, Excel, 268–272, 274
Outlook. *See also* attachment content; Calendar; messages
appointments, 484–489
Cached Exchange Mode, 435
categorizing items, 459–467
contact cards, 434–435
data sources, 178

events, 484–489
Focused Inbox, 448–449
Junk Mail filter, 448–449
@mentioning feature, 405–406
Options dialog, 27
presence information, 433
Scheduling Assistant, 500–501
searching address books, 412–413
Outlook notes, storing information in, 464–465
Outlook Options dialog, opening, 411

P

Page Break Preview view, Excel, 59
Page Down key, using, 55
Page Layout view, Excel, 59
page tabs, displaying, 10
Page Up key, using, 55
panes
and dialogs, 8
docking, 19
keyboard shortcuts, 518–519
paragraph borders and shading, configuring, 88–89
Paragraph dialog, opening, 82
paragraph formatting
alignment, 81–82
applying, 119
first letter as drop cap, 96
indents, 85–89
messages, 409
overview, 80–81
vertical spacing, 82–85
paragraph marks, displaying and hiding, 99
Paragraph Spacing option, 83–85
passwords, using to restrict access, 153–158
patterned backgrounds, applying to slides, 312
percentage (%) operator, Excel, 210
PERCENTILE.EXC function, Excel, 247
PERCENTILE.INC function, Excel, 247
photo albums, creating, 337–342, 358. *See also* pictures
Picture Format tool, 329–330
picture frame styles, 338–339
pictures. *See also* photo albums
animating on slides, 362–372, 395
artistic effects, 334
attributions, 334–337
cropping, 330–331

pictures (*continued*)
    editing and formatting, 329–334, 357
    framing, 332
    inserting, 328, 356
    managing in presentations, 324–329
    moving, 329, 356
    providing information about, 357
    removing backgrounds, 332–333
    resizing, 329, 356
    selecting, 329
pixels, storing graphics as, 326
Places list, accessing, 57
Plain Text message format, 402
PNG (Portable Network Graphic) files,
    PowerPoint, 327
PowerPoint. *See also* animation effects;
    presentations; slides
    animation effects, 363–372
    applying themes, 301–305
    BMP (bitmap) files, 327
    compressing media, 390–392
    content templates, 50
    editing and formatting pictures, 329–334
    file types, 65
    Format Background pane, 309
    Format Shape pane, 347
    GIF (Graphics Interchange Format) files, 327
    graphic formats, 326
    image library, 325
    inserting and formatting icons, 342–344,
    358–359
    JPEG (Joint Photographic Experts Group) files,
    327
    managing pictures, 324–329
    moving around in, 56
    Normal view, 60
    Notes Page view, 60
    Options dialog, 27
    Outline view, 60
    photo albums, 337–342, 358
    PNG (Portable Network Graphic) files, 327
    Reading view, 60
    shapes, 345–354
    Slide Sorter view, 60
    slide templates, 325
    SVG (Scalable Vector Graphic) files, 327, 344
.potm file type, 65
.potx file type, 65
.ppam file type, 65

.ppsm file type, 65
.ppsx file type, 65
.pptm file type, 65
.pptx file type, 65
presentations. *See also* PowerPoint; slides
    applying themes, 301–305
    basing on templates, 53
    closing, 72
    color schemes, 303–305
    creating, 52
    creating from Word documents, 299
    displaying, 62
    dividing into sections, 314–316, 322
    effect styles, 305
    font sets, 304–305
    hyperlinking to resources, 393
    merging sections in, 318
    moving around in, 56
    moving sections in, 317
    non-theme colors, 313
    opening, 57
    preparing source documents for, 299
    previewing, 302
    saving, 69
    themes, 321
    Title and Content template, 325
Print Layout view, Word, 59
printing
    mailing labels, 198
    messages, 471–472, 476
privacy, configuring for calendar, 494
procedures, adapting, 14–15
PRODUCT function, Excel, 245–246
Proofing group, Editor tool, 142
properties. *See* file properties

Q

QUARTILE functions, Excel, 247
Quick Access Toolbar
    adding commands to, 30–32
    customizing, 30–33
    displaying and customizing, 19, 31–32, 46–47
    displaying separator on, 33
    moving, 32
    moving buttons on, 33
    resetting, 33
Quick Click category, managing, 463–464

R

RAND function, Excel, 249
Read Mode view, Word, 59
Reading Pane, changing magnification, 428
Reading view, PowerPoint, 60
Recipient
    addressing messages to, 404
    troubleshooting in Outlook, 411–413
recipients list, filtering, 182–185
records
    mail merge process, 168
    refining for data sources, 181–185
    removing duplicates, 184
    sorting in data sources, 184–185
recurrences, configuring for calendar, 494–495,
    497–498
#REF! error, Excel, 226
rejecting and accepting tracked changes,
    141–142
relative references, Excel, 221–222, 224
reminders, configuring for calendar, 494, 497
Reply options for messages, 436, 438
Resolved comments, marking, 140
resolving email addresses, 405
Restrict Editing pane, displaying, 149
restricting
    access using passwords, 153–158
    actions in documents, 148–153
Review tab, Track Changes feature, 141
reviewers, managing for Track Changes, 131
Revisions pane
    closing, 138
    displaying changes in, 134–135
    displaying comments in, 137
    relocating and resizing, 138
RGB (Red, Green, Blue), specifying colors by, 313
ribbon
    adding room to, 13
    customizing, 34–38, 47
    features, 5–9
    hiding and redisplaying, 13, 17–18
    navigating, 517
    optimizing for touch interaction, 18
    resetting, 38
    Simplified versus Classic, 407–408
    and status bar, 12–13, 16–18

ribbon tabs
    custom groups, 37
    customizing, 36
    displaying, 17–18
    hiding and displaying, 34–36
    removing commands from, 36
    renaming, 36–37
Rich Text message format, 402
Right alignment, configuring, 81
Right Arrow, using, 55
Right Indent, configuring, 86
Right tab
    identifying, 98
    setting, 100
rulers and gridlines, displaying and hiding,
    61–62, 87

S

Save As dialog, displaying, 67–69, 516
Save commands, 6, 19
saves, adjusting time intervals between, 68
saving
    attachments to storage drives, 431–432
    and closing files, 67–72, 76
    mailing labels, 198
    messages externally, 471
    slides as pictures, 326
scaling options, selecting, 17
Scenario Manager dialog, Excel, 278
scenarios, Excel, 276–280
Schedule view, Calendar, 479
Scheduling Assistant, Outlook, 500–501
screen appearance, 14
screen resolution, 12, 16
screens, moving around, 55
ScreenTips
    Calendar, 486
    displaying, 7–8, 14, 28
    minimizing and turning off, 27
scroll arrows, using to navigate files, 54
Search feature, 5–6, 19, 40
sections
    deleting, 318
    dividing presentations into, 314–316, 322
    merging, 318
    moving in presentations, 317
    rearranging, 322

Sentence case, applying to text, 93
settings, managing, 9. *See also* file properties
shading and borders, configuring for
    paragraphs, 88–89
shapes
    adding text, 346
    connecting, 354
    drawing and modifying, 345–354, 359–360
    formatting, 350–353
    grouping, 353
    moving and modifying, 348–350
    moving on slides, 349
    resizing, 349
    rotating or flipping, 349–350
    selecting, 349
Share button, 10–11
Share pane, coauthoring documents, 160–161
SharePoint
    chatting in document on, 161
    connecting to, 23
Shift key. *See* keyboard shortcuts
shortcut menu, displaying, 519
Simple Markup view, displaying comments in, 136
Simplified versus Classic ribbon, 407–408
slide content, morphing, 372
Slide pane, 56
Slide Sorter view, PowerPoint, 56, 60, 314
slides. *See also* PowerPoint; presentations
    adding and removing, 320
    animating text and pictures, 395
    audio content, 380–385, 397
    backgrounds, 305–312, 321–322
    converting from Word styles, 296
    copying and importing, 294–299
    gradient backgrounds, 310–312
    hiding and deleting, 300–301
    inserting with content, 292–293
    maximizing on canvas, 62
    moving in presentations, 316–317
    moving shapes on, 349
    patterned backgrounds, 312
    rearranging, 322
    reusing, 295, 298
    saving as pictures, 326
    selecting, 296
    templates, 325
    textured backgrounds, 312
    video content, 386–389, 397–398
    watermarks, 312

slides and sections, rearranging, 316–318
SMALL function, Excel, 247
Sort & Filter menu, Excel, 262
sort order, reversing for messages, 457
sorting
    bulleted lists, 104
    data ranges, 260
    data using custom lists in Excel, 266–267
    records in data sources, 184–185
    worksheet data, 273–274
    worksheet data in Excel, 260–265
sound effects, adding to animations, 377
space, increasing between commands, 19
spacing, configuring, 82–85. *See also* character
    spacing
spelling issues, checking for, 142
splitting windows, 61–62
Start screen
    displaying and suppressing, 4–5, 27, 29
    suppressing, 52
status bar, 5, 11–18
STDEV functions, Excel, 245–246
storage drives, saving attachments to, 431–432
strikethrough text, applying, 92
styles
    applying to text, 107–112, 122–123
    outline levels, 112–114
Subject, including in messages, 405, 408
subscript characters, displaying, 92–93
SUBTOTAL function, Excel, 243–244, 247,
    249–250
subtotaling data, Excel, 268–272, 274
subtraction (–) operator, Excel, 210–212
SUM functions, Excel, 212, 218–221, 243, 245–246
summarizing data, Excel, 217–221, 235
superscript characters, displaying, 92–93
SVG (Scalable Vector Graphic) files, 327, 344
switching views of files, 61

T

tab character
    identifying, 97
    inserting, 100
    using to align text, 98
Tab key. *See* keyboard shortcuts
tab leader, specifying, 99
tab setting options, 98

tab stops
    removing, 101
    repositioning, 101
    setting, 100–101
tables
    filtering in Excel, 238–243, 257
    keyboard shortcuts, 518
tabs, aligning, 100–101
Tabs dialog, displaying, 99–100
task list, Calendar views, 484–489
templates. *See also* content templates; design
    templates
    and file creation, 50
    using with documents, 53
    using with files, 51
text
    adding to shapes, 345–346
    aligning with tab character, 98
    animating on slides, 395
    applying styles to, 107–112
    changing case of, 93
    copying formatting to, 95
    formatting while typing, 106
    highlighting, 94
text effects, applying, 91, 93. *See also* character
    formatting; fonts
text styles
    applying, 107–112, 122–123
    outline levels, 112–114
textured backgrounds, applying to slides, 312
themes. *See also* document themes
    adding to presentations, 321
    applying to presentations, 301–305
thumbnails, 8
time zones, configuring for calendar, 493, 496
title bar, 5–6
To primary message recipients, 404
tOGGLE cASE, applying to text, 93
tool tabs, 7. *See also* Mini Toolbar
toolbars, View Shortcuts, 60
touch interaction, optimizing ribbon for, 18
Touch mode, 13, 16
Track Changes feature, 128–132
tracked changes
    accepting and rejecting, 141–142
    displaying, 134–135
    displaying time and author of, 141

reviewing and processing, 140–142
specifying user name and initials, 27, 29

U

underlined text, formatting, 92
Unencrypted password protection, 153
Up Arrow, using, 55
upcoming features icon, 6
updates, managing, 25
UPPERCASE, applying to text, 93
User account menu button, 6
user interface
    Backstage view, 9–10
    collaboration tools, 10–11
    ribbon, 6–9, 12–18
    status bar, 11–18
    terminology, 3
    title bar, 6
    working in, 44

V

validation circles, removing in Excel, 256
validation criteria, Excel, 250
validation rules, editing in Excel, 255
#VALUE! error, Excel, 226
VAR functions, Excel, 245–246
variables, using to create data tables, 281
versions of documents, displaying, 147
vertical spacing, configuring, 82–85
video content, adding to slides, 386–389,
    397–398
View Shortcuts toolbar, 11, 60
views of files
    displaying, 59–62, 74–75
    switching, 61
VoIP (Voice over Internet Protocol) calls,
    initiating, 437

W

Watch Window, Excel, 228
watermarks, adding to slides, 312
Web Layout view, Word, 59
Week view, Calendar, 478, 481

windows
    changing, 24
    elements of, 5
    keyboard shortcuts, 514
    maximizing, 12, 16
    opening files n, 61
    personalizing appearance of, 23
    splitting, 61–62
Word
    browsing by object, 58
    character formatting, 89
    content templates, 50
    Display For Review options, 132–133
    Draft view, 59
    file types, 64
    Navigation pane, 58
    Options dialog, 27
    Outline view, 59
    Print Layout view, 59
    Read Mode view, 59
    Web Layout view, 59
Word documents. *See also* files; merged
        documents
    basing on templates, 53
    closing, 72
    coauthoring, 158–161, 166
    comparing and combining, 143–147, 165–166
    converting styles to slides, 296
    creating, 52
    creating presentations from, 299
    displaying, 62
    displaying versions of, 147
    marking up, 126–132, 163–164
    opening, 57
    saving, 69
    tracking changes to, 128–132
    viewing, 54–55

WordArt Styles, 91, 347
Work Week view, Calendar, 478, 481
workbooks. *See also* Excel
    basing on templates, 53
    closing, 72
    creating, 52
    displaying, 62
    opening, 57
    saving, 69
worksheet data, sorting in Excel, 260–265, 267,
        273–274

X

.xlam file type, 64
.xlsb file type, 64
.xlsm file type, 64
.xlsx file type, 64
.xltm file type, 64
.xltx file type, 64
.xml file type, 65
XML (Extensible Markup Language), 64
.xml file type, 64

Z

zigzag line, drawing, 106
zoom controls, using, 62
Zoom dialog opening, 61
Zoom Level button, 11
Zoom slider, 11